THE
SACRED BOOKS OF THE EAST

Translated by

VARIOUS ORIENTAL SCHOLARS

Edited by

F. MAX MÜLLER

Vol. 36

SACRED BOOKS OF THE EAST
Editor: F. Max Müller

These volumes of the Sacred Books of the East Series include translations of all the most important works of the seven non-Christian religions that have exercised a profound influence on the civilizations of the continent of Asia. The Vedic Brahmanic System claims 21 volumes, Buddhism 10, and Jainism 2; 8 volumes comprise Sacred Books of the Parsees; 2 volumes represent Islam; and 6 the two main indigenous systems of China. Translated by twenty leading authorities in the respective fields, the volumes have been edited by the late F. Max Müller. The inception, publication and the compilation of these books cover 34 years.

[ISBN: 81-208-0101-6] 50 Vols.

(Available in specially designed cartons)

VOLUMES

1, 15. THE UPANISHADS: in 2 Vols. *F. Max Müller*
2, 14. THE SACRED LAWS OF THE ÂRYAS: in 2 Vols. *Georg Bühler*
3, 16, 27, 28, 39, 40. THE SACRED BOOKS OF CHINA: in 6 Vols. *James Legge*
4, 23, 31. THE ZEND-AVESTA: in 3 Vols. *James Darmesteter & L.H. Mills*
5, 18, 24, 37, 47. PAHALVI TEXTS: in 5 Vols. *E.W. West*
6, 9. THE QUR'ÂN: in 2 Vols. *E.H. Palmer*
7. THE INSTITUTES OF VISH*N*U: *J. Jolly*
8. THE BHAGAVADGÎTÂ with the Sanatsujâtîya and the Anugîtâ: *K.T. Telang*
10. THE DHAMMAPADA: *F. Max Müller*
SUTTA-NIPÂTA: *V. Fausböll*
11. BUDDHIST SUTTAS: *T.W. Rhys Davids*
12, 26, 41, 43, 44. THE *S*ATAPATHA-BRÂHMA*N*A: in 5 Vols. *J. Eggeling*
13, 17, 20. VINAYA TEXTS: in 3 Vols. *T.W. Rhys Davids & H. Oldenberg*
19. THE FO-SHO-HING-TSAN-KING: *Samuel Beal*
21. THE SADDHARMA-PU*ND*ARÎKA or THE LOTUS OF THE TRUE LAWS: *H. Kern*
22, 45. JAINA SÛTRAS: in 2 Vols. *Hermann Jacobi*
25. MANU: *Georg Bühler*
29, 30. THE G*RI*HYA-SÛTRAS: in 2 Vols. *H. Oldenberg & F. Max Müller*
32, 46. VEDIC HYMNS: in 2 Vols. *F. Max Müller & H. Oldenberg*
33. THE MINOR LAW-BOOKS: *J. Jolly*
34, 38. THE VEDÂNTA SÛTRAS: in 2 Vols. with *S*ankarâcârya's Comm.: *G. Thibaut*
35, 36. THE QUESTIONS OF KING MILINDA: in 2 Vols.: *T.W. Rhys Davids*
42. HYMNS OF THE ATHARVA-VEDA: *M. Bloomfield*
48. THE VEDÂNTA-SÛTRAS with Râmânuja's *S*rîbhâshya: *G. Thibaut*
49. BUDDHIST MAHÂYÂNA TEXTS: *E.B. Cowell, F. Max Müller & J. Takakusu*
50. INDEX: *M. Winternitz*

The Questions of King Milinda

Translated from Pali by

T.W. RHYS DAVIDS

PART II

MOTILAL BANARSIDASS PUBLISHERS
PRIVATE LIMITED • DELHI

Reprint: Delhi, 1965, 1969, 1975, 1982, 1988, 1993, 1999, 2006
First Published by the Oxford University Press, 1894

ISBN: 81-208-0137-7

MOTILAL BANARSIDASS
41 U.A. Bungalow Road, Jawahar Nagar, Delhi 110 007
8 Mahalaxmi Chamber, 22 Bhulabhai Desai Road, Mumbai 400 026
203 Royapettah High Road, Mylapore, Chennai 600 004
236, 9th Main III Block, Jayanagar, Bangalore 560 011
Sanas Plaza, 1302 Baji Rao Road, Pune 411 002
8 Camac Street, Kolkata 700 017
Ashok Rajpath, Patna 800 004
Chowk, Varanasi 221 001

UNESCO COLLECTION OF REPRESENTATIVE WORKS—Indian Series
This book has been accepted in the Indian Translation Series of the UNESCO Collection of Representative Works jointly sponsored by the United Nations Educational, Scientific and Cultural Organization (UNESCO) and the Government of India.

Printed in India
BY JAINENDRA PRAKASH JAIN AT SHRI JAINENDRA PRESS,
A-45 NARAINA, PHASE-I, NEW DELHI 110 028
AND PUBLISHED BY NARENDRA PRAKASH JAIN FOR
MOTILAL BANARSIDASS PUBLISHERS PRIVATE LIMITED,
BUNGALOW ROAD, DELHI 110 007

RASHTRAPATI BHAVAN,
NEW DELHI-4
June 10, 1962

I am very glad to know that the Sacred Books of the East, published years ago by the Clarendon Press, Oxford, which have been out-of-print for a number of years, will now be available to all students of religion and philosophy. The enterprise of the publishers is commendable and I hope the books will be widely read.

S. RADHAKRISHNAN

PUBLISHER'S NOTE

First, the man distinguished between eternal and perishable. Later he discovered within himself the germ of the Eternal. This discovery was an epoch in the history of the human mind and the *East was the first to discover it.*

To watch in the Sacred Books of the East the dawn of this religious consciousness of man, must always remain one of the most inspiring and hallowing sights in the whole history of the world. In order to have a solid foundation for a comparative study of the Religions of the East, we must have before all things, complete and thoroughly faithful translation of their Sacred Books in which some of the ancient sayings were preserved because they were so true and so striking that they could not be forgotten. They contained eternal truths, expressed for the first time in human language.

With profoundest reverence for Dr. S. Radhakrishnan, President of India, who inspired us for the task; our deep sense of gratitude for Dr. C. D. Deshmukh & Dr. D. S. Kothari, for encouraging assistance; esteemed appreciation of UNESCO for the warm endorsement of the cause; and finally with indebtedness to Dr. H. Rau, Director, Max Müller Bhawan, New Delhi, in procuring us the texts of the Series for reprint, we humbly conclude.

CONTENTS.

PAGE

INTRODUCTION.

Chinese books on Nâgasena xi
The Buddhist canon xv
Vasubandhu's reference to Nâgasena . . . xvii
Kshemendra's reference to Milinda . . . xvii
The Mahâva*m*sa on Assagutta and Vattaniya . . xviii
The Kathâ Vatthu xx
Milinda and other authorities on the soul theory . xxi
The Milinda later than the Kathâ Vatthu . . . xxvi

TRANSLATION OF THE TEXT.

Book IV. The Solving of Dilemmas.

41st Dilemma. Why should houses (Wihâras) be built for the houseless ones? 1
42nd Dilemma. Was not the Buddha immoderate in food? 4
43rd Dilemma. Was not Bakkula said to be superior (in health) to the Buddha? 8
44th Dilemma. Why is the Buddha's teaching called both new and old? 13
45th Dilemma. Did not the Bodisat once kill animals in sacrifice? 16
46th Dilemma. Did not the Bodisat once abuse the Buddha? 20
47th Dilemma. Was not Kassapa the Buddha less powerful than the potter? 23
48th Dilemma. Why is the Buddha called both Brahman and king? 25
49th Dilemma. Did not the Buddha teach for hire? . 31
50th Dilemma. Did not the Buddha once doubt? (See No. 34.) 38

	PAGE
51st Dilemma. Was not the Buddha taught by others?	43
52nd Dilemma. Why can there be only one Buddha at a time?	47
53rd Dilemma. Did not the Buddha put the Order above himself?	51
54th Dilemma. As a layman can reach Arahatship, why enter the Order?	56
55th Dilemma. Did not the Buddha, having tried and abandoned asceticism, nevertheless still insist on it?	60
56th Dilemma. Men sometimes throw off the robes. Why not test candidates before initiation?	63
57th Dilemma. How is it that Arahats suffer bodily pain?	75
58th Dilemma. Why cannot an offender, who is not aware of his offence, enter the Path	78
59th Dilemma. How can a guilty Sama*n*a purify gifts?	82
60th Dilemma. The 'soul' in water	85
61st Dilemma. Why does the Order trouble itself about learning, and about buildings and gifts?	92
62nd Dilemma. Why cannot a layman, who can become an Arahat, continue as one?	96
63rd Dilemma. How is it that an Arahat can do wrong?	98
64th Dilemma. What is there that is, but not in the world?	101
65th Dilemma. What is there that is without a cause?	103
66th Dilemma. Karma-born, cause-born, and season-born	107
67th Dilemma. What becomes of dead devils?	108
68th Dilemma. Why did not the Buddha promulgate all the Rules of the Order at once?	109
69th Dilemma. How does the sun get cool?	111
70th Dilemma. Why is the sun hotter in winter?	112
71st Dilemma. How can Vessantara's giving away of his children be approved?	114
72nd Dilemma. Why did the Bodisat undergo penance?	132
73rd Dilemma. Which is stronger, virtue or vice?	144
74th Dilemma. Do the dead derive advantage from gifts given here?	151
75th Dilemma. Dreams and sleep	157
76th Dilemma. Is death ever premature?	162

PAGE

77th Dilemma. How can there be wonders at the graves of Arahats? 174
78th Dilemma. Cannot all men be converted? . . . 176
79th Dilemma. Is Nirvâ*n*a all bliss, or partly pain? . 181
80th Dilemma. The form, figure, duration, &c., of Nirvâ*n*a 186
81st Dilemma. The realisation of Nirvâ*n*a . . . 195
82nd Dilemma. The place of Nirvâ*n*a 202

Book V. The Problem of Inference.

§ 1. How can you know that the Buddha ever lived? . 206
4. The ordinary city, and its architect, shops, and inhabitants 208
5. The City of Righteousness, and its architect . 211
6. The flower bazaar therein 212
7. The perfume bazaar therein 214
8. The fruit bazaar therein 215
10. The antidote bazaar therein 217
11. The medicine bazaar therein 218
12. The ambrosia bazaar therein 219
13–20. The jewel bazaar therein, and the seven Jewels of the Truth 220
21. The general store bazaar therein 229
22. The inhabitants of the City of Righteousness . 231
23. The generals in the City of Righteousness . . 234
The chaplains in the City of Righteousness . . 234
The lamplighters in the City of Righteousness . 235
The peace-officers in the City of Righteousness . 236
The shop-keepers in the City of Righteousness . 237
The drunkards (!) in the City of Righteousness . 238
The watchmen in the City of Righteousness . 238
The lawyers and judges in the City of Righteousness 238
The bankers in the City of Righteousness . . 239
24. The conclusion drawn by inference 240

Book VI. The Voluntary Extra Vows.

§ 1. Can laymen attain Nirvâ*n*a? 244
6. The twenty-eight advantages of the vows . . 251
7. The eighteen good qualities that come from keeping them 252

PAGE

§ 10. No Arahatship without having kept them . . 254
12–15. Similes 255
16. He who, being unworthy, takes the vows . . 261
18. He who, being worthy, takes the vows . . 264
20. Details of the thirteen extra vows . . . 268
24. The example of Upasena 270
25. The thirty graces of the true recluse . . . 271
26. The example of Sâriputta 273

Book VII. Similes of Arahatship.

§ 1. Detailed list of these similes, sixty-seven being still preserved, and thirty-eight being now lost . 275
19. Wonders at the conclusion of Nâgasena's solution of the three hundred and four puzzles . . 373
20. Conversion of Milinda the king 373
21. Milinda enters the Order, and becomes an Arahat 374

Additions and Corrections 377
Index of Proper Names 379
Index of Subjects 381

Transliteration of Oriental Alphabets adopted for the Translations of the Sacred Books of the East . 385

INTRODUCTION.

I HAVE first to notice a few points as to the history of the Milinda book which have either come to light since the former Introduction was written, or which I then omitted to notice.

Mr. Bunyiu Nanjio in his Catalogue of Chinese Buddhist Books[1] mentions a Chinese book called Nâ-sien Pi*kh*iu *K*in (that is 'The Book of the Bhikshu Nâgasena' Sûtra)[2]. I have been so fortunate as to receive detailed information about this book both from Dr. Serge d'Oldenbourg in St. Petersburg and from M. Sylvain Lévi in Paris. Professor Serge d'Oldenbourg forwarded to me, in the spring of 1892, a translation into English (which he himself had been kind enough to make) from a translation into Russian by Mr. Ivanovsky, of the Chinese Introduction, and of various episodes in the Chinese which seemed to differ from the Pâli. This very valuable aid to the interpretation of the Milinda, which the unselfish courtesy of these two Russian scholars intended thus to place at my disposal, was most unfortunately lost in the post; and I have only been able to gather from a personal interview with Professor d'Oldenbourg that the Introduction was a sort of *G*âtaka story in which the Buddha appeared as a white elephant[3].

By a curious coincidence this regrettable loss has been

---

[1] Called on the title-page 'Catalogue of the Chinese Translation of the Buddhist Tripi*t*aka.' But this must surely be a mistake. It includes a number of works which are not translations at all, and translations of a large number of others which do not belong to the Pi*t*akas.

[2] No. 1358 in the Catalogue. Translated under the Eastern Tsin Dynasty, 317-420.

[3] As there is nothing about this curious Introduction in either of M. Specht's papers to be mentioned immediately, it seems possible that there are really three Chinese books on the same subject.

since made good by the work of two French scholars. Mons. Sylvain Lévi forwarded to the Ninth International Congress of Orientalists, held in London in the autumn of 1892, a careful study on the subject by M. Edouard Specht, preceded by an introductory essay by himself.

It appears from this paper, which excited much interest when it was read, that there are, not one, but two separate and distinct works extant in China under the name of Nâ-sien Pi*kh*iu *K*in, the one inserted in the Korean collection made in that country in 1010 A.D., and the other printed in the collection of Buddhist books published under the Sung in 1239. Neither the date nor the author of either version seems to be known, but Mr. Bunyiu Nanjio states of his work, which is probably one of the two, that it was composed between 317 and 420 A.D.[1] The Korean book gives much less of the matter contained in our books II and III than the later work in the Sung collection, the former containing only 13,752 characters while the latter has 22,657. In the matter of the order of the questions also the later of the two Chinese books follows much more closely the order found in the present translation than does the work found in the Korean collection.

This paper has since been published in the Proceedings of the Congress[2], and it gives translations of several episodes on questions in which the Chinese is said to throw light on the Pâli. Both M. Specht and M. Sylvain Lévi seem to think that the two Chinese books were translations of older recensions of the work than the one preserved in Pâli. This argument does not seem to me, as at present advised, at all certain. It by no means follows that a shorter recension, merely because it is shorter, must necessarily be older than a longer one. It is quite as possible that the longer one gave rise to the shorter ones.

[1] It would be very interesting to have this point decided; namely, whether the volume in the India Office Library is identical with either of the two very different books in Paris. If not, we have, then, still another Chinese book on Milinda.

[2] Vol. i. pp. 520–529.

The story of a discussion between Nâgasena and Milinda is no doubt, if the arguments in the Introduction to Part I are of any avail, an historical romance with an ethical tendency. In constant repetition, after it had become popular, it is precisely those parts which do not appeal so easily to the popular ear (because they deal, not with ordinary puzzles, but with dilemmas or with the higher mysteries of Arahatship), that would be naturally omitted. I do not go so far as to say that it must have been so. But I venture to think that for a critical judgment as to the comparative dates of the three works on the same subject, now known to exist, we must wait till translations of the whole of the two independent Chinese versions are before us. And further that the arguments must then turn on quite other considerations than the very ambiguous conclusions to be drawn merely from the length or shortness of the different treatment in each case. It is very much to be hoped therefore that M. Specht will soon give us complete versions of the two Chinese works in question.

At present it can only be said that we have a very pretty puzzle propounded to us, a puzzle much more difficult to solve than those which king Milinda put to Nâgasena the sage. If the shorter version (or rather paraphrase, for it does not seem to be a version at all in our modern sense)—that from the Korea—be really the original, how comes it that the other Chinese book, included in a collection made two centuries later, should happen to differ from it in the precise parts in which it, the supposed original, differs from the Pâli? Surely the only probable hypothesis would be that of the Chinese books, both working on the same original, the later is more exact than the earlier: and that we simply have here one more instance of an already well-known characteristic of Chinese reproductions of Indian books—namely, that the later version is more accurate than the older one. The later a Chinese 'translation' the better, in the few cases where comparison is possible, it has proved to be (that is, the nearer to our idea of what a translation should be);

and Tibetan versions are better, as a rule, than the best of the Chinese.

Since the publication of this very interesting paper, M. Sylvain Lévi has had the great kindness to send me an advance proof of a more complete paper, to be published in Paris, in which M. Specht and himself have made a detailed analysis of the three versions, setting out over against the English translation of each question (as contained in the first volume of the present work) the translations of it as they appear in each of the Chinese versions. I have not been able by a study of this analysis to add anything to the admirable summary of the conclusions as to the relations of these two books to one another and to the Pâli which are given by M. Specht in his article in the Proceedings of the Ninth Congress. The later version is throughout much nearer to the Pâli; but neither of the two give more than a small portion of it, the earlier does not seem to go much further than our Volume I, page 99 (just where the Pâli has the remark, 'Here end the questions of king Milinda'), and the later, though it goes beyond this point, apparently stops at Volume I, page 114.

These details are of importance for the decision of the critical question of the history of the Milinda. The book starts with an elaborate and very skilful introduction, giving first an account of the way in which Nâgasena and Milinda had met in a previous birth, then the life history, in order, of each of them in this birth, then the account of how they met. Throughout the whole story the attention is constantly directed to the very great ability of the two disputants, and to the fact that they had been specially prepared through their whole existence for this great encounter, which was to be of the first importance for religion and for the world. This introductory story occupies in my translation thirty-nine pages. Is it likely that so stately an entrance hall should have really been built to lead only into one or two small rooms?—to two chapters occupying only sixty pages more? Is it not more probable that the original architect had a better sense of proportion? As an Introduction to the book as we have it in these volumes the story told in those thirty-nine pages is very much in place; as an Introduction to the first two chapters only, or to the first two and a portion of the third, it is quite incongruous. And accordingly we find in the very beginning of the Introduction a kind of table of contents in which the shape of the whole book, as we have it here, is foreshadowed in detail, and in due proportion. This will have to be taken into account when, with full translations of the two Chinese books before us, we shall have to consider whether they are really copies of the original statue, or whether they are interesting fragments.

I ought not to close this reference to the labours of MM. Lévi and Specht without calling attention to a slip of the pen in one expression used by M. Sylvain Lévi regarding the Milinda[1]. He says, 'La science ne connaissait jusqu'ici de cet ouvrage qu'un texte écrit en Pali et incorporé dans le canon Singhalais?' Now there is, accurately speaking, no such thing as a Sinhalese canon of the Buddhist Scriptures, any more than there is a French or an English canon of the Christian Scriptures. The canon of the three Pi*t*akas, settled in the valley of the Ganges (probably at Patna in the time of Asoka), has been adhered to, it is true, in Ceylon, Burma, and Siam. But it cannot properly be called either a Ceylonese or a Burmese or a Siamese canon. In that canon the Milinda was never incorporated. And not only so, but the expression used clearly implies that there is some other canon. Now there has never been any other canon of the Buddhist Scriptures besides this one of the three Pi*t*akas. Many Buddhist books, not incorporated in the canon, have been composed in different languages—Pâli, Sanskrit, Chinese, Tibetan, Japanese, Sinhalese, Burmese, Siamese, &c.—but no new canon, in the European meaning of the phrase, has ever been formed.

One meets occasionally, no doubt, in European books on Buddhism allusions or references to a later canon

[1] 'Transactions of the Ninth International Congress of Orientalists,' vol. i, p. 518.

supposed to have been settled at the Council of Kanishka. The blunder originated, I believe, with Mr. Beal. But in the only account of that Council which we possess, that of Yuan Thsang[1], there is no mention at all of any new canon having been settled. The account is long and detailed. An occurrence of so extreme an importance would scarcely have escaped the notice of the Chinese writer. But throughout the account the canonicity of the three Pi*t*akas is simply taken for granted. The members of the Council were chosen exclusively from those who knew the three Pi*t*akas, and the work they performed was the composition of three books—the Upade*s*a, the Vinaya Vibhâshâ, and the Abhidharma Vibhâshâ. The words which follow in the Chinese have been differently interpreted by the European translators. Julien says:

'They (the members of the Council) thoroughly explained the three Pi*t*akas, and thus placed them above all the books of antiquity[2].'

Beal, on the other hand, renders:

'Which (namely, which three books) thoroughly explained the three Pi*t*akas. There was no work of antiquity to be compared with (placed above) their productions[3].'

It is immaterial which version best conveys the meaning of the original. They both clearly show that, in the view of Yuan Thsang, the Council of Kanishka did not establish any new canon. Since that time the rulers of China, Japan, and Tibet have from time to time published collections of Buddhist books. But none of these collections even purports to be a canon of the Scriptures. They contain works of very various, and some quite modern, ages and authors: and can no more be regarded as a canon of the Buddhist Scriptures than Migne's voluminous collection of Christian books can be called a new canon of the Christian Scriptures.

[1] Julien's translation, vol. i, pp. 173-178, and Mr. Beal's own translation, i, 147-157. There are two or three incidental references to the Council in other works. See my 'Buddhism,' p. 239.

[2] St. Julien, 'Voyages des Pelerins Bouddhistes,' vol. i, pp. 177, 178.

[3] Beal, 'Buddhist Records of the Western World,' vol. i, p. 155.

This was already pointed out in my little manual, 'Buddhism,' published in 1877, and it is a pity that references in subsequent books to a supposed canon settled at Kanishka's Council have still perpetuated the blunder. M. Sylvain Lévi, for whose genius and scholarship I have the profoundest respect, does not actually say that there was such a canon; but his words must lead readers, ignorant of the facts, to imply that there was one.

I have also to add that M. Barth has called attention[1] to the fact that M. Sylvain Lévi has added another service to those already mentioned as rendered by him to the interpretation of the Milinda, by a discussion of the reference to our book in the Abhidharma-kosa-vyâkhyâ, referred to in my previous Introduction, p. xxvi. This discussion was published in a periodical I have not seen[2]. But it seems that M. Lévi, with the help of two Chinese translations, has been able to show that the citation is not only in the commentary, but also in the text, of Vasubandhu's work. M. Léon Feer has been kind enough to send me the actual words of the reference, and they will be found published in the 'Journal of the Royal Asiatic Society' for 1891, p. 476.

Professor Serge d'Oldenbourg has also been good enough to point out to me that the two Cambridge MSS. of Kshemendra's Bodhisattvâvadâna-kalpalatâ read Milinda (not Millinda as given by Râjendra Lâl Mitra[3]) as the name of the king referred to in the 57th Avadâna, the Stûpavadâna. I had not noticed this reference to the character in our historical romance. It comes in quite incidentally, the Buddha prophesying to Indra that a king Milinda would erect a stûpa at Pâtaligrâma. There is no allusion to our book, and the passage is only interesting as showing that the memory of king Milinda still survived in India at the time when Kshemendra wrote in the eleventh century A.D.

Another reference to one of the characters in the Milinda

[1] In the 'Revue de l'Histoire des Religions' for 1893 (which has only just reached me), p. 258.

[2] The 'Comptes rendus des Séances de l'Académie des Inscriptions et Belles-lettres,' 1893, p. 232.

[3] 'Nepalese Buddhist Literature,' p. 60.

which has come to notice since the publication of part i, is in the closing words of the Attha-Sâlinî-Atthayo*g*anâ (a *t*îkâ on Buddhaghosa's first work, his commentary on the Dhamma Sanga*n*i), which was written in Siam after the twelfth century by *Ñ*ânakitti, and edited in 1890 at Galle, by Pa*ññ*âsekhara Unnânsê. On page 265 we read:

Vattaniya-senâsane ti Vi*ñgh*â*t*aviya*m* Vattaniya-senâsane. Tena vutta*m* Mahâva*m*se:

Assagutta-mahâthero pabhinna-Pa*t*isambhido
Sa*tth*i-bhikkhû sahassâni Vi*ñgh*a*tt*aviyam âdiya
Vattaniya-senâsanâ nabhasâ tattha-m-otarîti.

'The words Vattaniya-senâsane mean, "in the Vattaniya Hermitage in the Vindhya Desert." Therefore it is said in the Mahâva*m*sa:

'"The great Thera Assagutta, who knew so well the Pa*t*isambhidâ, bringing sixty thousand brethren from the Vattaniya Hermitage in the Vindhya Desert through the sky, descended there."'

This quotation is very interesting. It follows that in the original text of the Attha Sâlinî there is something about the Vattaniya Hermitage. And also that the author of this *T*îkâ must have had before him some text of our Mahâva*m*sa differing from ours, or perhaps some other Mahâva*m*sa. For the lines quoted do not occur in our text. The nearest approach to them is one line in the description of the assembly that came together at the consecration of the Mahâ Thûpa at Anurâdhapura in the year 157 B.C. It runs[1]:

Vi*ñgh*â*t*avi-Vattaniya-senasânâ[2] tu Uttaro
Thero sa*tth*i-sahassâni bhikkhû âdâya âgamâ.

'The thera Uttara came up bringing with him sixty thousand Bhikshus from the Vattaniya Hermitage [not Uttania Temple as Turnour translates] in the Vindhya Desert.'

The resemblance of the passages is striking. But all

[1] Chapter XXIX, p. 171, of Turnour's edition.

[2] Turnour has Vattaniyâ-senâsanu.

that can be concluded is that the author of our Mahâva*m*sa, Mahânâma, who wrote in the middle of the fifth century, knew of the Vattaniya Hermitage; and that the author of the text quoted by *Ñ*ânakitti (in a passage probably describing the same event) mentions an Assagutta as having come to the festival from his hermitage at Vattaniya.

Both these references are entirely legendary. In order to magnify the importance of the great festival held in Ceylon on the occasion referred to, it is related that certain famous members of the Buddhist order came, attended by many followers, through the sky, to take part in the ceremony. A comparison of this list with the previous list, also given in the Mahâva*m*sa[1], of the missionaries sent out nearly a hundred years before, by Asoka, will show that the names in the second list are in great part an echo of those in the first. But in selecting well-known names, Mahânâma in his second, fabulous, list has, according to the published text, also included that of the Vattaniya Hermitage, and, according to the new verse in the other text, has associated with that place the name of Assagutta, not found elsewhere except in the Milinda. In that book the residence of Assagutta is not specified—it is his friend Roha*n*a who lives at the Vattaniya, and the locality of the Vattaniya is not specified—it would seem from the statement at I, 25 (part i, p. 20 of this translation) that it was a day's journey from 'the Guarded Slope,' that is, in the Himâlayas. But geographical allusions are apt to be misleading when the talk is of Bhikshus who could fly through the air. And it seems the most probable explanation that the authors of these verses, in adopting these names, had the Milinda story in their mind.

[Turnour's reading of the name as Uttara, and not Assagutta, is confirmed by the Dîpava*m*sa, chap. XIX, verses 4–6, where all the fourteen names of the visitors from India are given (without any details as to the districts whence they came), and the corresponding name is also Uttara there.]

[1] Turnour, pp. 71–73.

The above sets out all the new information I have been able to glean about the Milinda since the publication of the Introduction to the first volume of this translation. I had hoped in this Introduction to discuss the doctrines, as apart from the historical and geographical allusions, of our author—comparing his standpoint with that of the earliest Buddhists, set out in the four great Nikâyas, with that of later books contained in the Pi*t*akas, and with that of still later works not included in the canon at all. I have to express my regret that a long and serious illness, culminating in a serious accident that was very nearly a fatal one, has deprived me altogether of the power of work, and not only prevented me from carrying out this perhaps too ambitious design, but has so long delayed the writing of this Introduction.

Only one of the preliminary labours to the intended Introduction was completed. I read through the Kathâ Vatthu, which has not yet been edited, with a view of ascertaining whether, at the time when that book was written, that is, in the time of Asoka, the kind of questions agitating the Buddhist community bore any relation to the kind of questions discussed by the author of our Milinda. As is well known, the Kathâ Vatthu sets out a number of points on which the orthodox school, that of the Theravâdins, differed in Asoka's time from the other seventeen schools (afterwards called collectively the Hînayâna) which had sprung up among the Buddhists between the time of the Buddha and that of Asoka. I published in the 'Journal of the Royal Asiatic Society' for 1892 a statement, both in the original Pâli and in English, of all the points thus discussed by the author of the Kathâ Vatthu, Moggaliputta Tissa Thera, giving (from the commentary) the names of the various schools against whom, in each instance, his remarks were directed.

It is now possible to judge from this analysis of the questions proposed, what were the subjects on which differences obtained among the early Buddhists. There are a number of points raised in Tissa's discussions which are also discussed by the author of the Milinda. In every instance the two authors agree in their views, Nâgasena in the Milinda always advocating the opinion which Tissa puts forward as that of the Thera-vâdins. This is especially the case with those points which Moggali-putta Tissa thinks of so much importance that he discusses them at much greater length than the others.

His first chapter, for instance, by far the longest in his book, is on the question whether, in the high and truest sense of the word, there can be said to be a 'soul'[1]. It is precisely this question which forms also the subject of the very first discussion between Milinda and Nâgasena, the conversation leading up to the celebrated simile of the chariot by which Nâgasena apparently convinces Milinda of the truth of the orthodox Buddhist view that there is really no such thing as a 'soul' in the ordinary sense[2]. On leaving the sage, the king returns to his palace, and the next day the officer who escorts Nâgasena there to renew the discussion, occupies the time to raise again the same question, and is answered by the simile of the musicians[3]. Not content with these two expositions of this important doctrine, the author of the Milinda returns again soon afterwards to the same point, which he illustrates by the simile of the palace[4], and further on in the book he takes occasion to discuss and refute the commonly held opinion that there is a soul in inanimate things, such as water[5].

It cannot be doubted that the authors of the Kathâ Vatthu and the Milinda were perfectly justified in putting this crucial question in the very forefront of their discussion —just as the Buddha himself, as is well known, made it the subject of the very first discourse he addressed to his earliest converted followers, the Anatta-lakkha*n*a Sutta, included both in the Vinaya and in the Aṅguttara Nikâya[6].

The history of ideas about the 'soul' has yet to be

[1] Kathâ Vatthu I, 1.
[2] Milinda, i, pp. 40–41.
[3] Milinda, i, p. 48.
[4] Milinda, i, pp. 86–89.
[5] Milinda, ii, pp. 85–87.
[6] Vinaya Texts (S. B. E. XIII), part i, pp. 100, 101, and Aṅguttara Nikâya.

written. But the outlines of it are pretty well established, and there is nothing to show that the Indian notions on the subject, apart perhaps from the subsidiary beliefs in Karma and transmigration, were materially different from those obtaining elsewhere. Already in prehistoric times the ancestors of the Indian peoples, whether Aryan by race or not, had come to believe, probably through the influence of dreams, in the existence inside each man of a subtle image of the man himself. This weird and intangible form left the body during sleep, and at death it continued in some way to live. It was a crude hypothesis found useful to explain the phenomena of dreams, of motion, and of life. And it was applied very indiscriminately to the allied phenomena in external things—the apparent life and motion, not only of animals, but also of plants and rivers, of winds and celestial bodies, being explained by the hypothesis of a soul within them. The varying conditions and appearances of the external world gave rise to the various powers and qualities ascribed to these external souls, and hence to whole systems of polytheism and mythology. And just as the gods, which never had any existence except in the ideas of their worshippers, were born and grew and changed and passed away with those ideas, so also the hypothesis of internal souls had, no less in India than elsewhere, a continual change, a continual development—and this not only as to ideas on the nature and origin of the internal human souls, but as to their relation to the external souls or gods. And when speculation, which loved to busy itself with these mysterious and fanciful hypotheses, had learnt to conjecture a unity behind the variety of external spirits, the relation of men's souls to the one great first cause, to God, became the subject of endless discussions, of varying views invented to harmonise with varying preconceived conceptions.

When Buddhism arose these hypotheses as to 'souls,' internal and external, formed the basis of all the widely differing, and very living and earnest, religious and philosophical speculations in the valley of the Ganges, where there then obtained that marvellous freedom of thought on all such subjects which has been throughout its history a distinguishing characteristic of the Indian people. Now there is one work, of more importance than any other in Buddhism, the collection of the Dialogues of Gotama the Buddha, brought together in the Dîgha and Ma*ggh*ima Nikâyas. It contains the views of the Buddha set out, as they appeared to his very earliest disciples, in a series of 185 conversational discourses, which will some day come to hold a place, in the history of human thought, akin to that held by the Dialogues of Plato. Is it a mere chance, or is it the actual result of the necessities of the case, that this question of 'souls' is put into the forefront of this collection, just as it is the point treated first and at the greatest length in the Kathâ Vatthu, and put first also in the Milinda?

The first of these 185 dialogues is the Brahma*g*âla Suttanta, the discourse called the Perfect Net, the net whose meshes are so fine that no folly of superstition, however subtle, can slip through—the clearing away of the rubbish before the foundations are laid for the new palace of good sense. In it are set out sixty-two varieties of existing hypotheses, and after each and all of them has been rejected, the doctrine of Arahatship is put forward as the right solution. The sixty-two heresies are as follows:

1–4. SASSATA-VÂDÂ. People who, either from meditation of three degrees, or fourthly through logic and reasoning, have come to believe that both the external world as a whole, and individual souls, are eternal.

5–8. EKA*KK*A-SASSATIKÂ. People who, in four ways, hold that some souls are eternal, while others are not.

a. Those who hold that God is eternal, but not the individual souls.

b. Those who hold that all the gods are eternal, but not the individual souls.

c. Those who hold that certain illustrious gods are eternal, but not the human souls.

d. Those who hold that while the bodily forms are not eternal, there is a subtle something, called Heart or Mind, or Consciousness, which is.

9–12. ANTÂNTIKÂ. People who chop logic about finity and infinity.

a. Those who hold the world to be finite.

b. Those who hold it to be infinite.

c. Those who hold it to be both.

d. Those who hold it to be neither.

13–16. AMARA-VIKKHEPIKÂ. People who equivocate about virtue and vice—

a. From the fear that if they express a decided opinion grief at possible mistake will injure them.

b. That they may form attachments which will injure them.

c. That they may be unable to answer skilful disputants.

d. From dullness and stupidity.

17, 18. ADHI*KK*A-SAMUPPANIKÂ. People who think that the origin of things can be explained without a cause.

19–50. UDDHAMA-ÂGHATANIKÂ. People who believe in the future existence of human souls.

a. Sixteen different phases of the hypothesis of a conscious existence after death.

b. Eight different phases of the hypothesis of an unconscious existence after death.

c. Eight different phases of the hypothesis of an existence between consciousness and unconsciousness after death.

51–57. UKKHEDA-VÂDÂ. People who teach the doctrine that there is a soul, but that it will cease to exist on the death of the body here, or at the end of a next life, or of further lives in higher and ever higher states of being.

58–62. DI*TTH*A-DHAMMIKA-NIBBÂNA-VÂDÂ. People who hold that there is a soul, and that it can attain to perfect bliss in this present world, or in whatever world it happens to be—

a. By a full, complete, and perfect enjoyment of the five senses.
b. By an enquiring mental abstraction (the First Dhyâna).
c. By undisturbed mental bliss, untarnished by enquiry (the Second Dhyâna).
d. By mental peace, free alike from joy and pain and enquiry (the Third Dhyâna).
e. By this mental peace plus a sense of purity (the Fourth Dhyâna).

Professor Garbe, in his just published 'Sankhya Philosophie[1],' holds that the first persons attacked in this list are the followers of the Sâṅkhya. The double view of the Sassata-vâdâ is no doubt the basis of the Sâṅkhya system. But the system contains much more, and it would be safer to say that we have here a warning against the philosophical view which afterwards developed into the Sâṅkhya, or rather which became afterwards a fundamental part of the Sâṅkhya. The Vedânta, in either of its forms, is not, it will be noticed, referred to in any one of the sixty-two divisions; but philosophical views forming part of the Vedânta may be traced in Nos. 5, 8, 10, 20, &c. The scheme is not intended as a refutation of the views, as a whole, held by any special school or individual, but as a statement of erroneous views on two special points, namely, the soul and the world. However this may be, we find an ample justification in this comprehensive and systematic condemnation of all current or possible forms of the soul-theory for the prominence which the author of the Milinda gives to the subject.

The other points on which the Milinda may be compared with the Kathâ Vatthu will need less comment. The discussion in the Milinda as to the manner in which the Divine Eye can arise in a man[2], is a reminiscence of the question raised in the Kathâ Vatthu III, 7 as to whether the eye of flesh can, through strength of dhamma, grow into the Divine Eye. The discussion in the Milinda as to

[1] Introduction, p. 57.
[2] Milinda, i, pp. 179-185.

how a layman, who is a layman after becoming an Arahat, can enter the Order[1], is entirely in accord with the opinion maintained, as against the Uttarâpathakâ, in the Kathâ Vatthu IV, 1. Our Milinda ascribes the verses,

'Exert yourselves, be strong, and to the faith,' &c.,

to the Buddha[2]. In the note on that passage I had pointed out that they are ascribed, not to the Buddha, but to Abhibhû in certain Pi*t*aka texts, and to the Buddha himself only in late Sanskrit works. In the exposition of Kathâ Vatthu II, 3 the verses are also ascribed to the Buddha. The proposition in the Kathâ Vatthu II, 8 that the Buddha, in the ordinary affairs of life, was not transcendental, agrees with Nâgasena's argument in the Milinda, part ii, pp. 8-12. The discussion in the Milinda as to whether an Arahat can be thoughtless or guilty of an offence[3] is foreshadowed by the similar points raised in the Kathâ Vatthu I, 2; II, 1, 2, and VIII, 11. And the two dilemmas, Nos. 65 and 66, especially as to the cause of space, may be compared with the discussion in Kathâ Vatthu VI, 6, as to whether space is self-existent.

The general result of a comparison between these two very interesting books of controversial apologetics seems to me to be that the differences between them are just such as one might expect (*a*) from the difference of date, and (*b*) from the fact that the controversy in the older book is carried on against members of the same communion, whereas in the Milinda we have a defence of Buddhism as against the outsider. The Kathâ Vatthu takes almost the whole of the conclusions reached in the Milinda for granted, and goes on to discuss further questions on points of detail. It does not give a description of Arahatship in glowing terms, but discusses minor points as to whether the realisation of Arahatship includes the Fruits of the three lower paths[4], or whether all the qualities of an Arahat are free from the Âsavas[5], or whether the knowledge of his

[1] Milinda, ii, pp. 96-98 (compare 57-59).
[2] Milinda, ii, p. 60.
[3] Milinda, ii, pp. 98 foll.
[4] Kathâ Vatthu IV, 9.
[5] Kathâ Vatthu IV, 3.

emancipation alone makes a man an Arahat[1], or whether the breaking of the Fetters constitutes Arahatship, and whether the insight into Arahatship suffices to break all the Fetters[2], and so on.

The discussion of these details gives no opportunity for the enthusiastic eloquence of the author of our Milinda, and the very fact of his eloquence argues a later date. But there can be no doubt as to the superiority of his style. And I still adhere to the opinions expressed in the former Introduction that the work, as it stands in the Pâli, is of its kind (that is, as a book of apologetic controversy) the best in point of style that had then been written in any country; and that it is the masterpiece of Indian prose.

T. W. RHYS DAVIDS.

Temple,
May, 1894.

[1] Kathâ Vatthu V, 1.

[2] Kathâ Vatthu V, 10, and X, 1.

THE QUESTIONS

OF

KING MILINDA.

BOOK IV.

The Solving of Dilemmas.

Chapter 5.

[DILEMMA THE FORTY-FIRST.

ON DWELLING-PLACES.]

1. [211] 'Venerable Nâgasena, the Blessed One said:

"In friendship of the world anxiety is born,
In household life distraction's dust springs up,
The state set free from home and friendship's ties,
That, and that only, is the recluse's aim [1]."

[1] This is the opening verse of the Muni Sutta (in the Sutta Nipâta I, 12). It is quoted again below, p. 385 of the Pâli text. The second line is, in the original, enigmatically terse, and runs simply, 'From a home dust arises.' This Fausböll renders (in the S. B. E., vol. x, part ii, p. 33), 'From household life arises defilement,' the word for dust (rago) being often used figuratively in the sense of something that disfigures, is out of place in the higher life. It is the distracting effect of household cares that the recluse has to fear.

'But on the other hand he said:

"Let therefore the wise man,
Regarding his own weal,
Have pleasant dwelling-places built,
And lodge there learned men [1]."

'Now, venerable Nâgasena, if the former of these two passages was really spoken by the Tathâgata, then the second must be wrong. But if the Tathâgata really said: "Have pleasant dwelling-places built," then the former statement must be wrong. This too is a double-edged problem, now put to you, which you have to solve.'

2. [212] 'Both the passages you have quoted, O king, were spoken by the Tathâgata. And the former is a statement as to the nature of things, an inclusive statement, a statement which leaves no room for anything to be supplemented to it, or to be added to it in the way of gloss [2], as to what is seemly and appropriate and proper for a recluse, and as to the mode of life which a recluse should adopt, the path he should walk along, and the practice he should follow. For just, O king, as a deer in the forest, wandering in the woods, sleeps wherever he desires, having no home and no

---

[1] This is a very famous verse, found first in the Vinaya (*K*ullavagga VI, 1, 5), and quoted in the Introduction to the *G*âtakas (Fausboll, vol. i, p. 93; compare vol. iv, p. 354), translated in my 'Buddhist Birth Stories,' vol. i, p. 132. Hîna*n*-kumburê adds the context:

'Then shall they preach to him the Truth,
The Truth dispelling every grief,
Which Truth when here a man perceives,
He's freed from stains, and dies away.'

[2] On these expressions compare above, p. 170 (p. 113 of the text).

dwelling-place, so also should the recluse be of opinion that

"In friendship of the world anxiety is born,
In household life distraction's dust springs up."

3. 'But when the Blessed One said:

"Have pleasant dwelling-places built,
And lodge there learned men,"

that was said wit' respect to two matters only. And what are those two? The gift of a dwelling-place (Wihâra) has been praised and approved, esteemed and highly spoken of, by all the Buddhas. And those who have made such a gift shall be delivered from rebirth, old age, and death. This is the first of the advantages in the gift of a dwelling-place. And again, if there be a common dwelling-place (a Wihâra) the sisters of the Order will have a clearly ascertained place of rendezvous, and those who wish to visit (the brethren of the Order)[1] will find it an easy matter to do so. Whereas if there were no homes for the members of the Order it would be difficult to visit them. This is the second of the advantages in the gift of a dwelling-place (a Wihâra). It was with reference to these two matters only that it was said by the Blessed One:

"Have pleasant dwelling-places built,
And lodge there learned men."

[213] 'And it does not follow from that that the sons of the Buddha[2] should harbour longings after the household life.'

[1] The words in brackets are added from Hîna/i-kumburê.

[2] That is, the members of the Order.

'Very good, Nâgasena! That is so, and I accept it as you say.'

[Here ends the dilemma as to dwelling-places.]

[DILEMMA THE FORTY-SECOND.

MODERATION IN FOOD.]

4. 'Venerable Nâgasena, the Blessed One said: "Be not remiss as to (the rules to be observed) when standing up (to beg for food). Be restrained in (matters relating to) the stomach [1]."

'But on the other hand he said:

"Now there were several days, Udâyin, on which I ate out of this bowl when it was full to the brim, and ate even more [2]."

'Now if the first rule be true, then the second statement must be false. But if the statement be true, then the rule first quoted must be wrong.

[1] This verse has not yet been traced. The first half of it occurs in a different connection at Dhammapada, verse 168, which I have rendered (at 'Buddhism,' p. 65), 'Rise up and loiter not!' without any reference at all to food. This was in accordance with the view taken of the passage, both by Prof. Fausböll, who renders it (p. 31 of his edition of the Pâli), 'Surgat, ne sit socors,' and by Prof. Max Müller, who renders it (S. B. E., vol. x, part i, p. 47), 'Rouse thyself, do not be idle!' And I still think (especially noting such passages as Dhammapada, verses 231, 232, and the verse quoted in the Commentary, p. 126 of Fausböll, from *G*âtaka IV, 496, &c.) that this was the original meaning in that connection. But here the words must clearly be taken as referring to food, and it is very remarkable that the commentator on the Dhammapada (see p. 335 of Fausböll's edition) takes them in that sense also even in the other connection. It is a striking instance of the way in which commentators impart a purely technical sense into a general ethical precept.

[2] From the Mahâ Udâyi Sutta (Ma*gg*h*i*ma Nikâya, No. 77).

This too is a double-edged problem, now put to you, which you have to solve.'

5. 'Both the passages you have quoted, O king, were spoken by the Blessed One. But the former passage [214] is a statement as to the nature of things, an inclusive statement, a statement which leaves no room for anything to be supplemented to it, or added to it in the way of gloss, a statement of what is true and real and in accordance with the facts, and that cannot be proved wrong, a declaration made by the prophets, and sages, and teachers, and Arahats, and by the Buddhas who are wise for themselves alone (Pa*kk*eka-Buddhas), a declaration made by the Conquerors, and by the All-wise Ones, a declaration made too by the Tathâgata, the Arahat, the Supreme Buddha himself. He who has no self-control as regards the stomach, O king, will destroy living creatures, will take possession of what has not been given to him, will be unchaste, will speak lies, will drink strong drink, will put his mother or his father to death, will slay an Arahat, will create a schism in the Order, will even with malice aforethought wound a Tathâgata. Was it not, O king, when without restraint as to his stomach, that Devadatta by breaking up the Order, heaped up for himself karma that would endure for a kalpa[1]? It was on calling to mind this, O king, and many other things of the same kind, that the Blessed One declared:

"Be not remiss as to (the rules to be observed)

[1] See above, p. 164 (p. 109 of the Pâli text). These passages show that Dr. Morris's note in the 'Journal of the Pâli Text Society,' 1885, requires modification. See also below, IV, 8, 88, and the passages quoted by him in the 'Journal' for 1886.

when standing up (to beg for food). Be restrained in (matters relating to) the stomach."

6. 'And he who has self-control as regards the stomach gains a clear insight into the Four Truths, realises the Four Fruits of the life of renunciation[1], and attains to mastery over the Four Discriminations[2], the Eight Attainments[3], and the Six Modes of Higher Knowledge[4], and fulfils all that goes to constitute the life of the recluse. Did not the parrot fledgling, O king, by self-restraint as to his stomach, cause the very heaven of the great Thirty-Three to shake, and bring down Sakka, the king of the gods, to wait upon him[5]? It was on calling to mind this, O king, and many other things of a similar kind, that the Blessed One declared:

"Be not remiss as to (the rules to be observed) when standing up (to beg for food). Be restrained in (matters relating to) the stomach."

7. 'But when, O king, the Blessed One said: "Now there were several days, Udâyi, on which I ate out of this bowl when it was full to the brim, and ate even more," that was said by him who had completed his task, who had finished all that he had to do, who had accomplished the end he set before him, who had overcome every obstruction, by the self-dependent[6] Tathâgata himself about himself.

---

[1] Sâmañña. [2] Patisambhidâ. [3] Samâpatti. [4] Abhiññâ.

[5] This story will be found in the two Suka Gâtakas (Nos. 429 and 430 in Fausböll). I had not succeeded in tracing it when the list at vol. i, p. xxvi, was drawn up; it should therefore be added there.

[6] Sayambhunâ, 'whose knowledge is not derived from any one else.' (Sayambhu-ñâna-wû says Hînati-kumburê.) Burnouf's proposition ('Lotus,' p. 336) to take it in the sense of 'who has no other substratum or raison d'être than himself' cannot be accepted, in spite of Childers's approbation.

Just, O king, as it is desirable that a sick man to whom an emetic, or a purge, or a clyster has been administered, should be treated with a tonic; **[215]** just so, O king, should the man who is full of evil, and who has not perceived the Four Truths, adopt the practice of restraint in the matter of eating. But just, O king, as there is no necessity of polishing, and rubbing down [1], and purifying a diamond gem of great brilliancy, of the finest water, and of natural purity; just so, O king, is there no restraint as to what actions he should perform, on the Tathâgata, on him who hath attained to perfection in all that lies within the scope of a Buddha [2].'

'Very good, Nâgasena! That is so, and I accept it as you say.'

[Here ends the dilemma as to restraint in eating.]

---

[1] Nighamsanâ. Compare the use of nighamsati at *K*ullavagga V, 27, 2.

[2] This is much more than a mere injunction not to gild refined gold. It comes very near to the enunciation of the dangerous doctrine that the holy man is above the law, and that nothing he does can be wrong. It is curious how frequently one finds this proposition cropping up in the most unexpected places, and the history of religious belief is full of instances of its pernicious effect on the most promising movements. When one considers the great influence of our author's work, it becomes especially interesting to note how the doctrine has never, among the orthodox Buddhists, who read the Pâli Scriptures, been extended from the Buddha himself to his followers, and from moderation in food to matters of more vital import in the life of a church. And this is the more remarkable as the Tantra works of the corrupt Buddhism of Nepal and Tibet show how fatal has been the result of the doctrine among those Buddhists who had lost the guiding support of the older Scriptures.

[DILEMMA THE FORTY-THIRD.

BAKKULA'S SUPERIORITY TO THE BUDDHA.]

8. 'Venerable Nâgasena, it was said by the Blessed One:

"A Brahman am I, O brethren, devoted to self-sacrifice[1], pure-handed at every time; this body that I bear with me is my last, I am the supreme Healer and Physician[2]."

'But on the other hand the Blessed One said:

"The chief, O brethren, among those who are disciples of mine, in the matter of bodily health, is Bakkula[3]."

'Now it is well known that diseases arose several times in the body of the Blessed One. So that if, Nâgasena, the Tathâgata was supreme, then the statement he made about Bakkula's bodily health must be wrong. But if the Elder named Bakkula was really chief among those who were healthy, then that statement which I first quoted must be

---

[1] Yâkayogo. See Sutta Nipâta III, 5, 1; Anguttara Nikâya III, 79, 2; and below, p. 225 (of the Pâli text).

[2] This passage has not yet been traced in the Pitakas, and the context is therefore unknown. But the word Brahman must of course be applied to the Buddha here in the sense, not of one belonging to the Brahman caste, but of Arahat. Hînati-kumburê adds, as a gloss, bâhita-pâpa-brâhmanayek, 'brahman because he has suppressed evil in himself.' On this explanation see my note to the forty-eighth dilemma, which is devoted to the discussion of this difficulty.

On the Buddha as the Great Physician see Sutta Nipâta III, 7, 13; Magghima Nikâya I, 429; Sumangala Vilâsinî, 67, 255; and Milinda, pp. 110, 169 (of the Pâli text).

[3] Anguttara Nikâya I, 14, 4. The reading adopted by our author agrees with that of the Simhalese MSS. put by Dr. Morris into the text.

wrong. This too is a double-edged problem, now put to you, which you have to solve.'

9. 'Both the quotations you have made, O king, are correct[1]. But what the Blessed One said about Bakkula was said of those disciples who had learnt by heart the sacred words, and studied them, and handed down the tradition, which in reference to the characteristics (each of them in some one point) had in addition to those which were found in him himself[2]. [216] For there were certain of the disciples of the Blessed One, O king, who were "meditators on foot," spending a whole day and night in walking up and down in meditation. But the Blessed One was in the habit of spending the day and night in meditation, not only walking up and down but also sitting and lying down. So such, O king, of the disciples as were "meditators on foot[3]" surpassed him in that particular. And there were certain of the disciples of the Blessed One, O king, who were "eaters at one sitting," who would not, even to save their lives, take more than one meal a day. But the

[1] Here, as always, they are repeated in full in the text.

[2] This passage is very ambiguous. Hînan-kumburê renders it: 'with reference to what was found in himself, and besides that (with reference) to the disciples who had learnt &c. . . . . tradition.' He translates agamânam and the two following words, as relative compounds, by âgama-dhâri-wû, &c., and in this I have followed him. But he supplies an 'and' after the last, thus taking them as accusatives in dependence on sandhâya, and that cannot be right. It seems forced to separate bâhirânam so much from the other genitives with which it stands in the text, and yet it is so impossible to make sense of the passage in any other way, that one would like to know the readings of all the MSS.

[3] '*K*akkhupâla and others' adds Hînan-kumburê. (For the story of *K*akkhupâla, see the commentary on the Dhammapada, verse 1.)

Blessed One was in the habit of taking a second, or even a third. So such, O king, of the disciples as were "eaters at one sitting" surpassed him in that particular. And in a similar way, O king, a number of different things have been told, each one of one or other of the disciples. But the Blessed One, O king, surpassed them all in respect of uprightness, and of power of meditation, and of wisdom, and of emancipation, and of that insight which arises out of the knowledge of emancipation, and in all that lies within the scope of a Buddha. It was with reference to that, O king, that he said:

"A Brahman am I, O brethren, devoted to self-sacrifice, pure-handed at every time; this body that I bear with me is my last, I am the supreme Healer and Physician."

10. 'Now one man, O king, may be of good birth, and another may be wealthy, and another full of wisdom, and another well educated, and another brave, and another adroit; but a king, surpassing all these, is reckoned supreme. Just in that way, O king, is the Blessed One the highest, the most worthy of respect, the best of all beings. And in so far as the venerable Bakkula was healthy in body, that was by reason of an aspiration (he had formed in a previous birth)[1]. For, O king, when Anoma-dassî, the Blessed One, was afflicted with a disease, with wind in his stomach, and again when Vipassî, the Blessed One, and sixty-eight thousand of his disciples, were afflicted with a disease, with greenness of blood[2], he,

[1] See, for other instances of such aspirations, above, vol. i, p. 5.

[2] Ti*n*a-pupphaka-roga. There is a flower called ti*n*a-puppha, and this may be a skin disease named after it. But pupphaka at *G*âtaka III, 541, means blood, and the disease may

being at those times an ascetic, had cured that disease with various medicines, and attained (thereby) to such healthiness of body (in this life) that it was said of him :

"The chief, O brethren, among those who are disciples of mine, in the matter of bodily health, is Bakkula."

11. 'But the Blessed One, O king, whether he be suffering, or not suffering, from disease ; whether he have taken, or not taken, upon himself the observance

---

be so called because the blood was turned by it to the colour of grass (tina). Hînati-kumburê (who gives these legends of the previous births of Bakkula at much greater length, adding others from the time of the Buddhas Padumuttara and Kassapa, and giving the story also of his present birth) says that the disease arose from contact with wind which had been poisoned through blowing over a Upas tree (p. 296 of the Simhalese version). But he does not explain the name of the disease, which occurs only here.

In his present birth Bakkula is said to have been born at Kosâmbî, in a wealthy family. His mother, understanding that to bathe a new-born child in the Jumna would ensure him a long life, took him down to the river. Whilst he was there being bathed, a huge fish swallowed him. But the fish, caught at Benares, was sold to a wealthy but childless man there, and on being cut open, the babe was found in it unhurt.

The mother hearing the news of this marvel, went in great state and with haste to Benares and claimed the child. Thereupon an interesting lawsuit arose, and the king of Benares, thinking it unjust to deprive the purchaser of a fish of anything inside it, and also unjust to deprive a mother of her child, decided that the child belonged equally to both. So he became the heir of both families, and was therefore called Bak-kula, 'the two-family-one' (Bak=Bâ=Dvâ). On the real derivation of Bakkula, see Dr. Morris in the 'Journal of the Pâli Text Society,' 1886, pp. 94-99. We need not quarrel with a false etymology which shows us so clearly the origin of the legend. Then Bakkula enjoys great prosperity in the orthodox three palaces, and at eighty years of age, being still in vigorous health, enters the Order.

of special vows [1],—there is no being like unto the Blessed One. [217] For this, O king, has been said by the Blessed One, the god of gods, in the most excellent Sa*m*yutta Nikâya [2]:

"Whatsoever beings, O brethren, there may be—whether without feet, or bipeds, or four-footed things, whether with a body, or without a body, whether conscious or unconscious, or neither conscious nor not—the Tathâgata is acknowledged to be the chief of all, the Arahat, the Buddha Supreme."'

'Very good, Nâgasena! That is so, and I accept it as you say [3].'

[Here ends the problem as to the superiority of Bakkula to the Buddha.]

[1] The Dhutangas, enumerated below, p. 351 (of the Pâli text).

[2] Sa*m*yutta Nikâya XLIV, 103.

[3] This piece of casuistry is not so entirely at variance with the context of the second passage (quoted from the Aṅguttara I, 14) as would seem at first sight. The answer practically amounts to this, that though each of many disciples may be superior to the Buddha in certain bodily qualities, or even in the special vows known as Dhutangas, yet he surpasses them in the 'weightier matters of the law.' It is true that one of the instances given, that of the *th*âna-*k*aṅkamikâ, is not included in the list of Dhutangas, and in the long enumeration in the Aṅguttara of those of the disciples who were 'chief' in any way, 'weightier matters of the law' are not overlooked. But 'meditation on foot' is of the same nature as the acknowledged Dhutangas, and none of the five special points in which Nâgasena places especially the superiority of the Buddha (uprightness, &c.), is mentioned in the Aṅguttara. Nevertheless the logical reply to the problem proposed would have been that in the Aṅguttara the superiority spoken of is over other disciples, and not over the Buddha.

[DILEMMA THE FORTY-FOURTH.

THE ORIGINALITY OF THE BUDDHA'S TEACHING.]

12. 'Venerable Nâgasena, it has been said by the Blessed One:

"The Tathâgata, O brethren, the Arahat, the Buddha supreme[1], is the discoverer of a way that was unknown[2]."

'But on the other hand he said:

"Now I perceived, O brethren, the ancient way, the ancient path, along which the previous Buddhas walked[2]."

'If, Nâgasena, the Tathâgata be the discoverer of a way not previously found out, then it must be wrong that it was an ancient way that he perceived, an ancient path along which previous Buddhas walked. But if the way he perceived were an ancient way, then the statement that it was unknown must be wrong. This too is a double-edged problem, now put to you, which you have to solve.'

13. 'Both the quotations you make, O king, are accurate. And both the statements so made are correct. When the previous Tathâgatas, O king, had disappeared, then, there being no teacher left, their way too disappeared. And it was that way—though then broken up, crumbled away, gone to ruin, closed in, no longer passable, quite lost to view—[**218**] that the Tathâgata, having gained a

[1] Supreme, that is, in comparison with the Pa*kk*eka Buddhas, 'Buddhas for themselves alone:' whereas the 'altogether Buddha' can not only see the truth for himself, but also persuade others of it.

[2] These two quotations are from the Sa*m*yutta Nikâya XXI, 58 and X, 2, 65, says Mr. Trenckner, but I cannot trace them in M. Feer's edition.

thorough knowledge of it, saw by the eye of his wisdom[1], (and knew it) as the way that previous Buddhas trod. And therefore is it that he said:

"Now I perceived, O brethren, the ancient way, the ancient path along which previous Buddhas walked."

'And it was a way which—there being, through the disappearance of previous Tathâgatas, no teacher left—was a way then broken up, crumbled away, gone to ruin, closed in, and lost to view, that the Tathâgata made now passable again. And therefore is it that he said:

"The Tathâgata, O brethren, the Arahat, the Buddha supreme, is the discoverer of a way that was unknown."

14. 'Suppose, O king, that on the disappearance of a sovran overlord, the mystic Gem of Sovranty lay concealed in a cleft on the mountain peak, and that on another sovran overlord arriving at his supreme dignity, it should appear to him. Would you then say, O king, that the Gem was produced by him[2]?'

'Certainly not, Sir! The Gem would be in its original condition. But it has received, as it were, a new birth through him.'

'Just so, O king, is it that the Blessed One, gaining a thorough knowledge of it by the eye of

---

[1] 'The wisdom arising from the perception of the Four Noble Truths' is Hînań-kumburê's gloss.

[2] The wondrous Gem-treasure of the king of kings (the Ve*l*uriya, etymologically the same as beryl, but probably meaning cat's-eye) is supposed, like the other mystic treasures, to come to him of its own accord, on his becoming sovran overlord. See my 'Buddhist Suttas,' p. 256 (S. B. E., vol. xi).

his wisdom, brought back to life and made passable again the most excellent eightfold way in its original condition as when it was walked along by the previous Tathâgatas,—though that way, when there was no teacher more, had become broken up, had crumbled away, had gone to ruin, was closed in, and lost to view. And therefore is it that he said:

"The Tathâgata, O brethren, the Arahat, the Buddha supreme, is the discoverer of a way that was unknown."

15. 'It is, O king, as when a mother brings forth from her womb the child that is already there, and the saying is that the mother has given birth to the child. Just so, O king, did the Tathâgata, having gained a thorough knowledge of it by the eye of his wisdom, bring into life, and make passable again, a way that was already there, though then broken up, crumbled away, gone to ruin, closed in, and lost to view.

'It is as when some man or other finds a thing that has been lost, and the people use the phrase: "He has brought it back to life." [219] And it is as when a man clears away the jungle, and sets free[1] a piece of land, and the people use the phrase: "That is his land." But that land is not made by him. It is because he has brought the land into use that he is called the owner of the land. Just so, O king, did the Tathâgata, having gained a thorough knowledge of it by the eye of his wisdom, bring back to life, and make passable again, a way that was already there, though then broken up, crumbled

[1] Nîharati. Âvara*n*aya kara ganneya says Hîna*t*i-kumburê.

away, gone to ruin, closed in, no longer passable, and lost to view. And therefore is it that he said:

"The Tathâgata, O brethren, the Arahat, the Buddha supreme, is the discoverer of a way that was unknown."'

'Very good, Nâgasena! That is so, and I accept it as you say.'

[Here ends the dilemma as to the way of Nirvâ*n*a.]

[DILEMMA THE FORTY-FIFTH.

THE BUDDHA'S KINDNESS.]

16. 'Venerable Nâgasena, it was said by the Blessed One:

"Already in former births when I was a man had I acquired the habit of inflicting no hurt on living beings.[1]."

'But on the other hand it is said[2]:

"When he was Lomasa Kassapa, the Rishi, he had hundreds of living creatures slain and offered the great sacrifice, the 'Drink of Triumph[3].'"'

---

[1] This passage has not yet been traced in the Pi*t*akas.

[2] The identical words are not found, but they are a summary of the Lomasa Kassapa *G*âtaka (No. 433 in Prof. Fausböll's edition, and see especially vol. iii, p. 517, line 25).

[3] Vâ*g*apeyya, which Professor Fausböll (loc. cit., p. 518) spells vâ*k*apeyya, and a Burmese MS. he quotes spells vâdhapeyya (characteristically enough,—the scribe not understanding the word, and thinking it must have been derived from vadha, makes what he thinks must be a correction). The Sanskrit form of the word is vâ*k*apêya, the drink or draught of battle or victory, name of that one of the seven Soma sacrifices which a king offered when desirous of attaining to sovran overlordship. In the allied legend

'Now, Nâgasena, if it is true what the Buddha said, that, in his former births as a man, he inflicted no hurt on living beings, then the saying that, as Lomasa Kassapa, he had hundreds of living creatures slain must be false. But if he had, then the saying that he inflicted no hurt on living beings must be false. This too is a double-edged problem, now put to you, which you have to solve.'

17. 'The Blessed One did say, O king, that already in former births, when he was a man, he had acquired the habit of inflicting no hurt on living beings. And Lomasa Kassapa, the Rishi, did have hundreds of living creatures slain, and offered the great sacrifice, the "Drink of Triumph." **[220]** But that was done when he was out of his mind through lust, and not when he was conscious of what he was doing.'

'There are these eight classes of men, Nâgasena, who kill living beings—the lustful man through his lust, and the cruel man through his anger, and the dull man through his stupidity, and the proud man through his pride, and the avaricious man through his greed, and the needy man for the sake of a livelihood, and the fool in joke, and the king in the way of punishment. These, Nâgasena, are the eight classes of men who kill living beings. The Bodisat, venerable Nâgasena, must have been acting in accordance with his natural disposition when he did so.'

'No, it was not, O king, an act natural to him that the Bodisat did then. If the Bodisat had been led, by natural inclination, to offer the great sacrifice, he would not have uttered the verse:

---

of king Lomapâda's sacrifice (Râmâya*n*a I, 8, 11 foll.) it is the a*s*va-medha, the horse sacrifice, which is offered.

"Not the whole world, Sayha, the ocean girt,
With all the seas and hills that girdle it,
Would I desire to have, along with shame[1]."

'But though, O king, the Bodisat had said that, yet at the very sight of *K*andavatî (Moon-face), the princess[2], he went out of his mind and lost command of himself through love. And it was when thus out of his mind, confused and agitated, that he, with his thoughts all perplexed, scattered and wandering, thus offered the great sacrifice, the "Drink of Triumph,"—and mighty was the outpour of blood from the necks of the slaughtered beasts!

'Just, O king, as a madman, when out of his senses, will step into a fiery furnace, and take hold of an infuriated venomous snake, and go up to a rogue elephant, and plunge forwards into great waters, the further shore of which he cannot see, and trample through dirty pools and muddy places[3], and rush into thorny brakes, and fall down precipices, and feed himself on filth, and go naked through the streets, and do many other things improper to be done—just so was it, O king, that at the very sight of *K*andavatî, the princess, the Bodisat went out of his mind, and then only acted as I have said[4].

18. **[221]** 'Now an evil act done, O king, by one out of his mind, is even in this present world not considered as a grievous offence, nor is it so in

[1] This verse is found not only in the 433rd *G*âtaka (loc. cit.), but also in the Sayha *G*âtaka, No. 310, a shorter recension of the same story.

[2] Hîna*t*i-kumburê here summarises the whole story.

[3] *K*andanikâ and o*l*igalla. See Aṅguttara III, 57, 1; Mag*gh*ima I, 11, 448; Thera Gâthâ 567; *K*ullavagga V, 17, 1. Hîna*t*i-kumburê spells the second word with an ordinary l.

[4] The text repeats the last paragraph.

respect of the fruit that it brings about in a future life. Suppose, O king, that a madman had been guilty of a capital offence, what punishment would you inflict upon him?'

'What punishment is due to a madman? We should order him to be beaten and set free. That is all the punishment he would have.'

'So then, O king, there is no punishment according to the offence of a madman. It follows that there is no sin in the act done by a madman, it is a pardonable act. And just so, O king, is it with respect to Lomasa Kassapa, the Rishi, who at the mere sight of *K*andavatî, the princess, went out of his mind, and lost command of himself through love. It was when thus out of his mind, confused and agitated, that he, with his thoughts all perplexed, scattered and wandering, thus offered the great sacrifice, the "Drink of Triumph,"—and mighty was the outpour of blood from the necks of the slaughtered beasts! But when he returned again to his natural state, and recovered his presence of mind, then did he again renounce the world, and having regained the five powers of insight, became assured of rebirth in the Brahma world.'

'Very good, Nâgasena! That is so, and I accept it as you say.'

[Here ends the dilemma about Lomasa Kassapa[1].]

[1] It is very instructive to notice the way in which our author looks upon the historical Buddha and the various heroes of the Gâtaka Stories as so absolutely identical that he feels obliged to defend the conduct of all the 'types' as earnestly as he would that of the Buddha himself. There is no such conception in the Pi*t*akas, and the whole tone of our author's argument reveals the lateness of his date as compared with the Pi*t*akas.

[DILEMMA THE FORTY-SIXTH.
THE MOCKING OF THE BUDDHA.]

19. 'Venerable Nâgasena, it was said by the Blessed One of Six-tusks, the elephant king,

"When he sought to slay him, and had reached him
with his trunk,
He perceived the yellow robe, the badge of a
recluse,
Then, though smarting with the pain, the thought
possessed his heart,—
'He who wears the outward garb the Arahats wear
Must be scatheless held, and sacred, by the good[1].'"

'But on the other hand it is said:

"When he was *G*otipâla, the young Brahman, he reviled and abused Kassapa the Blessed One, the Arahat, the Buddha supreme, with vile and bitter words, calling him a shaveling and a good-for-nothing monk[2]."

'Now if, Nâgasena, the Bodisat, even when he was an animal, respected the yellow robe, **[222]** then the statement that as *G*otipâla, a Brahman, he reviled and abused the Blessed One of that time, must be false. But if as a Brahman, he reviled and abused the Blessed One, the statement that when he was Six-tusks, the elephant king, he respected the yellow robe, must be false. If when the Bodisat was an animal, though he was suffering severe and cruel and bitter pain, he respected the yellow robe

[1] From the *Kh*addanta *G*âtaka, No. 514 (Fausböll, vol. v, p. 49); with which compare the Kâsâva *G*âtaka, No. 221 (vol. ii, p. 196).

[2] This has not been found in these words, but Mr. Trenckner refers to Ma*ggh*ima Nikâya, No. 81. Compare also *G*âtaka I, 43.

which the hunter had put on, how was it that when he was a man, a man arrived at discretion, with all his knowledge mature, he did not pay reverence, on seeing him, to Kassapa the Blessed One, the Arahat, the Buddha supreme, one endowed with the ten powers, the leader of the world, the highest of the high, round whom effulgence spread a fathom on every side, and who was clad in most excellent and precious and delicate Benares cloth made into yellow robes? This too is a double-edged problem, now put to you, which you have to solve.'

20. 'The verse you have quoted, O king, was spoken by the Blessed One. And Kassapa the Blessed One, the Arahat, the Buddha supreme, was abused and reviled by *G*otipâla the young Brahman with vile and bitter words, with the epithets of shaveling and good-for-nothing monk. But that was owing to his birth and family surroundings. For *G*otipâla, O king, was descended from a family of unbelievers, men void of faith. His mother and father, his sisters and brothers, the bondswomen and bondsmen, the hired servants and dependents in the house, were worshippers of Brahmâ, reverers of Brahmâ; and harbouring the idea that Brahmans were the highest and most honourable among men, they reviled and loathed those others who had renounced the world. It was through hearing what they said that *G*otipâla, when invited by Gha*t*ikâra the potter to visit the teacher, replied: "What's the good to you of visiting that shaveling, that good-for-nothing monk?"

[223] 21. 'Just, O king, as even nectar when mixed with poison will turn sour, just as the coolest water in contact with fire will become warm, so was

it that *G*otipâla, the young Brahman, having been born and brought up in a family of unbelievers, men void of faith, thus reviled and abused the Tathâgata after the manner of his kind. And just, O king, as a flaming and burning mighty fire, if, even when at the height of its glory, it should come into contact with water, would cool down, with its splendour and glory spoilt, and turn to cinders, black as rotten blighted [1] fruits—just so, O king, *G*otipâla, full as he was of merit and faith, mighty as was the glory of his knowledge, yet when reborn into a family of unbelievers, of men void of faith, he became, as it were, blind, and reviled and abused the Tathâgata. But when he had gone to him, and had come to know the virtues of the Buddhas which he had, then did he become as his hired servant; and having renounced the world and entered the Order under the system of the Conqueror, he gained the fivefold power of insight, and the eightfold power of ecstatic meditation, and became assured of rebirth into the Brahma heaven.'

'Very good, Nâgasena! That is so, and I accept it as you say.'

[Here ends the dilemma about *G*otipâla.]

---

[1] Niggu*nd*i, which Hîna*t*i-kumburê merely repeats. See *G*âtaka III, 348; IV, 456; Dhammapada Commentary, p. 209; Aṅguttara IV, 199; and Dr. Morris's restoration of Dîpava*m*sa XII, 32, in the Introduction to vol. ii of his Aṅguttara.

[DILEMMA THE FORTY-SEVENTH.

THE HELPLESSNESS OF A BUDDHA.]

22. 'Venerable Nâgasena, this too has been said by the Blessed One:

"Ghaṭîkâra the potter's dwelling-place remained, the whole of it, for three months open to the sky, and no rain fell upon it[1]."

'But on the other hand it is said:

"Rain fell on the hut of Kassapa the Tathâgata[1]."

'How was it, venerable Nâgasena, that the hut of a Tathâgata, the roots of whose merits were so widely spread[2], got wet? One would think that a Tathâgata should have the power to prevent that. If, Nâgasena, Ghaṭîkâra the potter's dwelling was kept dry when it was open to the sky, it cannot be true that a Tathâgata's hut got wet. But if it did, then it must be false that the potter's dwelling was kept dry. This too is a double-edged problem, now put to you, which you have to solve.'

23. 'Both the quotations you have made, O king, are correct. [224] Ghaṭîkâra the potter was a good man, beautiful in character, deeply rooted in merit, who supported his old and blind mother and father. And when he was absent, the people, without so much as asking his leave, took away the thatch from his dwelling to roof in with it the hut of the Tathâgata. Then, unmoved and unshaken at his thatch being thus removed, but filled rather

[1] Both these quotations are from the Maggh*ima Nikâya, No. 31 (the Ghaṭîkâra Suttanta).

[2] Ussanna-kusala-mûla. See *G*âtaka I, 145.

with a well-grounded and great joy the like of which cannot be found, an immeasurable bliss sprang up in his heart at the thought: "May the Blessed One, the chief of the world, have full confidence in me." And thereby did he obtain merit which brought forth its good result even in this present life.

24. 'And the Tathâgata, O king, was not disturbed by that temporary inconvenience (of the falling rain). Just, O king, as Sineru, the king of the mountains, moves not, neither is shaken, by the onslaught of innumerable gales[1]—just as the mighty ocean, the home of the great waters, is not filled up, neither is disturbed at all, by the inflow of innumerable great rivers—just so, O king, is a Tathâgata unmoved at temporary inconvenience.

'And that the rain fell upon the Tathâgata's hut happened out of consideration for the great masses of the people. For there are two circumstances, O king, which prevent the Tathâgatas from themselves supplying (by creative power) any requisite of which they may be in need[2]. And what are the two? Men and gods, by supplying the requisites of a Buddha on the ground that he is a teacher worthy of gifts, will thereby be set free from rebirth in states of woe. And lest others should find fault, saying: "They seek their livelihood by the working of miracles." If, O king, Sakka had kept that hut dry, or even Brahmâ himself, even then that action would have been faulty, wrong, and worthy of censure. For people might then say: "These Buddhas by

[1] Aneka-sata-sahassa-vâta-sampahârena. Perhaps 'by the battle (raging round it) of innumerable gales,' the onslaught of the winds being not against it, but against one another.

[2] Literally 'from receiving any self-created requisite.'

their dexterity[1] befool and lord it over the world." That is the reason why such action would have been better left undone. The Tathâgatas, O king, do not ask for any advantage; and it is because they ask for nothing that they are held blameless.'

'Very good, Nâgasena! That is so, and I accept as you say.'

[Here ends the dilemma about Gha*t*ikâra the potter.]

[DILEMMA THE FORTY-EIGHTH.

WHY GOTAMA CLAIMED TO BE A BRAHMAN.]

[**225**] 25. 'Venerable Nâgasena, this too was said by the Blessed One:

"A Brahman am I, O brethren, devoted to self-sacrifice[2]."

'But on the other hand he declared:

"A king am I, Sela[3]."

'If, Nâgasena, the Blessed One were a Brahman, then he must have spoken falsely when he said he was a king. But if he were a king, then he must have spoken falsely when he said he was a Brahman. He must have been either a Khattiya or a Brahman. For he could not have belonged, in the same birth, to two castes. This too is a double-edged problem, now put to you, which you have to solve.'

[1] Vibhûsa*m* katvâ. Daksha-kriyâ ko*t*a says Hîna*t*i-kumburê. The expression has not been found elsewhere.

[2] This passage has already been quoted above (IV, 4, 55). It has not been traced in the Pi*t*akas.

[3] These words from the Sela Sutta (Sutta Nipâta III, 7, 7) have also been already discussed above (IV, 3, 33, 34).

26. 'Both the quotations you have made, O king, are correct. But there is good reason why the Tathâgata should have been both Brahman and also king.'

'Pray what, Nâgasena, can be that reason?'

'Because all evil qualities, not productive of merit are in the Tathâgata suppressed, abandoned, put away, dispelled, rooted out, destroyed, come to an end, gone out, and ceased, therefore is it that the Tathâgata is called a Brahman[1]. A Brahman[2], O king, means one who has passed beyond hesitation, perplexity, and doubt. And it is because the Tathâgata has done all this, that therefore also is he called a Brahman. A Brahman, O king, means one who has escaped from every sort and class of becoming, who is entirely set free from evil and from stain, who is dependent on himself[3], and it is because the Tathâgata is all of these things, that therefore also is he called a Brahman. A Brahman, O king, means one who cultivates within himself the highest and best of the excellent and supreme

[1] This argument is based on the false etymology that brâhmano=bâhita-pâpo ('he in whom evil is suppressed'), adopted by Hînati-kumburê above at IV, 4, 55. Buddhaghosa, in the Sumangala, p. 244, has another derivation: Brahmam anatîti brâhmano. As Brahmam has not been found elsewhere except as the accusative of Brahmâ the name of the god, and as anati only occurs in this passage, it might be contended that Buddhaghosa means an 'invoker of Brahmâ.' But I think he is correct in his etymology, and intends to interpret the word Brahman as 'intoner of prayer.'

[2] The Arahat-Brahman says Hînati-kumburê.

[3] Asahâyo, literally 'has no friend.' I am not sure that I have rightly understood this term, which I have not found elsewhere applied to the Arahat. Hînati-kumburê merely repeats the word.

conditions of heart[1]. And it is because the Tathâgata does this that therefore also is he called a Brahman. A Brahman, O king, means one who carries on the line of the tradition of the ancient instructions concerning the learning and the teaching of sacred writ, concerning the acceptance of gifts, concerning subjugation of the sènses, self-control in conduct, and performance of duty. And it is because the Tathâgata carries on the line of the tradition of the ancient rules enjoined by the Conquerors[2] regarding all these things, that therefore also is he called a Brahman. [226] A Brahman, O king, means one who enjoys the supreme bliss of the ecstatic meditation. And it is because the Tathâgata does this, that therefore also is he called a Brahman. A Brahman, O king, means one who knows the course and revolution of births in all forms of existence. And it is because the Tathâgata knows this, that therefore also is he called a Brahman. The appellation "Brahman," O king, was not given to the Blessed One by his mother, nor his father, not by his brother, nor his sister, not by his friends, nor his relations, not by spiritual teachers of any sort, no, not by the gods. It is by reason of their emancipation that this is the name of the Buddhas, the Blessed Ones. From the moment when, under the Tree of Wisdom, they had overthrown the armies of the Evil One, had suppressed in themselves all evil qualities not productive of merit, and had attained to the knowledge of the Omniscient

[1] Dibba-vihâro; rendered divya-viharana by Hînañ-kumburê. It cannot mean here 'state of being a deva in the kamaloka' as rendered by Childers.

[2] That is, of course, the previous Buddhas.

Ones, it was from the acquisition of this insight, the appearance in them of this enlightenment, that this true designation became applied to them,—the name of "Brahman." And that is the reason why the Tathâgata is called a Brahman [1].'

27. 'Then what is the reason why the Tathâgata is called a king?'

'A king means, O king, one who rules and guides the world, and the Blessed One rules in righteousness over the ten thousand world systems, he guides the whole world with its men and gods, its evil spirits and its good ones [2], and its teachers, whether Sama*n*as or Brahmans. That is the reason why the Tathâgata is called a king. A king means, O king, one who, exalted above all ordinary men, making those related to him rejoice, and those opposed to him mourn; raises aloft the Sunshade of Sovranty, of pure and stainless white, with its handle of firm hard wood [3], and its many hundred ribs [4],—the symbol of his mighty fame and glory. And the Blessed One, O king, making the army of the Evil One, those given over to false doctrine, mourn; filling the hearts of those, among gods or men, devoted to sound doctrine, with joy; **[227]** raises aloft over the ten thousand world systems the Sunshade of his Sovranty, pure and stainless in the whiteness of emancipation,

---

[1] This is a striking instance of argument in a circle. The word Brahman is first interpreted in its technical Buddhist sense of Arahat, and then the Buddha, as Arahat, is called a Brahman. The only paragraph based on the real transition of meaning in the term is that referring to the holding up of tradition.

[2] Samâraka*m* sabrahmaka*m*, 'with its Mâras and Brahmas.'

[3] Ara*t*u, says Hîna*t*i-kumburê; that is wood from the heart of the tree.

[4] Salâkâ, which Hîna*t*i-kumburê repeats, adding 'of the highest wisdom.'

with its hundreds of ribs fashioned out of the highest wisdom, with its handle firm and strong through long suffering,—the symbol of his mighty fame and glory. That too is the reason why the Tathâgata is called a king. A king is one who is held worthy of homage by the multitudes who approach him, who come into his presence. And the Blessed One, O king, is held worthy of homage by multitudes of beings, whether gods or men, who approach him, who come into his presence. That too is the reason why the Tathâgata is called a king. A king is one who, when pleased with a strenuous servant, gladdens his heart by bestowing upon him, at his own good pleasure, any costly gift the officer may choose[1]. And the Blessed One, O king, when pleased with any one who has been strenuous in word or deed or thought, gladdens his heart by bestowing upon him, as a selected gift, the supreme deliverance from all sorrow,—far beyond all material gifts[2]. That too is the reason why the Tathâgata is called a king. A king is one who censures, fines[3], or executes the man who trans-

[1] Varitam varam. 'A gift appropriate to the service approved of' says Hînati-kumburê. And the word is not in Childers. But compare the use of varam varati at Gâtaka III, 493.

[2] Asesa-kâma-varena, for which Hînati-kumburê has asesa-kâmâvakarayem. Mr. Trenckner adds a ka, which, as being entirely superfluous, he puts in brackets. There can be but little doubt that the corrected reading is asesa-kâmâvakarena, and that the literal rendering would be 'gladdens him by that which has left in it nothing connected with (life in) the world of sense; to wit, deliverance from all sorrow' (that is deliverance from samsara).

Parimutti, which I have not found in the Pitakas, and which is not in Childers, occurs above (p. 112 of the Pâli text) in the same connection.

[3] Gâpeti. See my notes above on vol. i, p. 240, and below on VII, 5, 10. The Simhalese has here dhana-dânaya karanneya, where dânaya must be gâni.

gresses the royal commands. And so, O king, the man who, in shamelessness or discontent, transgresses the command of the Blessed One, as laid down in the rules of his Order, that man, despised, disgraced and censured, is expelled from the religion of the Conqueror. That too is the reason why the Tathâgata is called a king. A king is one who in his turn proclaiming laws and regulations according to the instructions laid down in succession by the righteous kings of ancient times, and thus carrying on his rule in righteousness, becomes beloved and dear to the people, desired in the world, and by the force of his righteousness establishes his dynasty long in the land. And the Blessed One, O king, proclaiming in his turn laws and regulations according to the instructions laid down in succession by the Buddhas of ancient times, and thus in righteousness being teacher of the world,—he too is beloved and dear to both gods and men, desired by them, and by the force of his righteousness he makes his religion last long in the land. That too is the reason why the Tathâgata is called a king.

'Thus, O king, so many are the reasons why the Tathâgata should be both Brahman and also king, that the ablest of the brethren could scarcely in an æon enumerate them all. Why then should I dilate any further? Accept what I have said only in brief.'

'Very good, Nâgasena! That is so, and I accept it as you say.'

[Here ends the dilemma as to the Buddha belonging to two castes.]

[DILEMMA THE FORTY-NINTH.

GIFTS TO THE BUDDHA.]

[**228**] 28. 'Venerable Nâgasena, it has been said by the Blessed One:

"Gifts chaunted for in sacred hymns
Are gifts I must not take.
All those who see into the Truth
Do this their practice make.
The Buddhas all refused to chaunt for wage;
This was their conduct still
Whene'er the Truth prevailed
Through every age[1]."

'But on the other hand the Blessed One, when preaching the Truth, or talking of it, was in the habit of beginning with the so-called "preliminary discourse," in which giving has the first place, and goodness only the second[2]. So that when gods and men heard this discourse of the Blessed One, the lord of the whole world, they prepared and gave gifts, and the disciples partook of the alms thus brought about. Now if, Nâgasena, it be true what the Blessed One said, that he accepted no gifts earned by the chaunting of sacred words, then it was wrong that the Blessed One put giving thus

[1] This stanza occurs no less than five times in those portions of the Pi*t*akas already published. See Sutta Nipâta I, 4, 6 and III, 4, 27, and Sa*m*yutta Nikâya VII, 1, 8, VII, 1, 9, and VII, 2, 1. The rhythm of the Pâli is strikingly beautiful, and is quite spoilt in the rendering.

[2] See, for instance, Dîgha Nikâya V, 28; Mahâvagga I, 7, 5 and 10; V, 1, 9; VI, 26, 8; and *K*ullavagga VI, 4, 5. As there is a doubt about the spelling, Fausböll at *G*âtaka I, 8, and I, 30, and our MSS. of the Dîgha reading ânupubbi-kathâ, whereas Childers and Oldenberg read anupubbi-kathâ, it is perhaps worth mentioning that the Si*m*halese has the short a.

into the foreground. But if he did rightly in so emphasizing the giving of gifts, then it is not true that he accepted no gifts earned by the utterance of sacred words. And why so? Because if any one worthy of offerings should praise to the laity the good results to them of the bestowal of alms, they, hearing that discourse, and pleased with it, will proceed to give alms again and again. And then, whosoever enjoy that gift, they are really enjoying that which has been earned by the utterance of sacred words. This too is a double-edged problem, now put to you, which you have to solve.'

29. 'The stanza you quote, O king, was spoken by the Blessed One. And yet he used to put the giving of alms into the forefront of his discourse. But this is the custom of all the Tathâgatas—first by discourse on almsgiving to make the hearts of hearers inclined towards it, and then afterwards to urge them to righteousness. This is as when men, O king, give first of all to young children things to play with—[**229**] such as toy ploughs [1], tip-cat sticks [2], toy wind-mills [3], measures made of leaves [4], toy carts,

[1] All these articles are mentioned in the Dîgha Nikâya I, 1, 14. Buddhaghosa explains the first word (vaṅkaka*m*) as toy ploughs. Hoops the Indian children do not have, probably for want of suitable roads.

[2] Gha*t*ika*m*, which is, according to Buddhaghosa, a game played by striking a short stick with a long one; and according to Hîna*t*i-kumburê the game called in Si*m*halese kalli. Clough has this word, but simply explains it as a game so called.

[3] *K*ingulaka*m*, which is, according to Buddhaghosa, a little wheel made of cocoa-nut leaves, which is set turning by the impact of the wind. Hîna*t*i-kumburê says 'an œmbaruwa (twirling thing) made of cocoa-nut leaves.'

[4] Pattâ*lh*aka*m*. Buddhaghosa and the Si*m*halese agree in rendering this 'toy measures.'

and bows and arrows—and afterwards appoint to each his separate task. Or it is as when a physician first causes his patients to drink oil for four or five days in order to strengthen them, and to soften their bodies; and then afterwards administers a purge. The supporters of the faith, O king, the lordly givers, have their hearts thus softened, made tender, affected. Thereby do they cross over to the further shore of the ocean of transmigration by the aid of the boat of their gifts, by the support of the causeway of their gifts. And (the Buddha), by this (method in his teaching), is not guilty of "intimation[1]."'

30. 'Venerable Nâgasena, when you say "intimation" what are these intimations?'

'There are two sorts, O king, of intimation—bodily and verbal. And there is one bodily intimation which is wrong, and one that is not; and there is one verbal intimation which is wrong, and one that is not. Which is the bodily intimation which is wrong? Suppose any member of the Order, in going his rounds for alms, should, when choosing a spot to stand on, stand where there is no room[2], that is a bodily intimation which is wrong. The true members of the Order will not accept any alms so asked for, and the individual who thus acts is despised, looked down upon, not respected, held blameworthy, disregarded, not well thought of, in the religion of the Noble Ones; he is reckoned as

[1] Viññatti. It is a breach of rules for a member of the Order to ask, in words, for an alms. For a Buddha to lay stress, in a discourse, on the advantages of almsgiving does not, Nâgasena means, make him guilty of this offence.

[2] And thus cause an obstruction, and attract attention to the fact that he is there. I do not know of any such prohibition in the Vinaya.

one of those who have broken their (vows as to) means of livelihood. And again, O king, suppose any member of the Order, in going his round for alms, should stand where there is no room, and stretch out his neck like a peacock on the gaze, in the hope: "Thus will the folk see me"—that too is a bodily intimation which is wrong. True brethren will not accept an alms so asked for, and he who thus acts is regarded like the last. And again, O king, suppose any member of the Order should make a sign with his jaw, or with his eyebrow, or with his finger—[230] that too is a bodily intimation which is wrong. True brethren will not accept an alms so asked for, and he who thus acts is regarded the same way.

31. 'And which is the bodily intimation which is not wrong? If a brother, on going his round for alms, be self-possessed, tranquil, conscious of his acts; if he stand, wherever he may go, in the kind of spot that is lawful; if he stand still where there are people desirous to give, and where they are not so desirous, if he pass on[1];—that is a bodily intimation which is not wrong. Of an alms so stood for the true members of the Order will partake; and the individual who thus asks is, in the religion of the Noble Ones, praised, thought highly of, esteemed, and reckoned among those whose behaviour is without guile, whose mode of livelihood is pure. For thus has it been said by the Blessed One, the god over all gods:

"The truly wise beg not, for Arahats scorn to beg.

[1] The author has *K*ullavagga VIII, 5, 2 in his mind, where the signs (of their being willing or not) are specified.

The good stand for their alms, thus only do they beg[1]."

32. 'Which is the verbal intimation which is wrong? In case, O king, a brother intimate his wish for a number of things, requisites of a member of the Order—robes and bowls and bedding and medicine for the sick—that is a verbal intimation which is wrong. Things so asked for the true members of the Order (Ariyâ) will not accept; and in the religion of the Noble Ones the individual who acts thus is despised, looked down upon, not respected, held blameworthy, disregarded, not well thought of—reckoned rather as one who has broken his (vows as to) means of livelihood. And again, O king, in case a brother should, in the hearing of others, speak thus: "I am in want of such and such a thing;" and in consequence of that saying being heard by the others he should then get that thing—that too is a verbal intimation which is wrong. True members of the Order will not use a thing so obtained, and he who acts thus is regarded like the last. And again, O king, in case a brother, dilating in his talk[2], give the people about him to understand: "Thus and thus should gifts be given to the Bhik-

---

[1] From *G*âtaka III, 354. The words are there ascribed, not to the Buddha, but to the Bodisat in the story.

The word translated Arahats is Ariyâ, which is taken here, as elsewhere, as a dissyllable, and pronounced Aryâ. It is the same as our word Aryans, and is rendered above Noble Ones. I do not think that it is applied exclusively to Arahats.

[2] Va*k*î-vipphârena. The expression has not been found elsewhere, nor is it in Childers. The Si*m*halese has: 'dilating on the words obtaining in this religion.' I presume it means, that not content with praising almsgiving in general, he particularises. Compare Mahâvagga VI, 37.

khus," and in case they, on hearing that saying, should bring forth from their store anything so referred to—that too is a verbal intimation which is wrong. True members of the Order will not use a thing so obtained, and he who acts thus is regarded like the last. [**231**] For when Sâriputta, the Elder, O king, being ill in the night-time, after the sun had set, and being questioned by Moggallâna, the Elder, as to what medicine would do him good, broke silence; and through that breach of silence obtained the medicine—did not Sâriputta then, saying to himself: "This medicine has come through breach of silence; let not my (adherence to the rules regarding) livelihood be broken," reject that medicine, and use it not[1]? So that too is a verbal intimation which is wrong. True members of the Order will not use a thing so obtained, and he who acts thus is regarded like the last.

33. 'And what is the verbal intimation which is right? Suppose a brother, O king, when there is necessity for it, should intimate among families either related to him, or which had invited him to spend the season of Was with him[2], that he is in want of medicines—this is a verbal intimation which is not wrong. True members of the Order will partake of things so asked for; and the individual who acts thus is, in the religion of the Noble Ones, praised, thought highly of, esteemed, reckoned among those whose mode of livelihood is pure,

[1] This story has not yet been traced; but the Simhalese (p. 317) gives it at great length.

[2] Ñâti-pavâritesu kulesu. Compare Pâkittiya 39 ('Vinaya Texts,' vol. i, p. 39).

approved of the Tathâgatas, the Arahats, the Supreme Buddhas. And the alms that the Tathâgata, O king, refused to accept of Kasî-Bhâradvâ*g*a, the Brahman[1], that was presented for the sake of testing him with an intricate puzzle which he would have to unwind[2], for the sake of pulling him away, of convicting him of error, of making him acknowledge himself in the wrong. Therefore was it that the Tathâgata refused that alms, and would not partake thereof.'

34. 'Nâgasena, was it always, whenever the Tathâgata was eating, that the gods infused the Sap of Life from heaven into the contents of his bowl, or was it only into those two dishes—the tender boar's flesh, and the rice porridge boiled in milk—that they infused it[3]?'

'Whenever he was eating, O king, and into each morsel of food as he picked it up—just as the royal cook takes the sauce and pours it over each morsel in the dish while the king is partaking of it[4]. **[232]** And so at Vera*ñg*â, when the Tathâgata was eating the cakes[5] made of dried barley, the gods moistened each one with the Sap of Life, as they placed it

[1] See Sutta Nipâta I, 4. The Si*m*halese always has a long î in Kasî.

[2] Âve*th*ana. Compare the use of all these terms above, II, 1, 3 (vol. i, p. 46).

[3] There is nothing about this infusion of the Sap of Life (dibba*m* oga*m*) in the published texts of the Pi*t*akas. But it is mentioned in the account in the *G*âtaka Commentary of the second meal referred to ('Buddhist Birth Stories,' p. 92). The other is, of course, the Buddha's last meal, 'Book of the Great Decease,' IV, 14-23 (in my 'Buddhist Suttas,' pp. 71-73).

[4] Hîna*t*i-kumburê gives here a great deal of additional matter (pp. 314-324).

[5] Pulake; which the Si*m*halese renders peti.

near him[1]. And thus was the body of the Tathâgata fully refreshed.'

'Great indeed was the good fortune, Nâgasena, of those gods that they were ever and always so zealous in their care for the body of the Tathâgata! Very good, Nâgasena! That is so, and I accept it as you say.'

[Here ends the problem as to the Buddha's mode of livelihood.]

[DILEMMA THE FIFTIETH.

ON THE BUDDHA'S AFTER-DOUBT[2].]

35. 'Venerable Nâgasena, your people say:

"The Tathâgata gradually, through millions of years, through æon after æon[3], brought his omniscient wisdom to perfection for the sake of the salvation of the great masses of the people[4]."

'But on the other hand (they say)[5]:

"Just after he had attained to omniscience his

[1] I am not sure what meal is here referred to. The Buddha is twice said to have taken meals at Verañgâ (in the Sutta Vibhaṅga, pp. 6, 11; Pârâgika I, 2 and I, 4). In neither case is there any mention of these cakes. But the former of the two may be the one referred to, as it took place in a time of drought.

[2] Compare my manual 'Buddhism,' p. 41.

[3] Literally 'through four Asaṅkheyyas and a lak of Kappas.'

[4] This passage has not yet been traced in the Piṭakas, and the word samuddharanâ (rendered 'salvation') does not occur elsewhere in published texts. It means literally 'bringing safe to shore.' Compare samuddhaṭa at Saddhammopâyana 143 in the 'Journal of the Pâli Text Society' for 1887, p. 44.

[5] See 'Vinaya Texts,' vol. i, p. 85, and Saṃyutta Nikâya VI, 1. The words are very slightly different.

heart inclined, not to the proclamation of the Truth, but to rest in peace."

'So that, Nâgasena, just as if an archer, or an archer's pupil, who had practised archery for many days with the object of fighting, should, when the day of the great battle had come, draw back—just so did the Tathâgata, who through countless ages had gradually matured his omniscience for the sake of bringing safe to the shore (of salvation) the great masses of the people, turn back, on the day when that omniscience had been reached, from proclaiming the Truth. Just as if a wrestler who through many days had practised wrestling should, when the day of the wrestling match[1] had come, draw back—just so did the Tathâgata, who through countless ages had gradually matured his omniscience for the sake of bringing safe to the shore (of salvation) the great masses of the people, turn back, on the day when that omniscience had been reached, from proclaiming the Truth.

'Now was it from fear, Nâgasena, that the Tathâgata drew back, or was it from inability to preach[2], or was it from weakness, or was it because he had not, after all, attained to omniscience? [233] What was the reason of this? Tell me, I pray, the reason, that my doubts may be removed. For if for so long a time he had perfected his wisdom with the object of saving the people, then the statement that he hesitated to announce the Truth must be wrong. But if that be true, then the other statement must be false. This too is a double-edged problem,

[1] Compare Sumangala Vilâsinî, p. 85.

[2] Apâka*t*atâya, not found elsewhere. I follow the Si*m*halese, which has bœna kiya*n*ta no dœnena bœwin.

now put to you,—a problem profound, a knot hard to unravel,—which you have to solve.'

36. 'The statements in both the passages you quote, O king, are correct. But that his heart inclined, not to the preaching of the truth, but to inaction, was because he saw, on the one hand, how profound and abstruse was the Doctrine[1], how hard to grasp and understand, how subtle, how difficult to penetrate into; and, on the other, how devoted beings are to the satisfaction of their lusts, how firmly possessed by false notions of Individualism[2]. And so (he wavered) at the thought: "Whom shall I teach? And how can I teach him?"—his mind being directed to the idea of the powers of penetration which beings possessed.

'Just, O king, as an able physician, when called in to a patient suffering from a complication of diseases, might reflect: "What can be the treatment, what the drug, by which this man's sickness can be allayed?"—just so, O king, when the Tathâgata called to mind how afflicted were the people by all the kinds of malady which arise from sin, and how profound and abstruse was the Doctrine, how subtle, and how difficult to grasp, then at the thought: "Whom can I teach? And how shall I teach him?" did his heart incline rather to inaction than to preaching—[234] his mind being directed to the powers of penetration which beings possessed.

'And just, O king, as a king, of royal blood, an anointed monarch, when he calls to mind the many

[1] 'Of Arahatship' is Hînaṅi-kumburê's gloss.

[2] Sakkâya-diṭṭhi. The belief in being, instead of in becoming; the belief in the permanence of individuality. See my 'Hibbert Lectures,' pp. 211-214.

people who gain their livelihood in dependence on the king—the sentries and the body-guard, the retinue of courtiers, the trading folk, the soldiers and the royal messengers, the ministers and the nobles[1]—might be exercised at the thought: "How now, in what way, shall I be able to conciliate them all?"—just so when the Tathâgata called to mind how profound and abstruse was the Doctrine, how subtle, and how difficult to grasp, and how devoted beings were to the satisfaction of their lusts, how firmly possessed by false notions of Individualism, then at the thought: "Whom shall I teach? And how shall I teach him?" did his heart incline rather to inaction than to preaching—his mind being directed to the powers of penetration which beings possessed.

37. 'And this, too, is an inherent necessity in all Tathâgatas that it should be on the request of Brahmâ that they should proclaim the Dhamma. And what is the reason for that? All men in those times, with the ascetics and the monks, the wandering teachers and the Brahmans, were worshippers of Brahmâ, reverers of Brahmâ, placed their reliance on Brahmâ. And therefore, at the thought: "When so powerful and glorious, so famous and renowned, so high and mighty a one has shown himself inclined (to the Dhamma), then will the whole world of gods and men become inclined to it, hold it fitting, have faith in it"—on this ground, O king, the Tathâgatas preached the Dhamma when requested to do so by Brahmâ. For just, O king, as what a sovran or a minister of state shows homage to, or offers worship to, that will the rest of mankind, on

[1] On this list see below, IV, 6, 11.

the ground of the homage of so powerful a personage, show homage to and worship—just so, O king, when Brahmâ had paid homage to the Tathâgatas, so would the whole world of gods and men. For the world, O king, is a reverer of what is revered. And that is why Brahmâ asks of all Tathâgatas that they should make known the Doctrine, and why, on so being asked, they make it known[1].'

'Very good, Nâgasena! The puzzle has been well unravelled, most able has been your exposition. That is so, and I accept it as you say.'

[Here ends the problem as to the Buddha's hesitation to make the Doctrine known.]

Here ends the Fifth Chapter.

---

[1] Hînaṅ-kumburê here gives a page of description—not found in the Pâli—of the episode of Brahmâ's request to the Buddha. The oldest account of this episode has been already translated in vol. xiii of the 'Sacred Books of the East,' in 'Vinaya Texts,' part i, pp. 84–88.

Book IV. Chapter 6.

[Dilemma the Fifty-first.

Contradictory Statements as to the Buddha's Teacher.]

1. [235] 'Venerable Nâgasena, this too has been said by the Blessed One:

"I have no teacher, and the man
Equal to me does not exist.
No rival to me can be found
In the whole world of gods and men[1]."

'But on the other hand he said:

"Thus then, O brethren, Â*l*âra Kâlâma, when he was my teacher and I was his pupil, placed me on an equality with himself, and honoured me with exceeding great honour[2]."

---

[1] This verse is found three times in the Pi*t*akas—in the Mahâvagga I, 6, 8, in the Ariya-pariyesana Sutta (Ma*ggh*ima Nikâya I, 171), and in the Aṅgulimâla Sutta (Ma*ggh*ima Nikâya, No. 86). It occurs with other stanzas of a similar tendency, and many of the lines in those stanzas are repeated, but with variations and in a different order, by the author of the Lalita Vistara (pp. 526, 527 of Râ*g*endra Lâl Mitra's edition). One verse is found there in two detached lines which run thus in the Sanskrit:—

Â*k*âryyo na hi me kas*k*it, sad*ri*so me na vidyate

and

Sadevâsuragandharvvo nâsti me pratipudgala*h*.

Hîna*t*i-kumburê renders pa*t*ipuggalo, not by 'rival,' but by 'superior.'

[2] Mr. Trenckner has pointed out that this quotation is found in two Suttas, Nos. 85 and 100 in the Ma*ggh*ima Nikâya.

'Now if the former of these statements be right, then the second must be wrong. But if the second be right, then the first must be wrong. This too is a double-edged problem, now put to you, which you have to solve.'

2. 'Both the quotations you have made, O king, are accurate. But when he spoke of Â*l*âra Kâlâma as his teacher, that was a statement made with reference to the fact of his having been his teacher while he (Gotama) was still a Bodisat and before he had attained to insight and to Buddhahood; and there were five such teachers, O king, under whose tuition the Bodisat spent his time in various places—his teachers when he was still a Bodisat, before he had attained to insight and to Buddhahood. And who were these five?

3. 'Those eight Brahmans who, just after the birth of the Bodisat, took note of the marks on his body—**[236]** Râma, and Dha*g*a, and Lakkha*n*a, and Mantî[1], and Ya*ññ*a[2], and Suyâma, and Subho*g*a[3], and Sudatta[4]—they who then made known his future glory, and marked him out as one to be carefully guarded—these were first his teachers[5].

---

[1] Hîna*t*i-kumburê reads *G*âtimantî. It may be noted that Hardy (Manual of Buddhism, p. 149), who omits Ya*ññ*a, gives *G*âti and Manta as two separate names, and spells the last two names Bho*g*a Sudanta.

[2] So also the Si*m*halese, p. 329. But the *G*âtaka Commentary (verse 270 at vol. i, p. 50) has konda*ññ*a.

[3] The *G*âtaka Introduction (loc. cit.) has Bho*g*a. The Si*m*halese has Subho*g*a.

[4] Hîna*t*i-kumburê agrees here with Hardy in reading Sudanta.

[5] This episode has not been traced in the Pi*t*akas. The Si*m*halese here gives also the detail of the one and two fingers, found in the *G*âtaka, and translated in my 'Buddhist Birth Stories,' p. 72.

'And again, O king, the Brahman Sabbamitta of distinguished descent, who was of high lineage in the land of Udi*kk*a[1], a philologist and grammarian, well read in the six Vedaṅgas[2], whom Suddhodana the king, the Bodisat's father, sent for, and having poured out the water of dedication from a golden vase, handed over the boy to his charge, to be taught—this was his second teacher[3].

'And again, O king, the god who raised the agitation in the Bodisat's heart, at the sound of whose speech the Bodisat, moved and anxious, that very moment went out from the world in his Great Renunciation—this was his third teacher[4].

---

[1] In the North-West. See *G*âtaka I, 140, &c.

[2] *Kh*a*l*aṅgavanta*m*. These are phonetics, prosody, grammar, exegesis, astronomy, and ritual. I was wrong in taking Childers's interpretation of this word at 'Buddhist Birth Stories,' p. 72.

[3] This episode is also not in the Pi*t*akas. On o*n*o*g*eti see Mahâvagga I, 22, 18. Sabbamitra is given in the Thera Gâthâ, I, 150, as the name of a Thera, and in the Divyâvadana, p. 420, as the name of Asoka's herald or court crier.

[4] There is nothing about any such devatâ in the Pi*t*akas. Hîna*t*i-kumburê takes it to mean the god who took the outward appearance of the four visions—an old man, a sick man, a dead man, and a recluse. But in that story—which is not related in the Pi*t*akas of the Buddha, though it is referred to in connection with him at Buddhava*m*sa XXVI, p. 16—the god does not speak. The only god whose words are said, in any of the later Pâli legends, to have agitated the Bodisat's heart at that moment, was the Evil One himself; and that only in one version of the legend, the Pâli authority for which I cannot give. It is in Hardy's 'Manual,' p. 157, where the speech of the Evil One, placed at *G*âtaka I, 63 at a later time, is said to have been made at the moment of the Renunciation. Even if it be not a mere blunder of Hardy's to put it at that time, still it cannot be the speech referred to by our author. For the startling doctrine that the Evil One himself was one of the Bodisat's teachers would never have been smuggled in, as it were, by concealing the identity of the spirit referred to under

'And again, O king, Â*l*âra Kâlâma—he was his fourth teacher.

'And again, O king, Uddaka the son of Râma—he was his fifth teacher.

'These, O king, are the five who were his teachers when he was still a Bodisat, before he had attained to insight and to Buddhahood. But they were teachers in worldly wisdom. And in this Doctrine that is transcendental, in the penetrating into the wisdom of the omniscient ones—in that there is no one who is above the Tathâgata to teach him. Self-dependent for his knowledge is the Tathâgata, without a master, and that is why it was said by the Tathâgata:

"I have no teacher, and the man
Equal to me does not exist.
No rival to me can be found
In the whole world of gods and men."'

'Very good, Nâgasena! That is so, and I accept it as you say.'

[Here ends the dilemma as to the Buddha's teachers.]

---

the generic term of devatâ. Now in the Fo-pan-hin-tsi-*k*in (Nanjio, No. 680), a Chinese work of the beginning of the seventh century A. D., we find in the sixteenth kwuen or chapter (if one may trust the abstract given in Beal's 'Romantic Legend,' p. 131) that a Devaputra named Tsao-ping is said to have spoken to the Bodisat at the moment of the Renunciation. It is scarcely open to doubt that our author had in his mind an earlier form of that episode. But if so it is the only proved case of his having Sanskrit, and not Pâli works, as his authority.

[DILEMMA THE FIFTY-SECOND.

WHY MUST THERE BE ONLY ONE BUDDHA AT A TIME ?]

4. 'Venerable Nâgasena, this too was said by the Blessed One:

"This is an impossibility, an occurrence for which there can be no cause, that in one world two Arahat Buddhas supreme should arise at one and the same time [**237**]—such a thing can in no wise be[1]."

'But, Nâgasena, when they are preaching, all the Tathâgatas preach (the Doctrine as to) the thirty-seven constituent elements of insight[2]; when they are talking, it is of the Four Noble Truths that they talk; when they are instructing, it is in the three Trainings[3] that they instruct; when they are teaching, it is the practice of zeal[4] that they teach. If, Nâgasena, the preaching of all the Tathâgatas is one, and their talk of the same thing, and their training the same, and their teaching one, why then should not two Tathâgatas arise at the same time? Already by the appearance of one Buddha has this world become flooded with light. If there should be a second Buddha the world would be still more illuminated by the glory of them both. When they were exhorting two Tathâgatas would exhort at ease; when they were instructing two Tathâgatas would instruct at ease. Tell me the reason of this, that I may put away my doubt.'

---

[1] Aṅguttara Nikâya I, 15, 10.

[2] These divisions of the seven 'Jewels of the Law' of Arahatship are set out in my 'Buddhist Suttas,' pp. 62–63.

[3] Adhisîla, adhi*k*itta, and adhipa*ññ*â.

[4] Appamâda.

5. 'This world system, O king, is a one-Buddha-supporting world; that is, it can bear the virtue of only a single Tathâgata. If a second Tathâgata were to arise the world could not bear him, it would shake and tremble, it would bend, this way and that, it would disperse, scatter into pieces, dissolve, be utterly destroyed. Just as a boat, O king, might be able to carry one passenger across. Then, when one man had got on board, it would be well trimmed and able to bear his weight[1]. But if a second man were to come like to the first in age and caste and strength and size and stoutness of body and build of frame, and he too should get on board the boat—would that boat be able, O king, to carry them both?'

'Certainly not, Sir! it would shake and tremble; it would bend, this way and that; it would break into pieces, be shattered, dissolved, and utterly destroyed; it would sink into the waves.'

'Just so, O king, with this world, if a second Tathâgata were to appear. Or suppose, O king, that a man [**238**] had eaten as much food as he wanted, even so that he had filled himself with nourishment up to the throat, and he—thus satiated[2], regaled, filled with good cheer, with no room left for more, drowsy and stiff as a stick one cannot bend—were again to eat as much food as he had eaten before—would such a man, O king, then be at ease?'

'Certainly not, Sir! If he were to eat again, but once more, he would die.'

---

[1] Samupâdikâ, for which the Si*m*halese has sama bara wannîya, usûlana sulu wannîya.

[2] Dhâto; not in Childers, but see *G*âtaka II, 247, Mahâvagga VI, 25, 1, and below, IV, 6, 29.

'Well, no more could this world bear a second Tathâgata, than that man could bear a second meal.'

6. 'But how is that, Nâgasena? Would the earth tremble at a too great weight of goodness?'

'Suppose, O king, there were two carts quite filled with precious things up to the top [1], and people were to take the things from the one cart and pile them up on the other, would that one be able to carry the weight of both?'

'Certainly not, Sir! The nave of its wheels would split, and the spokes would break, and the circumference would fall to pieces, and the axle-tree would break in twain [2].'

'But how is that, O king? Would the cart come to pieces owing to the too great weight of goods?'

'Yes, it would.'

7. 'Well, just so, O king, would the earth tremble owing to the too great weight of goodness. But that argument has been adduced to make the power of the Buddhas known [3]. Hear another fitting reason why two Buddhas could not appear at the same

[1] Literally 'mouth.' I presume a small uncovered bullock cart is meant, like that figured in Plate 57 in Cunningham's 'Bharhut Tope.' The chariot on the other hand is of the shape given in Plates 3, 34, 35 of Fergusson's 'Tree and Serpent Worship.' The usual form of the bullock cart has also a hood, or cover, as clearly shown in Fergusson's Plate No. 65, and Cunningham's Plate No. 34. But the one here referred to cannot have had the cover over it, for then the supposition that more goods were piled on to it, when full, would be an impossible one. I know of no other passage where the mukha, literally 'mouth,' of a cart is mentioned, and I may possibly be wrong in rendering it 'top.'

[2] This simile has already been used in the Vessantara Dilemma above, I, 173.

[3] Our author himself here confesses that his thoughts are more on edification than on logic.

time. If, O king, two Buddhas were to arise together, then would disputes arise between their followers, and at the words: "Your Buddha, our Buddha," they would divide off into two parties—just as would the followers of two rival powerful ministers of state. This is the other [239] reason, O king, why two Buddhas could not appear at the same time.

8. 'Hear a further reason, O king, why two Buddhas could not appear at the same time. If that were so, then the passage (of Scripture) that the Buddha is the chief would become false, and the passage that the Buddha takes precedence of all would become false, and the passage that the Buddha is the best of all would become false. And so all those passages where the Buddha is said to be the most excellent, the most exalted, the highest of all, the peerless one, without an equal, the matchless one, who hath neither counterpart nor rival—all would be proved false. Accept this reason too as in truth a reason why two Buddhas cannot arise at once.

9. 'But besides that, O king, this is a natural characteristic of the Buddhas, the Blessed Ones, that one Buddha only should arise in the world. And why? By reason of the greatness of the virtue of the all-knowing Buddhas. Of other things also, whatever is mighty in the world is singular. The broad earth is great, O king, and it is only one. The ocean is mighty, and it is only one. Sineru, the king of the mountains, is great; and it is only one. Space is mighty, and it is only one. Sakka (the king of the gods) is great, and he is only one. Mâra (the Evil One, Death) is great, and he is only one. Mahâ-Brahmâ is mighty, and he is only one.

A Tathâgata, an Arahat Buddha supreme, is great; and he is alone in the world. Wherever any one of these spring up, then there is no room for a second. And therefore, O king, is it that only one Tathâgata, an Arahat Buddha supreme, can appear at one time in the world.'

'Well has the puzzle, Nâgasena, been discussed by simile adduced and reason given. Even an unintelligent man on hearing this would be satisfied; how much rather one great in wisdom as myself. Very good, Nâgasena! That is so, and I accept it as you say.'

[Here ends the dilemma as to why there should be only one Buddha at a time in the world.]

[DILEMMA THE FIFTY-THIRD.

WHY SHOULD GIFTS BE GIVEN TO THE ORDER RATHER THAN TO THE BUDDHA?]

[240] 10. 'Venerable Nâgasena, the Blessed One said to his mother's sister[1], Mahâ-Pa*g*âpatî the Gotamî, when she was about to give him a cloth wrapper for use in the rainy season[2]:

"Give it, O Gotamâ, to the Order. If the Order is presented by you with it, then will you have paid homage thereby alike to the Order and to me[3]."

'But what, Nâgasena? Is not the Tathâgata of

[1] There is no general word in Pâli for aunt or uncle. There are separate expressions for each of the degrees of relationship expressed by those words in English—mother's brother, father's sister, &c.

[2] Vassika-sâ*t*ikâ. See the note at 'Vinaya Texts,' vol. ii, p. 225 (Sacred Books of the East, vol. xvii).

[3] From the *G*anta Sutta (Ma*gg*h*i*ma Nikâya, No. 142). See Mr. Trenckner's note.

greater weight and importance, and more worthy of gifts than even the jewel treasure of the Order, that the Tathâgata should have told his aunt, when about to present him with a wrapper for the rainy season which she herself had carded and pressed and beaten and cut and woven [1], to give it to the Order! If, Nâgasena, the Tathâgata were really higher and greater and more excellent than the Order, then he would have known that a gift given to him would be most meritorious, and therefore would not have told her to give it to the Order. But inasmuch as the Tathâgata, Nâgasena, puts himself not in the way of gifts to himself, gives no occasion for such gifts, you see that he then told his aunt to give that wrapper rather to the Order.'

11. 'The quotation you make, O king, is correct, and the Blessed One did so direct his aunt's gifts [2]. But that was not because an act of reverence paid to himself would bear no fruit, or because he was unworthy to receive gifts, but it was out of kindness and mercy that he, thinking: "Thus will the Order in times to come, when I am gone, be highly thought of;" magnified the excellence which the Order really had, in that he said: "Give it, O Gotamî, to the Order. If you present the Order with it, thus will you have paid homage alike to the Order and to me." Just as a father, O king, while he is yet alive, exalts in the midst of the assembly of ministers, soldiers, and royal messengers, of

[1] The translation of these five technical terms of cloth-making is doubtful. The Simhalese (p. 335) has piñgana, sindina, pothita, kaina, wiyana.

[2] The Simhalese (p. 335) here gives at length the story of Pagâpatî's gift, at the time when Gotama returned, as the Buddha, to Kapilavatthu.

sentries, body guards, and courtiers [1]—yea, in the presence of the king himself—the virtues which his son really possesses, thinking: "If established here he will be honoured of the people in times to come;" so was it out of mercy and kindness that the Tathâgata, thinking: "Thus will the Order, in times to come, when I am gone, be highly thought of;" magnified the excellence which the Order really had, in that he said: "Give it, O Gotamî, to the Order. If you present the Order with it, thus will you have paid homage alike to the Order and to me."

12. [**241**] 'And by the mere gift of a wrapper for the rainy season, the Order, O king, did not become greater than, or superior to, the Tathâgata. Just, O king, as when parents anoint their children with perfumes, rub them, bathe them, or shampoo them [2], does the son by that mere service of theirs become greater than, or superior to, his parents?'

'Certainly not, sir! Parents deal with their children as they will, whether the children like it or not [3]. And therefore do they anoint them with perfumes, shampoo, or bathe them.'

'And just so, O king, the Order did not become greater than, or superior to, the Tathâgata merely by the fact of that gift; and although the Tathâgata, whether the Order liked it or not, told his aunt to give the wrapper to the Order.

13. 'Or suppose, O king, some man should bring a complimentary present to a king, and the king should present that gift to some one else—to a soldier or a

---

[1] On this list see above, p. 234 of the Pâli text (IV, 5, 36).

[2] On these words compare Aṅguttara Nikâya II, 4, 2.

[3] Akâmakaranîyâ. Compare Vimâna Vatthu X, 6 and Dîgha Nikâya II, 46.

messenger, to a general or a chaplain,—would that man become greater than, or superior to, the king, merely by the fact that it was he who got the present[1]?'

'Certainly not, Sir! That man receives his wage from the king, from the king he gains his livelihood; it was the king who, having placed him in that office, gave him the present.'

'And just so, O king, the Order did not become greater than, or superior to, the Tathâgata merely by the fact of that gift. The Order is, as it were, the hired servant of the Tathâgata, and gains its livelihood through the Tathâgata. And it was the Tathâgata who, having placed it in that position, caused the gift to be given it.

14. 'And further the Tathâgata, O king, thought thus: "The Order is by its very nature worthy of gifts. I will therefore have this thing, my property though it be, presented to it," and so he had the wrapper given to the Order. For the Tathâgata, O king, magnifies not the offering of gifts to himself, but rather to whomsoever in the world is worthy of having gifts presented to him. For this was said, O king, by the Blessed One, the god over all gods, in the most excellent Ma*ggh*ima Nikâya, **[242]** in the religious discourse entitled Dhamma-dâyâda, when he was exalting the attainment of being content with little:

"He would become the first of my Bhikkhus, the most worthy of presents and of praise[2]."

15. 'And there is not, O king, in the three worlds

---

[1] The same simile has already occurred, vol. i, p. 220 (IV, 2, 22).

[2] Ma*ggh*ima Nikâya, vol. i, p. 13 (in Mr. Trenckner's edition for the Pâli Text Society).

any being whatever more worthy of gifts, greater or more exalted or better, than the Tathâgata. It is the Tathâgata who was greatest and highest and best. As it was said, O king, by Mâ*n*ava-gâmika the god, in the most excellent Sa*m*yutta Nikâya, as he stood before the Blessed One in the midst of the assembly of gods and men:

"Of all the Râ*g*agaha hills Mount Vipula's acknowledged chief,
Of the Himâlayas Mount White, of planetary orbs the sun,
The ocean of all waters, of constellations bright the moon[1]—
In all the world of gods and men the Buddha's the acknowledged Lord[2]!"

'And those verses of Mâ*n*ava the god, O king, were well sung, not wrongly sung, well spoken, not wrongly spoken, and approved by the Blessed One[3]. And was it not said by Sâriputta, the Commander of the faith:

"There is but one Confession, one true Faith,
One Adoration of clasped hands stretched forth
—That paid to Him who routs the Evil One,
And helps us cross the ocean of our ills[4]!"

[1] This must have been composed after the moon god had become established in belief as the husband, or lord, of the Nakshatras, or lunar mansions. For it cannot, of course, be intended that the moon is itself a constellation.

[2] Sa*m*yutta Nikâya III, 2, 10 (vol. i, p. 67 of the Pâli Text Society's edition).

[3] These phrases of approval are commonly used in the Pi*t*akas of words uttered by any one whose sayings would not, of themselves, carry weight. So in the Dîgha III, 1, 28 and in the Ma*ggh*ima I, 385.

[4] This verse has not yet been traced in the Pi*t*akas. In

'And it was said by the Blessed One himself, the god over all gods:

"There is one being, O brethren, who is born into the world for the good and for the weal of the great multitudes, out of mercy to the world, for the advantage and the good and the weal of gods and men. And what is that being? A Tathâgata, an Arahat Buddha supreme [1].'"

'Very good, Nâgasena! That is so, and I accept it as you say.'

[Here ends the dilemma as to the precedence of the Order over the Buddha.]

[DILEMMA THE FIFTY-FOURTH.

IS IT MORE ADVANTAGEOUS TO BE A LAYMAN, OR TO ENTER THE ORDER?]

16. 'Venerable Nâgasena, it was said by the Blessed One:

"I would magnify, O brethren, the Supreme Attainment [2] either in a layman or in a recluse. Whether he be a layman, O brethren, or a recluse, the man who has reached the Supreme Attainment

---

the Thera Gâthâ we have a collection of verses ascribed to Sâriputta, but this is not one of them. The literal translation is: 'There is but one feeling of faith, but one taking of refuge, but one stretching forth of the hands (with joined palms, in adoration—that paid) to the Buddha, who puts to rout the armies of the Evil One, and is able to make (us) cross (the ocean of continual becomings).' The taking of refuge meant is the confession, the repetition of which characterises a man as a Buddhist—'I take my refuge in the Buddha, &c.'

[1] Aṅguttara Nikâya I, 13, 1.

[2] That is, of insight and of the practice of right conduct.

shall overcome all the difficulties inherent therein, shall win his way even to the excellent condition of Arahatship[1]." [243]

'Now, Nâgasena, if a layman, clad in white robes, enjoying the pleasures of sense, dwelling in a habitation encumbered with wife and children[2], making constant use of the sandal wood of Benares[3], of garlands and perfumes and unguents, accepting gold and silver, wearing a turban inlaid with jewels and gold, can, having reached the Supreme Attainment, win his way to the excellent condition of Arahatship—and if a recluse, with his shaven head and yellow robes, dependent for his livelihood on the alms of other men, perfectly fulfilling the fourfold code of morality[4], taking upon himself and carrying out the hundred and fifty precepts[5], con-

---

[1] Sa*m*yutta Nikâya XLIV, 24, says Mr. Trenckner. The passage has not yet been reached in M. Léon Feer's edition for the Pâli Text Society. Hîna*t*i-kumburê (p. 341) renders *ñ*âya by nirwâna.

[2] Literally 'a bed encumbered, &c.' See below, p. 348 of the Pâli text, where the question, as here, is whether such a layman can attain to the Nirvâ*n*a of Arahatship.

[3] So the Buddha says of himself (Aṅguttara Nikâya III, 38), that, in the days when he was a layman, he never used any sandal wood except that from Benares.

[4] I don't know what these four Sîlakkhandhas are. Morality is described in the Pi*t*akas as threefold, fivefold, or tenfold, according as the Sîlas, in three divisions (as translated in my 'Buddhist Suttas,' vol. xi of the 'Sacred Books of the East,' pp. 189–200), are referred to; or the first five, or the whole ten, of the moral precepts (the Buddhist Ten Commandments) set out in my 'Buddhism,' p. 160. This reference to four divisions of the moral code is foreign to the Pi*t*akas, at least as we yet know them.

[5] The Diya*ddh*esu sikkhâpada-satesu. It is clear from the Aṅguttara Nikâya III, 83 that the precepts referred to are those of the Pâtimokkha (translated by me at the beginning of 'Vinaya

ducting himself according to the thirteen extra vows [1] without omitting any one of them, can also, having reached the Supreme Attainment, win his way to the excellent condition of Arahatship—then, Sir, what is the distinction between the layman and the recluse? Your austerity is without effect, your renunciation is useless, your observance of the precepts is barren, your taking of the extra vows is vain. What is the good of your therein heaping up woes to yourselves, if thus in comfort the condition of bliss can be reached?'

17. 'The words you ascribe to the Blessed One, O king, are rightly quoted. And that is even so. It is the man who has reached to the Supreme Attainment who bears the palm. If the recluse, O king, because he knows that he is a recluse, should neglect the Attainments, then is he far from the fruits of renunciation, far from Arahatship—how much more if a layman, still wearing the habit of the world, should do so! But whether he be a layman, O king, or a recluse, he who attains to the supreme insight, to the supreme conduct of life, he too will win his way to the excellent condition of Arahatship.

18. 'But nevertheless, O king, it is the recluse who is the lord and master of the fruit of renunciation. And renunciation of the world, O king, is full of gain, many and immeasurable are its advantages, its profit can no man calculate. Just, O king, as no man can put a measure, in wealth, on the

Texts,' vol. xvii of the 'Sacred Books of the East'), notwithstanding the fact that the actual number of these rules is 227.

[1] The Dhutangas: see above, IV, 5, 10, and the enumeration below at the translation of p. 351 of the Pâli text.

value of a wish-conferring gem, [244] saying: "Such and such is the price of the gem"—just so, O king, is the renunciation of the world full of gain, many and immeasurable are its advantages, its profit can no man calculate—no more, O king, than he could count the number of the waves in the great ocean, and say: "So and so many are the waves in the sea!"

19. 'Whatsoever the recluse, O king, may have yet to do, all that doth he accomplish straightway, without delay. And why is that? The recluse, O king, is content with little, joyful in heart, detached from the world, apart from society, earnest in zeal, without a home, without a dwelling-place, righteous in conduct, in action without guile, skilled in duty and in the attainments—that is why whatsoever may lie before him yet to do, that can he accomplish straightway, without delay—just as the flight of your javelin [1], O king, is rapid because it is of pure metal, smooth, and burnished, and straight, and without a stain.'

'Very good, Nâgasena! That is so, and I accept it as you say.'

[Here ends the dilemma as to the recluse having no advantages over the layman.]

---

[1] Nârâ*k*a. As Childers expresses a doubt as to the character of this weapon, I would refer to the Ma*ggh*ima I, 429, *G*âtaka III, 322, and Milinda, pp. 105, 418 (of Mr. Trenckner's text).

[DILEMMA THE FIFTY-FIFTH.

ASCETICISM.]

20. 'Venerable Nâgasena, when the Bodisat was practising austerity[1], then there was found no other exertion the like of his, no such power, no such battling against evil, no such putting to rout of the armies of the Evil One, no such abstinence in food, no such austerity of life. But finding no satisfaction in strife like that, he abandoned that idea, saying:

"Not even by this cruel asceticism am I reaching the peculiar faculty, beyond the power of man, arising from insight into the knowledge of that which is fit and noble[2]. May there not be now some other way to wisdom[3]?"

'But then, when weary of that path he had by another way attained to omniscience, he, on the other hand, thus again exhorted and instructed his disciple in that path (he had left, saying):

[245] "Exert yourselves, be strong, and to the faith
The Buddhas taught devote yourselves with zeal.
As a strong elephant a house of reeds,
Shake down the armies of the Evil One[4]."

[1] See 'Buddhist Birth Stories,' pp. 90, 91; and Ma*ggh*ima Nikâya I, 240–246.

[2] Alamariya-dassana-*ñâ*n*a-visesa*m*. I am not sure of the exact meaning of this compound. For alamariya the Si*m*halese has here (p. 343) sarva*gñ*atâ, and renders the whole 'do I arrive at a superhuman condition, at the distinctive faculty which is able to see into omniscience,' and on IV, 8, 21 it gives a slightly different but practically identical rendering, 'I shall not reach that superhuman condition which can distinguish or which suffices for insight into the supreme omniscience.'

[3] That is the wisdom of Buddhahood. The passage is from the Ma*ggh*ima Nikâya I, 246 (quoted also below, IV, 8, 21).

[4] This is a very famous stanza. It is put into the mouth of

'Now what, Nâgasena, is the reason that the Tathâgata exhorted and led his disciples to that path which he had himself abandoned, which he loathed?'

21. 'Both then also, O king, and now too, that is still the only path. And it is along that path that the Bodisat attained to Buddhahood. Although the Bodisat, O king, exerting himself strenuously, reduced the food he took till he had decreased it to nothing at all[1], and by that disuse of food he became weak in mind, yet when he returned little by little to the use of solid food, it was by that path that before long he attained to Buddhahood. And that only has been the path along which all the Tathâgatas reached to the attainment of the insight of omniscience. Just as food is the support of all beings, as it is in dependence on food that all beings live at ease, just so is that the path of all the Tathâgatas to the attainment of the insight of omniscience. The fault was not, O king, in the exertion, was not in the power, not in the battle waged against evil, that the Tathâgata did not then, at once, attain to Buddhahood. But the fault was in the disuse of food, and the path itself (of austerity) was always ready for use.

22. 'Suppose, O king, that a man should follow a path in great haste, and by that haste his sides

Abhibhû at Thera Gâthâ, verse 256, and in the Samyutta Nikâya VI, 2, 4, §§ 18 and 23; and also, in its Sanskrit form, into the mouth of the Buddha at the Divyâvadana, p. 300, and into the mouth of the gods at ibid. p. 569. It is possibly another instance of our author having Sanskrit, and not Pâli, authorities in his mind, that he ascribes it here to the Buddha, and not to Abhibhû, the Elder.

[1] The Simhalese has here six pages of description of the austerities not found in the Pâli text.

should give way[1], or he should fall a cripple on the ground, unable to move, would there then be any fault, O king, in the broad earth that that man's sides had given way?'

'Certainly not, Sir! The great earth is always ready. How should it be in fault? The fault was in the man's own zeal which made him fail.'

'And just even so, O king, the fault was not in the exertion, not in the power, not in the battle waged against evil, that the Tathâgata did not then, at once, attain to Buddhahood. But the fault was in the disuse of food, and the path itself was always ready—**[246]** just as if a man should wear a robe, and never have it washed, the fault would not be in the water, which would always be ready for use, but in the man himself. That is why the Tathâgata exhorted and led his disciples along that very path. For that path, O king, is always ready, always right.'

'Very good, Nâgasena! That is so, and I accept it as you say.'

[Here ends the dilemma as to the path.]

[1] Pakkha-hato: 'should become like one whose two hands are ruined' says the Simhalese here (p. 349), but at p. 411 (on p. 276 of the Pâli) it translates the same term, 'whose hands and feet are broken.' It is literally 'should become side-destroyed,' and may mean paralysed.

[DILEMMA THE FIFTY-SIXTH.

THE BACKSLIDERS.]

23. 'Venerable Nâgasena, this doctrine of the Tathâgatas is mighty, essentially true, precious, excellent, noble, peerless, pure and stainless, clear and faultless. It is not right to admit a layman who is merely a disciple[1] into the Order. He should be instructed as a layman still, till he have attained to the Fruit of the First Path[2], and then be admitted. And why is this? When these men, still being evil, have been admitted into a religion so pure, they give it up, and return again to the lower state[3], and by their backsliding the people is led to think: "Vain must be this religion of the Sama*n*a Gotama, which these men have given up." This is the reason for what I say.'

24. 'Suppose, O king, there were a bathing tank[4], full of pure clear cold water. And some man, dirty, covered with stains and mud, should come there, and without bathing in it should turn back again, still dirty as before. Now in that matter whom would the people blame, the dirty man, or the bathing tank?'

'The dirty man, Sir, would the people blame,

---

[1] Tâva*t*aka*m*. I take this word, in the sense of 'mere,' as an accusative in agreement with gihim (see the use of the word at pp. 107, 115, 241 of the Pâli text), and not as an accusative of motion, 'into so great a sâsana*m*.'

[2] That is till he be converted, till he has 'entered the stream.' See 'Buddhism,' p. 101.

[3] That is, of a layman.

[4] Ta*l*âka, which Childers wrongly renders 'pond, pool, lake.' It is always an artificial tank, reservoir. See *K*ullavagga X, 1, 6; *G*âtaka I, 239; Milinda, pp. 66, 81, 296.

saying: "This fellow came to the bathing tank, and has gone back as dirty as before. How could the bathing tank, of itself, cleanse a man who did not care to bathe? What fault is there in the tank?"'

'Just so, O king, [247] has the Tathâgata constructed a bathing tank full of the excellent waters of emancipation[1],—the bath of the good law. Whosoever of conscious discerning beings are polluted with the stains of sin, they, bathing in it, can wash away all their sins. And if any one, having gone to that bathing tank of the good law, should not bathe in it, but turn back polluted as before, and return again to the lower state, it is him the people would blame, and say: "This man entered religion according to the doctrine of the Conquerors, and finding no resting-place within it, has returned again to the lower state. How could the religion of the Conquerors, of itself, cleanse him who would not regulate his life in accordance with it? What fault is there in the system?"

25. 'Or suppose, O king, that a man afflicted with dire disease should visit a physician skilled in diagnosis[2], knowing an efficacious and lasting method of cure, and that that man should then not let himself be treated, but go back again as ill as before. Now therein whom would the people blame, the sick man or the doctor?'

'It is the sick man, Sir, they would blame, say-

[1] '**Vimutti**: of the nectar of the Nirvâ*n*a which is the highest fruit of Arahatship' is Hîna*t*i-kumburê's gloss.

[2] **Roguppatti-kusala*m***: 'skilled in the threefold origin of disease' says the Si*m*halese (p. 351). See also pp. 248, 272 of the Pâli text.

ing: "How could the physician, of himself, cure this man, who would not let himself be treated? What fault is there in the doctor?"'

'Just so, O king, has the Tathâgata deposited in the casket of his religion the ambrosial medicine (of Nirvâ*n*a) which is able to entirely suppress all the sickness of sin, thinking: "May all those of conscious sentient beings who are afflicted with the sickness of sin drink of this ambrosia, and so allay all their disease." And if any one, without drinking the ambrosia, should turn back again with the evil still within him, and return once more to the lower state, it is he whom the people will blame, saying: "This man entered religion according to the doctrine of the Conquerors, and finding no resting-place within it, has returned again to the lower state. How could the religion of the Conquerors, of itself, cure him who would not regulate his life in accordance with it? What fault is there in the system?"

[1] 26. 'Or suppose, O king, a starving man were to attend at a place where a mighty largesse of food[2] given for charity was being distributed, and then should go away again, still starving, without eating anything. Whom then would the people blame, the starving man, or the feast of piety?'

'It is the starving man, Sir, they would blame, saying: **[248]** "This fellow, though tormented with hunger, still when the feast of piety was provided for him, partook of nothing, and went back as hungry as before. How could the meal, of which he

[1] The Si*m*halese (p. 352) inserts here 'Give me, Sir, I pray you, another simile,' and then goes on 'Then suppose, O king, &c.'

[2] Bhatta, perhaps rice, as the food par excellence.

would not eat, enter, of itself, into his mouth? What fault is there in the food?"'

'Just so, O king, has the Tathâgata placed the most excellent, good, auspicious, delicate ambrosial food, surpassing sweet, of the realisation of the impermanency of all things[1], into the casket of his religion, thinking: "May all those of conscious sentient beings who feel within them the torment of sin[2], whose hearts are deadened by cravings, feeding upon this food, allay every longing that they have for future life in any form, in any world." And if any one, without enjoying this food, should turn back, still dominated by his cravings, and return once more to the lower state, it is he whom the people will blame, saying: "This man entered religion according to the doctrine of the Conquerors, and finding no resting-place within it, has returned again to the lower state. How could the religion of the Conquerors, of itself, purify him who would not regulate his life in accordance with it? What fault is there in the system?"'

27. 'If the Tathâgata, O king, had let a householder be received into the Order only after he had been trained in the first stage of the Excellent Way, then would renunciation of the world no longer indeed be said to avail for the putting away of evil qualities, for purification of heart—then would there be no longer any use in renunciation. It would be as if a man were to have a bathing tank excavated

[1] Kayâgata-sati: literally 'intentness of mind on (the truth relating to) bodies.'

[2] Kilesa-kilant-aggh*att*â. Compare *kh*âtaggh*a*tta*m*, *G*â-taka I, 345.

by the labour of hundreds (of workpeople[1]), and were then to have a public announcement made: "Let no one who is dirty go down into this tank! Let only those whose dust and dirt have been washed away, who are purified and stainless, go down into this tank!" Now would that bath, O king, be of any use to those thus purified and stainless?'

'Certainly not, Sir! The advantage they would have sought in going into the bath they would have already gained elsewhere. Of what use would the bath be to them then?'

'Just so, O king, had the Tathâgata ordained that only laymen who had already entered the first stage of the Excellent Way should be received into the Order, then would the advantage they seek in it have been already gained. Of what use would the renunciation be to them then?

28. 'Or suppose, O king, that a physician, a true follower of the sages of old[2], one who carries (in his memory) the ancient traditions and verses[3], a practical man[4], skilled in diagnosis, and master of an efficacious and lasting system of treatment, who had collected (from medicinal herbs) a medicine able to cure every disease, were to have it announced: **[249]** "Let none, Sirs, who are ill come to visit me! Let the

[1] Stonemasons and sculptors are implied as well as navvies. Compare my note at 'Buddhist Suttas,' p. 262.

[2] Sabhâva-isi-bhattiko. Compare Siva-bhattiko (Saivite) at Mahâva*m*sa, chapter 93, line 17. In râ*g*a-bhattiko (above, p. 142 of the Pâli text) the connotation is different. The Si*m*halese (p. 353) repeats the phrase.

[3] Suta-manta-dharo, which the Si*m*halese repeats.

[4] Atakkiko: 'without the theories (vitarka) resorted to by those ignorant of the practice of medicine' says Hîna*t*i-kumburê.

healthy and the strong visit me!" Now, would then, O king, those men free from illness and disease, healthy and jubilant, get what they wanted from that physician?'

'Certainly not, Sir! What men want from a physician, that would they have already obtained otherwise. What use would the physician be to them?'

'Just so, O king, had the Tathâgata ordained that only those laymen who had already entered the first stage of the Excellent Way should be received into the Order, then would the advantages they seek in it have been already gained elsewhere. Of what use would the renunciation be to them then?

29. 'Or suppose, O king, that some had had many hundreds of dishes of boiled milk-rice prepared[1], and were to have it announced to those about him: 'Let not, Sirs, any hungry man approach to this feast of charity. Let those who have well fed, the satisfied, refreshed, and satiated[2], those who have regaled themselves, and are filled with good cheer, —let them come to the feast." Now would any advantage, O king, be derived from the feast by those men thus well fed, satisfied, refreshed, satiated, regaled, and filled with good cheer?'

'Certainly not, Sir! The very advantage they would seek in going to the feast, that would they have already attained elsewhere. What good would the feast be to them?'

'Just so, O king, had the Tathâgata ordained that

[1] As Agâtasattu is said to have done for Devadatta at *G*âtaka I, 186.

[2] See above, IV, 6, 5.

only those laymen who had already entered the first stage of the Excellent Way should be received into the Order, thus would the advantages they seek in it have been already gained elsewhere. Of what use would the renunciation be to them?

30. 'But notwithstanding that, O king, they who return to the lower state manifest thereby five immeasurably good qualities in the religion of the Conquerors. And what are the five? They show how glorious is the state (which those have reached who have entered the Order), how purified it is from every stain, how impossible it is for the sinful to dwell within it together (with the good), how difficult it is to realise (its glory), how many are the restraints to be observed within it.

31. 'And how do they show the mighty glory of that state? Just, O king, as if a man, poor, and of low birth, without distinction [1], deficient in wisdom, were to come into possession of a great and mighty kingdom, it would not be long before he would be overthrown, utterly destroyed [2], and deprived of his glory. For he would be unable to support his dignity. [250] And why so? Because of the greatness thereof. Just so is it, O king, that whosoever are without distinction, have acquired no merit, and are devoid of wisdom, when they renounce the world according to the religion of the Conquerors, then, unable to bear that most excellent renunciation, overthrown, fallen, and deprived of their glory, they return to the lower state. For they are unable to

[1] Nibbisesa, not in Childers; but see, for instance, *G*âtaka II, 32.

[2] Paridha*m*sati. Compare below, IV, 7, 8 (p. 265 of the Pâli).

carry out the doctrine of the Conquerors. And why so? Because of the exalted nature of the condition which that doctrine brings about. Thus is it, O king, that they show forth the mighty glory of that state.

32. 'And how do they show how purified that state is from every stain? Just, O king, as water, when it has fallen upon a lotus, flows away, disperses, scatters, disappears, adheres not to it. And why so? Because of the lotus being pure from any spot. Just so, O king, when whosoever are deceitful, tricky, crafty, treacherous, holders of lawless opinions, have been admitted into the religion of the Conquerors, it is not long before they disperse, and scatter, and fall from that pure and stainless, clear and faultless [1], most high and excellent religion, and finding no standing-place in it, adhering no longer to it, they return to the lower state. And why so? Because the religion of the Conquerors has been purified from every stain. Thus is it, O king, that they show forth the purity of that state from every stain.

33. 'And how do they show how impossible it is for the sinful to dwell within it together with the good? Just, O king, as the great ocean does not tolerate the continuance in it of a dead corpse [2], but whatever corpse may be in the sea, that does it bring quickly to the shore, and cast it out on to the dry land. And why so? Because the ocean is

[1] Nikka*n*t*aka-pa*nd*ara: literally 'thornless and yellow-white.' The second of these epithets of the religion (sâsana) is applied to it above, IV, 6, 23 (p. 250 of the Pâli). The Si*m*halese merely repeats them.

[2] On this curious belief see the note above on IV, 3, 39 (p. 187 of the Pâli).

the abode of mighty creatures. Just so, O king, when whosoever are sinful, foolish, with their zeal evaporated, distressed, impure, and bad, have been admitted into the religion of the Conquerors, it is not long before they abandon that religion, and dwelling no longer in it—the abode of the mighty, the Arahats, purified, and free from the Great Evils[1]—they return to the lower state. And why so? Because it is impossible for the wicked to dwell in the religion of the Conquerors. Thus is it, O king, that they show forth the impossibility of the sinful to abide within it together with the good.

34. 'And how do they show how difficult a state it is to grasp? Just, O king, as archers who are clumsy, untrained, ignorant, and bereft of skill, are incapable of high feats of archery, such as hair-splitting[2], but miss the object, and shoot beyond the mark. And why so? Because of the fineness and minuteness of the horse-hair. [251] Just so, O king, when foolish, stupid, imbecile[3], dull, slow-minded

---

[1] They are lust, dulness, delusion, and ignorance.

[2] Vâlaggavedha*m*, 'hair-splitting;' which is also used in the Pi*t*akas in the secondary sense we too have given to it.

[3] E*l*amûga, supposed to mean literally 'deaf and dumb;' but often (if not always) used in this secondary sense. See *G*âtaka I, 247, 248 (where both MSS. read elamûga), and Ma*gg*hima Nikâya I, 20 (where Mr. Trenckner has an interesting note). In both places the fifth century commentators explain the word by lâla-mukha, 'drivelling,' supposing it to be derived from elâ, 'saliva,' and mukha, 'mouth.' This is certainly wrong, for the last part of the compound is mûka, 'dumb.' The fact is that the word was a puzzle, even then. The meaning assigned to it by both Pâli and Sanskrit lexicographers of 'deaf and dumb' has not yet been confirmed by a single passage either in Pâli or Sanskrit. And as e*d*a, 'sheep,' is common in both, in its longer form of e*d*aka, e*l*aka, the compound probably meant originally 'as dumb

fellows renounce the world according to the doctrine of the Conquerors, then they, unable to grasp the exquisitely fine and subtle distinctions of the Four Truths, missing them, going beyond them, turn back before long to the lower state. And why so? Because it is so difficult to penetrate into the finenesses and subtleties of the Truths. This is how they show forth the difficulty of its realisation.

35. 'And how do they show how many are the restraints to be observed within it? Just, O king, as a man who had gone to a place where a mighty battle was going on, when, surrounded on all sides by the forces of the enemy, he sees the armed hosts crowding in upon him, will give way, turn back, and take to flight. And why so? Out of fear lest he should not be saved in the midst of so hot a fight. Just so, O king, when whosoever are wicked [1], unrestrained, shameless, foolish, full of ill-will, fickle, unsteady, mean and stupid, renounce the world under the system of the Conquerors, then they, unable to carry out the manifold precepts, give way, turn back, and take to flight, and so before long return to the lower state. And why so? Because of the multiform nature of the restraints to be observed in the religion of the Conquerors. Thus is it, O king, that they show forth the manifoldness of the restraints to be observed.

as a sheep,' which would be a quite satisfactory basis for the secondary sense of 'imbecile,' in which alone it can be traced in Pâli. For the Sanskrit form e*d*amûka Böhtlingk-Roth give only lexicographers as authority. So elâ, 'saliva,' is in Pâli only a lexicographer's word, and may have been invented to explain e*l*amûga, and ane*l*agalâ vâkâ, as at Sumangala, p. 282.

[1] Pâkata. Hîna*t*i-kumburê says (p. 356) pâpakalâwû, which suggests a different reading.

36. 'As on that best of flowering shrubs, O king, the double jasmine[1], there may be flowers that have been pierced by insects, and their tender stalks being cut to pieces, they may occasionally fall down. But by their having fallen is not the jasmine bush disgraced. For the flowers that still remain upon it pervade every direction with their exquisite perfume. Just so, O king, whosoever having renounced the world under the system of the Conquerors, return again to the lower state, are, like jasmine flowers bitten by the insects and deprived of their colour and their smell, colourless as it were in their behaviour, and incapable of development. But by their backsliding is not the religion of the Conquerors put to shame. For the members of the Order who remain in the religion pervade the world of gods and men with the exquisite perfume of their right conduct.

37. 'Among rice plants that are healthy **[252]** and ruddy there may spring up a kind of rice plant called Karumbhaka[2], and that may occasionally fade. But by its fading are not the red rice plants disgraced. For those that remain become the food of kings. Just so, O king, whosoever having renounced the world under the system of the Conquerors return again to the lower state, they, like Karumbhaka plants among the red rice, may grow not, nor attain development, and may even occasionally relapse into the lower state. But by their backsliding is not the religion of the Conquerors put to shame,

[1] Vassikâ. So also above, IV, 3, 32 (p. 183 of the Pâli).

[2] 'A yellowish white kâwalu sort' says Hîna*t*i-kumburê, and Clough renders kâwalu by 'a species of panic grass' (panicum glaucum). The word has only been found in this passage.

for the brethren that remain stedfast become fitted even for Arahatship.

38. 'On one side, O king, of a wish conferring gem a roughness [1] may arise. But by the appearance of that roughness is not the gem disgraced. For the purity that remains in the gem fills the people with gladness. And just so, O king, whosoever having renounced the world under the system of the Conquerors return again to the lower state, they may be rough ones and fallen ones in the religion. But by their backsliding is not the religion of the Conquerors put to shame, for the brethren who remain stedfast are the cause of joy springing up in the hearts of gods and men.

39. 'Even red sandal wood of the purest sort, O king, may become in some portion of it rotten and scentless. But thereby is not the sandal wood disgraced. For that portion which remains wholesome and sweet scatters and diffuses its perfume all around. And just so, O king, whosoever having renounced the world under the system of the Conquerors return again to the lower state, they, like the rotten part of the sandal wood, may be as it were thrown away in the religion. But by their backsliding is not the religion of the Conquerors put to shame. For the brethren who remain stedfast pervade, with the sandal wood perfume of their right conduct, the world of gods and men.'

'Very good, Nâgasena! By one appropriate simile after another, by one correct analogy after another have you most excellently made clear the

[1] Kakkasa*m*. The Si*m*halese (p. 357) has left out this clause, evidently by mistake only.

faultlessness of the system of the Conquerors, and shown it free from blame. And even those who have lapsed make evident how excellent that system is.'

[Here ends the dilemma as to those who have lapsed.]

[DILEMMA THE FIFTY-SEVENTH.

WHY HAVE ARAHATS NO POWER OVER THEIR BODIES?]

40. 'Venerable Nâgasena, your (members of the Order) say: **[253]**

"There is one kind of pain only which an Arahat suffers, bodily pain, that is, and not mental[1]."

'How is this, Nâgasena? The Arahat keeps his mind going by means of the body. Has the Arahat no lordship, no mastery, no power over the body?'

'No, he has not, O king.'

'That, Sir, is not right that over the body, by which he keeps his mind going, he should have neither lordship, nor mastery, nor power. Even a bird, Sir, is lord and master and ruler over the nest in which he dwells.'

41. 'There are these ten qualities, O king, inherent in the body, which run after it, as it were, and accompany it from existence to existence[2]. And what are the ten? Cold and heat, hunger and thirst,

---

[1] This passage has not yet been traced in the Pi/akas. An almost identical phrase has already been quoted, as said by the Buddha himself, at II, 1, 4 (p. 44 of the Pâli).

[2] Bhave bhave anuparivattanti. See IV, 4, 41 (p. 204 of the Pâli).

the necessity of voiding excreta, fatigue and sleepiness, old age, disease, and death. And in respect thereof, the Arahat is without lordship, without mastery, without power.'

'Venerable Nâgasena, what is the reason why the commands of the Arahat have no power over his body, neither has he any mastery over it? Tell me that.

'Just, O king, as whatever beings are dependent on the land, they all walk, and dwell, and carry on their business in dependence upon it. But do their commands have force, does their mastery extend over it?'

'Certainly not, Sir!'

'Just so, O king, the Arahat keeps his mind going through the body. And yet his commands have no authority over it, nor power.'

42. 'Venerable Nâgasena, why is it that the ordinary man suffers both bodily and mental pain?'

'By reason, O king, of the untrained state of his mind. Just, O king, as an ox when trembling with starvation might be tied up with a weak and fragile and tiny rope of grass or creeper. But if the ox were excited [1] then would he escape, dragging the fastening with him. Just so, O king, when pain comes upon him whose mind is untrained, then is his mind excited, and the mind so excited bends his body this way and that and makes it grovel on the ground, [254] and he, being thus untrained in mind, trembles [2] and cries, and gives forth terrible

[1] Parikupati, not in Childers; but see above, IV, 1, 38 (p. 118 of the Pâli).

[2] Tasati. Mr. Trenckner points out (p. 431) that two MSS.

groans. This is why the ordinary man, O king, suffers pain as well in body as in mind.'

43. 'Then why, Sir, does the Arahat only suffer one kind of pain—bodily, that is, and not mental?'

'The mind of the Arahat, O king, is trained, well practised, tamed, brought into subjection, and obedient, and it hearkens to his word. When affected with feelings of pain, he grasps firmly the idea of the impermanence of all things, so ties his mind as it were to the post of contemplation, and his mind, bound to the post of contemplation, remains unmoved, unshaken, becomes stedfast, wanders not—though his body the while may bend this way and that and roll in agony by the disturbing influence of the pain. This is why it is only one kind of pain that the Arahat suffers—bodily pain, that is, and not mental.'

44. 'Venerable Nâgasena, that verily is a most marvellous thing that when the body is trembling the mind should not be shaken. Give me a reason for that.'

'Suppose, O king, there were a noble tree, mighty in trunk and branches and leaves. And when agitated by the force of the wind its branches should wave. Would the trunk also move?'

'Certainly not, Sir!'

'Well, O king, the mind of the Arahat is as the trunk of that noble tree.'

'[1] Most wonderful, Nâgasena, and most strange!

---

read rasati and one sarati. The Simhalese rendering (p. 359), bhaya wanneya, confirms the reading he has adopted.

[1] The Simhalese (p. 360) has four lines here that are not in the Pâli.

Never before have I seen a lamp of the law that burned thus brightly through all time.'

[Here ends the dilemma as to the Arahat's power over his body.]

[DILEMMA THE FIFTY-EIGHTH.

THE LAYMAN'S SIN.]

45. **[255]** 'Venerable Nâgasena, suppose a layman had been guilty of a Pârâgika offence[1], and some time after should enter the Order. And neither he himself should be aware that when still a layman he had so been guilty, nor should any one else inform him, saying: "When a layman you were guilty of such an offence." Now if he were to devote himself to the attainment of Arahatship[2], would he be able so to comprehend the Truth as to succeed in entering upon the Excellent Way?'

'No, O king, he would not.'

'But why not, Sir?'

'That, in him, which might have been the cause of his grasping the Truth has been, in him, destroyed. No comprehension can therefore take place.'

46. 'Venerable Nâgasena, your people say: "To him who is aware (of an offence) there comes

[1] This, for a member of the Order, would be either unchastity, theft, murder, or putting forward false claims to extraordinary holiness. See 'Vinaya Texts,' part i, pp. 3-5. But Hînati-kumburê takes the word Pârâgika here in the sense of matricide, parricide, injuring a Bo Tree, murder of an Arahat, wounding a Tathâgata, or rape of a nun.

[2] Tathattâya. Rahat phala pinisa pilipadane wî nam, says the Simhalese (p. 361).

remorse. When remorse has arisen there is an obstruction in the heart. To him whose heart is obstructed there is no comprehension of the Truth [1]."

'Why should there then be no such comprehension to one not aware of his offence, feeling no remorse, remaining with a quiet heart. This dilemma touches on two irreconcilable statements. Think well before you solve it.'

47. 'Would selected seed [2], O king, successfully sown in a well-ploughed, well-watered, fertile soil, come to maturity?'

'Certainly, Sir!'

'But would the same seed grow on the surface of a thick slab of rock?'

'Of course not.'

'Why then should the same seed grow in the mud, and not on the rock?'

'Because on the rock the cause for its growth does not exist. Seeds cannot grow without a cause.'

'Just so, O king, the cause by reason of which his comprehension of the Truth (his conversion) might have been brought about, has been rooted out in him. Conversion cannot take place without a cause.'

48. '[Give me, Sir, another simile [3].']

'Well, O king, will sticks and clods and cudgels [4]

---

[1] This passage has not yet been traced in the Pi*t*akas.

[2] Sârada*m* bîgam. 'Seed which will give sâra.' It has nothing to do with sâradam, 'autumn.' See Sa*m*yutta Nikâya XXII, 24.

[3] Added from the Si*m*halese (p. 362). It is not in the Pâli.

[4] Laku*t*a, not in Childers. But see below (p. 301 of the Pâli text). It is probably the same Dravidian word as appears in the Sanskrit dictionaries as lagu*d*a.

and clubs find a resting-place in the air, in the same way as they do on the ground?'

'No, Sir.'

'But what is the reason why they come to rest on the earth, when they will not stand in the air?'

'There is no cause in the air for their stability, and without a cause they will [256] not stand.'

'Just so, O king, by that fault of his the cause for his conversion has been removed. And without a cause there can be no conversion. Now will fire, O king, burn in water in the same way as it will on land?'

'No, Sir.'

'But why not?'

'Because in water the conditions precedent for burning do not exist. And there can be no burning without them.'

'Just so, O king, are the conditions precedent to conversion destroyed in him by that offence of his. And when the conditions which would bring it about are destroyed there can be no conversion.'

49. 'Venerable Nâgasena, think over this matter once more. I am not yet convinced about it. Persuade me by some reason how such obstruction can occur in the case of one not aware of his offence, and feeling therefore no remorse.'

'Would the Halâhala[1] poison, O king, if eaten by

---

[1] There is a curious confusion about this word. It is found in post-Buddhistic Sanskrit in the sense of a particular sort of strong poison, and in this sense it occurs also in the Ģâtaka Commentary I, 271; III, 103; and in the Tela-ka*t*âha-gâthâ, verse 82. In none of these passages is the nature of the poison at all explained; it is taken for granted as a well-known powerful poison. But above (p. 122 of the Pâli), and at *G*âtaka I, 47, 48, it is used in

a man who did not know he had eaten it, take away his life?'

'Yes, Sir.'

'Just so, O king, is there an obstruction to his comprehension of the Truth, who, without being aware of it, has committed a sin. And would fire, O king, burn a man who walked into it unawares?'

'Yes, Sir.'

'Well, just so in the case you put. Or would a venomous snake, if it bit a man without his knowing it, kill him?'

'Yes, Sir.'

'Well, just so in the case you put. And is it not true that Samana Kolañña, the king of Kaliṅga,—when surrounded by the seven treasures of a sovereign overlord he went mounted on his state elephant to pay a visit to his relatives,—was not able to pass the Tree of Wisdom, though he was not aware that it was there[1]? Well, of the same kind is the reason why one who has committed an offence, even though he know it not, is nevertheless incapable of rising to the knowledge of the Truth.'

'Verily, Nâgasena, this must be the word of the Conqueror. To find any fault with it were vain. And this (explanation of yours) must be the meaning of it. I accept it as you say.'

[Here ends the dilemma of the layman's sin.]

---

the sense of kolâhala, 'noise' (compare the Sanskrit halahalâ, used as a cry or call). In this sense it is probably a mere imitation of the supposed sound. In the sense of poison its derivation is doubtful.

[1] This must be the incident referred to at Gâtaka IV, 232, though the name of the king is given (on the previous page) simply as Kâliṅgo and not as Samana-kolañño.

[DILEMMA THE FIFTY-NINTH.

THE GUILTY RECLUSE.]

50. [**257**] 'Venerable Nâgasena, what is the distinction, what the difference, between a layman who has done wrong, and a Sama*n*a (member of the Order) who has done wrong? Will they both be reborn in like condition? Will the like retribution happen to both? Or is there any difference?'

'There are, O king, ten qualities which abound in the guilty Sama*n*a, distinguishing him from the guilty layman. And besides that, in ten ways does the Sama*n*a purify the gifts that may be given him.

51. 'And what are the ten qualities which abound in the guilty Sama*n*a, distinguishing him from the guilty layman? The guilty Sama*n*a, O king, is full of reverence for the Buddha, for the Law, for the Order, and for his fellow-disciples; he exerts himself in putting questions about, and in recitation of (the sacred texts); he is devoted to learning, though he has done wrong. Then, O king, the guilty one entering the assembly, enters it decently clad, he guards himself alike in body and mind through fear of rebuke, his mind is set upon exerting himself (towards the attainment of Arahatship), he is of the companionship of the brethren. And even, O king, if he does wrong he lives discreetly. Just, O king, as a married woman sins only in secret and in privacy, so does the guilty Sama*n*a walk discreetly in his wrongdoing. These are the ten qualities, O king, found in the guilty Sama*n*a, distinguishing him from the guilty layman.

52. 'And what are the ten ways in which, besides,

he purifies a gift given to him? He purifies it in that he wears an invulnerable coat of mail[1]; in that he is shorn in the fashion of the characteristic mark of renunciation used by the seers of old[2]; in that he is one who is included in the multitude of the brethren; in that he has taken his refuge in the Buddha, the Law, and the Order; in that he dwells in a lonely spot suitable for the exertion (after Arahatship); in that he seeks after the treasure of the teaching of the Conquerors; in that he preaches the most excellent law (Dhamma); in that his final destiny is to be reborn in the island of truth[3]; in that he is possessed of an honest belief that the Buddha is the chief of all beings; in that he has taken upon himself the keeping of the Uposatha day. These, O king, are the ten ways in which, besides, he purifies a gift given to him.

53. [258] 'Even, O king, when thoroughly fallen, a guilty Sama*n*a yet sanctifies the gifts of the supporters of the faith—just as water, however thick, will wash away slush, and mud and dirt and stains—just as hot, and even boiling water will put a mighty blazing fire out—just as food, however nasty, will allay the faintness of hunger. For thus, O king, hath it been said by the god over all gods in the most excellent Ma*ggh*ima Nikâya in the chapter "On gifts[4]:"

[1] 'The threefold robes, the Arahad-dha*g*a, for the suppression of all evil, worn by all the Buddhas' adds the Si*m*halese (p. 364). Compare above, vol. i, p. 190.

[2] The Rishis; 'who were gaining the Swarga-moksha' adds the Si*m*halese. (It was before the days of Arahatship.)

[3] Dhamma-dîpa, that is to reach Arahatship, Nirvâ*n*a. Compare the *G*âtaka stanza, IV, 121, verse 3.

[4] The Dakkhi*n*â Vibhaṅga, No. 12 in the Vibhaṅga Vagga, No. 142 in the whole Nikâya.

"Whene'er a good man, with believing heart,
Presents what he hath earned in righteousness
To th' unrighteous,—in full confidence
On the great fruit to follow the good act—
Such gift is, by the giver, sanctified." '

'Most wonderful, Nâgasena, and most strange! We asked you a mere ordinary question, and you, expounding it with reasons and with similes, have filled, as it were, the hearer with the sweet taste of the nectar (of Nirvâ*n*a [1]). Just as a cook, or a cook's apprentice, taking a piece of ordinary nutmeg, will, treating it with various ingredients, prepare a dish for a king—so, Nâgasena, when we asked you an ordinary question, have you, expounding it with reasons and similes, filled the hearer with the sweet taste of the nectar of Nirvâ*n*a.'

[Here ends the dilemma as to the guilty recluse.]

[1] Amata-madhura*m* savanûpaga*m* akâsi. Hîna*t*i-kumburê (p. 365) understands this differently, and has apparently read amata*m* madhura*m*. For he translates 'filled the hearer with the taste of Nirvâ*n*a, and adorned the least of the people with the ear-ring of Arahatship.' It is difficult to see where he finds 'the least of the people,' and there is no authority for rendering savanûpaga*m* by 'ear-ring.' Amata as an epithet of the state of mind called by Western writers Nirvâ*n*a (which is only one of many names applied in the Buddhist books themselves to Arahatship) has nothing to do with immortality. As this wrong notion of the use of the word has led to much confusion, I have considered in an appendix all the passages in which the epithet occurs.

[DILEMMA THE SIXTIETH.

THE SOUL IN WATER.]

54. 'Venerable Nâgasena, this water when boiling over the fire gives forth many a sound, hissing and simmering[1]. Is then, Nâgasena, the water alive? Is it shouting at play? [259] or is it crying out at the torment inflicted on it?'

'It is not alive, O king, there is no soul or being in water. It is by reason of the greatness of the shock of the heat of the fire that it gives forth sounds, hissing and simmering.'

'Now, venerable Nâgasena, there are false teachers who on the ground that the water is alive reject the use of cold water, and warming the water feed themselves on tepid foods of various kinds[2].

'These men find fault with you and revile you, saying: "The Sakyaputtiya Sama*n*as do injury to the souls of one function[3]." Dispel, remove, get rid of this their censure and blame.'

55. 'The water is not alive, O king. Neither is there therein either soul or being. And it is the

[1] *Kikki/*âyati *ki/iki/*âyati. The English words entirely fail in representing the sound of these striking words (in which the *k* is pronounced as ch). They recur Mahâvagga VI, 26, 7 and Puggala Pa*ññ*atti 3, 14.

[2] Veka*/*ika-veka*/*ikam. Hîna*/*i-kumburê renders this by hu*n*u-hu*n*uye*m*, and hu*n*u is the Pâli u*n*ha. But the expression may be compared with vika*/*a, 'filth' (used for food), at Mahâvagga VI, 14, 6. On the belief of the *G*ains in the 'water-life,' see the Âyâra*n*ga Sutta I, 1, 3 (in vol. xxii of the S. B. E., p. 5).

[3] Ekindriya*m* *g*îva*m*. The belief in such a soul is to be understood as held by the teachers referred to, not by Buddhists. Hîna*/*i-kumburê's translation implies that the one function meant is prâ*n*a. Compare the heretical opinions described in the Dîgha II, 20, and 26.

great shock of the heat of the fire that makes it sound, hissing and simmering. It is like the water in holes in the ground, in ponds and pools and lakes, in reservoirs, in crevices and chasms, in wells, in low-lying places, and in lotus-tanks[1], which before the mighty onset of the hot winds[2] is so deeply affected that it vanishes away. But does the water in that case, O king, give forth many a sound, hissing and simmering?'

'Certainly not, Sir.'

'But, if it were alive, the water would then also make some sound. Know therefore, O king, that there is no soul, neither being, in water; and that it is the greatness of the shock of the heat of the water that makes it give forth sounds.

56. 'And hear another reason, O king, for the same thing. If water, O king, with grains of rice in it, is put in a vessel and covered up, but not placed over the fireplace, would it then give forth sound?'

'No, Sir. It would remain quiet and unmoved.'

'But if you were to put the same water, just as it is in the vessel, over a fireplace[3], and then light up the fire, would the water remain quiet and motionless?'

---

[1] This list recurs in almost identical terms below, p. 296 (of the Pâli text). See also above, II, 1, 10 (vol. i, p. 55).

[2] Vâtâtapa, not 'heat and wind' as Böhtlingk-Roth understand it in their rendering of vâtâtapika. See 'Vinaya Texts,' III, 159 and Sa*m*yutta XXII, 12.

[3] Uddhane. This word is always rendered 'oven' in the dictionaries. But I doubt whether there were ovens at all, in our sense, in those times, and in any case, the word certainly means a fireplace made of bits of brick between which the wood for the fire is laid. We must imagine the bricks to be laid, as a general rule, in a triangle. I have often seen both Si*m*halese peasants, and Tamils from the Madras Presidency, boiling their rice in the open over such extemporised fireplaces in pots either placed on the

'Certainly not, Sir. It would move and be agitated, become perturbed and all in commotion, waves would arise in it, it would rush up and down and in every direction [260], it would roll up and boil over[1], and a garland of foam would be formed above it.'

---

bricks, or more usually suspended from three sticks meeting above the centre of the space between the bricks. That this, and this only, is the sense in which the word is used in Pâli is clear from a comparison of the passages in which it is used, though of course in huts the fireplace, though of the same kind, would be a more permanent structure. I have not traced the word in the Pi*t*akas. In the *G*âtaka Commentary I, 68 we find that smoke usually rises uddhanato. This it would not do from an oven. At *G*âtaka I, 33 and Dhammapada Commentary 176 uddhane âropetvâ must mean 'lifted up on to' not 'put into.' At *G*âtaka I, 346 the speaker says he will take the uddhana-kapallâni, and the rice with ingredients for the curry, up on to the flat roof of the house, and there cook and eat them. These are the bits of brick to make, not an oven, but a fireplace of. At *G*âtaka II, 133 the husband wrings the neck of the parrot (the parrot of the Arabian Nights, chap. 2, I may add) and throws it uddhanantaresu 'into the space (between the bricks) of the fireplace.' At *G*âtaka III, 178 and Dhammapada Commentary 263 we hear of meat boiled on the uddhana. In the Rasavâhini (quoted in the 'Journal of the Pâli Text Society,' 1884, p. 53) the context shows that a fireplace or hearth, not an oven, is meant. Finally above (p. 118 of the Pâli) we hear of a cauldron being mounted on to an uddhana, and the fire being lighted under it.

The derivation is uncertain. The Sanskrit lexicographers give various forms of the word—always with the meaning 'oven'—uddhâna, udvâna, uddhmâna (this last probably influenced by a supposition that the word was connected with dham). The Si*m*halese is uduna, and though 'fireplace' is better than 'oven,' we have really no corresponding word in English. The gypsies, who are Indian in origin, should have a name for it. But I only find in their vocabularies yogongo-tan, which means simply aggi*th*âna.

[1] Uttarati patarati. 'Itirenneya pœtirenneya' says the Si*m*halese.

'But why so, O king, when water in its ordinary state remains quiet and motionless?'

'It is because of the powerful impulse of the heat of the fire that the water, usually so still, gives forth many a sound, bubbling and hissing.'

'Then thereby know, O king, that there is no soul in water, neither being; and that it is the strong heat of the fire that causes it to make sounds.

57. 'And hear another reason, O king, for the same thing. Is there not water to be found in every house put into water-pots with their mouths closed up?'

'Yes, Sir.'

'Well, does that water move, is it agitated, perturbed, in commotion, does it form into waves, does it rush up and down and in every direction, does it roll up and roll over[1], is it covered with foam?'

'No! That water is in its ordinary state. It remains still and quiet.'

'But have you ever heard that all this is true of the water in the great ocean? and that rearing up[2] it breaks against the strand with a mighty roar?'

'Yes, I have both heard of it, and have seen it myself—how the water in the great ocean lifts itself up a hundred, two hundred, cubits high, towards the sky.'

'But why, whereas water in its ordinary state remains motionless and still, does the water in the ocean both move and roar?'

'That is by reason of the mighty force of the

[1] Uttarati patarati, the second of which the Si*m*halese (p. 368) omits here. See p. 117 of the Pâli.

[2] Ussakkitvâ, 'continually pumping up,' says the Si*m*halese.

onset of the wind, whereas the water in the water-jars neither moves nor makes any noise, because nothing shakes it.'

'Well, the sounds given forth by boiling water are the result, in a similar way, [261] of the great heat of the fire.'

58. 'Do not people cover over the dried-up mouth of a drum[1] with dried cow-leather?'

'Yes, they do.'

'Well, is there any soul or being, O king, in a drum?'

'Certainly not, Sir.'

'Then how is it that a drum makes sounds?'

'By the action or effort of a woman or a man.'

'Well, just as that is why the drum sounds, so is it by the effect of the heat of the fire that the water sounds. And for this reason also you might know, O king, that there is no soul, neither being, in water; and that it is the heat of the fire which causes it to make sounds[2].

59. 'And I, too, O king, have something yet further to ask of you—thus shall this puzzle be thoroughly threshed out. How is it? Is it true of every kind of vessel that water heated in it makes noises, or only of some kinds of vessels?'

'Not of all, Sir. Only of some.'

'But then you have yourself, O king, abandoned the position you took up. You have come over to my side—that there is no soul, neither being, in water. For only if it made noises in whatever

---

[1] Bheri-pokkharam, which the Si*m*halese renders bheri-mukha. Compare Vimâna Vatthu 18, 10, where pokkhara is a sort of drum.

[2] A similar analogy has been used above, vol. i, p. 48.

vessel it were heated could it be right to say that it had a soul. There cannot be two kinds of water—that which speaks, as it were, which is alive, and that which does not speak, and does not live. If all water were alive, then that which the great elephants, when they are in rut, suck up in their trunks, and pour out over their towering frames, or putting into their mouths take right into their stomachs—that water, too, when crushed flat between their teeth, would make a sound. And great ships, a hundred cubits long, heavily laden, full of hundreds of packages of goods, pass over the sea—the water crushed by them, too, would make sounds. [262] And mighty fish, leviathans with bodies hundreds of leagues long[1], since they dwell in the great ocean, immersed in the depths of it, must, so living in it, be constantly taking into their mouths and spouting out the ocean—and that water, too, crushed between their gills or in their stomach, would make sounds. But as, even when tormented with the grinding and crushing of all such mighty things, the water gives no sound, therefore, O king, you may take it that there is no soul, neither being, in water.'

'Very good, Nâgasena! With fitting discrimination has the puzzle put to you[2] been solved. Just, Nâgasena, as a gem of inestimable value which had come into the hands of an able master goldsmith, clever and well trained, would meet with due appreciation, estimation, and praise—just as a rare pearl

[1] Their names are given. On this belief see above, III, 7, 10 (vol. i, p. 130) and *K*ullavagga IX, 1, 3.

[2] Desâgato, 'based on the teaching of the Omniscient One,' says Hîna*t*i-kumburê, who therefore apparently read desanâgato.

at the hands of a dealer in pearls, a fine piece of woven stuff at the hands of a cloth merchant[1], or red sandal wood at the hands of a perfumer—just so in that way has this puzzle put to you been solved with the discrimination it deserved.'

[Here ends the dilemma as to the water-life.]

Here ends the Sixth Chapter[2].

[1] Dussika, a word only found, so far as I know, here and below at V, 4 (p. 331 of the Pâli), where see the note.

[2] Sakala-*g*ana mano-mandanîyya-wû srî-saddharmâdâsayehi sha*t*wana vargaya nimiyeya, says the Si*m*halese.

BOOK IV. CHAPTER 7.

[DILEMMA THE SIXTY-FIRST.

THE OBSTACLES.]

1. 'Venerable Nâgasena, the Blessed One said:

"Live, O brethren, devoted to and taking delight in that which has no Papañkas (none of those states of mind which delay or obstruct a man in his spiritual growth[1])."

'What is that which has no Papañkas?'

'The fruit of Conversion has no Papañkas, O king, the fruit of that stage of the Path in which those live who will be only once, or not all reborn, the fruit of Arahatship has no Papañkas.'

'But if that be so, Nâgasena, [**263**] then why do the brethren concern themselves with recitation of, with asking questions about the discourses, and the pieces in mixed prose and verse, and the expositions, and the poems, and the outbursts of emotion, and the passages beginning "Thus he said," and the birth-stories, and the tales of wonder, and the extended treatises[2]? Why do they trouble themselves about new buildings[3], about gifts and offerings to the Order?'

---

[1] This passage has not yet been traced in the Piṭakas.

[2] These are the well-known navangâni, the nine divisions into which the Scriptures are divided. See Maggh*ima Nikâya I, 133; Aṅguttara Nikâya IV, 6, &c.

[3] Navakammena palibuggh*anti. The Simhalese adds khaṇḍa-phulla-paṭisaṃkharaṇayen, 'repairing dilapidations.'

2. 'They who do all these things, O king, are working towards attainment of freedom from the Papañkas, (that is of Arahatship[1]). For whereas, O king, all those of the brethren who are pure by nature, those upon whose hearts an impression has been left by good deeds done in a former birth[2], can (get rid of the Papañkas, can) become Arahats, in a moment—those on the other hand whose minds are much darkened by evil[3] can only become Arahats by such means as these.

3. 'Just, O king, as while one man who has sown a field and got the seed to grow can, by the exertion of his own power, and without any rampart or fence, reap the crop—whereas another man when he has got the seed to grow must go into the woods, and cut down sticks and branches and make a fence of them, and thus only reap the crop—in the same way those who are pure by nature, upon whose hearts an impression has been left by good deeds done in a former birth, can, in a moment, become Arahats, like the man who gathers the crop without a fence. But those, on the other hand, whose minds are darkened by the evil they have done can only become Arahats by such means as these—like the man who can only reap his crop if he builds the fence.

4. 'Or just, O king, as there might be a bunch of fruits on the summit of a lofty mango tree. Then

---

[1] This is (very properly) added in the Simhalese, for the two are practically identical. Hereafter it throughout renders nippapañko hoti by 'become an Arahat.'

[2] Vâsita-vâsanâ. See above, vol. i, p. 18.

[3] Mahârâgakkhâ, 'evil done both in this and in former births' is here to be understood.

whoever possesses the power of Iddhi could take those fruits[1], but whoever had not, he would have first to cut sticks and creepers and construct a ladder, and by its means climb up the tree and so get at the fruit. In the same way those who are by nature pure, and upon whose hearts an impression has been left by good deeds done in a former birth, may attain, in a moment, to Arahatship, like the man getting the fruit by the power of Iddhi. But those, on the other hand, whose minds are darkened by the evil they have done can only become Arahats by such means as these, like the man who only gets the fruit by means of the ladder he has made.

5. **[264]** 'Or just, O king, as while one man who is clever in business will go alone to his lord and conclude any business he has to do, another man, rich though he may be, must by his riches bring others to his service, and by their help get the business done—and it is for the business' sake that he has to seek after them. In the same way those who are by nature pure, upon whose hearts an impression has been left by good deeds done in a former birth, may reach, in a moment, to the attainment of the Six Transcendent Qualities[2], like the man who does the business alone by himself. Whereas those brethren whose minds are darkened by the evil they have done can only by such means as these realise the gains of renunciation, like the man who through others' help brings his business to the desired end.

---

[1] By the simple process of going through the air to the top of the tree.

[2] Chasu abhiññâsu vasîbhâva*m* pâpu*n*anti.

6. 'For recitation is of great good, O king, and asking questions, and superintending building work, and seeing to gifts and offerings is of great good—each of them to one or other of the spiritual objects which the brethren seek to obtain. Just, O king, as there might be some one of the ministers or soldiers or messengers or sentries or body-guards or attendants who was especially serviceable and useful to the king, but when he had any business given him to do they would all help him—just so are all these things of assistance when those objects have to be attained. When all men, O king, shall have become by nature pure, then will there be nothing left for a teacher [1] to accomplish. But so long as there is still need of discipleship [2], so long will even such a man, O king, as the Elder Sâriputta himself (though he had attained to the summit of wisdom by reason of his having been, through countless ages, deeply rooted in merit), yet find it impossible, without discipleship, to attain to Arahatship [3]. Therefore is it, O king, that hearing (the Scriptures) is of use, and recitation of them, and asking questions about them. And therefore is it that those also who are addicted to

[1] 'Who is a Buddha' adds Hînati-kumburê (p. 372).

[2] Savanena, literally 'bearing.'

[3] Âsavakkhayam, literally 'to the destruction of the Âsavas;' that is, of the Great Evils, which are lust, dulness, becoming, and ignorance. Mr. Trenckner marks this passage as corrupt, but Hînati-kumburê seems to have had the same reading before him as Mr. Trenckner has selected from his MSS., except that he has not had any mark of punctuation after the word hoti.

The particular occasion on which Sâriputta became finally free from the Âsavas is related in the Dîgha-nakha Suttanta, No. 74 in the Magghima Nikâya (vol. i, p. 50 of Mr. Trenckner's edition for the Pâli Text Society).

these things, becoming free from the obstacles thereto, attain to Arahatship[1].'

'Right well have you made me understand this puzzle, Nâgasena. That is so, and I accept it as you say.'

[Here ends the dilemma as to the obstacles.]

[DILEMMA THE SIXTY-SECOND.

THE LAY ARAHAT.]

7. 'Venerable Nâgasena, your people say: "Whosoever has attained, as a layman, to Arahatship, one of two conditions are possible to him, and no other—either that very day he enters the Order, or he dies away, for beyond that day he cannot last[2]."

[265] 'Now if, Nâgasena, he could not, on that day, procure a teacher or preceptor, or a bowl and set of robes[3], would he then, being an Arahat, admit himself, or would he live over the day, or would some other Arahat suddenly appear by the power of Iddhi and admit him, or would he die away?'

'He could not, O king, because he is an Arahat, admit himself. For any one admitting himself to

---

[1] Literally 'therefore is it that recitation, &c., is a condition free from the obstacles, and unmade' (the Unmade being also one of the many epithets of Arahatship).

[2] This passage has not yet been traced in the Piṭakas.

[3] All these are necessary to one who is a candidate for admission to the Order—the teacher and preceptor being, as it were, his proposer and seconder; and no one being admitted who is not already provided with a bowl and a set of robes.

the Order is guilty of theft[1]. And he could not last beyond that day. Whether another Arahat should happen, or not, to arrive, on that very day would he die away.'

'Then, Nâgasena, by whatever means attained, the holy condition of Arahatship is thereby also lost, for destruction of life is involved in it.'

8. 'It is the condition of laymanship which is at fault, O king. In that faulty condition, and by reason of the weakness of the condition itself, the layman who, as such, has attained to Arahatship must either, that very day, enter the Order or die away. That is not the fault of Arahatship, O king. It is laymanship that is at fault, through not being strong enough.

'Just, O king, as food, that guards the growth and protects the life of all beings, will, through indigestion, take away the life of one whose stomach is unequal to it, whose internal fire is low and weak—just so if a layman attains Arahatship when in that condition unequal to it, then by reason of the weakness of the condition he must, that very day, either enter the Order or die away.

'Or just, O king, as a tiny blade of grass when a heavy rock is placed upon it will, through its weakness, break off and give way—just so when a layman attains Arahatship, then, unable to support Arahatship in that condition, he must, that very day, either enter the Order or die away.

'Or just, O king, as a poor weak fellow of low birth and little ability, if he came into possession of

[1] 'Inasmuch as he would be taking a dress to which he was not entitled' is Hînati-kumburê's gloss.

a great and mighty kingdom, would be unable to support the dignity of it [1]—just so if a layman attains to Arahatship, then is he unable, in that condition, to support it. [266] And that is the reason why he must, on that very day, either enter the Order or die away.'

'Very good, Nâgasena! That is so, and I accept it as you say.'

[Here ends the dilemma as to the lay Arahat.]

[DILEMMA THE SIXTY-THIRD.

THE FAULTS OF THE ARAHAT.]

9. 'Venerable Nâgasena, can an Arahat be thoughtless [2]?'

'The Arahats, O king, have put thoughtlessness far from them. They are never inadvertent.'

'But can an Arahat be guilty of an offence?'

'Yes, O king.'

'In what respect?'

'In the construction of his cell [3], or in his intercourse (with the other sex) [4], or in imagining the wrong time (for the midday meal) to be the right

---

[1] We have had the same simile above, IV, 6, 30.

[2] Compare the note on *K*ullavagga V, 9, 5.

[3] Which must not exceed certain dimensions, &c. See the 6th Sa*m*ghâdisesa ('Vinaya Texts,' I, pp. 8, 9).

[4] Sa*ñk*aritte. Perhaps only the 5th Sa*m*ghâdisesa (loc. cit.) is here referred to, but Hîna*t*i-kumburê (p. 375) takes it in a much more extended sense, as referring to all the restrictions, as to time and place, &c., laid down for the guidance of the brethren in their relations with women.

time[1], or when he has been invited (to a meal[2]) forgetting the invitation, or in taking to be "left over[3]" food which has not been left over.'

'But, venerable Nâgasena, your people say: "Those who commit offences do so from one of two reasons, either out of carelessness or out of ignorance[4]."

'Now, is the Arahat careless that he commits offences?'

'No, O king.'

'Then if the Arahat commits offences, and yet is not careless, he must be capable of thoughtlessness.'

'He is not capable of thoughtlessness, and yet the Arahat may be guilty of offences.'

'Convince me then by a reason. What is the reason of this?'

10. 'There are two kinds of sins, O king—those which are a breach of the ordinary moral law, and those which are a breach of the Rules (of the Order). And what is a breach of the ordinary moral law? The ten modes of evil action[5] (killing, theft,

[1] It is curious that the well-known rule as to not eating solid food after sunturn at noon is not expressly stated in the Pâtimokkha, or indeed anywhere in the Vinaya. But it is often implied. See, for instance, the 37th Pâkittiya Rule; Mahâvagga VI, 19, 2; VI, 33, 2; VI, 40, 3; *K*ullavagga V, 25, &c.

[2] See the Pâ*k*ittiya Rules, Nos. 32 and 46.

[3] A Bhikkhu may not, except for certain special reasons, such as sickness, either keep or eat food which has been left over after the principal meal. See the 35th Pâ*k*ittiya Rule. Hîna*t*i-kumburê (pp. 374–376) goes at great length into the full meaning of these five technical terms of the Buddhist Canon Law, giving examples under each.

[4] Not traced as yet. 'Ignorance of the Sikshâpadas' says the Si*m*halese (p. 376).

[5] Dasa akusala-kamma-pathâ. See Childers sub voce.

unchastity, lying, slander, harsh language, frivolous talk, covetousness, malice, and false doctrine). These things are against the moral law. And what is a breach of the Rules? Whatever is held in the world as unfitting and improper for Samanas, but is not wrong for laymen—things concerning which the Blessed One laid down rules for his disciples, not to be transgressed by them their lives long. Eating after sunturn, O king, is not wrong to those in the world, but is wrong to those in the religion (the Order) of the Conquerors. Doing injury to trees and shrubs is no offence in the eyes of the world, but it is wrong in the religion. The habit of sporting in the water is no offence to a layman, but it is wrong in the religion. And many other things of a similar kind, O king, are right in the world, but wrong in the religion of the Conquerors. This is what I mean by a breach of the Rules. Now the Arahat (he in whom the Great Evils are destroyed) is incapable of sinning against whatever is moral law, but he may unawares be guilty of an offence against the rules of the Order. **[267]** It is not within the province of every Arahat to know everything, nor indeed in his power. He may be ignorant of the personal or family name of some woman or some man. He may be ignorant of some road over the earth. But every Arahat would know about emancipation, and the Arahat gifted with the six modes of transcendental knowledge[1] would know what lies within their scope, and an omniscient Tathâgata, O king, would know all things.'

[1] Chalabhiññâo—which every Arahat is not.

'Very good, Nâgasena! That is so, and I accept it as you say.'

[Here ends the dilemma as to the faults of the Arahat.]

[DILEMMA THE SIXTY-FOURTH.

WHAT IS, BUT NOT IN THE WORLD.]

11. 'Venerable Nâgasena, there are to be seen in the world Buddhas, and Pa*kk*eka-Buddhas, and disciples of the Tathâgatas, and sovran overlords, and kings over one country, and gods and men;—we find rich and poor, happy and miserable;—we find men who have become women, and women who have become men—there are good deeds and evil, and beings experiencing the result of their virtue or their vice;—we find creatures born from eggs, and in the water, and in sediment, or springing into life by the mere apparitional birth; creatures without feet, bipeds and quadrupeds, and creatures with many feet;—we find Yakkhas and Rakkhasas, and Kumbha*nd*as, and Asuras, and Dânavas, and Gandhabbas, and Petas and Pisâ*k*as, and Kinnaras, and Mahoragas, and Nâgas and Supa*nn*as [1], and magicians and sorcerers;—there are elephants, and horses, and cattle, and buffaloes, and camels, and asses, and goats, and sheep, and deer, and swine, and lions, and tigers, and leopards, and bears, and wolves, and hyenas, and dogs, and jackals, and many kinds of birds;—there is gold and silver, and the pearl, and

[1] Fairies and goblins of various degrees and powers, most of them not mentioned in the Pi*t*akas.

the diamond, and the chauk, and rock, and coral, and the ruby, and the Masâra stone, and the cat's-eye, and crystal, and quartz, and iron ore [1], and copper, and brass [2], and bronze;—there is flax, and silk, and cotton, and hemp [3], and wool;—there is rice, and paddy, and barley, and millet, and kudrûsa grain, and beans [4], and wheat, and oilseed, and vetches;—there are perfumes prepared from roots, and sap, and pith, and bark, and [268] leaves, and flowers, and fruit, and of all other sorts;—we find grass, and creepers, and shrubs, and trees, and medicinal herbs, and forests, and rivers, and mountains, and seas, and fish, and tortoises,—all is in the world. Tell me, Sir, what there is, then, which is not in the world.'

12. 'There are three things, O king, which you cannot find in the world. And what are the three? That which, whether conscious or unconscious, is not subject to decay and death—that you will not find. That quality of anything, (organic or inorganic), which is not impermanent—that you will not find. And in the highest sense there is no such thing as being possessed of being [5].'

---

[1] Kâ*l*a-loha, 'black metal' (not found in the Pi*t*akas).

[2] Va*tt*a-loha, 'round metal.' I can only guess what this is. The Si*m*halese has simply wa*t*aloha, which is equally unintelligible. The word occurs again below (p. 331 of the Pâli), and Hîna*t*i-kumburê there renders it tœ*t*i, which is a particular kind of brazen vessel.

[3] Two kinds are mentioned, sâ*n*a and bhaṅga. I don't know the difference between them. The Si*m*halese has sana and bañkâlpê.

[4] Three kinds of Phaseoli are mentioned, Varaka, Mugga, and Mâsa.

[5] Paramatthena sattûpaladdhi natthi. It is very curious

'Very good, Nâgasena! That is so, and I accept it as you say.'

[Here ends the puzzle as to what is not in the world.]

[DILEMMA THE SIXTY-FIFTH.

THINGS WITHOUT A CAUSE.]

13. 'Venerable Nâgasena, there are found beings in the world who have come into existence through Karma, and others who are the result of a cause, and others produced by the seasons[1]. Tell me—is there any thing that does not fall under any one of these three heads?'

'There are two such things, O king. And what are the two? Space, O king, and Nirvâna.'

'Now do not spoil the word of the Conquerors, Nâgasena, nor answer a question without knowing what you say!'

'What, pray, is it I have said, O king, that you should address me thus?'

'Venerable Nâgasena, that is right what you said in respect of space. But with hundreds of reasons

that both here, and in the analogous phrase at III, 5, 6 (p. 71 of the Pâli), Hînati-kumburê should merely repeat the words in the text. Both of these curt summaries of the deepest Buddhist doctrine were probably as ambiguous to him as they are to us. The literal translation of the phrase here would be, 'In the highest sense there is no acquisition of a being.' As in Buddhism being cannot strictly be predicated of any thing, or of any god or animal or man,—each is really only becoming—the sense probably meant must be very nearly as I have ventured to render.

[1] Utu-nibbattâ; which the Simhalese repeats. See the next dilemma on 'Karma-born, cause-born, and season-born.'

did the Blessed One proclaim to his disciples the way to the realisation of Nirvâ*n*a. And yet you say that Nirvâ*n*a is not the result of any cause!'

'No doubt, O king, the Blessed One gave hundreds of reasons for our entering on the way to the realisation of Nirvâ*n*a. But he never told us of a cause out of which Nirvâ*n*a could be said to be produced.'

14. 'Now in this, Nâgasena, we have passed from darkness into greater darkness, **[269]** from a jungle into a denser jungle, from a thicket into a deeper thicket—inasmuch as you say there is a cause for the realisation of Nirvâ*n*a, but no cause from which it can arise. If, Nâgasena, there be a cause of the realisation of Nirvâ*n*a, then we must expect to find a cause of the origin of Nirvâ*n*a. Just, Nâgasena, as because the son has a father, therefore we ought to expect that that father had a father—or because the pupil has a teacher, therefore we ought to expect that the teacher had a teacher—or because the plant came from a seed, therefore we ought to expect that the seed too had come from a seed[1]—so, Nâgasena, if there be a reason for the realisation of Nirvâ*n*a, we ought to expect that there is a reason too for its origin,—just as if we saw the top of a tree, or of a creeper, we should conclude that it had a middle part, and a root.'

'Nirvâ*n*a, O king, is unproduceable, and no cause for its origin has been declared.'

'Come now, Nâgasena, give me a reason for this. Convince me by argument, so that I may know how

[1] Compare the argument based above, II, 3, 2, on this and similar series.

it is that while there is a cause that will bring about the realisation of Nirvâ*n*a, there is no cause that will bring about Nirvâ*n*a itself.'

15. 'Then, O king, give ear attentively, and listen well, and I will tell you what the reason is. Could a man, O king, by his ordinary power, go up from hence to the Himâlaya, the king of mountains?'

'Yes, Sir, he could.'

'But could a man, by his ordinary power, bring the Himâlaya mountains here?'

'Certainly not, Sir.'

'Well! therefore is it that while a cause for the realisation of Nirvâ*n*a can be declared, the cause of its origin can not. And could a man, O king, by his ordinary power cross over the great ocean in a ship, and so go to the further shore of it?'

'Yes, Sir, he could.'

'But could a man **[270]** by his ordinary power bring the further shore of the ocean here?'

'Certainly not, Sir.'

'Well! so is it that while a cause for the realisation of Nirvâ*n*a can be declared, the cause of its origin can not. And why not? Because Nirvâ*n*a is not put together of any qualities.'

16. 'What, Sir! is it not put together?'

'No, O king. It is uncompounded, not made of anything. Of Nirvâ*n*a, O king, it cannot be said that it has been produced, or not been produced, or that it can be produced[1], that it is past or future or present, that it is perceptible by the eye or the ear or the nose or the tongue, or by the sense of touch.'

'But if so, Nâgasena, then you are only showing

[1] The Si*m*halese is here (p. 381) expanded.

us how Nirvâ*n*a is a condition that does not exist [1]. There can be no such thing as Nirvâ*n*a.'

'Nirvâ*n*a exists, O king. And it is perceptible to the mind. By means of his pure heart, refined and straight, free from the obstacles [2], free from low cravings, that disciple of the Noble Ones who has fully attained can see Nirvâ*n*a.'

17. 'Then what, Sir, is Nirvâ*n*a? Such a Nirvâ*n*a (I mean) as can be explained by similes [3]. Convince me by argument how far the fact of its existence can be explained by similes.'

'Is there such a thing, O king, as wind?'

'Yes, of course.'

'Show it me then, I pray you, O king—whether by its colour, or its form, whether as thin or thick, or short or long!'

'But wind, Nâgasena, cannot be pointed out in that way [4]. It is not of such a nature that it can be taken into the hand or squeezed. But it exists all the same.'

'If you can't show me the wind, then there can't be such a thing.'

'But I know there is, Nâgasena. That wind

---

[1] Natthidhamma*m* nibbânam upadisatha. Compare the use of atthi-dhamma*m* nibbâna*m*, at p. 316 (of the Pâli). I take the compound to mean either 'has the quality (or condition) of not existing,' or 'is a condition that is not.' And the latter is more in harmony with the analogous phrase atthisattâ devâ (p. 317 of the Pâli) since that can only mean 'gods, which are beings that are.'

[2] Lust, malice, pride, sloth, and doubt.

[3] Hîna*t*i-kumburê puts the stop, not after nibbâna*m* as Mr. Trenckner does, but after opammehi.

[4] On the connotation of upadassayitu*m*, see pp. 316, 347, of the Pâli.

exists I am convinced [1], [271] though I cannot show it you.'

'Well! just so, O king, does Nirvâ*n*a exist, though it cannot be shown to you in colour or in form [2].'

'Very good, Nâgasena! That is so, and I accept it as you say.'

[Here ends the dilemma as to Nirvâ*n*a.]

[DILEMMA THE SIXTY-SIXTH.

MODES OF PRODUCTION.]

18. 'Venerable Nâgasena, what are they who are said, in this connection, to be "Karma-born," and "cause-born," and "season-born"? And what is it that is none of these?'

'All beings, O king, who are conscious, are Karma-born (spring into existence as the result of Karma). Fire, and all things growing out of seeds, are cause-born (the result of a pre-existing material cause). The earth, and the hills, water, and wind—all these are season-born (depend for their existence on reasons connected with weather). Space and Nirvâ*n*a exist independently alike of Karma, and cause,

[1] Me hadaye anupavi*tth*a*m*, literally 'has entered into my heart.' But Hîna*t*i-kumburê takes vâto atthîti as dependent on *g*ânâmi, and renders these three words by 'it (the wind) has entered into my heart,' and then adds, by way of gloss, 'and has struck against my body, and travels through the sky.' In another passage below, IV, 8, 65 (p. 317 of the Pâli), this same word anupavi*tth*a*m* recurs in a clause the sense of which is doubtful; and there Hîna*t*i-kumburê explains it quite differently. It looks very much as if we had here an idiom peculiar to our author; but one cannot of course be sure on any such point till the Pi*t*akas are all published.

[2] The same simile is used below, p. 317 (of the Pâli).

and seasons. Of Nirvâ*n*a, O king, it cannot be said that it is Karma-born or cause-born or season-born; that it has been, or has not been, or can be produced, that it is past or future or present, that it is perceptible by the eye or the nose or the ear or the tongue or by the sense of touch. But it is perceptible, O king, by the mind. By means of his pure heart, refined and straight, free from the obstacles, free from low cravings, that disciple of the Noble Ones who has fully attained can see Nirvâ*n*a.'

'Well has this delightful puzzle, venerable Nâgasena, been examined into, cleared of doubt, brought into certitude. My perplexity has been put an end to as soon as I consulted you, O best of the best of the leaders of schools!'

[Here ends the dilemma as to modes of production.]

[DILEMMA THE SIXTY-SEVENTH.

DEAD DEMONS.]

19. 'Venerable Nâgasena, are there such things as demons (Yakkhâ) in the world?'

'Yes, O king.'

'Do they ever leave that condition' (fall out of that phase of existence)?

'Yes, they do.'

'But, if so, why is it that the remains of those dead Yakkhas are never found, nor any odour of their corpses smelt?'

'**[272]** Their remains are found, O king, and an odour does arise from their dead bodies. The remains of bad Yakkhas can be seen in the form of worms and beetles and ants and moths and snakes and scorpions and centipedes, and birds and wild beasts.'

'Who else, O Nâgasena, could have solved this puzzle except one as wise as you!'

[Here ends the dilemma as to dead demons.]

[DILEMMA THE SIXTY-EIGHTH.

THE METHOD OF PROMULGATING THE RULES.]

20. 'Venerable Nâgasena, those who were teachers of the doctors in times gone by—Nârada[1], and Dhammantari[2], and Aṅgîrasa[3], and Kapila[4], and Ka*nd*araggisâma, and Atula, and Pubba Ka*kk*âyana[5]—all these teachers knowing thoroughly, and of themselves, and without any omission, the rise of disease and its cause and nature and progress and cure and treatment and management[6],—each of them composed his treatise en bloc, taking time by the forelock, and pointing out that in such and such a body such and such a disease would arise. Now no one of these

[1] No doubt the celebrated Devârshi is meant, though it is odd to find him in a list of physicians.

[2] In Sanskrit Dhanvantarî, the physician of the gods. He is mentioned in the *G*âtaka IV, 496, with Bho*g*a and Vetara*n*î, as a well-known physician of old famous for the cure of snake-bite.

[3] The connection of Aṅgîrasa with the physicians is due to the charms against disease to be found in the Atharva-veda.

[4] Kapila is known in the Brahman literature as a teacher of philosophy rather than of medicine.

[5] Probably 'the Eastern Ka*kk*âyana,' but nothing is known of these last three names. Hîna*t*i-kumburê calls all seven 'Rishis.'

[6] Siddhâsiddha*m*, for which Hîna*t*i-kumburê (p. 385), who merely repeats all the other terms, has sâdhyâsâdhya.

was omniscient. Why then did not the Tathâgata, who was omniscient, and who knew by his insight of a Buddha what would happen in the future, determining in advance that for such and such an occasion such and such a rule would be required, lay down the whole code of rules at once; instead of laying them down to his disciples from time to time as each occasion arose, when the disgrace (of the wrong act) had been already noised abroad, when the evil was already wide spread and grown great, when the people were already filled with indignation[1]?'

21. 'The Tathâgata, O king, knew very well that in fulness of time the whole of the hundred and fifty Rules[2] would have to be laid down to those men. But the Tathâgata, O king, thought thus: "If I were to lay down the whole of the hundred and fifty Rules at once the people would be filled with fear **[273]**, those of them who were willing to enter the Order would refrain from doing so, saying, 'How much is there here to be observed! how difficult a thing is it to enter religion according to the system of the Sama*n*a Gotama'—they would not trust my words, and through their want of faith they would be liable to rebirth in states of woe. As occasion arises therefore, illustrating it with a religious discourse, will I lay down, when the evil has become manifest, each Rule."'

'A wonderful thing is it in the Buddhas, Nâgasena, and a most marvellous that the omniscience of the Tathâgata should be so great. That is just so,

[1] This question has already been discussed above, III, 6, 2 (I, 116).

[2] The rules of the Pâtimokkha are 227 in number, but without the Sekhiyas they are 152.

venerable Nâgasena. This matter was well understood by the Tathâgata—how that hearing that so much was to be observed, men[1] would have been so filled with fear that not a single one would have entered religion according to the system of the Conquerors. That is so, and I accept it as you say[2].'

[Here ends the dilemma as to the method in which the Rules were laid down.]

[DILEMMA THE SIXTY-NINTH.
THE HEAT OF THE SUN.]

22. 'Venerable Nâgasena, does this sun always burn fiercely, or are there times when it shines with diminished heat?'

'It always burns fiercely, O king, never gently.'

'But if that be so, how is it that the heat of the sun is sometimes fierce, and sometimes not[3]?'

23. 'There are four derangements[4], O king, which happen to the sun, and affected by one or other of these its heat is allayed. And what are the four? The clouds, O king, and fog[5], and

[1] Sattâ, literally 'beings,' but that means human beings, men and women, as no others (gods, Nâgas, animals, &c.) were admitted to the Order. See Mahâvagga I, 63; I, 76, 1; *K*ullavagga X, 17, 1.

[2] In the Introductory Stories to the Rules it is often stated, how, when a Bhikkhu had done some act, the people were indignant, the brethren heard that and reported the matter to the Blessed One, who then, and then only, laid down the Rule prohibiting that act. But these Introductory Stories are really later than the Rules.

[3] Here Hîna*t*i-kumburê (pp. 386–7) goes into great details, giving instances, and quoting verses.

[4] Rogâ, literally 'diseases.'

[5] Mahikâ. Childers gives frost as the only meaning of this word.

smoke[1], and eclipses[2]—these are the four derangements which happen to the sun, and it is when affected by one or other of these that its heat is allayed.'

'Most wonderful, Nâgasena, and most strange [274] that even the sun, so transcendent in glory, should suffer from derangement—how much more then other, lesser, creatures. No one else could have made this explanation except one wise like you!'

[Here ends the dilemma as to the heat of the sun.]

[DILEMMA THE SEVENTIETH.
THE SEASONS.]

24. 'Venerable Nâgasena, why is it that the heat of the sun is more fierce in winter than in summer?'

'In the hot season, O king, dust is blown up[3] into clouds, and pollen[4] agitated by the winds rises up into the sky, and clouds multiply in the heavens, and gales blow with exceeding force. All these crowded and heaped together shut off the rays of the sun, and so in the hot season the heat of the sun is diminished. But in the cold season, O king, the earth below is at rest, the rains above are

[1] Megho, literally 'rain-cloud.' But clouds of smoke are meant, as is clear from the parallel passage loc. cit. which has dhumarago, but see *K*ullavagga XII, 1, 3 (from which the whole section IV, 7, 23 is derived).

[2] Râhu.

[3] Anupahata*m*. Compare Dr. Morris's note in the 'Journal of the Pâli Text Society,' 1884, p. 75, on Therâ Gâthâ 625.

[4] Re*n*û. Perhaps this should again be rendered dust. See the verse at *G*âtaka I, 117 (which is nearly the same as Divyâvadâna, p. 491).

in reserve[1], the dust is quiet, the pollen wanders gently through the air, the sky is free from clouds, and very gently do the breezes blow. Since all these have ceased to act the rays of the sun become clear, and freed from every obstruction the sun's heat glows and burns. This, O king, is the reason why the heat of the sun is more fierce in winter than in summer.

'So it is when set free from the obstacles besetting it that the sun burns fiercely, which it cannot do when the rains and so on are present with it.'

['Very good, Nâgasena! That is so, and I accept it as you say[2].']

[Here ends the dilemma of the seasons[3].]

Here ends the Seventh Chapter[4].

---

[1] Mahâ-megho upa*tth*ito hoti, which is very ambiguous. The Si*m*halese (p. 389) has mahâ meghaya pa*t*an-gannâ-*l*ada wanneya.

[2] Inserted from Hîna*t*i-kumburê.

[3] There is great uncertainty at present as to the views held, first in the Pi*t*akas and later in the Commentaries, regarding the calculation of time and the division of years into months and seasons. Our author here seems to regard the year as divided into two seasons only, Hemanta and Gimha. But Hemanta is usually supposed to last only from the 1st November (that is the middle of Kattika) to the beginning of March (that is the middle of Phagguni), Gimhâna for the next four months (March 1st–June 30th), and Vassâna the remaining four (July–October)—the year being thus divided into three equal cold, hot, and rainy seasons. At Mahâvagga VIII, 24, 3 there is a division of the year into unequal dry and wet seasons (utu and vassâna), and at *G*âtaka I, 86 it is said that vasanta-samayo begins when hemanta ends at the full moon of Phagguni. As our author places the characteristic events of the rainy season in the hot season, he cannot have had the division into three seasons in his mind.

[4] 'Of the excellent Saddharmâdâsa' says the Si*m*halese.

Book IV. Chapter 8.

[DILEMMA THE SEVENTY-FIRST.

VESSANTARA'S GIVING[1].]

1. 'Venerable Nâgasena, do all the Bodisats give away their wives and children, or was it only Vessantara the king who did so?'

'All of them do so, not Vessantara only.'

[**275**] 'Do they then give them away with their own consent?'

'The wife, O king, was a consenting party. But the children, by reason of their tender age, lamented. Had they thoroughly understood, they too would have approved.'

'A hard thing, Nâgasena, was it that the Bodisat carried out, in that he gave away his own children, his only ones dearly beloved, into slavery to the Brahman. And this second action was harder still, that he bound his own children, his only ones, and dearly beloved, young and tender though they were, with the jungle rope, and then, when he saw them being dragged along[2] by the Brahman,—their hands

[1] We have seen above, IV, 1, 41 (I, 178), how Hînaʼi-kumburê expanded the story of Vessantara, which had aroused also in our author a greater enthusiasm than any of the many other subjects that he treats. Here too the Si*m*halese translator fairly runs riot over the 'mighty giving of the glorious king, and expands the ten pages of the Pâli into thirty-three pages of his version (pp. 389-421), whereas usually one page of the Si*m*halese covers very nearly a page of the Pâli.

[2] Anuma*gg*iyante. See Mr. Trenckner's note. But the

bruised by the creeper,—yet could look on at the sight. And this third action was even harder still, that when his boy ran back to him, after loosing the bonds by his own exertion, then he bound him again with the jungle rope and again gave him away. And this fourth action was even harder still, that when the children, weeping, cried: "Father dear, this ogre is leading us away to eat us!" he should have appeased them by saying: "Don't be afraid." And this fifth action was even harder still, that when the prince, *G*âli, fell weeping at his feet, and besought him, saying: "Be satisfied, father dear, only keep Ka*n*hâginâ (his little sister). I will go away with the ogre. Let him eat me!"—that even then he would not yield. And this sixth action was even harder still, that when the boy *G*âli, lamenting, exclaimed: "Have you a heart of stone then, father, that you can look upon us, miserable, being led away by the ogre into the dense and haunted jungle, and not call us back?"—that he still had no pity. And this seventh action was even harder still, that when his children were thus led away to nameless horrors until they passed gradually to their bitter fate[1], out of sight—that then his heart did not break, utterly break! What, pray, has the man who seeks to gain merit to do with bringing sorrow on others! Should he not rather give himself away?'

2. 'It is because what he did, O king, was so

Si*m*halese (p. 390) has at mardanaya ko*l*a welannawun dœka.

[1] Rû*l*arû*l*assa bhîmabhîmassa. The Si*m*halese (p. 390) omits these words, giving other details in place of them, and as they occur only here I am not sure of their meaning.

difficult, that the sound of the fame of the Bodisat was spread abroad among gods and men through the ten thousand world systems—[276] that the gods exalt him in heaven; and the Titans in the Titan-world, and the Garu*d*as in their abodes, and the Nâgas in the Nâga-world, and the Yakshas where they dwell—that through the ages the reputation of this his glory has been handed down by successive tradition—till now, to-day, it has reached to this meeting of ours, at which we sitting are, forsooth, disparaging and casting a slur on that gift[1], debating whether it were well given or ill! But that high praise, O king, shows forth the ten great qualities of the intelligent, and wise, and able, and subtle-minded Bodisats. And what are the ten? Freedom from greed, the not clinging (to any worldly aim), self-sacrifice, renunciation, the never turning back again (to the lower state), the equal delicacy and greatness, the incomprehensibility, the rarity, and the peerlessness of Buddhahood. In all these respects is it that the fame of that giving shows forth the great qualities of the Bodisats.'

3. 'What, venerable Nâgasena? he who gives gifts in such a way as to bring sorrow upon others—does that giving of his bring forth fruit in happiness, does it lead to rebirth in states of bliss?'

'Yes, O king. What can be said (to the contrary)?'

'I pray you, Nâgasena, give me a reason for this.'

'Suppose, O king, there were some virtuous Sama*n*a or Brahman, of high character, and he were

---

[1] Vikittentâ vikopentâ. Hîna*t*i-kumburê (p. 410) has 'angrily finding fault with.' Compare above, vikopanâ, at p. 266 (of the Pâli).

paralysed, or a cripple [1], or suffering from some disease or other, and some man desirous of merit were to have him put into a carriage, and taken to the place he wished to go to. Would happiness accrue to that man by reason thereof, would that be an act leading to rebirth in states of bliss?'

'Yes, Sir. What can be said (to the contrary)? That man would thereby acquire a trained elephant, or a riding-horse, or a bullock-carriage, on land a land-vehicle and on water a water-vehicle, in heaven a vehicle of the gods [2] and on earth one that men could use,—from birth to birth there would accrue to him that which in each would be appropriate and fit,—and joys appropriate would come to him, and he would pass from state to state of bliss, and by the efficacy of that act mounting on the vehicle of Iddhi he would arrive at the longed-for goal, the city of Nirvâ*n*a itself.'

'But then, O king, a gift given in such a way as to bring sorrow upon others does bring forth fruit in happiness, does lead to rebirth in states of bliss **[277]**,—inasmuch as that man by putting the cart-bullocks to pain would attain such bliss.

4. 'And hear another reason, O king, for the same thing. Suppose some monarch were to raise from his subjects a righteous tax, and then by the issue of a command were to bestow thereout a gift, would that monarch, O king, enjoy any happiness on that account, would that be a gift leading to rebirth in states of bliss?'

---

[1] Pakkha-hato vâ pî*th*a-sappî vâ. See the note above on IV, 6, 22.

[2] Devayâna, on which compare Sutta Nipâta, verse 139 (Vasala Sutta 24).

'Certainly, Sir. What can be said against it? On that account the monarch would receive a hundred thousandfold, he might become a king of kings, a god above the gods, or Brahmâ lord of the Brahma gods, or a chief among the Samanas, or a leader of the Brahmans, or the most excellent among the Arahats.'

'Then, O king, a gift given in such a way as to bring sorrow upon others does bring forth fruit in happiness, does lead to rebirth in states of bliss—inasmuch as that monarch by giving as a gift what was gained by harassing his people with taxation would enjoy such exceeding fame and glory.'

5. 'But, venerable Nâgasena, what was given by Vessantara the king was an excessive gift; in that he gave his own wife as wife to another man, and his own children, his only ones, into slavery to a Brahman. And excessive giving is by the wise in the world held worthy of censure and of blame. Just, Nâgasena, as under too much weight the axle-tree of a cart would break, or a ship would sink, as his food would disagree with him who ate too much, or the crops would be ruined by too heavy rain, or bankruptcy would follow too lavish generosity, or fever would come from too much heat, or a man would go mad from excessive lust, or become guilty of an offence through excessive anger, or fall into sin through excessive stupidity, or into the power of robbers through too much avarice, or be ruined by needless fear, or as a river would overflow through excessive inflow, or a thunderbolt fall through too much wind, or porridge boil over through too hot a fire, or a man who wandered

about too much[1] would not live long—just so, Nâgasena, is excessive giving held by the wise in the world as worthy of censure and of blame. And as king Vessantara's gift was excessive [**278**] no good result could be expected from it.'

6. 'Giving exceedingly[2], O king, is praised, applauded, and approved by the wise in the world; and they who give away anything as a gift just as it may occur to them[3], acquire fame in the world as very generous givers. Just, O king, as when a man has taken hold of a wild root which by its extraordinary virtues is divine, that moment he becomes invisible even to those standing within arm's length—just as a medicinal herb by the exceeding power of its nature will utterly kill pain, and put an end to disease—just as fire burns by its exceeding heat, and water puts that fire out by its exceeding cold—just as by its exceeding purity a lotus remains undefiled by water or by mud—just as a (magic) gem by the extraordinary virtue inherent in it procures the granting of every wish—just as lightning by its marvellous quick sharpness cleaves asunder even the diamonds, pearls, and crystals—just as the earth by its exceeding size can support men, and snakes, and wild beasts, and birds, and the waters,

[1] Atisa*ñk*ârena, which the Si*m*halese merely repeats. The meaning is doubtful. The use of sa*ñk*âra at *G*âtaka II, 112 has suggested the above rendering.

[2] The whole of this answer turns on the ambiguity of the prefix ati, which may mean either 'very much' or 'too much.'

[3] Yâdisa*m* kîdisa*m*. The meaning of this idiom cannot be controlled by parallel passages, as I know of none. Hîna*t*i-kumburê (pp. 412–413) construes yâdisa*m* as an accusative dependent on atidânadâyî; 'Those who give away anything as a gift, acquire fame in the world as exceeding givers of that.'

and rocks, and hills, and trees—just as the ocean by its exceeding greatness can never be quite filled—just as Sineru by its mighty weight remains immoveable, and space by the greatness of its wide extent is infinite, and the sun by its mighty glory dissipates the darkness—just as the lion in the greatness of its lineage is free from fear—just as a wrestler in the greatness of his might easily lifts up his foe—just as a king by the excellence of his justice becomes overlord, and a Bhikkhu by reason of his very righteousness becomes an object of reverence to Nâgas, and Yakshas, and men, and Mâras—just as a Buddha by the excellence of his supremacy is peerless—just so, O king, is exceeding generosity praised, applauded, and approved by the wise in the world; and they who give away anything as a gift, just as it may occur to them, acquire in the world the fame of being nobly generous. And by his mighty giving Vessantara the king, O king, was praised, and lauded, and exalted, and magnified, and famous throughout the ten thousand world systems, and by reason, too, of that mighty giving is it that he, the king Vessantara, has, now in our days, become the Buddha, the chief of gods and men.

7. 'And now, O king, tell me—is there anything in the world which should be withheld as a gift, and not bestowed, when one worthy of a gift, one to whom it is one's duty to give[1], is there?'

---

[1] Dakkhi*n*eyya. We have no word in English to express the full meaning of this word. It was an idea that was common ground to our Buddhist apologist, and to the Brahman opponents whom he always has in view, that there were certain people to whom gifts ought to be given, and the being worthy was one of the conditions precedent to belonging to this class. Of course the

'There are ten sorts of gifts, Nâgasena, in the world that are commonly disapproved of as gifts. And what are the ten? Strong drink, Nâgasena, and festivals in high places[1], and women, and buffaloes, and suggestive [279] paintings[2], and weapons, and poison, and chains, and fowls, and swine, and false weights and measures. All these, Nâgasena, are disapproved of in the world as gifts, and those who give such presents become liable to rebirth in states of woe.'

'I did not ask you, O king, what kinds of gifts are not approved of. But this, O king, I asked: "Is there anything in the world which ought to be withheld, and not bestowed as a gift, if one worthy of a gift were present?"'

'No, Sir. When faith arises in their hearts some give food to those worthy of gifts, and some give clothes, and some give bedding, and some give dwellings, and some give mats or robes, and some give slave girls or slaves, and some give fields or premises, and some give bipeds or quadrupeds, and

Brahmans held that to be a Brahman was another condition, but the Buddhist, who inherited the idea from them, had discarded this part of the conception. See, for the Brahman view, Eggeling's *S*atapatha-Brâhma*n*a II, 114, 344.

[1] Sama*gg*a-dâna*m*. Childers under sama*gg*â gives only the meaning 'assembly,' but it is clear from *K*ullavagga V, 26; VI, 2, 7; the Sutta Vibhaṅga II, 267, and Sumaṅgala I, 84, that the word, at least as a masculine (which it is here), has the technical sense of one of those orgies in high places which were common in so many parts of the world in very early times, and were due in India to Kolarian influences. The 'giving' (dâna) of such a sama*gg*a would doubtless mean the providing of the necessary food, seats, cushions, &c.

[2] *K*itta-kamma*m*. See my note on Pa*t*ibhâna-*k*itta*m* at 'Vinaya Texts,' III, 172.

some give a hundred[1] or a thousand or a hundred thousand, and some give the kingdom itself, and some give away even their own life.'

'But then, O king, if some give away even their own lives, why do you so violently attack[2] Vessantara, that king of givers, for the virtuous bestowal of his child and wife? Is there not a general practice in the world, an acknowledged custom, according to which it is allowable for a father who has fallen into debt, or lost his livelihood, to deposit[3] his son in pledge, or sell him?'

'Yes, that is so.'

'Well, in accordance therewith was it that Vessantara, O king, in suffering and distress at not having obtained the insight of the Omniscient Ones, pledged and sold his wife and children for that spiritual treasure. So that he gave away what other people had given away, he did what other people had done. Why then do you, O king, so violently attack him, the king of givers?'

---

[1] I. e. pieces of money, which it would be against the rules for a member of the Buddhist Order to accept. But the donees in all these cases are not necessarily Buddhists.

[2] Paripâtesi, not in Childers; but see *G*âtaka II, 208; and below, p. 367 (of the Pâli text). Hîna*t*i-kumburê has here nindâ karanne, and just below apasâdanaya karanne.

[3] Âvapitu*m*, not in Childers. Dr. Morris, in the 'Journal of the Pâli Text Society' for 1886, p. 157, compares the Sanskrit root vyap, but this does not help us much. Hîna*t*i-kumburê (p. 414) has 'an tœneka œpaye hinduwanna*t*a,' which means, I think, 'to deposit as a pledge in some place or other.' At all events œpa, the ordinary word now in use in Ceylon courts for 'bail,' may very well be actually derived from vâpa. And the passage at *G*âtaka I, 321 is an exact parallel to our phrase here, for there the Bodisat, when an elephant, gives away his teeth and tusks as vâpana for the insight of the Omniscient Ones.

8. 'Venerable Nâgasena, I don't blame him for giving, but for not having made a barter[1] with the beggar, and given away himself rather, instead of his wife and children.'

[280] 'That, O king, would be an act of a wrong doer, to give himself when he was asked for his wife and children. For the thing asked for, whatever it is, is that which ought to be given. And such is the practice of the good. Suppose, O king, a man were to ask that water should be brought, would any one who then brought him food have done what he wanted?'

'No, Sir. The man who should have given what he first asked to be brought would have done what he wanted.'

'Just so, O king, when the Brahman asked Vessantara the king for his wife and children, it was his wife and children that he gave. If the Brahman, O king, had asked for Vessantara's body, then would Vessantara have not saved his body, he would neither have trembled nor been stained (by the love of self), but would have given away and abandoned his own body. If, O king, any one had come up to Vessantara the king, and asked of him, saying: "Become my slave," then would he have given away and abandoned his own self, and in so giving would he have felt no pain.

9. 'Now the life of king Vessantara, O king, was a good thing shared in by many—just as meats when cooked are shared in by many, or as a tree covered with fruit is shared in by many flocks of

[1] Niminitvâ, also not in Childers; but see *G*âtaka III, 63, 221.

birds. And why so? Because he had said to himself: "Thus acting may I attain to Buddhahood." As a man in need, O king, who is wandering about in his search after wealth, will have to pass along goat-tracks, and through jungles full of stakes and sticks[1], and doing merchandise by sea and land, will devote his actions, words, and thoughts to the attainment of wealth—just so, O king, did Vessantara, the king of givers, who was longing for the treasure of Buddhahood, for the attainment of the insight of the Omniscient Ones, by offering up to any one who begged of him his property and his corn, his slave girls and his slaves, his riding animals and carriages, all that he possessed, his wife and children and himself, seek after the Supreme Enlightenment. Just, O king, as an official who is anxious for the seal[2], and for the office of the custody thereof **[281]**, will exert himself to the attainment of the seal by sacrificing everything in his house—property and corn, gold and silver, everything—just so, O king, did Vessantara, the king of givers, by giving away all that he had, inside his house and out[3], by giving even his life for others, seek after the Supreme Enlightenment.

10. 'And further, O king, Vessantara, the king of givers, thought thus: "It is by giving to him precisely what he asks for, that I shall be of service

[1] A*g*apatha*m* sa*n*kupatha*m* vettapatha*m* ga*kkh*ati. Hîna*t*i-kumburê, at p. 416, repeats the words with a gloss on the two last words, which I have followed.

[2] Mudda-kâmo; mudra-na*m* ganam perekkuwa, says Hîna*t*i-kumburê, p. 416.

[3] Bâhirabbhantara*m* dhana*m* datvâ. I am not sure that I have rightly understood this phrase, which the Si*m*halese merely repeats.

to the Brahman:" and therefore did he bestow upon him his wife and children. It was not, O king, out of dislike to them that he gave them away, not because he did not care to see them more, not because he considered them an encumbrance or thought he could no longer support them, not (in annoyance) with the wish of being relieved of what was not pleasant to him—but because the jewel treasure of omniscience was dear to him, for the sake of the insight of the Omniscient Ones, did he bestow that glorious gift,—immeasurable, magnificent, unsurpassed—of what was near and dear to him, greatly beloved, cherished as his own life, his own children and his wife! For it has been said, O king, by the Blessed One, the god of gods, in the *K*ariyâ Pi*t*aka[1]:

"'Twas not through hatred[2] of my children sweet,
'Twas not through hatred of my queen, Maddî,
Thraller of hearts[3]—not that I loved them less—
But Buddhahood more, that I renounced them all."

[1] *K*ariyâ Pi*t*aka I, 9, 53.

[2] Dessa, that is dreshya, from dvish. Compare diso, 'an enemy.' It occurs also at *K*ariyâ Pi*t*aka I, 4, 7; 5, 3; 8, 16 (quoted *G*âtaka IV, 406); II, 4, 11; III, 1, 6 (quoted *G*âtaka I, 46); III, 2, 16; 3, 10; 6, 18. The effect of the use of this rare poetical word is lost in the English version.

[3] Maddî and Ka*n*hâ*g*inâ, the names of Vessantara's wife and daughter, mean respectively 'enthraller (of men's minds),' and 'the dark conquerors (of hearts).' As Vessantara is used in the Ma*gg*h*i*ma (I, 386, line 5) as an adjective, not a name, and is applied to the Buddha, it too must have a special meaning. But it can scarcely be connected with Vai*s*ya, while we have a very famous epithet in vai*s*vânara, so often applied to the sacred fire as 'common good to all men.' The insertion of the t would explain the shortening of the â, and though there seems to be no sufficient reason for any alteration at all of the older term, this is

11. 'Now at that time, O king, Vessantara, when he had given away his wife and children, entered the leaf hut, and sat down there. And heavy grief fell upon him distressed by his exceeding love for them, and his very heart[1] became hot, and hot breath, too much to find its way through the nose, came and went through his mouth, and tears rolled in drops of blood from his eyes. Such was the grief, O king, with which Vessantara gave to the Brahman his wife and children in the thought that his practice of giving should not be broken in upon. But there were two reasons, O king, why he thus gave them away. What are those two? That his practice of giving should not be interrupted was one; the other was that as a result of his so doing his children, distressed by living with him only on wild roots and fruits, should eventually be set free by their new master. [282] For Vessantara knew, O king: "No one is capable of keeping my children as slaves. Their grandfather will ransom the children, and so they will come back to me." These are the two reasons why he gave his children away to the Brahman.

12. 'And further, O king, Vessantara knew: "This Brahman is worn out, aged, well stricken in years, weak and broken, leaning on a stick, he has drawn near the end of his days, his merit is small, he will not be capable of keeping my children as

probably the real derivation of Vessantara. And the whole legend may well be due to previous stories of the world-wide beneficence of Agni Vais*v*ânara, or of the sun as Vais*v*ânara.

[1] Hadaya-vatthu, 'like a broth-pot foaming over,' is Hîna*t*i-kumburê's explanation of this phrase (pena nœgena mas sœliyak men h*ri*daya wastuwa, p. 417).

slaves." Would a man be able, O king, by his ordinary power, to seize the moon and the sun[1],

---

[1] *K*andima-suriye. We should say 'the sun and the moon,' and I cannot think the difference of phraseology is entirely without significance. While the Brahmans put their own caste and order first, the Buddhist texts talk of 'Sama*n*as and Brahmans,' 'Khattiyas and Brahmans.' This has, and no doubt rightly, been held significant of the opinion of the authors. Why should the fact of their always referring, in similar compounds, to the moon before the sun, and to women before men, be less so? Now it is almost always taken for granted that the Buddhists were reformers, as opposed to the Brahmans, who wanted to run still in the ancient grooves. But there is another side of the question that has been entirely overlooked. There is ample evidence in their literature that (at least in certain directions, more especially of religious thought) the Brahmans had been constantly progressive, and their Brâhma*n*as are really the result of reform following on reform. To use a parallel drawn from modern politics, Buddhists are to Brahmans much more like Socialists to Liberals than like Liberals to Conservatives. The Brahmans had worked out in their minds no new complete system, and when they reformed they left the roots of the old order of things in the ground. But in the momentous change from matriarchate to patriarchate they threw all their power and influence on the side of the newer conception. And when, like Kronos to Jupiter, the old gods gave place to the new, it was they who worked out the newer set of ideas—more especially heaven or sun-worship as against moon-worship and all that it involved. We must not forget that a change of dynasty, or of precedence, among the gods was of more importance to men in those times than a change of dynasty among earthly kings. And though the Buddhists it is true, as we ourselves now, cared for none of these things, and were busied with other discussions than the precedence of the sun and moon, they quite quietly and naturally, when they had to choose, adopted the form of words which did not imply an acceptance of the Brahman position, whose system in other matters they were trying, if not to storm, at least to turn.

We are here in the midst of questions too vast to be discussed with profit in a note. But Buddhism certainly arose among those sections of the community least influenced by the reforms the Brahmans supported. And there is evidence, in the precedence the

mighty and powerful as they are, keeping them in a basket or a box, to use them, deprived of their light, as plates?'

'Certainly not, Sir.'

'Neither, O king, could any one whatever keep in use, as his slaves, the children of Vessantara, who were to the world like the moon and the sun in glory.

13. 'And hear another reason, O king, for the same thing[1]. That wondrous gem, O king, of a sovran overlord, bright and beautiful, with its eight facets so well cut, four cubits in thickness, and in circumference[2] as the nave of a cart-wheel, could no man, wrapping it up in a cloth and putting it into a basket, keep and use as a hone[3] to grind his scissors[4] upon. And neither, O king, could any one soever keep in use, as his slaves, the children of Vessantara, like to the jewels of the lord of the world in glory.

14. 'And hear, O king, another reason. Just as the elephant king Uposatha[5], gentle and handsome, eight cubits in height and nine in girth and length, showing the signs of rut in three places on his body, all white, sevenfold firm[6], could never by any one

Buddhists gave to women and to the moon, that the older ideas had not, even then, died out.

[1] These words are repeated before each of the following similes.

[2] Pari*n*âha, which Childers is wrong in rendering 'breadth,' when not qualified by âyâma (wa*t*a œttâwû, says the Si*m*halese, p. 418).

[3] Nisâna; karagal, says Hîna*t*i-kumburê.

[4] Satthaka, see *K*ullavagga V, 11, 1.

[5] The mythic fairy elephant of the *K*akkavatti (not a snake king as Prof. E. Müller has it, 'Journal of the Pâli Text Society,' 1888, p. 16). See my note at 'Buddhist Suttas,' p. 254.

[6] Sattappati*tth*ito. The Si*m*halese merely repeats this ambiguous word (compare IV, 8, 57).

be covered up with a saucer[1] or a winnowing fan[1], could never be put into a cowpen like a calf, or made use of as one [283]; just so could no one whatever keep in use, as his slaves, the children of Vessantara, who were, in the world, like Uposatha the elephant king.

15. 'And hear, O king, another reason. Just, O king, as the mighty ocean is great in length and breadth, and deep, not to be measured, and hard to cross, impossible to fathom or to cover up, and no one could close it in and make use of it as a single ferry, just so could no one whatever keep in use, as his slaves, the children of Vessantara, as esteemed in the world as the mighty ocean.

16. 'And hear another reason, O king. Just as the Himâlaya, the king of the mountains, five leagues high, and three thousand leagues in extent at the circumference, with its ranges of eight and forty thousand peaks, the source of five hundred rivers, the dwelling-place of multitudes of mighty creatures[2], the producer of manifold perfumes, enriched with hundreds of magical drugs, is seen to rise aloft, like a cloud, in the centre (of the earth); like it, O king, could no one whatever keep in use, as his slaves, the children of Vessantara, as esteemed in the world as Himâlaya, the mountain king.

'And hear another reason, O king. Just as a

[1] Suppena vâ sarâvena vâ. Hînati-kumburê renders the first of these words by kullaka, which is a winnowing-basket; and the second by malâwaka, which I do not understand. But the use of sarâva at Gâtaka I, 8, 14 and Sumaṅgala I, 298 seems to me to confirm Childers's rendering.

[2] Mahâbhûta: 'Yakshas' says Hînati-kumburê, p. 419. Compare above, p. 250 (of the Pâli).

mighty bonfire burning on a mountain top would be visible afar off in the darkness and the gloom of night, so was Vessantara the king well known among men, and therefore could no one whatever keep in use, as his slaves, the children of so distinguished a man—for just as at the time of the flowering of the Nâga trees[1] in the Himâlaya mountains, when the soft winds (of spring)[2] are blowing, the perfume of the flowers is wafted for ten leagues, or for twelve [**284**], so was the sound of the fame of king Vessantara noised abroad, and the sweet perfume of his righteousness wafted along for thousands of leagues, even up to the abodes of the Akani*tth*a, (the highest of all) gods, passing on its way the dwelling places of the gods and Asuras, of the Garu*d*as and Gandhabbas, of the Yakshas and Râkshasas, of the Mahoragas and Kinnaras, and of Indra the monarch of the gods[3]! Therefore is it that no one could keep his children as slaves.

---

[1] Nâga-puppha-samaye. Hîna*t*i-kumburê says, 'at the time when the Nâ trees bloom.' The Nâ or Nâga is the Mesua ferea, whose lovely flowers, like those of the Champak, are still in special request for laying before the images of the Buddha in Buddhist temples. I am told that these so-called flowers are not flowers at all, botanically speaking, but young shoots. But it is one of the most beautiful sights in a Ceylon landscape to see this splendid forest tree, lofty and wide-spreading as it is, one mass of what look like red blossoms from crown to root. For at the 'bloom time' it casts all its green leaves, and has the appearance of a scarlet bell. No wonder that this was thought supernatural, and that the tree should be called the Nâga tree. Its timber is so valuable that in Anglo-Indian the tree is called the 'Iron-wood' tree. But it may be regretted that the commercial spirit of the European has substituted this hard name for the 'Fairy tree' of the native languages.

[2] U*g*u-vâta, which the Si*m*halese repeats.

[3] Compare vol. i, pp. 38, 175.

17. 'And the young prince *G*âli, O king, was instructed by his father, Vessantara, in these words: "When your grandfather, my child, shall ransom you with wealth that he gives to the Brahman, let him buy you back for a thousand ounces of gold[1], and when he ransoms your sister Ka*n*hâ*g*inâ let him buy her back for a hundred slaves and a hundred slave girls and a hundred elephants and a hundred horses and a hundred cows and a hundred buffaloes and a hundred ounces of gold. And if, my child, your grandfather should take you out of the hands of the Brahman by word of command, or by force, paying nothing, then obey not the words of your grandfather, but remain still in subjection[2] to the Brahman." Such was his instruction as he sent him away. And young *G*âli went accordingly, and when asked by his grandfather, said:

"As worth a thousand ounces, Sir,
My father gave me to this man;
As worth a hundred elephants,
He gave the girl Ka*n*hâ*g*inâ."'

'Well has this puzzle, Nâgasena, been unravelled, well has the net of heresy been torn to pieces, well has the argument of the adversaries been overcome and your own doctrine been made evident, well has the letter (of the Scriptures) been maintained while

[1] Nikkha-sahassa*m*. See my 'Ancient Coins and Measures,' pp. 6, 14; Sa*m*yutta Nikâya II, 3, 9, 9 (*G*âtaka I, 375, IV, 97; Aṅguttara III, 73, 3).

[2] Anuyâyino. Not found elsewhere, and not in Childers. But anuyâyati occurs below (p. 391 of the text) and an ânuyâyin at Sutta Nipâta V, 7, 3, 4 and Tela-ka*t*âha-gâthâ 25 (compare 41). Hîna*t*i-kumburê (p. 470) has anuwa hœsirew.

you have thus explained its spirit! That is so, and I accept it as you say.'

[Here ends the dilemma as to Vessantara's gift of his wife and children.]

[DILEMMA THE SEVENTY-SECOND.
PENANCE.]

18. 'Venerable Nâgasena, did all the Bodisats go through a period of penance, or only Gotama?'

'Not all, O king, but Gotama did.'

'Venerable Nâgasena, if that be so, it is not right that there should be a difference between Bodisat and Bodisat.'

[285] 'There are four matters, O king, in which there is such difference. And what are the four? There is a difference as to the kind of family (in which they are born [1]), there is a difference as to their place in the period (which has elapsed since the succession of Buddhas began [2]), there

[1] Kula-vemattatâ. Those Bodisats who are to become Buddhas in their then lives may be born either in a Brahman or in a Kshatriya family, but in no other.

[2] Addhâna-vemattatâ, which is ambiguous, as 'period-difference' may mean different things according to the interpretation given to 'period.' Now the Bodisat theory has never been thoroughly worked out in detail. It is clear from the statements given in pp. 38–58 of my 'Buddhist Birth Stories' that the Bodisat who became Gotama the Buddha was held to have been in existence throughout the whole period in which the former twenty-four Buddhas appeared, and this is probably the 'period' intended. Hînaᵹi-kumburê's version (p. 421) is as ambiguous as the Pâli. Spence Hardy gives at p. 87 of his 'Manual of Buddhism' what purports to be a translation of our passage. But it is only a loose paraphrase, and he interprets this 'period-difference' as simply

is a difference as to the length of their individual lives[1], there is a difference as to their individual size[2]. In these four respects, O king, there is a difference between Bodisat and Bodisat. But there is no difference between any of the Buddhas, who are alike in bodily beauty[3], in goodness of character, in power of contemplation and of reasoning, in emancipation, in the insight arising from the knowledge of emancipation, in

---

identical with the next one in the list, the 'length-of-life-difference'—which must be wrong.

It must be remembered that the Bodisats referred to throughout this dilemma are exclusively men—not those mentioned in the *G*âtakas (who are all Bodisats of the historical Buddha), but only those Bodisats who became Buddhas in the same life—that is, the Buddhas themselves before they reached Buddhahood.

[1] Âyu-vemattatâ. This may be due to either of two causes—in the first place they may be born as creatures whose allotted period of life varies. Thus the Bodisat was twenty times Sakka, the king of the gods; and his life would then have lasted hundreds of thousands of years. But he was 106 times an animal of some kind, and then his life would have been of course much shorter. Again, in his births as a man (more than 350 times, see the table in my 'Buddhist Birth Stories,' p. ci), the average duration of men's lives will have varied, according to Buddhist theory, from many centuries down to only a few years. It is in this second sense only that (with Hîna*t*i-kumburê) we must suppose the phrase âyu-vemattatâ to be used—thus excluding all the Bodisats except such as were men. But in the *G*âtaka stories the average age of man is (with one or two exceptions) normal.

[2] Pamâ*n*a-vemattatâ, which we must also understand to refer only to the varying average size of mankind, which, according to Buddhist theory, is very great at the commencement, and very small at the close, of a Kalpa. For it is only the men-Bodisats, and only in each series the last man-Bodisat (just before he became 'Buddha'), concerning whom this question of penance could arise.

[3] Rûpe, which the Si*m*halese repeats (p. 422), and which cannot here mean bodily form only.

the four bases of confidence[1], in the ten powers of a Tathâgata[2], in the sixfold special know-

[1] *K*atu-vesâra*gg*e. They are the confidence that no one—Sama*n*a or Brahman, God or Mâra—can reprove him by saying: (1) 'The qualities which you maintain to be those of a Buddha have not been attained by you;' or (2) 'The Great Evils which you maintain to have ceased in an Arahat have not ceased in you;' or (3) 'The qualities which you say are dangerous (in the higher life) are not really dangerous to one who practises them;' or (4) 'The aim which you held before others in preaching your Dhamma will not lead him who follows it to the destruction of sorrow.' The list will be found in the Aṅguttara Nikâya IV, 8 (where it is probably a quotation from one of the conversational Suttas). But the punctuation in Dr. Morris's edition should be corrected by putting full stops after each viharâmi. Childers gives a different explanation under vesâra*gg*a, but his interpretation must be altered to that here given, which is the only correct one.

[2] These have not been found in any Pi*t*aka text, but Burnouf gives them in a note to the 'Lotus de la Bonne Loi' (p. 781) from the *G*inâlaṅkâra. He says the expression dasabalo is found as applied to the Buddha 'à chaque instant dans les textes,' but this is not the case, so far at least as the older texts are concerned. In one of the old verses preserved at the Mahâvagga I, 22, 13, and quoted in the *G*âtaka (vol. i, p. 84), dasabalo occurs as an epithet of the Buddha, but among the numerous epithets applied in the Buddhava*m*sa to the various Buddhas the term does not occur, nor have I been able to find it in the published portions of any of the great Nikâyas. (Ten Nâga-balas are ascribed to the Buddha in Buddhava*m*sa, p. 39, but these seem to be different.) Buddha-rakkhita, the author of the *G*inâlaṅkâra, probably lived at about the eleventh or twelfth century A.D., and Hardy's paraphrase of his interpretations (in the 'Manual of Buddhism,' pp. 380, 381) is throughout inaccurate. As therefore it is precisely the growth of ideas about the Buddha that is of prime importance in the history of Buddhism, I give here Buddha-rakkhita's explanation, adding the Sanskrit names as given in the Mahâvyutpatti, § 8:—

1. *Th*a*n*â*th*ana-*ñ*â*n*a-bala*m*	Sthânasthâna-*gñ*âna-balam	(1)
2. Sabbatha-gâminî-patipadâ	Karma-vipâka	(5)
3. Aneka-dhâtu-nânâ-dhâtu	Nânâdhimukti	(4)
4. Sattâna*m* nânâdhimuttikatâ	Nânâdhatu	(3)

ledge[1], in the fourteenfold knowledge of Buddha[2], in the eighteen characteristics of a Buddha[3]—in a word, in all the qualities of a Buddha. For all the Buddhas are exactly alike in all the Buddha-qualities.'

'But if, Nâgasena, that be so, what is the reason that it was only the Gotama Bodisat who carried out the penance?'

'Gotama the Bodisat had gone forth from the world, O king, when his knowledge[4] was immature, and his wisdom was immature. And it was when he was bringing that immature knowledge to maturity that he carried out the penance.'

19. 'Why then, Nâgasena, was it that he thus went forth with knowledge and with wisdom immatured? Why did he not first mature his knowledge, and then, with his knowledge matured, renounce the world?'

'When the Bodisat, O king, saw the women of his harem all in disorder[5], then did he become dis-

5. Vipâka-vemattatâ . . .	Indriya-parâpara	(7)
6. Sa*m*kilesa-vodâna-vatthu .	Sarvatra-gâminî-pratipad . .	(2)
7. Indriya-paropariya . . .	Sa*m*kilesa-vyavadâna-vyu*tth*âna	(6)
8. Pubbe-nivâsânussate . .	Purva-nivasânusm*ri*ti . . .	(8)
9. Dibba-*k*akkhu	*K*yut-utpatti	(9)
10. Asava-kkhaya	Âsrava-kshaya	(10)

Some of these terms are found in the Dharma-saṅgraha, Anecdota Oxoniensia, vol. i, part 5, pp. 16, 51.

[1] *Kh*a-asâdhâra*n*a-*ñ*â*n*a, not yet found elsewhere.

[2] Possibly the above ten with four others.

[3] The details of these eighteen are given by Spence Hardy in the 'Manual of Buddhism,' p. 381, but he does not mention his authority. Hîna*t*i-kumburê (p. 422) merely repeats the Pâli.

[4] 'Of the four Truths' is Hîna*t*i-kumburê's gloss.

[5] See *G*âtaka I, 61. But the whole episode is told in the Pi*t*akas, not of the Bodisat, but of Yasa (Mahâvagga I, 7).

gusted, and in him thus disgusted discontent sprang up. And on perceiving that his heart was filled with discontent, a certain god of those that wait on Death (Mâra) thought: "This now is the time to dispel that discontent of his heart," and standing in the air he gave utterance to these words: "O honourable one! O fortunate one! Be not thou distressed. On the seventh day from this the heavenly treasure of the Wheel shall appear to thee, with its thousand spokes, its tire, and its nave, complete and perfect; and the other treasures, those that walk on earth and those that travel through the sky, shall come to thee of their own accord; and the words of command of thy mouth shall bear sway over the four great continents and the two thousand dependent isles; and thou shalt have above a thousand sons, heroes mighty in strength to the crushing out of the armies of the foe; and with those sons surrounding thee thou, master of the Seven Treasures, shalt rule the world!" [286] But even as if a bar of iron, heated the livelong day and glowing throughout, had entered the orifice of his ear, so was it that those words, O king, entered the ear of the Bodisat. And to the natural distress he already felt there was added, by that utterance of the god, a further emotion, anxiety, and fear. Just as a mighty fiery furnace, were fresh fuel thrown on it, would the more furiously burn—just as the broad earth, by nature moist, and already swampy through the water dripping on it from the vegetation and the grass that have arisen on it, would become more muddy still when a great rain cloud had poured out rain upon it—so to the distress that he already felt there was added, by that utterance of the god, a further emotion, anxiety, and fear.'

20. 'But tell me, Nâgasena, if the heavenly Wheel-treasure had, on the seventh day, appeared to the Bodisat, would he, the Wheel having appeared, have been turned back from his purpose?'

'No Wheel-treasure appeared, O king, on the seventh day to the Bodisat. For rather that was a lie that was told by that god with the object of tempting him. And even had it appeared, yet would not the Bodisat have turned aside. And why not? Because the Bodisat, O king, had firmly grasped (the facts of) the impermanence (of all things, of) the suffering (inherent in existence as an individual, of) the absence of a soul (in any being made up of the five Skandhas), and had thus arrived at the destruction of the attachment (to individuality which arises from lust, or from heresy, or from dependence upon outward acts, or from delusions as to the possession of a permanent soul)[1]. The water, O king, which flows into the river Ganges from the Anottata lake, and from the Ganges river into the great ocean, and from the great ocean into the openings into the

[1] Upâdânakkhaya*m* patto. Childers says that the destruction of these upâdânas 'constitutes Arahatship.' I know of no authority for this, and it is incompatible with the Buddhist theory of Arahatship that any Arahat should go through such a period of penance as our author supposes the Bodisat to have done after he had reached this 'destruction of the upâdânas.' The perception of the first of the above facts, the impermanence of all things and beings (ani*kk*am), constitute indeed the 'entrance upon the path' (see above, p. 25), and of course the upâdânas are destroyed in every Arahat, but that is very different from Childers's conclusion, which would make the terms convertible.

regions under the earth[1]—would that water, after it had once entered that opening, turn back and flow again into the great ocean, and from the great ocean into the Ganges river, and from the Ganges river into the Anottata lake?'

[287] 'Certainly not, Sir.'

'In the same way, O king, it was for the sake of that last existence of his that the Bodisat had matured merit through the immeasurable æons of the past. He had now reached that last birth, the knowledge of the Buddhas had grown mature in him, in six years he would become a Buddha, all-knowing, the highest being in the world. Would then the Bodisat, for the sake of the Wheel-treasure, turn back?'

'Certainly not, Sir.'

'No! Though the great earth, O king, with all its peaks and mountain ranges, should turn back, yet the Bodisat would not before he had attained to Buddhahood. Though the water of the Ganges should flow backwards up the stream, yet the Bodisat would not turn back before he had attained to Buddhahood. Though the mighty ocean with its immeasurable waters[2] should dry up like the water in the footprint of a cow[3], yet would not the Bodisat turn back before he had attained to Buddhahood. Though Sineru, the king of the moun-

[1] Pâtâla-mukha*m*, which the Si*m*halese repeats. There is a similar sequence in the Sa*m*yutta I, 5, 4.

[2] Aparimita-*g*ala-dharo. Hîna*t*i-kumburê, p. 424, has dhârî, which may either be the same in meaning as dharo, or refer to the dhârâ, the streams of water.

[3] Gopade; not in Childers, but compare Gopadaka, 'puddle,' in a similar connection at Sumaṅgala Vilâsinî I, 147 (where one MS. reads Gopade).

tains, should split up into a hundred or a thousand fragments, yet would not the Bodisat turn back before he had attained to Buddhahood. Though the sun and moon with all the stars should fall, like a clod, upon the ground, yet would not the Bodisat turn back before he had attained to Buddhahood. Though the expanse of heaven should be rolled up like a mat, yet would not the Bodisat turn back before he had attained to Buddhahood! And why not? Because he had torn asunder every bond.'

21. 'Venerable Nâgasena, how many bonds are there in the world?'

'There are these ten bonds in the world, O king, bound by which men renounce not the world, or turn back again to it. And what are the ten? A mother, O king, is often a bond, and a father, and a wife, and children, and relations, and friends, and wealth, and easy income, [**288**] and sovranty, and the five pleasures of sense. These are the ten bonds common in the world, bonds bound by which men renounce not the world or turn back to it. And all these bonds had the Bodisat, O king, burst through. And therefore could he not, O king, turn back.'

22. 'Venerable Nâgasena, if the Bodisat, on discontent arising in his heart at the words of the god, though his knowledge (of the four Truths) was yet imperfect, and his insight of a Buddha not mature, did nevertheless go forth into renunciation of the world, of what advantage was penance to him then? Ought he not rather, awaiting the maturity of his knowledge, to have lived in the enjoyment of all (suitable) foods?'

'There are, O king, these ten sorts of individuals who are despised and contemned in the world, thought shameful, looked down upon, held blameworthy, treated with contumely, not loved. And what are the ten? A woman without a husband, O king, and a weak creature, and one without friends or relatives, and a glutton, and one dwelling in a disreputable family, and the friend of sinners, and he whose wealth has been dissipated, and he who has no character, and he who has no occupation[1], and he who has no means. These are the ten despised and contemned in the world, thought shameful, looked down upon, held blameworthy, treated with contumely, not loved[2]. It was on calling these conditions to mind, O king, that this idea occurred to the Bodisat: "Let me not incur blame among gods and men as being without occupation or without means! Let me as a master in action, held in respect by reason of action, one having the supremacy which arises from action, one whose conduct is based upon action, one who carries action (into every concern of life)[3], one who has his dwelling in action, be constant in earnestness[4]." That was the spirit, O king, in which the Bodisat, when he was bringing his knowledge to maturity, undertook the practice of penance.'

23. 'Venerable Nâgasena, the Bodisat, when he was undergoing penance, said thus to himself:

[1] Kamma is here explained by Hînaʃi-kumburê by karmânta ('such as husbandry or merchandise').

[2] On this list of epithets compare above, p. 229 (of the Pâli).

[3] Kamma-dhoreyyo. The latter word is not in Childers. Hînaʃi-kumburê (p. 427) has karmayama usulannâ wû. It is the Sanskrit dhaureya, and the whole might be rendered 'like a beast of burden whose load is action.'

[4] Appamâdo—that constant theme of praise and exhortation in the early Buddhist books.

[289] "But it is not by this penance severe that I shall reach the peculiar faculty of the insight arising from the knowledge of that which is fit and noble—that insight beyond the powers of ordinary men. May there not be now some other way to the wisdom (of Buddhahood)[1]?"

'Was then the Bodisat, at that time, confused in his mind about the way[2]?'

'There are twenty-five qualities, O king, which are causes of weakness of mind, weakened by which the mind cannot successfully be devoted to the destruction of the Âsavas (the Great Evils—lust, becoming, delusion, and ignorance)[3]. And what are the twenty-five? Anger, O king, and enmity, and hypocrisy[4], and conceit[5], and envy, and avarice, and deceit[6],

[1] These words, already quoted above, IV, 6, 20 (p. 244 of the Pâli), are put into the mouth of the Bodisat, after the conclusion of the 'penance,' in the Mahâ Sa*kk*aka Sutta (M. I, 246), which is the chief Pi*t*aka text on the penance (the Dukkha-kârikâ). The Si*m*halese version here (p. 427) has already been given in the note on the former passage.

[2] The way to Buddhahood (not the way to Arahatship). This is Hîna*t*i-kumburê's explanation, which agrees with the context.

[3] It will be noticed that (the destruction of the Âsavas being Arahatship, not Buddhahood) this is really no reply.

[4] Makkho, 'depreciation of the good qualities of others,' says Hîna*t*i-kumburê, pp. 427, 564. But the use of the word at *G*âtaka I, 385; Mahâvagga I, 15, 4; *K*ullavagga III, 34, 2; Ma*gg*hima Nikâya I, 15, shows that concealing one's own faults is rather the meaning.

[5] Pâlâso; not in Childers. But see Anguttara Nikâya II, 6, 12; Puggala Pa*ññ*atti II, 2; Ma*gg*hima Nikâya I, 15, &c. This and the last are usually mentioned together (see for instance below, VII, 2, 18), and the contrast is 'concealing the faults one has, and laying claim to virtues one has not.'

[6] Mâyâ. It is noteworthy that this famous word, which plays so great a part in the later philosophies, and which is often sup-

and treachery, and obstinacy[1], and perverseness[2], and pride, and vainglory, and the intoxication (of exalted ideas about birth or health or wealth), and negligence in (well-doing), and intellectual inertness or bodily sloth[3], and drowsiness[4], and idleness, and friendship with sinners, and forms, and sounds, and odours, and tastes, and sensations of touch, and hunger, and thirst[5], and discontent[6]. These are the

posed to express a fundamental conception of the Buddhists, has not yet been traced, and will probably never be found, in the Pi*t*akas, in any other than this subordinate and purely ethical sense. So when Mr. Gough in his 'Philosophy of the Upanishads' says, p. 186, that 'pessimism, metempsychosis, and mâyâ (the primitive world fiction) are retained in Buddhism' he is as wrong about mâyâ as he is about metempsychosis. He is evidently still under the delusion that Buddhism teaches the transmigration of souls, and that it has inherited from such schoolmen as *S*aṅkarâ*k*ârya the theory of the mâyâ. This is as funny as the astounding blindness which makes him say (pp. 267, 268) 'there is no quest of verity, of an active law of righteousness (in Buddhism), but only a yearning after a lapse into the void' (!). The converse proposition would be nearer to the actual fact, and the Buddhist Avi*gg*â is quite different from the Mâyâ of the later Vedântists. How absolutely different is the world in which the thoughts of a Buddhist would move is shown by Hîna*ti*-kumburê's gloss: 'The mâyâ of concealing faults one has' (tamâge œti agu*n*a sa*m*gawana mâyâ).

[1] Thambho (not 'stupor,' as Childers has it). 'That obstinacy of mind (d*ridh*awû sit œti bawa) which will not bend to the exhortation of the great,' says the Si*m*halese.

[2] Sârambho; not merely 'clamour, angry talk,' as Childers has it. See the commentary on the word sârambhî at *G*âtaka III, 259, with which Hîna*ti*-kumburê here agrees. 'Contrariness' would be perhaps a better rendering.

[3] Thînamiddha*m*; so Hîna*ti*-kumburê (but he takes them as two).

[4] Tandî, as Hîna*ti*-kumburê reads (for Mr. Trenckner's nandî).

[5] Khudâ pipâsâ, which must be taken separately to make up the twenty-five. The Si*m*halese takes them as two.

[6] Arati, which the Si*m*halese (taking thîna and middha separately) omits.

twenty-five qualities, O king, which are causes of weakness of mind, weakened by which the mind cannot successfully be devoted to the destruction of the Âsavas. (And of these it was) hunger and thirst, O king, which had then seized hold of the body[1] of the Bodisat. And his body being thus, as it were, "possessed," his mind was not rightly devoted to the destruction of the Âsavas. Now the Bodisat, O king, through the immeasurable æons of the past, had followed after the perception of the Four Noble Truths through all of his successive births. Is it then possible that in his last existence, in the birth in which that perception was to arise, there should be any confusion in his mind as to the way? But nevertheless there arose, O king, in the Bodisat's mind the thought: "May there not now be some other way to the wisdom (of a Buddha)?" And already before that, O king, when he was only one month old, when his father the Sakya was at work (ploughing), the Bodisat, placed in his sacred cot for coolness under the shade of the *G*ambu tree, sat up crosslegged, and putting away passion, free from all evil conditions of heart, he entered into and remained in the first *Gh*âna—a state of joy and ease, born of seclusion, full of reflection, full of investigation, **[290]** and so into the second, and so into the third, and so into the fourth *Gh*âna[2].'

---

[1] Pariyâdiyi*m*su; literally 'were suffused as to the body of' (Hîna*ti*-kumburê has *s*arîrayehi vyâpta wû). The passive forms of this verb are always difficult to translate. See above, p. 254, and below, pp. 296, 297 (of the Pâli), and *K*ullavagga VI, 2, 6; VII, 2, 1.

[2] This passage follows in the Mahâ Sa*kk*aka Sutta immediately after the passage quoted above (Ma*ggh*ima Nikâya I, 246), and the

'Very good, Nâgasena! That is so, and I accept it as you say. It was whilst he was bringing his knowledge to maturity that the Bodisat underwent the penance.'

[Here ends the dilemma as to the penance undergone by the Bodisat.]

[DILEMMA THE SEVENTY-THIRD.

VIRTUE STRONGER THAN VICE.]

24. 'Venerable Nâgasena, which is the more powerful, virtue or vice?'

'Virtue, O king[1].'

'That is a saying, Nâgasena, which I cannot believe—that virtue is more powerful than vice. For there are to be seen here (in the world) men who destroy living creatures, who take to themselves what has not been given, who walk in evil in their lusts, who speak lies, who commit gang robberies on whole villages, who are highwaymen, sharpers, and swindlers, and these all according to their crime suffer the cutting off of their hands, or their feet, or their hands and feet, or their ears, or

incident is also related at *G*âtaka I, 57. But in both these books there is reference only to the first—not to the second, third, and fourth *Gh*ânas. As this is therefore only another instance of the difference between the Pi*t*akas and the more advanced views of our author, I have not translated the remaining *Gh*ânas. As will be seen from the version of them in my 'Buddhist Suttas from the Pâli' (S. B. E., vol. xi, p. 272), the idea that a mere baby could have practised these higher meditations would only become possible after the Buddha theory had been much more developed than it is in the Pi*t*akas.

[1] Kusala*m*. So it has been already laid down at III, 7, 7 (pp. 83, 84 of the Pâli), that merit (pu*ññ*a*m*) is more than demerit.

their nose, or their ears and nose, or the Gruel Pot, or the Chank Crown, or the Râhu's Mouth, or the Fire Garland, or the Hand Torch, or the Snake Strips, or the Bark Dress, or the Spotted Antelope, or the Flesh Hooks, or the Penny Cuts, or the Brine Slits, or the Bar Turn, or the Straw Seat, or they are anointed with boiling oil, or eaten by dogs, or are impaled alive, or are beheaded with a sword[1]. Some of them sin one night and that night experience the fruit of their sin, some sinning by night experience the next day, some sinning one day experience that day, some sinning by day experience that night, some experience when two days or three have elapsed. But all experience in this present visible world the result of their iniquity. And is there any one, Nâgasena, who from having provided a meal with all its accessories[2] for one, or two, or three, or four, or five, or ten, or a hundred, or a thousand (members of the Order), has enjoyed in this present visible world wealth or fame or happiness—(is there any one who) from righteousness of life, or from observance of the Uposatha, (has received bliss even in this life[3])?'

25. 'There are **[291]**, O king, four men who by giving gifts, and by the practice of uprightness, and by the keeping of Uposatha, even in their earthly bodies attained to glory in Tidasapura (the city of the gods).'

[1] This is a repetition of the list given above (I, 276–278), where the technical terms are explained. Compare Mr. William Andrews's book, 'Punishments in the Olden Time.'

[2] Saparivâra*m* dâna*m*. Pirikara-sahita-wû mahâ dan dî, says the Si*m*halese, p. 430.

[3] The words in brackets are supplied from Hîna*t*i-kumburê.

'And who, Sir, were they[1]?'

'Mandhâtâ the king, and Nimi the king, and Sâdhîna the king, and Guttila the musician[2].'

'Venerable Nâgasena, this happened thousands of births ago, and is beyond the ken of either of us two. Give me, if you can, some examples from that period (of the world) which is now elapsing in which the Blessed One has been alive.'

'In this present period, O king, the slave Pu*nn*aka, on giving a meal to Sâriputta the Elder, attained that day to the dignity of a treasurer (Se*tth*i), and he is now generally known as Pu*n*-*n*aka the Se*tth*i. The queen, the mother of Gopâla, who (being the daughter of poor peasant folk) sold her hair for eight pennies, and therewith gave a meal to Mahâ Ka*kk*âyana the Elder and his seven companions, became that very day the chief queen of king Udena. Suppiyâ, the believing woman, cut flesh from her own thigh to provide broth[3] for a sick Bhikkhu, and on the very next day the wound closed up, and the place became cured, with skin grown over it. Mallikâ, the queen who (when a poor flower girl) gave the last night's gruel (she had reserved for her own dinner) to the Blessed One, became that very day the chief queen of the king of Kosala[4]. Sumana, the garland maker, when he had

[1] The king himself has already mentioned them, in reverse order, above, I, 172.

[2] The legends will be found in full in the *G*âtaka stories numbered respectively, in Professor Fausböll's edition, 258, 533, 494, and 243.

[3] Pa*t*i*kkh*âdaniya*m*. See the note on Mahâvagga VI, 23, where this curious story is given in full.

[4] See *G*âtaka III, 495, 496 for this story. Âbhidosika*m* is not in Childers, but see the Sutta Vibhaṅga, Pârâ*g*ika I, 5, 6.

presented to the Blessed One eight bunches of jessamine flowers, came that very day into great prosperity. Eka-sâ*t*aka the Brahman, who gave to the Blessed One his only garment, received that very day the office of Sabba*tth*aka (Minister in general)[1]. All these, O king, came into the enjoyment of wealth and glory in their then existing lives.'

'So then, Nâgasena, with all your searching and enquiry you have only found six cases[2]?'

'That is so, O king.'

26. 'Then it is vice, Nâgasena, and not virtue which is the more powerful. For on one day alone I have seen ten men expiating their crimes by being impaled alive, and thirty even, and forty, and fifty, [**292**], and a hundred, and a thousand. And further, there was Bhaddasâla, the soldier in the service of the royal family of Nanda[3], and he waged war against king *K*andagutta[4]. Now in that war, Nâgasena, there were eighty Corpse Dances. For they say that when one great Head Holocaust has taken place (by which is meant the slaughter of ten thousand elephants, and a lac of horses, and five thousand charioteers, and a hundred ko*t*is of soldiers on foot), then the headless corpses arise and dance in frenzy over the battle-field. And all the men

[1] 'Received from the king the great honour (sammâna) called sabba*tth*aka,' says Hîna*t*i-kumburê, p. 431. But we find a particular office so called at *G*âtaka II, 57. (It is true the reading there is sabbatthaka, but Mr. Trenckner's reading is doubtless preferable.)

[2] All these cases have already been referred to above, I, 172.

[3] 'Nandagutta of the Brahman caste,' says the Si*m*halese, p. 431.

[4] 'Descended from the *S*âkya race,' adds Hîna*t*i-kumburê.

thus slain came to destruction through the fruit of the Karma of their evil deeds[1]. And therefore, too, do I say, Nâgasena, that vice is more powerful than virtue. And have you heard, Nâgasena, that in all this dispensation (since the time of Gotama the Buddha) the giving by the Kosala king has been unequalled?'

'Yes, I have heard so, O king.'

'But did he, Nâgasena, on account of his having given gifts so unequalled, receive in this present life wealth, or glory, or happiness?'

'No, O king, he did not.'

'Then, in that case, surely, Nâgasena, vice is more powerful than virtue?'

27. 'Vice, O king, by reason of its meanness, dies quickly away. But virtue, by reason of its grandeur, takes a long time to die. And this can be further examined into by a metaphor. Just, O king, as in the West Country[2] the kind of corn called Kumuda-bha*nd*ikâ, ripening quickly and being garnered in a month, is called Mâsalu (got in a month)[3], but the rices only come to perfection in six months or five. What then is the difference, what the distinction herein between Kumuda-bha*nd*ikâ and rice?

'The one is a mean plant, O king, the other a grand one. The rices are worthy of kings, meet for

[1] The Pâli being otherwise unintelligible, the above version has been expanded in accordance with the Si*m*halese interpretation. Kavandha as a living headless trunk occurs already in the Sutta Vibhaṅga, Pârâ*g*ika IV, 9, 3.

[2] Aparante. This may mean merely the western country (as at *G*âtaka I, 98), or may be a specific place name as Aparântika is in the 'Indian Antiquary,' VII, 263.

[3] So the Si*m*halese, which seems to follow a slightly different reading.

the king's table; the other is the food of servants and of slaves.

[293] 'Just so, O king, it is by reason of its meanness that vice dies quickly away. But virtue, by its grandeur, takes a long time to die.'

28. 'But, Nâgasena, it is just those things which come most quickly to their end which are in the world considered the most powerful. And so still vice must be the more powerful, not virtue. Just, Nâgasena, as the strong man who, when he enters into a terrible battle, is able the most quickly to get hold of his enemies' heads under his armpit[1], and dragging them along to bring them prisoners to his lord, that is the champion who is regarded, in the world, as the ablest hero—just as that surgeon who is able the most quickly to extract the dart, and allay the disease, is considered the most clever—just as the accountant who is able with the greatest speed to make his calculations, and with most rapidity to show the result, is considered the cleverest counter—just as the wrestler who is able the most quickly to lift his opponent up, and make him fall flat on his back, is considered the ablest hero—just so, Nâgasena, it is that one of these two things—virtue and vice—which most quickly reaches its end that is, in the world, the more powerful of the two.'

'The Karma of both the two, O king, will be made evident in future births; but vice besides that will by reason of its guilt be made evident at once, and in this present life. The rulers (Kshatriyas)

[1] Upakakkhake. The word is not in the Pâli dictionaries, but I follow Hîna*n*-kumburê, p. 432, who renders it Kisilla, and the context at the parallel passage, *G*âtaka I, 63 (see also *G*âtaka I, 158, and the Sutta Vibhanga II, 260).

of old, O king, established this decree: "Whosoever takes life shall be subject to a fine, and whosoever takes to himself what has not been given, and whosoever commits adultery, and whosoever speaks lies, and whosoever is a dacoit, and whosoever is a highwayman, and whosoever cheats and swindles. Such men shall be liable to be fined or beaten or mutilated or broken[1] or executed." And in pursuance thereof they held repeated enquiry, and then adjudged one or other punishment accordingly. But, O king, has there ever been by any one a decree promulgated: "Whosoever gives gifts, or observes a virtuous life, or keeps Uposatha, to him shall wealth be given, or honours?" And do they make continued enquiry, and bestow wealth or honours accordingly, as they do stripes or bonds upon a thief?'

'Certainly not, Sir.'

'Well, if they did so then would virtue too be made evident even in this life. **[294]** But as they neither make such enquiry concerning givers, nor bestow wealth and honours upon them, therefore is virtue not manifested now. And this is the reason, O king, why vice is made known in this life, whereas he (the giver) receives the more abundantly in the lives to come. And therefore it is virtue which, through the destructions brought about by Karma, is by far the more powerful of the two[2].'

'Very good, Nâgasena! Only by one wise as you could this puzzle have been so well solved.

---

[1] Bhettabbo, 'have their arms or legs broken.'

[2] In this sentence the translation follows Hînañ-kumburê, who has apparently had a different, and fuller, reading before him.

The problem put by me in worldly sense have you in transcendental sense made clear.'

[Here ends the dilemma as to virtue and vice.]

[DILEMMA THE SEVENTY-FOURTH. OFFERINGS TO THE DEAD.]

29. 'Venerable Nâgasena, these givers when they bestow their offerings, devote them specifically to former (relatives) now departed[1], saying: "May this gift benefit such and such." Now do they (the dead) derive any benefit therefrom?'

'Some do, O king, and some do not.'

'Which then are they that do, and which do not?'

'Those who have been reborn in purgatory, O king, do not; nor those reborn in heaven; nor those reborn as animals. And of those reborn as Pretas three kinds do not—the Vantâsikâ (who feed on vomit), the Khuppipâsino (who hunger and thirst), the Nigg*h*âma-ta*n*hikâ (who are consumed by thirst). But the Paradattûpa*g*îvino (who live on the gifts of others) they do derive profit, and those who bear them in remembrance do so too.'

'Then, Nâgasena, offerings given by the givers have run to waste[2], and are fruitless, since those

[1] Petâ; which are not ghosts, disembodied 'souls,' but new beings whose link of connection with the departed is, 'not soul,' but Karma.

[2] Vissota*m*, from sru. The Si*m*halese, p. 434, has âsthâna gata wanneya (for asthâna).

for whose benefit they are given derive no profit therefrom.'

'No, O king. They run not to waste, neither are fruitless. The givers themselves derive profit from them.'

'Then convince me of this by a simile.'

'Suppose, O king, people were to get ready fish and meat and strong drinks and rice and cakes, and make a visit on a family related to them. If their relatives should not accept their complimentary present, would that present be wasted or fruitless?'

'No, Sir, it would go to the owners of it.'

'Well, just so the givers themselves derive the profit. Or just, O king, **[295]** as if a man were to enter an inner chamber, and there were no exit in front of him, how would he get out?'

'By the way he entered.'

'Well, just so the givers themselves derive the profit.'

30. 'Let that pass, Nâgasena. That is so, and I accept it as you say. We will not dispute your argument. But, venerable Nâgasena, if the offerings made by such givers do advantage certain of the departed, and they do reap the result of the gifts, then if a man who destroys living creatures and drinks blood and is of cruel heart, were after committing murder or any other dreadful act, to dedicate it to the departed, saying: "May the result of this act of mine accrue to the departed"—would it then be transferred to them?'

'No, O king.'

'But what is the reason, what is the cause, that a good deed can accrue to them, and not an evil one?'

'This is really not a question you should ask, O king. Ask me no foolish question, O king, in the idea that an answer will be forthcoming. You will be asking me next why space is boundless, why the Ganges does not flow up stream, why men and birds are bipeds, and the animals quadrupeds!'

'It is not to annoy you that I ask this question, Nâgasena, but for the sake of resolving a doubt. There are many people in the world who are left-handed or squint[1]. I put that question to you, thinking: "Why should not also these unlucky ones have a chance[2] of bettering themselves?"'

'An evil deed, O king, cannot be shared with one who has not done it, and has not consented to it. People convey water long distances by an aqueduct. But could they in the same way remove a great mountain of solid rock?'

'Certainly not, Sir.'

'Well, just in that way can a good deed be shared, but a bad one cannot. And one can light a lamp with oil, but could one in the same way, O king, light it with water?'

[**296**] 'Certainly not, Sir.'

'Well, so is it that a good deed can be shared, but not an evil one. And husbandmen take water from a reservoir to bring their crops to maturity, but could they for the same purpose, O king, take water from the sea?'

---

[1] Vâmagâhino vi*k*akkhukâ. Neither of these words are in the dictionaries. Hîna*t*i-kumburê, p. 436, says, 'who spoil what they take hold of, and whose eyes have lost their cunning.'

[2] Otâra, which the Si*m*halese renders awakâ*s*aya; and in that sense the word is used at Ma*gg*h*ima Nikâya I, 334.

'Certainly not, Sir.'

'So again is it that though a good deed can be shared, an evil one cannot.'

31. 'But, venerable Nâgasena, why is that? Convince me of this by a reason. I am not blind, or unobservant. I shall understand when I have heard.'

'Vice, O king, is a mean thing, virtue is great and grand. By its meanness vice affects[1] only the doer, but virtue by its grandeur overspreads the whole world of gods and men.'

'Show me this by a metaphor.'

'Were a tiny drop of water to fall on the ground, O king, would it flow on over ten leagues or twelve?'

'Certainly not. It would only have effect[2] on that very spot of ground on which it fell.'

'But why so?'

'Because of its minuteness.'

'Just so, O king, is vice minute. And by reason of its littleness it affects the doer only, and cannot possibly be shared. But if a mighty rain cloud were to pour out rain satisfying the surface of the earth, would that water spread round about?'

'Certainly, Sir. That thunderstorm would fill up the depressions in the ground and the pools and ponds, and the gullies and crevices and chasms, and the lakes and reservoirs and wells and lotus-tanks, and the water would spread abroad for ten leagues or for twelve[3].'

[1] Pariyâdiyati. See the note above at IV, 8, 23.

[2] A similar metaphor is used below, IV, 8, 55 (p. 311 of the Pâli).

[3] This long list is made up of the two given above at pp. 35,

'But why so, O king?'

'Because of the greatness of the storm.'

'Just so, O king, is virtue great. And by reason of its abundance it can be shared by gods and men.'

'Venerable Nâgasena, why is it that vice is so limited, [297] and virtue so much more wide-reaching?'

'Whosoever, O king, in this world gives gifts, and lives in righteousness, and keeps Uposatha[1], he, glad, right glad, joyful, cheerful, happy, becomes filled with a sweet sense of trust and bliss, and bliss ruling in his heart his goodness grows still more and more abundantly. Like a deep pool of clear water, O king, and into which on one side the spring pours, while on the other the water flows away; so as it flows away it comes again, and there can be no failure there—so, O king, does his goodness grow more and more abundantly. If even through a hundred years, O king, a man were to keep on transferring[2] to others (the merit of) any good he

259 of the Pâli (Paragraphs II, 1, 10 and IV, 6, 55 of the translation).

[1] The Buddhist Sabbath. See 'Buddhism,' pp. 140, 141.

[2] Âva*gg*eya, which the Si*m*halese, p. 437, merely repeats, is ambiguous (literally 'cause to bend towards'). Compare *G*âtaka I, 74, 89, 108, 171; II, 243. In most places the meaning 'bend back or towards' comes to have the secondary sense of 're-flect.' But throughout this discussion there is an underlying reference to a very beautiful Buddhist conception that a man can transfer to others the merit of any good deed he has done. Thus at the end of a palm-leaf manuscript the copyist often adds the pious wish: 'May the merit of my having made this copy redound to the advantage of all men,' or words to that effect. And the preceding metaphor would seem to show that this must be the secondary sense here attached to 'causing to bend towards;'—the more he

had done, the more he gave it away the more would his goodness grow, and he would still be able to share it with whomsoever he would. This, O king, is the reason why virtue is so much the greater of the two.

32. 'But on doing evil, O king, a man becomes filled with remorse [1], and the heart of him who feels remorse cannot get away (from the thought of the evil he has done), it is forcibly bent back on it, thrown back on it, obtains no peace [2]; miserable, burning, abandoned of hope, he wastes away, and gaining no relief from depression [3], he is, as it were, possessed with his woe! Just, O king, as a drop of water, falling on a dry river bed with its mighty sandbanks rising and falling in undulations along its crooked and shifty course, gains not in volume, but is swallowed up on the very spot where it fell, just so, O king, is a man, when he has done wrong, overcome with remorse, and the heart of him who feels remorse cannot get away from the thought of the evil he has done, it is forcibly bent back on it, thrown back on it, obtains no peace; miserable, burning, abandoned of hope, he wastes away, and gaining no release from his depression, he is, as it

---

spends (as it were) his virtue, the more remains, just as however much the water flows away from the spring, still quite as much remains, and he can still share with others that which is left. The doctrine of imputed righteousness is not confined to Buddhists, but the Buddhist theory is really quite different from the corresponding Western ideas, even from the Catholic doctrine of the transference of the righteousness of saints.

[1] So already above, III, 7, 7 (I, 128).

[2] Patilîyati patikutati pativa*tt*ati na sampasârîyati. None of these words are in the dictionaries.

[3] Na parivaddhate; literally 'is not dilated.'

were, swallowed up of his woe. This is the reason, O king, why vice is so mean.'

'Very good, Nâgasena! That is so, and I accept it as you say.'

[Here ends the problem as to virtue and vice.]

[DILEMMA THE SEVENTY-FIFTH.

DREAMS.]

33. 'Venerable Nâgasena, men and women in this world see dreams pleasant and evil, things they have seen before and things they have not, things they have done before and things they have not, [298] dreams peaceful and terrible, dreams of matters near to them and distant from them, full of many shapes and innumerable colours. What is this that men call a dream, and who is it who dreams it?'

'It is a suggestion[1], O king, coming across the path of the mind which is what is called a dream. And there are six kinds of people who see dreams—the man who is of a windy humour[2], or of a bilious one, or of a phlegmatic one, the man who dreams dreams by the influence of a god, the man who does so by the influence of his own habits, and the man who does so in the way of prognostication[3]. And

[1] Nimittam, aramunuwa in the Si*m*halese, p. 438.

[2] Vâtiko, which Childers renders wrongly rheumatic. Wâta prak*ri*ti wû, says the Si*m*halese, p. 438.

[3] The Si*m*halese gives the different kinds of dreams seen by each of these six—the first dreams of journeys through space, the second of fire and conflagrations, the third of water, the fourth

of these, O king, only the last kind of dreams is true; all the rest are false.'

34. 'Venerable Nâgasena, when a man dreams a dream that is a prognostication, how is it? Does his own mind set out itself to seek the omen, or does the prognostication come of its own accord into the path of his mind, or does some one else come and tell him of it?'

'His own mind does not itself seek the omen, neither does any one else come and tell him of it. The prognostication comes of its own accord into his mind. It is like the case of a looking-glass, which does not go anywhere to seek for the reflection; neither does any one else come and put the reflection on to the looking-glass. But the object reflected comes from somewhere or other across the sphere over which the reflecting power of the looking-glass extends.'

35. 'Venerable Nâgasena, does the same mind which sees the dream also know: "Such and such a result, auspicious or terrible, will follow?"'

'No, that is not so, O king. After the omen has occurred he tells others, and then they explain the meaning of it.'

'Come, now, Nâgasena, give me a simile to explain this.'

'It is like the marks, O king, and pimples, and cutaneous eruptions which arise on a man's body to his profit or loss, to his fame or dishonour, to his praise or blame, to his happiness or woe. **[299]** Do

of good or bad things according as the god is kindly or malignant, the fifth of what he has himself seen or heard, and the last of his future gain or loss.

in that case the pimples come because they know: "Such and such is the event which we shall bring about?"'

'Certainly not, Sir. But according to the place on which the pimples have arisen, the fortune-tellers, making their observations, give decision, saying: "Such and such will be the result."'

'Well, in the same way, O king, it is not the same mind which dreams the dream which also knows: "Such and such a result, conspicuous or terrible, will follow." But after the omen has occurred he tells others, and they then explain the meaning of it.'

36. 'Venerable Nâgasena, when a man dreams a dream, is he awake or asleep?'

'Neither the one, O king, nor yet the other. But when his sleep has become light[1], and he is not yet fully conscious[2], in that interval it is that dreams are dreamt. When a man is in deep sleep, O king, his mind has returned home (has entered again into the Bhavaṅga)[3], and a mind thus shut in does not act, and a mind hindered in its action knows not the evil and the good, and he who knows not[4] has no dreams. It is when the mind is active that dreams are dreamt. Just, O king, as in the darkness and gloom, where no light is, no shadow will fall even on the most burnished mirror, so when a man is in deep sleep his mind has returned into itself, and

[1] Okkante middhe; 'like a monkey's sleep,' says Hînaṭi-kumburê.

[2] On bhavaṅga compare Abhidhammattha Saṅgaha III, 8.

[3] 'Like a bird that has re-entered its nest' is Hînaṭi-kumburê's gloss.

[4] Appaṭivigânantassa, 'does not know the distinctions between bliss and woe (sukha dukkha vibhâga),' says the Simhalese, p. 440.

a mind shut in does not act, and a mind inactive knows not the evil and the good, and he who knows not does not dream. For it is when the mind is active that dreams are dreamt. As the mirror, O king, are you to regard the body, as the darkness sleep, as the light the mind. Or again, O king, just as the glory of a sun veiled in fog is imperceptible, as its rays, though they do exist, are unable to pierce through, and as when its rays act not there is no light, so when a man is in deep sleep his mind has returned into itself, and a mind shut in does not act, and a mind inactive knows not the evil and the good, and he who knows not does not dream. For it is when the mind is active that dreams are dreamt. As the sun, O king, are you to regard the body, as the veil of fog sleep, [**300**] as the rays the mind.

37. 'Under two conditions, O king, is the mind inactive though the body is there—when a man being in deep sleep the mind has returned into itself, and when the man has fallen into a trance[1]. The mind of a man who is awake, O king, is excited, open, clear, untrammelled, and no prognostication occurs to one whose mind is so. Just, O king, as men seeking concealment avoid the man who is open, candid, unoccupied, and unreserved,—just so is it that the divine intention is not manifested to the wakeful man, and the man who is awake therefore sees no dream. Or again, O king, just as the qualities which lead to wisdom are found not in that brother whose mode of livelihood and conduct are wrong, who is the friend of sinners, wicked, insolent, devoid

[1] Nirodha, which the Si*m*halese repeats. Probably the fourth *Gh*âna is here referred to.

of zeal,—just so is it that the divine intention is not manifested to the wakeful man, and the man who is awake, therefore, sees no dream.'

38. 'Venerable Nâgasena, is there a beginning, a middle, and an end in sleep?'

'Yes, O king, there is.'

'Which then is the beginning, which the middle, and which the end?'

'The feeling of oppression and inability[1] in the body, O king, of weakness, slackness, inertness—that is the beginning of sleep. The light "monkey's sleep" in which a man still guards his scattered thoughts[2]—that is the middle of sleep. When the mind has entered into itself—that is the end of sleep. And it is in the middle stage, O king, in the "monkey's sleep" that dreams are dreamt. Just, O king, as when a man self-restrained with collected thoughts, stedfast in the faith, unshaken in wisdom, plunges deep into the woods far from the sound of strife, and thinks over some subtle matter, he there, tranquil and at peace, will master the meaning of it—just so a man still watchful, not fallen into sleep, but dozing in a "monkey's sleep," will dream a dream. **[301]** As the sound of strife, so, O king, are you to regard wakefulness, and as the lonely wood the "monkey's sleep." And as that man avoiding the sound of strife, keeping out of sleep, remaining in the middle stage, will master the meaning of that subtle matter, so the still watchful man, not fallen into sleep, but dozing in a "monkey's sleep," will dream a dream.'

[1] Onâho pariyonâho, 'obstruction, covering.' See the Tevi*gg*a Sutta, § 58.

[2] Voki*nn*aka*m s*aggati. 'Destroys sleep by scattered thoughts,' says the Si*m*halese, p. 441.

'Very good, Nâgasena! That is so, and I accept it as you say.'

[Here ends the dilemma as to dreams[1].]

[DILEMMA THE SEVENTY-SIXTH.

PREMATURE DEATH.]

39. 'Venerable Nâgasena, when beings die, do they all die in fullness of time, or do some die out of due season?'

'There is such a thing, O king, as death at the due time, and such a thing as premature death.'

'Then who are they whose decease is at the due time, and who are they whose decease is premature?'

'Have you ever noticed, O king, in the case of mango trees or *G*ambu trees or other fruit-bearing trees, that their fruits fall both when they are ripe and when they are not ripe?'

'Yes, I have.'

'Well, those fallen fruits, do they all fall at the due time, or do some fall prematurely?'

'Such of those fruits, Nâgasena, as are ripe and mature[2] when they fall, fall in fullness of time. But of the rest some fall because they are bored into by worms, some because they are knocked down by a

[1] It is not known whether the whole of this theory of dreams is taken from the Pi*t*akas, or whether it is an expansion of views there suggested. But the germs of the theory are certainly in the Pi*t*akas. Thus the Buddha is made at Ma*gg*h*ima Nikâya I, 249, 250 to say of himself that in his midday sleep he was neither stupefied nor the contrary (neither sammûlho nor asammûlho), which comes very near to the 'monkey's sleep' referred to throughout this dilemma.

[2] Vilînani, wilikun wû says Hîna*t*i-kumburê (p. 442).

long stick, some because they are blown down by the wind, some because they have become rotten—and all these fall out of due season[1].'

'Just so, O king, those men who die of the effect of old age, they die in fullness of time. But of the rest some die of the dire effect of the Karma (of evil deeds), some of excessive journeying[2], some of excessive activity.'

40. 'Venerable Nâgasena, those who die of Karma, or of journeying, or of activity, or of old age, they all die in fullness of time: and even he who dies in the womb, that is his appointed time, so that he too dies in fullness of time; and so of him who dies in the birth chamber **[302]**, or when he is a month old, or at any age up to a hundred years. It is always his appointed time, and it is in the fullness of time that he dies. So, Nâgasena, there is no such thing as death out of due season. For all who die, die at the appointed time.'

'There are seven kinds of persons, O king, who, there being still a portion of their appointed age to run, die out of time. And which are the seven? The starving man, O king, who can get no food, whose inwards are consumed[3]—and the thirsty man who can get no water, whose heart is dried up—and the man bitten by a snake, who, when consumed by the fierce energy of poison, can find no cure—and he who has taken poison, and when all his limbs are

[1] This simile has already been used above, IV, 3, 7 (I, 235).

[2] Gati-patibâ*l*hâ, gamana bâhulyatâwen says the Si*m*halese.

[3] Upahat-abbhantaro, 'whose interior is burnt by the fierceness of the stomach fire' (*g*a*th*arâgni-gaha*n*i), says Hîna*t*i-kumburê, p. 443.

burning, is unable to procure medicine—and one fallen into fire, who when he is aflame, can find no means of putting out the fire—and he who having fallen into water can find no firm ground to stand on—and the man wounded by a dart, who in his illness can find no surgeon—all these seven, there being still a portion of their appointed time to run, die out of due season. And herein (in all these seven cases) I declare that they are all of one nature[1]. In eight ways, O king, does the death of mortals take place—through excess of windy humour, or of bilious humour, or of phlegmatic humour, through the adverse union of these three, through variations in temperature, through inequality in protection, through (medical) treatment, and through the working of Karma[2]. And of these, O king, it is only death by the working of Karma that is death at the due season, all the rest are cases of death out of due season. For it is said:

"By hunger, thirst, by poison, and by bites,
Burnt, drowned, or slain, men out of time do die;
By the three humours, and by three combined,
By heats, by inequalities, by aids,
By all these seven men die out of time[3]."

41. **[303]** 'But there are some men, O king, who die through the working of some evil deed or other they have committed in a former birth. And of

[1] Hînaʈi-kumburê had apparently a different reading (perhaps ekamse na vadâmi). For he translates, p. 444, 'In this death I do not say that there is one cause.'

[2] As was noticed above on p. 112 (of the Pâli), some of these medical terms are very uncertain, and the Simhalese gives no help.

[3] Not traced in the Piʈakas.

these, O king, whosoever has starved others to death, after having been himself through many hundreds of thousands of years tormented by hunger, famished, exhausted, emaciated, and withered of heart, dried up, wasted away, heated, and all on fire within, will, either as youth or man or old man, die of hunger too. And that death will be to him a death at the appointed time[1]. Whosoever has put others to death by thirst, after having through many hundreds of thousands of years become a Preta consumed by thirst, thin and miserable, will himself too, either as youth or man or old man, die of thirst. And that death will be to him a death at the appointed time. Whosoever has put others to death by having them bitten by snakes, will, after wandering through many hundreds of thousands of years from existence to existence, in which he is constantly bitten by boa constrictors and black snakes, himself too, either as youth or man or old man, die of snake bite. And that will be to him a death at the appointed time. Whosoever has put others to death by poison will, after existing for many hundreds of thousands of years with burning limbs and broken body, and exhaling the odour of a corpse, himself too, either as youth or man or old man, die of poison. And that will be to him a death at the appointed time. Whosoever has put others to death by fire, he having wandered from purgatory[2] to purgatory, from one mass of burning charcoal to

[1] Sâmâyiko, 'timely,' but Childers says 'temporary,' and we have had the word above (p. 22 of the Pâli) in the sense of 'religious.' The Si*m*halese, p. 445, repeats the word.

[2] Yama-visaya, 'abode of the god of death.'

another, with burning and tortured limbs, for many hundreds of thousands of years, will himself too, either as youth or man or old man, be burnt to death. And that will be to him a death at the appointed time. Whosoever has put others to death by drowning, he having suffered many hundreds of thousands of years as a being disabled, ruined, broken, weak in limb, and anxious in heart, will himself too, either as youth or man or old man, die by drowning. And that will be to him a death at the appointed time. Whosoever has put others to death by the sword, **[304]** he having suffered for many hundreds of thousands of years (in repeated births as an animal) from cuts and wounds and blows and bruises, or (when born as a man) ever destroyed by weapons[1], will himself too, either as youth or man or old man, perish by the sword. And that will be to him a death at the appointed time.'

42. 'Venerable Nâgasena, the death out of due time that you also speak of—come now, tell me the reason for that.'

'As a great and mighty fire, O king, on to which dry grass and sticks and branches and leaves have been heaped, will nevertheless, when this its food has been consumed, die out by the exhaustion of the fuel. Yet such a fire is said to have gone out in fullness of time, without any calamity or accident (having happened to it). Just so, O king, the man who, when he has lived many thousands of days, when he is old and stricken in years, dies at last of

[1] Sarnâhato. Compare above, pp. 181, 254 of the Pâli, and Ma*ggh*ima Nikâya I, 337.

old age, without any calamity or accident having happened to him, is said to have reached death in the fullness of time. But if there were a great and mighty fire, O king, on to which dry grass and sticks and branches and leaves had been heaped, then if a mighty rain cloud were to pour out rain upon it, and it were thus to be put out, even before the fuel was consumed, could it be said, O king, that that great fire had gone out in fullness of time?'

'No, Sir, it could not.'

'But wherein would the second fire differ, in its nature, from the first?'

'The second one, Sir, which suffered from the onset of the rain—that fire would have gone out before its time.'

'Just so, O king, whosoever dies before his time does so in consequence of suffering from the attack of some disease,—from excess of windy humour, or of bilious humour, or of phlegmatic humour, or from the union of the three, or from variations in temperature, or from inequality in protection, or from treatment, or from hunger, or from thirst, or from fire, or from water, or from the sword. This, O king, is the reason why there is such a thing as dying before one's time.

43. 'Or again, O king, it is like a mighty storm cloud which, rising up into the heavens, should pour out rain, filling the valleys and the plains. That cloud would be said to have rained without calamity or accident. Just so, O king, the man who after having lived long, dies at last, when he is old and well stricken in years, without any calamity or accident having happened to him, of old age, is said to have

reached death in the fullness of time. **[305]** But if, O king, a mighty storm cloud were to rise up into the heavens, and as it did so were to be dissipated by a mighty wind, could it be said, O king, that that cloud had perished in due time?'

'No, Sir, it could not.'

'But wherein would the second cloud differ, in its nature, from the first?'

'The second one, Sir, which suffered from the onset of the whirlwind, would have been dissipated before its time.'

'Just so, O king, whosoever dies before his time does so in consequence of suffering from the attack of some disease,—from excess of windy humour, or of bilious humour, or of phlegmatic humour, or from the union of the three, or from variations in temperature, or from inequality in protection, or from treatment, or from hunger, or from thirst, or from fire, or from water, or from the sword. This, O king, is the reason why there is such a thing as dying before one's time.

44. 'Or again, O king, it is like a powerful and deadly snake, which being angered should bite a man, and to him that poison, no impediment and no accident happening to it, should bring death. That poison would be said, without impediment or accident, to have reached its aim. Just so, O king, the man who, having lived long, dies at last, when he is old and well stricken in years, without any calamity or accident having happened to him, of old age, he is said to have reached, unimpeded and uninterrupted, to the goal of his life, to have died in the fullness of time. But if a snake charmer were to give a drug to the man while he was suffering from

the bite, and thus get rid of the poison, could it be said that the poison was removed in the fullness of time?'

'No, Sir, it could not.'

'But wherein, O king, would the second poison differ, in its nature, from the first?'

'The second one, Sir, which was acted upon by the introduction of the drug, would have been removed before its end was attained.'

'Just so, O king, whosoever dies before his time does so in consequence of suffering from the attack of some disease,—from excess of windy humour, or of bilious humour, or of phlegmatic humour, or from the union of the three, or from variations in temperature, or from inequality in protection, or from treatment, or from hunger, or from thirst, or from fire, or from water, or from the sword. This, O king, is the reason why there is such a thing as dying before one's time.

45. 'Or again, O king, it is like the arrow discharged by an archer. [306] If that arrow should go to the very end of the line of the path along which it was natural for it to go, then it would be said to have reached that aim, without let or hindrance. Just so, O king, the man who, having lived long, dies at last, when he is old and well stricken in years, without any calamity or accident having happened to him, of old age, is said to have reached death, unimpeded and uninterrupted, in the fullness of time. But if, at the moment when the archer was discharging the arrow, some one should catch hold of it, could that arrow be said to have reached the end of the line of the path along which it was shot?'

'No, Sir, it could not.'

'But wherein, O king, would the second arrow differ, in its nature, from the first?'

'By the seizure which intervened, Sir, the course of the second arrow was arrested.'

'Just so, O king, whosoever dies before his time does so in consequence of suffering from the attack of some disease,—from excess of windy humour, or of bilious humour, or of phlegmatic humour, or from the union of the three, or from variations in temperature, or from inequality in protection, or from treatment, or from hunger, or from thirst, or from fire, or from water, or from the sword. This, O king, is the reason why there is such a thing as dying before one's time.

46. 'Or again, O king, it is like the brazen vessel which a man should strike. And by his striking thereof a note should be produced, and sound to the very end of the line of the path along which it was its nature to sound. It would then be said to have reached that aim without let or hindrance. Just so, O king, the man who, having lived long, dies at last, when he is old and well stricken in years, without any calamity or accident having happened to him, of old age, is said to have reached death, without let or hindrance, in the fullness of time. But if a man were to strike a brazen vessel, and by his striking thereof a note should be produced, but some one, before it had reached any distance, were to touch the vessel, and at his touching thereof the sound should cease, could then that sound be said to have reached the end of the line of the path along which it was its nature to sound?'

'No, Sir, it could not.'

'But wherein, O king, would the second sound differ, in its nature, from the first?'

'By the touching which intervened, Sir, that sound was suppressed[1].'

[**307**] 'Just so, O king, whosoever dies before his time does so in consequence of suffering from the attack of some disease,—from excess of windy humour, or of bilious humour, or of phlegmatic humour, or from the union of the three, or from variations in temperature, or from inequality in protection, or from treatment, or from hunger, or from thirst, or from fire, or from water, or from the sword. This, O king, is the reason why there is such a thing as dying before one's time.

47. 'Or again, O king, it is like the corn seed which had sprung up well in the field, and by means of a plentiful downpour of rain had become well laden far and wide[2] with many seeds, and had survived in safety to the time of standing crops, that corn would be said to have reached, without let or hindrance, to its due season. Just so, O king, the man who, having lived long, dies at last, when he is old and well stricken in years, without any calamity or accident having happened to him, of old age, is said to have reached death, without let or hindrance, in the fullness of time. But if that corn, after it had sprung up well in the field, should, deprived of water, die, could it be said to have reached its due season?'

---

[1] Uparato, for which Hînaʼi-kumburê, p. 449, has upahata wîyœyi.

[2] Otaka-vitaka-âki*nn*a. Gha*n*ayawû pata*l*awû âkîr*nn*awû says the Si*m*halese.

'No, Sir, it could not.'

'But wherein, O king, would the second crop differ, in its nature, from the first?'

'Oppressed by the heat which intervened, that crop, Sir, perished.'

'Just so, O king, whosoever dies before his time does so in consequence of suffering from the attack of some disease,—from excess of windy humour, or of bilious humour, or of phlegmatic humour, or from the union of the three, or from variations in temperature, or from inequality in protection, or from treatment, or from hunger, or from thirst, or from fire, or from water, or from the sword. This, O king, is the reason why there is such a thing as dying before one's time.

48. 'And have you ever heard, O king, of a young crop that, after it had come to ear, worms sprung up and destroyed down to the roots?'

'We have both heard of such a thing, Sir, and have seen it, too.'

'Well, O king, was that crop destroyed in season, or out of season?'

'Out of season, Sir. For surely if worms had not destroyed the crop it would have survived to harvest time.'

'What then, O king! on a disaster intervening the crop is lost, but if no injury is done it, it survives to the harvest?'

'That is so, Sir.'

[308] 'Just so, O king, whosoever dies before his time does so in consequence of suffering from the attack of some disease,—from excess of windy humour, or of bilious humour, or of phlegmatic humour, or from the union of the three, or from variations in temperature, or from inequality in protection, or from treatment, or from hunger, or from thirst, or from fire, or from water, or from the sword. This, O king, is the reason why there is such a thing as dying before one's time.

49. 'And have you ever heard, O king, of a crop that had grown, and was bent down by the weight of the grains of corn, the ears having duly formed[1], when a so-called Karaka rain (hail-storm)[2] falling on it, destroyed it?'

'We have both heard of such a thing, Sir, and have seen it, too.'

'Well, O king! would you say the crop was destroyed in season or out of season?'

'Out of season, Sir. For if the hail-storm had not come the crop would have lasted to harvest time.'

'What then, O king! on a disaster intervening the crop is lost, but if no injury is done it, it survives to the harvest?'

'That is so, Sir.'

'Just so, O king, whosoever dies before his time does so in consequence of suffering from the attack of some disease,—from excess of windy humour, or of bilious humour, or of phlegmatic humour, or from the union of the three, or from variations in temperature, or from inequality in protection, or from treatment, or from hunger, or from thirst, or from fire, or from water, or from the sword. This, O

[1] Mañgarita-patte, which the Simhalese renders karal patra œttâwû.

[2] Karaka-vassam is pâsâna-warsha in the Simhalese. If karaka originally meant 'hard shell,' it could have reached its ordinary meaning of 'water-pot,' from the fact that an empty half of a cocoa-nut shell is the most common form of cup.

king, is the reason why there is such a thing as dying before one's time.'

50. 'Most wonderful, Nâgasena, most strange! Right well have you explained, by reason and by simile, how it is that people die before their time. That there is such a thing as premature death have you made clear and plain and evident[1]. A thoughtless man even, Nâgasena, a puzzle-headed fellow, could by any one of your comparisons have come to the conclusion that premature deaths do occur;—**[309]** how much more an able man! I was convinced already, Sir, by the first of your similes, that such deaths happen, but nevertheless, out of the wish to hear still further and further solutions, I would not give in.'

[Here ends the dilemma as to premature deaths.]

[DILEMMA THE SEVENTY-SEVENTH.

WONDERS AT THE GRAVE.]

51. 'Venerable Nâgasena, are there wonders at the *K*etiyas (the mounds raised over the ashes) of all who have passed entirely away (of all the Arahats deceased)[2]?'

'Of some, O king, but not of others.'

'But of which, Sir, is this the case, and of which not?'

[1] Vibhûta*m* kata*m* is rendered prasiddha kara*n*a laddeya in the Si*m*halese, p. 451.

[2] Parinibbutâna*m*. The words in brackets are Hînai*t*i-kumburê's gloss. 'Of all who have been entirely set free' is an alternative, and perhaps a better, rendering.

'It is by the stedfast resolve, O king, of three kinds of people, that wonders take place at the *K*etiya of some person deceased who has been entirely set free. And who are the three? In the first place, O king, an Arahat, when still alive, may, out of pity for gods and men, make the resolve: "Let there be such and such wonders at my *K*etiya[1]." Then, by reason of his resolve, wonders happen there. Thus is it that wonders occur by the resolve of an Arahat at the *K*etiya of one entirely set free.

'And again, O king, the gods, out of pity for men, show wonders at the *K*etiya of one who has been entirely set free, thinking: "By this wonder may the true faith remain always established on the earth, and may mankind, believing, grow in grace!" Thus is it that wonders occur by the resolve of a god at the *K*etiya of one entirely set free.

'And again, O king, some woman or some man of believing heart, able, intelligent, wise, endowed with insight, may deliberately take perfumes, or a garland, or a cloth, and place it on the *K*etiya, making the resolve: "May such and such a wonder take place!" Thus is it that wonders occur by the resolve of human beings at the *K*etiya of one entirely set free.

52. 'These, O king, are the three kinds of people by whose stedfast resolve wonders take place at the *K*etiyas of Arahats deceased. And if there has been no such resolve, O king, by one of these, then

[1] Mr. Trenckner prints evam-nâma as qualifying *K*etiya. The Si*m*halese, p. 451, takes it as I have rendered.

is there no wonder at the *K*etiya even of one whose âsavas had been destroyed, who had attained to the sixfold insight, who was master of himself. And if there be no such wonder, then, O king, [310] one should call to mind the purity of conduct one has seen[1], and draw in trusting faith the conclusion: "Verily, this child of the Buddhas has been entirely set free!"'

'Very good, Nâgasena! That is so, and I accept it as you say.'

[Here ends the dilemma as to wonders at the grave.]

[DILEMMA THE SEVENTY-EIGHTH.

CONVERSION AND CONDUCT.]

53. 'Venerable Nâgasena, those who regulate their lives aright—do they all attain to insight into the Truth, or are there some of them who do not?'

'Some do, O king, and some do not.'

'Then which do, Sir, and which do not?'

'He who is born as an animal, O king, even though he regulate his life aright, will not attain to insight into the Truth, nor he who is born in

[1] These words are very ambiguous, and unfortunately the Sim-halese (p. 452), though much expanded, is equally so. The kind of wonder referred to throughout the dilemma is also doubtful. The only one of the kind mentioned, so far as I know, in the Pi*t*akas is that referred to in the 'Book of the Great Decease,' V, 26, where the placing of garlands on a *K*etiya produces calm in the heart. But it is difficult to believe that our author had merely a spiritual experience of this kind in his thoughts. The whole discussion points rather to the late date at which he wrote.

the Preta world, nor he who holds wrong views, nor the deceitful man, nor he who has slain his mother, or his father, or an Arahat, nor he who has raised up a schism in the Order, nor he who has shed a Buddha's blood, nor he who has furtively attached himself to the Order[1], nor he who has become a pervert[2], nor he who has violated a sister of the Order, nor he who, having been guilty of one or other of the thirteen grievous offences[3], has not been rehabilitated, nor a eunuch, nor an hermaphrodite—and whosoever is a human child under seven years of age, even though he regulate his life aright, will not attain to insight into the Truth. To these sixteen individuals there is no attainment of insight, O king, even though they regulate their life aright.'

54. 'Venerable Nâgasena, there may or may not be a possibility of insight to the fifteen you have first singled out for opposition[4]. But what is the reason why an infant, one under seven years of age, should not, even though he regulate his life aright, attain to insight? Therein there is still a puzzle left. For is it not admitted that in a child there is not passion, neither malice, nor dullness, nor pride, nor heresy, nor discontent, nor lustful thoughts? Being undefiled by sin, that which we call an infant is fit and ready (to the attainment

[1] Theyya-sa*m*vâsaka. See Mahâvagga I, 69, 4.

[2] Titthiya-pakkantaka, 'gone over to the Titthiyas.'

[3] Garukâpatti, which Hîna*t*i-kumburê takes to be equivalent to the Sa*m*ghâdisesa offences. This is doubtless correct, and the use of the phrase in that sense is a sign of our author's later date.

[4] Viruddhâ, 'placed in a class' (wœdœrum wû), says the Si*m*halese, p. 453. It is literally 'opposed,' and the idiom is curious.

even of Arahatship—how much more)[1] is he worthy to penetrate at a glance into the four truths!'

'The following is the reason, O king, for my saying **[311]** that an infant, even though he regulate his life aright, cannot attain to insight. If, O king, one under seven years of age could feel passion about things exciting to passion, could go wrong in things leading to iniquity, could be befooled in matters that mislead, could be maddened as to things that infatuate, could understand a heresy, could distinguish between content and discontent, could think out virtue and vice, then might insight be possible to him. But the mind of one under seven years of age, O king, is powerless and weak, mean, small, slight, obscure, and dull, whereas the essential principle of Nirvâ*n*a is transcendental, important, weighty, wide-reaching, and extensive. Therefore is it, O king, that the infant, with so imperfect a mind, is unable to grasp an idea so great. It is like the case of Sineru, O king, the king of the mountains, heavy and ponderous, wide-reaching and mighty as it is,—could now a man, by his ordinary strength and power and energy, root that mountain up[2]?'

'Certainly not, Sir.'

'But why not?'

'Because of the weakness of the man, and because of the mightiness of Sineru, the mountain king.'

---

[1] The words in brackets are added from the Si*m*halese.

[2] Similar metaphors have already been used in the 71st Dilemma (p. 283 of the Pâli) and in the 74th Dilemma (p. 295 of the Pâli).

'Just so, O king, is the relation of the infant's mind to Nirvâna[1].

55. 'And again, it is like the broad earth, O king, long and wide, great in expanse and extension, large and mighty—would now a tiny drop of water be able to wet and turn to mud that broad earth[2]?'

'Certainly not, Sir.'

'But why not, O king?'

'Because of the minuteness of the drop of water, and because of the greatness of the broad earth.'

'Just so, O king, is the relation of the infant's mind to Nirvâna.

[312] 56. 'Or again, O king, suppose there were weak and powerless, minute, tiny, limited, and dull fire—would it be possible, with so insignificant a fire, to overcome darkness and make light appear over the whole world of gods and men?'

'Certainly not, Sir.'

'But why not, O king?'

'Because of the dullness of the fire, and because of the greatness of the world.'

'Just so, O king, the mind of one under seven years of age is powerless and weak, limited, insignificant, obscure, and dull; it is veiled, moreover, with the thick darkness of ignorance. Hard would it be, therefore, for it to shine forth with the light of knowledge. And that is the reason, O king, why to an infant, to one under seven years of age, even though he order his conduct aright, there can be no attainment of insight into the Truth.

[1] In the text the whole comparison is repeated.

[2] For a similar metaphor see above, IV, 8, 31 (p. 296 of the Pâli).

57. 'Or again, O king, suppose there were a Sâlaka[1], minute in the measure of its body, and rendered lean by disease, and it on seeing an elephant king, which showed the signs of rut in three places, and was nine cubits in length, and three in breadth, and ten in girth, and seven in height[2], coming to its lair, were to begin to drag the elephant towards it with the view of swallowing it—now would the Sâlaka, O king, be able to do so[3]?'

'Certainly not, Sir.'

'But why not, O king?'

'Because of the minuteness of the Sâlaka's body, and because of the magnitude of the elephant king.'

'Just so, O king, the mind of one under seven years of age is powerless and weak, limited, insignificant, obscure, and dull. Grand and transcendental is the ambrosial essence of Nirvâ*n*a[4]. With that mind so powerless and weak, so limited, insignificant, obscure, and dull, he cannot penetrate into the grand and transcendental essence of Nir-

[1] It is unknown what this kimi (insect, vermin, small creature) is, and it is not mentioned elsewhere. Susruta mentions a *s*ârikâmukha insect, and as in one rare word at least, which the Pâli translator did not sufficiently understand to restore to the ordinary Pâli form (kalasi for karisi, see above, I, xxiii), we find la stood in our author's dialect for ri, there may be some connection between the two. It would be particularly interesting to be able to determine the species and habitat of this creature, as it might throw some light on the district in which our author flourished.

[2] These measurements differ slightly from those given above, IV, 8, 14 (p. 282 of the Pâli), for a fine elephant.

[3] Compare the tale of the frog who wanted to swallow the bull in Æsop's fables (not yet traced in the *G*âtakas). Is the Sâlaka a kind of frog, much smaller than ours?

[4] So Hîna*t*i-kumburê, p. 455.

vâ*n*a. And that is the reason, O king, why to an infant, one under seven years of age, even though he order his conduct aright, there can be no attainment to insight of the Truth.'

'Very good, Nâgasena! That is so, and I accept it as you say.'

[Here ends the dilemma on conversion and conduct.]

[DILEMMA THE SEVENTY-NINTH.

THE PAIN OF NIRVÂ*N*A[1].]

[313] 58. 'Venerable Nâgasena, how is it? Is Nirvâ*n*a all bliss, or is it partly pain[2]?'

---

[1] The following pages will seem only so much verbiage, and will convey no idea to a European reader, unless he realises that the Nirvâ*n*a discussed is of course not a salvation to be enjoyed by a 'soul' after death, and in some other world; but a state of mind to be realised and enjoyed by a man here, on this earth, in this life, and in this life only.

Though I had pointed this out already in 1876 the animistic interpretation of Nirvâ*n*a is still the prevalent one, and still continues to lead to endless confusion. Why is it then, the reader may ask, that our author does not contradict the Christian interpretation of the Buddhist summum bonum in so many words? Simply because it never occurred to him as possible. It was probably even as inconceivable to him as the Buddhist interpretation of it seems to be to most Western writers.

[2] This dilemma and the next have been translated into French in the 'Revue de l'histoire des Religions' for 1885 (vol. xi, pp. 336 and following). The author's name being given as Mr. Lewis da Sylva, of Colombo, the article as it stands is presumably a translation into French, made in Paris, of Mr. da Sylva's version in English from the Si*m*halese, which may account for the fact that there is scarcely a sentence which is not misleading.

'Nirvâ*n*a is all bliss, O king. There is no intermingling of pain in it.'

'That, Sir, is a saying we cannot believe—that Nirvâ*n*a is all bliss. On this point, Nâgasena, we maintain that Nirvâ*n*a must be alloyed with pain. And there is a reason for our adopting that view. What is that reason? Those, Nâgasena, who seek after Nirvâ*n*a are seen to practise exertion and application both of body and of mind, restraint in standing, walking, sitting, lying, and eating, suppression of sleep, subjugation of the organs of sense, renunciation of wealth and corn, of dear relatives and friends. But all those who are joyful and happy in the world take delight in, are devoted to, the five pleasures of sense—they practise and delight their eyes in many kinds of pleasurable forms, such as at any time they like the best—they practise and delight their ears in many kinds of pleasurable sounds of revelry and song, such as at any time they like the best—they practise and delight their sense of smell with many kinds of perfumes of flowers, and fruits, and leaves, and bark, and roots, and sap, such as at any time they like the best—they practise and delight their tongue with many kinds of pleasurable tastes of hard foods and of soft, of syrups, drinks, and beverages, such as at any time they like the best—they practise and delight their sense of touch with many kinds of pleasurable feelings, tender and delicate, exquisite and soft, such as at any time they like the best—they practise and delight their minds with many sorts of conceptions and ideas, pure and impure, good and bad, such as at any time they like the best. You, on the other hand, put a stop to and destroy, maim and mangle, put a drag on and restrain the development of your eye, and ear, and nose, and tongue, and body, and mind. Therefore is your body afflicted and your mind afflicted too, and your body being afflicted you feel bodily discomfort and pain, and your minds being afflicted you feel mental discomfort too and pain. Did not even Mâgandiya, the ascetic, find fault with the Blessed One, and say[1]: **[314]** "The Sama*n*a Gotama is a destroyer of increase[2]?"'

59. 'Nirvâ*n*a, O king, has no pain in it. It is bliss unalloyed. When you, O king, maintain that Nirvâ*n*a is painful, that which you call "painful" is not Nirvâ*n*a. It is the preliminary stage to the realisation of Nirvâ*n*a, it is the process of seeking after Nirvâ*n*a. Nirvâ*n*a itself is bliss pure and simple, there is no pain mixed with it. And I will give you an explanation of this. Is there such a thing, O king, as the bliss of sovranty which kings enjoy?'

'Most certainly.'

'And is there no pain, O king, mingled with that bliss?'

'No, Sir.'

'But surely then, O king, why is it that when their frontier provinces have broken out in revolt, the kings, to the end that they may bring the inhabitants of those provinces into subjection again, leave their homes, attended by their ministers and chiefs, their

[1] In the Mâgandiya Sutta, No. 75 in the Ma*ggh*ima Nikâya, at I, 502, where the speech will be f. Trenckner's valuable note.

[2] Bhûtaha*kk*e. See Pâli, reading Bhûtahu, and rendering Hîna*ñ*kumburê, p. 456, qaranayek. it 'anabhiw*r*idd

soldiers and their guards, and marching over ground even and uneven, tormented the while by gnats and mosquitoes and hot winds, engage in fierce fights, and suffer the presentiment of death?'

'That, venerable Nâgasena, is not what is called the bliss of sovranty. It is only the preliminary stage in the pursuit of that bliss. It is after they have thus, in pain, sought after sovranty, that they enjoy the bliss thereof. And thus that bliss, Nâgasena, is itself unmixed with pain, for the bliss of sovranty is one thing, and the pain another.'

'Just so, O king, is Nirvâ*n*a all bliss, and there is no pain mingled with it. Those who are in quest of Nirvâ*n*a afflict their minds and bodies it is true, restrain themselves in standing, walking, sitting, lying, and in food, suppress their sleep, keep their senses in subjection, abandon their very body and their life. But it is after they have thus, in pain, sought after Nirvâ*n*a, that they enjoy the Nirvâ*n*a which is bliss unalloyed—as kings do the bliss of sovranty after their foes have been put down. Thus is it, O king, that Nirvâ*n*a is all bliss, and there is no pain mingled with it. For Nirvâ*n*a is one thing, and the pain another.

[315] 60. 'And hear another explanation, O king, of the same thing. Is there such a thing, O king, as the bliss of knowledge which those teachers have who have passed through their course?'

'Yes, Sir, there is.'

'Well, is that bliss of knowledge alloyed with pain?'

'No.'

'What then, O king, is the good of their afflicting

themselves by bowing down before and standing up in the presence of their teachers; by drawing water, and sweeping out the cell, and placing tooth-sticks and washing-water ready; by living upon scraps left over; by doing service in shampooing, and bathing, and washing of the feet; by suppressing their own will, and acting according to the will of others; by sleeping in discomfort, and feeding on distasteful food?'

'That, Nâgasena, is not the bliss of knowledge, it is a preliminary stage in the pursuit thereof. It is after the teachers have, in pain, sought after knowledge, that they enjoy its bliss. Thus is it, Nâgasena, that the bliss of knowledge is unalloyed with pain. For that bliss of knowledge is one thing, and the pain another.'

'Just so, O king, is Nirvâ*n*a all bliss, and there is no pain mingled with it. Those who are in quest of Nirvâ*n*a afflict their minds and bodies it is true, restrain themselves in standing, walking, sitting, lying, and in food, suppress their sleep, keep their senses in subjection, abandon their very body and their life. But it is after they have thus, in pain, sought after Nirvâ*n*a, that they enjoy the Nirvâ*n*a which is bliss unalloyed—as teachers do the bliss of knowledge. Thus is it, O king, that Nirvâ*n*a is all bliss, and there is no pain mingled with it. For Nirvâ*n*a is one thing, and the pain another.'

'Very good, Nâgasena! That is so, and I accept it as you say.'

[Here ends the dilemma as to the pain of Nirvâ*n*a.]

[DILEMMA THE EIGHTIETH.

THE OUTWARD FORM OF NIRVÂ*N*A.]

61. 'Venerable Nâgasena, this Nirvâ*n*a that you are always talking of—can you make clear by metaphor, or explanation, or reason, or argument, the form, or figure, or duration [1], or measure of it?'

[316] 'Nirvâ*n*a, O king, has nothing similar to it. By no metaphor, or explanation, or reason, or argument can its form, or figure, or duration, or measure be made clear.'

'That I cannot believe, Nâgasena,—that of Nirvâ*n*a, which really after all is a condition that exists [2], it should be so impossible in any way to make us understand either the form, or figure, or duration, or measure! Give me some explanation of this.'

62. 'Very well, O king, I will do so. Is there such a thing, O king, as the great ocean?'

'Yes, the ocean exists.'

'Well, suppose some one were to ask you, saying: "How much water is there, your majesty, in the sea, and how many are the creatures that dwell therein?" When that question had been put, how would you answer him?'

'I should reply thus to such a question: "My good fellow! this is an unaskable thing that you ask me. No one ought to ask such a question. It

[1] So the Pâli (vaya*m*). But the Si*m*halese has wâsaya, 'dwelling-place,' throughout §§ 56 and 57.

[2] Atthi-dhammassa nibbânassa. The Si*m*halese, p. 459, translates 'the form, &c., of the quality (dharma) of Nirvâ*n*a'—as if the Pâli were nibbâna-dhammassa. But see next page, note 2.

is a point that should be left alone. The physicists[1] have never examined into the ocean in that way. And no one can measure the water there, or count the creatures who dwell therein." Thus, Sir, should I make reply.'

63. 'But why, O king, would you make such a reply about the ocean which, after all, is really an existing condition of things[2]. Ought you not rather to count and tell him, saying: "So and so much is the water in the sea, and so and so many are the creatures that dwell therein?"'

'That would be impossible, Sir. The question is beyond one's power.'

'As impossible as it is, O king, to tell the measure of the water in the sea, or the number of the creatures dwelling therein, though after all the sea exists, so impossible is it in any of the ways you suggest to tell the form, or figure, or duration, or measure of Nirvâ*n*a, though after all it is a condition that does exist. [**317**] And even, O king, if one of magical powers, master over mind, were to be able to count the water and the creatures in the sea, even he could not tell the form or the figure, the duration or the measure of Nirvâ*n*a.

64. 'And hear another explanation of the same thing, O king. Are there, O king, among the gods certain of them called "The Formless Ones[3]?"'

---

[1] Lokakkhâyikâ, 'those who have in former days enquired into and described the world,' says the Si*m*halese.

[2] Atthidhammassa again, which Hîna*t*i-kumburê now renders œti swabhawawû. 'Pourquoi réponds-tu ainsi au sujet de l'etat naturel du grand océan,' says the French. (Compare above, p. 270 of the Pâli.)

[3] Arûpakâyikâ. It is very odd that Hîna*t*i-kumburê takes the word here, and in the answer, as a feminine singular, and still

'Yes, Sir. I have heard there are such.'

'Well, O king, can you make clear by metaphor, or explanation, or reason, or argument the form, or figure, or duration[1], or size of these gods, the "Formless Ones?"'

'No, I cannot.'

'Then, O king, there are none.'

'The Formless Ones, Sir, do exist; and yet it is impossible in any of the ways you suggest to explain either their form or figure, either their duration or their size.'

'As impossible as it is, O king, to tell the form or figure, the duration or the size of the gods called "Formless Ones," though they after all are beings that exist[2], so impossible is it in any of the ways you suggest to explain the form or the figure, the duration or the measure of Nirvâ*n*a, though after all it is a condition that does exist.'

65. 'Venerable Nâgasena, I will grant you that Nirvâ*n*a is bliss unalloyed, and yet that is impossible to make clear, either by simile or explanation, by reason or by argument, either its form or its figure, either its duration or its size. But is there no quality of Nirvâ*n*a which is inherent also in other

more so that the French translation takes it throughout as a masculine singular. But the Si*m*halese throughout the sequel treats it properly as a plural nominative; and there can be little doubt that the inhabitants, or some of the inhabitants, of the 'Formless Realm,' the Arûpâva*k*ara or Arûpa-brahma-loka, are referred to. But this name is different from those given to any of these gods in Childers, and I cannot trace it in the Pi*t*akas as applied to any of them.

[1] I follow the Pâli, which still has vaya*m*. The Si*m*halese has here and below winâ*s*aya.

[2] Atthisattana*m* yeva, which the Si*m*halese, p. 460, represents merely by œttâwû.

things[1], and is such that it can be made evident by metaphor[2]?'

'Though there is nothing as to its form which can be so explained, there is something, O king, as to its qualities which can.'

[318] 'O happy word, Nâgasena! Speak then, quickly, that I may have an explanation of even one point in the characteristics of Nirvâ*n*a. Appease the fever of my heart. Allay it by the cool sweet breezes of your words!'

'There is one quality of the lotus, O king, inherent in Nirvâ*n*a, and two qualities of water, and three of medicine, and four of the ocean, and five of food, and ten of space, and three of the wish-conferring gem, and three of red sandal wood, and three of the froth of ghee, and five of a mountain peak.'

66. 'Venerable Nâgasena, that one quality of the lotus which you said was inherent in Nirvâ*n*a,—which is that?'

'As the lotus, O king, is untarnished by the water[3], so is Nirvâ*n*a untarnished by any evil dispositions. This is the one quality of the lotus inherent in Nirvâ*n*a.'

---

[1] A*ññ*ehi anupavi*tth*a*m*; 'not previously explained by others,' says Hîna*t*i-kumburê. Neither rendering is altogether satisfactory. Perhaps 'of which you have been convinced by others,' in agreement with the use of the word above, p. 270 of the Pâli.

[2] In the French of Mr. da Sylva this sentence runs (p. 342): 'Mais vénérable, n'y a-t-il pas une vertu du Nirvâna dont on puisse percevoir quelque ressemblance.'

[3] That is, no drop of water adheres to the lotus, though it is surrounded by water and water may fall on it. For instances of the frequent similes drawn from this fact see below, V, 14; and Dhammapada 401; Sutta Nipâta II, 14, 17; III, 9, 32; IV, 6, 9. The French translation is: 'de même que le lotus élève fièrement sa tête au-dessus de l'eau' (!).

67. 'Venerable Nâgasena, those two qualities of water which you said were inherent in Nirvâ*n*a,—which are they?'

'As water, O king, is cool and assuages heat, so also is Nirvâ*n*a cool, and assuages the fever arising from all evil dispositions. This is the first quality of water inherent in Nirvâ*n*a. And again, O king, as water allays the thirst of men and beasts when they are exhausted and anxious, craving for drink, and tormented by thirst, so does Nirvâ*n*a allay the thirst of the craving after lusts, the craving after future life, and the craving after worldly prosperity[1]. This is the second quality of water inherent in Nirvâ*n*a.'

68. 'Venerable Nâgasena, those three qualities of medicine, which you said were inherent in Nirvâ*n*a, —which are they?'

[319] 'As medicine, O king, is the refuge of beings tormented by poison, so is Nirvâ*n*a the refuge of beings tormented with the poison of evil dispositions. This is the first quality of medicine inherent in Nirvâ*n*a. And again, O king, as medicine puts an end to diseases, so does Nirvâ*n*a put an end to griefs. This is the second quality of medicine inherent in Nirvâ*n*a. And again, O king, as medicine is ambrosia[2], so also is Nirvâ*n*a ambrosia. This is the third quality of medicine inherent in Nirvâ*n*a.'

---

[1] On these fundamental conceptions see my notes in 'Buddhist Suttas,' pp. 148, 149, where it is shown that the three 'cravings' which end in Nirvâ*n*a are pretty much the same as the lust of the flesh, theism, and materialism.

[2] Amata, the translation of which word by 'immortality' has given rise to so much confusion. So the French here says 'la médecine a le pouvoir de combattre la mort,' which is nearly as bad. See the Appendix.

69. 'Venerable Nâgasena, those four qualities of the ocean which you said were inherent in Nirvâ*n*a, —which are they?'

'As the ocean, O king, is free from (empty of) corpses[1], so also is Nirvâ*n*a free from (empty of) the dead bodies of all evil dispositions[2]. This, O king, is the first quality of the ocean inherent in Nirvâ*n*a. And again, O king, as the ocean is mighty and boundless, and fills not with all the rivers that flow in to it; so is Nirvâ*n*a mighty and boundless, and fills not with all beings (who enter in to it). This is the second quality of the ocean inherent in Nirvâ*n*a. And again, O king, as the ocean is the abode of mighty creatures, so is Nirvâ*n*a the abode of great men—Arahats, in whom the Great Evils and all stains have been destroyed, endowed with power, masters of themselves. This is the third quality of the ocean inherent in Nirvâ*n*a. And again, O king, as the ocean is all in blossom[3], as it were, with the innumerable and various and fine flowers of the ripple of its waves, so is Nirvâ*n*a all in blossom, as it were, with the innumerable and

[1] See on this belief above, IV, 3, 39 (I, 259).

[2] The word used here for free, empty (su*ññ*a), has again given rise to the most odd misconceptions. As Nirvâ*n*a is hence called Sunyatâ, 'emptiness,' Christian writers (taking Nirvâ*n*a as a name for some kind of future life) have very naturally thought, in trying to fasten some meaning upon emptiness in a future life, that it must mean 'annihilation of a soul,' and have labelled Buddhism as Nihilism! The real meaning is really very simple, and entirely ethical (not metaphysical or animistic):

'Men may rise on stepping stones
Of their dead selves to higher things.'

See below, IV, 8, 78, for a metaphor founded on a similar idea.

[3] Sa*m*kusumito, only found here. Compare 'garlands, vitvam,' I, 175, 176.

various and fine flowers of purity, of knowledge, and of emancipation. This is the fourth quality of the ocean inherent in Nirvâ*n*a.'

[320] 70. 'Venerable Nâgasena, those five qualities of food which you said were inherent in Nirvâ*n*a, —which are they?'

'As food, O king, is the support of the life of all beings, so is Nirvâ*n*a, when it has been realised, the support of life, for it puts an end to old age and death. This is the first quality of food inherent in Nirvâ*n*a. And again, O king, as food increases the strength of all beings, so does Nirvâ*n*a, when it has been realised, increase the power of Iddhi of all beings. This is the second quality of food inherent in Nirvâ*n*a. And again, O king, as food is the source of the beauty of all beings, so is Nirvâ*n*a, when it has been realised, the source to all beings of the beauty of holiness. This is the third quality of food inherent in Nirvâ*n*a. And again, O king, as food puts a stop to suffering in all beings, so does Nirvâ*n*a, when it has been realised, put a stop in all beings to the suffering arising from every evil disposition. This is the fourth quality of food inherent in Nirvâ*n*a. And again, O king, as food overcomes in all beings the weakness of hunger, so does Nirvâ*n*a, when it has been realised, overcome in all beings the weakness which arises from hunger and every sort of pain. This is the fifth quality of food inherent in Nirvâ*n*a.'

71. 'Venerable Nâgasena, those ten qualities of space which you said were inherent in Nirvâ*n*a,— which are they?'

'As space, O king, neither is born nor grows old, neither dies nor passes away nor is reborn (has a future life to spring up into), as it is incompressible, cannot be carried off by thieves, rests on nothing, is the sphere in which birds fly, is unobstructed, and is infinite; [321] so, O king, Nirvâ*n*a is not born, neither does it grow old, it dies not, it passes not away, it has no rebirth (no future life to spring up into), it is unconquerable, thieves carry it not off, it is not attached to anything[1], it is the sphere in which Arahats move, nothing can obstruct it, and it is infinite. These are the ten qualities of space inherent in Nirvâ*n*a.'

72. 'Venerable Nâgasena, those three qualities of the wish-conferring gem which you said were inherent in Nirvâ*n*a,—which are they?'

'As the wishing-gem, O king, satisfies every desire, so also does Nirvâ*n*a. This is the first quality of the wishing-gem inherent in Nirvâ*n*a. And again, O king, as the wishing-gem causes delight, so also does Nirvâ*n*a. This is the second quality of the wishing-gem inherent in Nirvâ*n*a. And again, O king, as the wishing-gem is full of lustre, so also is Nirvâ*n*a. This is the third quality of the wishing-gem inherent in Nirvâ*n*a.'

73. 'Venerable Nâgasena, those three qualities of red sandal wood which you said were inherent in Nirvâ*n*a,—which are they?'

[1] Anissita*m*, so below, p. 351 of the Pâli, the dhutaṅga*m* is said to be anissita*m*. The translation is difficult. In our passage here Hînaṅ-kumburê (p. 464) renders it, as applied both to space and to Nirvâ*n*a, by 'having no âsrawa.' Below, as applied to the vows (dhutaṅgas), he renders it (p. 512) by 'unconnected with craving' (t*r*ish*n*ânis*r*ita). 'Self-dependent' or 'untarnished (by reliance on external things') would suit the context in all three passages.

'As red sandal wood, O king, is hard to get, so is Nirvâ*n*a hard to attain to. This is the first quality of red sandal wood inherent in Nirvâ*n*a. And again, O king, as red sandal wood is unequalled in the beauty of its perfume, so is Nirvâ*n*a. This is the second quality of red sandal wood inherent in Nirvâ*n*a. And again, O king, as red sandal wood is praised by all the good, so is Nirvâ*n*a praised by all the Noble Ones. This is the third quality of red sandal wood inherent in Nirvâ*n*a.'

74. [**322**] 'Venerable Nâgasena, those three qualities of the skimmings of ghee[1] which you said were inherent in Nirvâ*n*a,—which are they?'

'As ghee is beautiful in colour, O king, so also is Nirvâ*n*a beautiful in righteousness. This is the first quality of the ghee inherent in Nirvâ*n*a. And again, O king, as ghee has a pleasant perfume, so also has Nirvâ*n*a the pleasant perfume of righteousness. This is the second quality of ghee inherent in Nirvâ*n*a. And again, O king, as ghee has a pleasant taste, so also has Nirvâ*n*a. This is the third quality of ghee inherent in Nirvâ*n*a.'

75. 'Venerable Nâgasena, those five qualities of a mountain peak which you said were inherent in Nirvâ*n*a,—which are they?'

'As a mountain peak is very lofty, so also is Nirvâ*n*a very exalted. This is the first quality of a mountain peak inherent in Nirvâ*n*a. And again, O king, as a mountain peak is immoveable, so also is Nirvâ*n*a. This is the second quality of a mountain peak inherent in Nirvâ*n*a. And again, O king,

[1] This is butter made of buffaloes' milk, and is highly esteemed in India.

as a mountain peak is inaccessible, so also is Nirvâna inaccessible to all evil dispositions. This is the third quality of a mountain peak inherent in Nirvâna. And again, O king, as a mountain peak is a place where no plants can grow, so also is Nirvâna a condition in which no evil dispositions can grow. This is the fourth quality of a mountain peak inherent in Nirvâna. And again, O king, as a mountain peak is free alike from desire to please and from resentment, so also is Nirvâna. This is the fifth quality of a mountain peak inherent in Nirvâna.'

[323] 'Very good, Nâgasena! That is so, and I accept it as you say.'

[Here ends the problem as to the form of Nirvâna.]

[DILEMMA THE EIGHTY-FIRST.

THE TIME OF NIRVÂNA.]

76. 'Venerable Nâgasena, your people say[1]: "Nirvâna is not past, nor future, nor present, nor produced, nor not produced, nor producible[2]."

'In that case, Nâgasena, does the man who, having ordered his life aright, realises Nirvâna, realise something already produced, or does he himself produce it first, and then realise it?'

'Neither the one, O king, nor the other. And nevertheless, O king, that principle of Nirvâna (nibbâna-dhâtu) which he, so ordering his life aright, realises—that exists.'

---

[1] Not yet traced in the Pitakas.

[2] 'By the action of Karma as a pre-existing cause' is to be understood.

'Do not, venerable Nâgasena, clear up this puzzle by making it dark! Make it open and plain as you elucidate it. With a will, strenuous in endeavour, pour out upon it all that has been taught you. It is a point on which this people is bewildered, plunged into perplexity, lost in doubt. Dissipate this guilty uncertainty; it pierces like a dart[1]!'

77. 'That principle of Nirvâ*n*a, O king, so peaceful, so blissful, so delicate, exists. And it is that which he who orders his life aright, grasping the idea of all things (of the Confections, Sa*m*khâras) according to the teachings of the Conquerors, realises by his wisdom—even as a pupil, by his knowledge, makes himself, according to the instruction of his teacher, master of an art.

'And if you ask: "How is Nirvâ*n*a to be known[2]?" it is by freedom from distress and danger, by confidence, by peace, by calm, by bliss, by happiness, by delicacy, by purity, by freshness[3].

78. 'Just, O king, as a man being burnt in a blazing fiery furnace heaped up with many faggots of dry sticks, when he has freed himself from it by

[1] Bhind' eta*m* anto-dosa-salla*m*; 'break and take away the dart of the guilt (dosa) of that doubt which has arisen in my inmost being (satana),' says Hîna*t*i-kumburê. It is literally 'break this dart of guilt within.' The meaning is clear enough (except as to whether the guilt is the speaker's or 'this people's'). To break a dart in a wound would be no kindness, and that cannot have been the author's idea. To bring out the meaning one must amplify a little, and I should have followed the Sim-halese had it not seemed preferable to leave the personality of the guilty one as ambiguous in the translation as in the text.

[2] Hîna*t*i-kumburê, p. 467, does actually put these words into Nâgasena's mouth.

[3] Sîtalato, literally 'by cold.' See the note above on III, 6, 6 (I, 119).

a violent effort, and escaped into a cool place, [**324**] would experience supreme bliss—just so whosoever orders his life aright, he by his careful thinking will realise the supreme bliss of Nirvâ*n*a, in which the burning heat of the threefold fire (of lust, malice, and delusion)[1] has all gone out. As the furnace, O king, so should you regard this threefold fire, as the man fallen into the fire the man who is ordering his life aright, as the cool place Nirvâ*n*a.

79. 'Or again, O king, as a man fallen into a pit full of the dead bodies of snakes and dogs and men, of ordure, and of refuse, when, finding himself in the midst of it entangled in the hair of the corpses, he had by a violent effort escaped into a place where no dead bodies were, would experience supreme bliss—just so whosoever orders his life aright, he by his careful thinking will realise the supreme bliss of Nirvâ*n*a, from which the corpses of all evil dispositions have been removed[2]. As a corpse, O king, so should you regard the four pleasures of sense, as the man fallen among corpses the man who is ordering his life aright, as the place free from corpses Nirvâ*n*a.

80. 'Or again, O king, as a man (fallen among enemies with drawn swords in their hands)[3], quaking with fear and terror, agitated and upset in mind, when with a violent effort he has freed himself from them, and escaped into a strong refuge, a firm place of security, experiences supreme bliss—just so whosoever orders his life aright, he by his careful thinking will realise the supreme bliss of Nirvâ*n*a,

[1] Râga, dosa, moha.

[2] Compare above, IV, 8, 69, and the note there.

[3] The words in brackets are added from the Si*m*halese, p. 467.

in which fear and terror have been put away. As the terror, O king, so should you regard the anxiety which arises again and again on account of birth, old age, disease, and death, as the terrified man the man who is ordering his life aright, as the place of refuge Nirvâ*n*a.

81. 'Or again, O king, as a man fallen on a spot filthy with dirt, and slime, and mud, when with a violent effort he has got rid of the mud, and escaped to a clean and spotless place, would experience supreme bliss—just so whosoever orders his life aright, he by his careful thinking will realise the supreme bliss of Nirvâ*n*a, from which the stains and mud of evil dispositions have been removed. As the mud, O king, [**325**] so should you regard income, and honour, and praise [1], as the man fallen into the mud the man who is ordering his life aright, as the clean and spotless place Nirvâ*n*a.

82. 'And if again you should ask: "How does he who orders his life aright realise that Nirvâ*n*a?" (I should reply), He, O king, who orders his life aright grasps the truth as to the development of all things [2], and when he is doing so he perceives therein birth, he perceives old age, he perceives disease, he perceives death. But he perceives not therein either happiness or bliss, he perceives not therein, whether in the beginning, or the middle, or the end, anything worthy of being laid hold of (as lasting satisfaction) [3]. As a man, O king, if a mass of iron

---

[1] So also at *G*âtaka IV, 222 (verse 48).

[2] Sa*m*khârâna*m* paratta*m* sammasati. Compare Dharmapada, verse 374.

[3] Gayhûpagam; so the Si*m*halese.

had been heated the livelong day[1], and were all glowing, scorching, and red hot, would find no spot on it, whether at one end or in the middle or at the other end, fit to be taken hold of—just so, O king, he who orders his life aright grasps the truth of the development of things, and in doing so he perceives therein birth, he perceives old age, he perceives disease, he perceives death. But he perceives not therein either happiness or bliss, he perceives not therein, whether in the beginning, or in the middle, or in the end, anything fit to be taken hold of (as a lasting satisfaction).

83. 'And discontent arises in his mind when he thus finds nothing fit to be relied on as a lasting satisfaction, and a fever takes possession of his body[2], and without a refuge or protection, hopeless, he becomes weary of repeated lives[3]. As if a man had fallen into a burning and blazing mighty fiery furnace, and saw no refuge from it, no way of escape, he would, hopeless, be weary of the fire—just so, O king, discontent arises in his mind when he thus finds nothing fit to be relied on as a lasting satisfaction, and a fever takes possession of his body, and without a refuge or protection, hopeless, he becomes weary of repeated births.

84. 'And in the mind of him who thus perceives

---

[1] Divasa-santatta. So Hînati-kumburê, and compare Magghima Nikâya I, 453, and Gâtaka IV, 118 (where the reading is diva-santatta). See also above, p. 46 of the Pâli.

[2] For dâho okkamati, Hînati-kumburê may have had a different reading. He renders dahadiya selawenneya, 'sweat shapes' (sic for 'forms').

[3] Bhavesu; literally 'of becomings' ('in any of the three worlds,' adds the Simhalese).

the insecurity of transitory life, (of starting afresh in innumerable births)[1] the thought arises: "All on fire is this endless becoming, burning, and blazing! Full of pain is it, of despair! If only one could reach a state in which there were no becoming, there would there be calm, that would be sweet—the cessation of all these conditions[2], the getting rid of all these defects[3] (of lusts, of evil, and of Karma), the end of cravings, the absence of passion, peace, Nirvâ*n*a!" And therewith does his mind leap forward into that state in which there is no becoming, and then has he found peace, [**326**] then does he exult and rejoice[4] at the thought: "A refuge have I gained at last!" Just, O king, as a man who, venturing into a strange land, has lost his way, on becoming aware of a path, free from jungle, that will lead him home, bounds forward along it, contented in mind, exulting and rejoicing at the thought: "I have found the way at last!"—just so in him who thus perceives the insecurity of transitory births there arises the thought: "All on fire is this endless becoming, burning, and blazing! Full of pain is it, and despair! If only one could reach a state in which there were no becoming, there would there be calm, that would be sweet—the cessation of all these conditions, the getting rid of all these defects, the end of cravings, the absence of passion, peace, Nirvâ*n*a!" And therewith does his mind leap forward into that state in which there is no becoming,

[1] Pavatte. I have included Hîna*n*-kumburê's explanation of this word, for which there is no equivalent in English.

[2] Sa*m*khârâ, sa*m*khâra-dharmayangê says the Si*m*halese.

[3] Upadhi; the Si*m*halese (p. 470) has simply kle*s*ayan.

[4] Paha*m*sîyati kuhûyati, both words only found here.

and then has he found peace, then does he exult and rejoice at the thought: "A refuge have I found at last!" And he strives with might and main along that path, searches it out, accustoms himself thoroughly to it, to that end does he make firm his self-possession, to that end does he hold fast in effort, to that end does he remain stedfast in love (toward all beings in all the worlds), and still to that does he direct his mind again and again, until gone far beyond the transitory, he gains the Real, the highest fruit (of Arahatship)[1]. And when he has gained that, O king, the man who has ordered his life aright has realised, (seen face to face,) Nirvâ*n*a[2]!'

'Very good, Nâgasena! That is so, and I accept it as you say.'

[Here ends the problem as to the time of Nirvâ*n*a[3].]

[1] Appavattam okkamati, Apraw*ri*ttiya yayi kiyana lada Arhat-phalaya*t*a pœmi*n*enneya, says Hîna*t*i-kumburê.

[2] This paragraph is an excellent example of the difficulty of doing anything like justice in translations to the most instructive and valuable passages in our Buddhist texts. It is in the Pâli full of eloquence, and even in the Si*m*halese, though there too much expanded, it is powerful and striking. To a Buddhist it must have been inspiring and touching to the last degree, carefully led up to, as it is, with masterly skill, by our author. But it is so full of terms untranslateable into English, and with difficulty even comprehensible to minds saturated with Western ideas, that every translation must be inadequate, and any attempt to reproduce the real beauty of its style must be a failure.

[3] How almost impossible it is for a reader with pre-conceived delusions to grasp the plain sense of such passages may be seen from the strange note which the French translator has added at the end of this clear and eloquent description. He says, 'La conclusion de ce Jâtaka (sic!) paraît être que le dévot bouddhiste peut

[DILEMMA THE EIGHTY-SECOND.

THE PLACE OF NIRVÂ*N*A.]

85. 'Venerable Nâgasena, does there exist the spot—either in the direction of the East, or of the South, or of the West, or of the North, either above, or below, or on the horizon—where Nirvâ*n*a is stored up[1]?'

'There is no spot, O king,—either in the East, or the South, or in the West, or the North, either above, or below, or on the horizon—where Nirvâ*n*a is.'

'But if so, Nâgasena, then neither can Nirvâ*n*a exist, and those who realise it, their realisation is vain. And I will give you an explanation of this. Just, Sir, as there are on the earth fields in which crops can be grown, flowers from which perfumes come, bushes on which flowers can grow, trees on which fruits can ripen, mines from which gems can be dug, so that whosoever desires any of these things can go there and get it—just so, Nâgasena, if [**327**] Nirvâ*n*a exists one must expect there to be some place, where it is produced[2]. But since there is not, therefore I declare that there can be no Nirvâ*n*a, and those who realise it, their realisation is vain.'

86. 'There is no spot, O king, where Nirvâ*n*a is

---

atteindre Nirvâna dans cette vie même. Il est fâcheux que l'auteur ne se soit pas expliqué plus catégoriquement sur cette question intéressante' (!).

[1] Sannihita*m* perhaps 'is situate.' Hîna*t*i-kumburê has pihi*t*iye, 'can be got.'

[2] I*kkh*itabbo. See above, p. 269 of the Pâli.

situate, and yet Nirvâ*n*a is, and he who orders his life right will, by careful attention, realise Nirvâ*n*a. Just as fire exists, and yet there is no place where fire (by itself) is stored up. But if a man rubs two sticks together the fire comes;—just so, O king, Nirvâ*n*a exists, though there is no spot where it is stored up. And he who orders his life aright will, by careful attention, realise Nirvâ*n*a.

87. 'Or again, O king, just as there are the seven treasures of the king of kings—the treasure of the wheel, and the treasure of the elephant, and the treasure of the horse, and the treasure of the gem, and the treasure of the woman, and the treasure of the finance minister, and the treasure of the adviser. But there is no spot where these treasures are laid up. When a sovran conducts himself aright they appear to him of their own accord [1]—just so, O king, Nirvâ*n*a exists, though there is no place where it is stored up. And he who orders his life aright will, by careful attention, realise Nirvâ*n*a.'

88. 'Venerable Nâgasena, let it be granted that there is no place where Nirvâ*n*a is stored up. But is there any place on which a man may stand and, ordering his life aright, realise Nirvâ*n*a?'

'Yes, O king, there is such a place.'

'Which then, Nâgasena, is that place?'

'Virtue, O king, is the place. For if grounded in virtue, and careful in attention—whether in the land of the Scythians [2] or the Greeks, whether in China or

[1] This is stated in regard to each of the seven in the standard passage on these seven treasures, translated in my 'Buddhist Suttas,' pp. 251–259.

[2] Sakâ. Hîna*t*i-kumburê has sadly blundered over this, to him, strange word. He actually translates it 'one's own.'

Tartary[1], whether in Alexandria[2] or in Nikumba, whether in Benares or in Kosala, whether in Kashmîr or in Gandhâra[3], whether on a mountain top[4] or in the highest heavens[5]—wheresoever he may be, the man who orders his life aright will realise Nirvâ*n*a. [328] Just, O king, as the man who has eyes wherever he may be—in the land of the Scythians or the Greeks, in China or in Tartary, in Alexandria, Nikumba, Benares, or Kosala, in Kashmîr or in Gandhâra, on a mountain top or in the highest heavens—will be able to behold the expanse of heaven and to see the horizon facing him—just so, O king, will he who orders his conduct aright and is careful in attention—whether in the land of the Scythians or the Greeks, whether in China or Tartary, whether in Alexandria, or Benares, or Kosala, or Nikumba, whether in Kashmîr or in Gandhâra, whether on a mountain top or in the highest heavens—wheresoever he may be, attain to the realisation of Nirvâ*n*a.'

'Very good, Nâgasena! You have preached to me of Nirvâ*n*a, and of the realisation thereof, you have set forth the advantages of virtue, you have explained the supreme attainment, you have raised aloft the standard of the Truth, you have established the eye of Truth, you have shown how right means adopted by those of high aims will be neither

[1] Vilâta, the Si*m*halese has Milâta.

[2] That is Alexandria on the Indus. See the Introduction to the first part, p. xxiii.

[3] All these names are discussed, ibid. pp. xliii, xliv.

[4] Naga-muddham. Hîna*t*i-kumburê understands this as the top of Mount Meru, Sakka's heaven.

[5] Brahma-loke.

barren nor unfruitful. That is so, and I accept it as you say[1].'

[Here ends the problem of the place of Nirvâ*n*a.]

[Here ends the Eighth Chapter[2].]

---

[1] In the Si*m*halese, pp. 472, 473, this last paragraph is much expanded.

[2] The Si*m*halese has Sakala-*g*ana-mano-nandanîyawû me Srî-saddharmâdâsayehi a*t*aweni wargaya nimiyeya.

BOOK V.

THE PROBLEM OF INFERENCE.

[329] 1. Now Milinda the king went up to the place where Nâgasena was, and bowed down before him, and took his seat on one side. And when so seated he, longing to know, to hear, and to remember, and longing to make the light of knowledge arise and to break in pieces his ignorance, roused up in himself courage and zeal, and, full of self-possession and thoughtfulness, spake thus to Nâgasena:

2. 'Venerable Nâgasena, tell me, have you ever seen the Buddha[1]?'

'No, O king.'

'Then have your teachers ever seen the Buddha?'

'No, Sire.'

'So you say, venerable Nâgasena, that you have never seen the Buddha, and that your teachers have never seen the Buddha. Therefore, Nâgasena, the Buddha did not exist. There is no clear evidence, in that case, of a Buddha.'

'But did those Kshatriyas of old exist, who were the founders of the line of kings from which you come?'

'Certainly, Sir. How can there be any doubt about that?'

'Well, O king. Have you ever seen them?'

'No, Sir.'

[1] A similar question has been already asked above, III, 5. 1 (I, 109).

'And those who instructed you—the family chaplains, and officers of the staff, and those who lay down the law, and ministers of state—have they ever seen those Kshatriyas of old?'

'No, Sir.'

'If then neither have you seen them, nor your teachers, where are they? There is no clear evidence, in that case, of those Kshatriyas of old!'

3. 'But, Nâgasena, the royal insignia they used are still to be seen—[330] the white sunshade of state, and the crown, and the slippers, and the fan with the yak's tail, and the sword of state, and the priceless throne—and by these can we know and believe that the Kshatriyas of old lived once.'

'Just so, O king, can we know that Blessed One and believe in him. For there is a reason for our knowledge and belief that the Blessed One was. And what is that reason?—The royal insignia used by that Blessed One, by him of knowledge and insight, the Arahat, the Buddha Supreme, are still to be seen—the four Means of keeping oneself ready and mindful, and the fourfold Great Struggle, and the four steps to Iddhi, and the five Organs of the moral sense, and the five moral Powers, and the seven forms of the wisdom of the Arahats, and the Noble Eightfold Path [1]—and by these can the whole

[1] These are the famous thirty-five constituent qualities that make up Arahatship (that is, that state of mind which, from another point of view and by another of its numerous names, is also called Nirvâ*n*a). They formed the subject of the last discourse delivered by Gotama before his death to his disciples ('Book of the Great Decease,' III, 61), and on my translation of that passage ('Buddhist Suttas,' pp. 60-63) I have added a note giving all the details.

It is perhaps worthy of remark that both here and twice else-world of gods and men know and believe that that Blessed One existed once. By this reason, on this ground, by this argument, through this inference, can it be known that the Blessed One lived.

"He who, himself set free in that bless'd state
In which the Upadhis have ceased to be,
—Lusts, sin, and Karma,—has brought safe ashore,
Saved from the sea of woe, great multitudes—
Only by inference can it be known
That he, the best of men, existed once [1]."'

4. 'Venerable Nâgasena, give me an illustration.'

'Just, O king, as the architect of a city [2], when he wants to build one, would first search out a pleasant spot of ground, with which no fault can be found, even, with no hills or gullies in it, free from rough ground and rocks, not open to the danger of attack. And then, when he has made plain any rough places there may still be on it, he would clear it thoroughly of all stumps and stakes, and would proceed to build there a city fine and regular, measured out into suitable quarters [3], with trenches and ramparts thrown up around it [4], with strong gateways, watch-towers, and battlements, with wide squares and open places and junctions (where two roads meet) and cross-ways (where four

where, at pp. 37, 335 (of the Pâli), our author reverses the order of Nos. 4 and 5—the five moral Powers and the five Organs (of the higher sense)—which are really only the same mental qualities looked at from two different points of view.

[1] These verses have not been traced as yet in the Pi*t*akas.

[2] There is another parable of the architect above, p. 34 of the Pâli (I, 53 of the translation).

[3] Bhâgaso mita*m*, an expression constantly recurring.

[4] Ukki*nn*a. See *G*âtaka IV, 106.

roads meet)[1], with cleanly and even high roads[2], with regular lines of open shops (bazaars), well provided with parks, and gardens, and lakes, and lotus-ponds, and wells, adorned with many kinds of temples to the gods, free from every fault. And then when the city stood there in all its glory, he would go away to some other land. And in course of time that city might become mighty and prosperous, filled with stores of food, **[331]** peaceful, glorious, happy, free from distress and calamity, the meeting-place of all sorts and conditions of men. Then nobles and brahmans, merchants and work-people; soldiers mounted on elephants, and on horses, and on chariots; infantry, and bowmen, and swordsmen; standard-bearers, officers, and camp-followers[3]; high-born warriors whose delight is in war, fighting champions, men mighty as elephants, heroes, men who fight in buckskin[4], devoted fighting-men born of slaves in great houses or of the privates in the royal army[5]; troops of professional wrestlers[6];

---

[1] According to the dictionaries each of those four words (kakkara, katukka, sandhi, and singhâtaka) means either a square, or a place where four roads meet. The Simhalese has âpana-katushka-sandhi œti, omitting the last and certainly inexact in its rendering of the first word. Sandhi I have only met with here in this sense.

[2] Râga-maggam; literally 'the king's highways,' which also only occurs here.

[3] For pinda-dâvikâ Hînati-kumburê (who at p. 475 gives the Pâli of all this) reads pinda-dayakâ.

[4] Vammino yodhino. But both Hînati-kumburê here, and the parallel passage in the Samañña Phala Sutta (D. II, 14), read Kamma-yodhino.

[5] For Bhatti-putta Hînati-kumburê reads Bhata-puttâ.

[6] These two (Bhati-puttâ and Malla-ganâ) are omitted in the Dîgha.

cooks and curry makers, barbers and bathing attendants, smiths and florists, workers in gold and silver and lead and tin and copper and brass[1] and iron, and jewellers; messengers; potters, salt gatherers[2], tanners, carriage builders, carvers in ivory[3], rope makers, comb makers, cotton-thread spinners, basket makers, bow manufacturers, bowstring makers, arrow fletchers, painters, dye manufacturers, dyers, weavers, tailors, assayers of gold[4], cloth merchants[5], dealers in perfumes, grass cutters, hewers of wood, hired servants[6], people who live by gathering flowers and fruits and roots in the woods, hawkers of boiled rice, sellers of cakes, fishmongers, butchers, dealers in strong drinks, play actors, dancers, acrobats[7], conjurors, professional bards[8], wrestlers

[1] Vattakârâ. See the note above on IV, 7, 11 (p. 267 of the Pâli).

[2] Lonakârâ, 'salt makers.' But Hînati-kumburê reads lohakârâ and translates lokuruwo, 'workers in metal.'

[3] Dantakârâ, which in the Simhalese is simply repeated. There is no such word in Clough.

[4] Heraññikâ. Childers says 'royal treasurer,' and Hînati-kumburê 'coiners of silver mâsakas' (ran masu tanannoya), but Subhûti (in his Simhalese gloss on Abhidhâna Padîpikâ, verse 343) renders it 'judgers of gold' (ran balannâ); and that this is right is shown by the context in the passage of the Sumaṅgala Vilâsinî (p. 315), where the probably identical word heraññaka is used.

[5] Dussika. Hînati-kumburê renders this word here by pili welendo, 'cloth-sellers,' but above (p. 262 of the Pâli) by sâyam kârako, 'dice manufacturers.'

[6] It is instructive that men working for hire are put here among the lowest sort of work-people, while the slave born in the house stands in the best company.

[7] Laṅghakâ. Pinum kârayo, 'turners of summersets' in the Simhalese. See Gâtaka I, 431, and above, pp. 31, 191 of the Pâli.

[8] Vetâlikâ. Vetâliyehi maṅgalâshtaka kiyannâwû in

(boxers), corpse burners, casters out of rotten flowers[1], savages[2], wild men of the woods[3], prostitutes, swingers and jumpers[4], and the slave girls of bullies—people of many countries, people from Scythia, Bactria, China, and Vilâta; people of Uggeni, of Bhârukakkha, of Benares, of Kosala, and of the border lands; people from Magadha, and Sâketa, and Suraṭṭha, and the West; from Koṭumbara and Madhura, from Alexandria, Kashmîr, and Gandhâra[5],—all these coming to take up their residence there, and finding the new city to be regular, faultless, perfect, and pleasant, would know: "Able indeed must that architect have been by whom this city was built!"

5. 'Just so, O king, that Blessed One, peerless, unequalled, unapproached, incomparable, admirable beyond all measure by weight or calculation, of infinite virtue, full of virtue and perfection, boundless in wisdom and glory and zeal and power, who, when he had attained to the summit of all the perfections

the Simhalese (Wandi-bhaṭṭayo according to Subhûti on Abhidhâna Padîpikâ 369).

[1] Pupphakkhadakâ. A well-known low caste whose duty it was to remove flowers offered on the shrines of the gods after they had faded. At Thera Gâthâ, verse 620, this is called one of the meanest of occupations.

[2] Venâ. Hînaṅi-kumburê has 'lute makers,' but this must be wrong.

[3] The Simhalese says simply Weddahs (Wœddas), the well-known interesting wild men of Ceylon.

[4] Lâsikâ, 'those,' says the Simhalese, 'who as if intoxicated with joy jump about and leap and dance.' But I think it is connected with the ancient usages to which the lascivious swinging of the Saivites and Vallabhâkâryas owes its origin.

[5] On all these names see the Introduction to part I, pp. xliii, xliv. Aparântaka and Pâtheyyaka might there have been added, as well as puratthimo ganapado (from p. 42).

of the Buddhas, [332] overthrew Mâra and all his hosts,—he, bursting asunder the net of heresy, and casting aside ignorance, and causing wisdom to arise, and bearing aloft the torch of Truth, reached forward to Buddhahood itself, and so, unconquered and unconquerable in the fight, built this city of Righteousness. And the Blessed One's City of Righteousness, O king, has righteousness for its rampart, and fear of sin for its moat, and knowledge for the battlement over its city gate, and zeal for the watch-tower above that, and faith for the pillars at its base, and mindfulness for the watchman at the gate, and wisdom for the terrace above, and the Suttantas for its market-place, and the Abhidhamma for its cross-ways, and the Vinaya (the Canon Law) for its judgment hall, and constant self-possession for its chief street. And in that street, O king, these bazaars are open—a flower bazaar, and a fruit bazaar, and an antidote bazaar, and a medicine bazaar, and an ambrosia bazaar, and a bazaar for precious stones, and a bazaar for all manner of merchandise.'

6. 'But what, venerable Nâgasena, is the flower bazaar of the Blessed One, the Buddha?'

'There are certain subjects for meditation, O king, that have been made known by the Blessed One, by him of knowledge and insight, by the Arahat, the Buddha Supreme. And they are these. The idea of the impermanence (of every thing and of every being), the idea of the absence of any abiding principle (any soul in any thing or any being), the idea of the impurity and the idea of the danger connected with the body, the idea of getting rid of evil dispositions, the idea of freedom from passion, the idea of peace, the idea of dissatisfaction with the things of the world, the idea of the transitory nature of all conditions, the idea of ecstatic trance, the ideas of a corpse in the various stages of decay, the ideas of a place of execution in all its various horrors, the idea of love to all beings, the idea of pity for all beings, the idea of sympathy with all beings, the idea of equanimity in all the changing circumstances of life, the idea of death, and the idea of the body[1]. These, O king, are the subjects for meditation prescribed by the Blessed One. And of these, whoever, longing to be delivered from old age and death, takes any one as the subject of his meditation, by that meditation does he become set free from passion, set free from malice, set free from dullness, set free from pride, set free from wrong views, by that does he cross the ocean of Sa*m*sâra, and stem the torrent of cravings, and cleanse himself of the threefold stain[2], and destroy within himself all evil; and so, entering that glorious city, spotless and stainless, pure and white, [333] ageless and deathless, where all is security and calm and bliss—the city of Nirvâ*n*a—he emancipates his mind in Arahatship! And this, O king, is what is called "The Blessed One's bazaar of flowers."

"Take with you Karma as the price,
And go ye up to that bazaar,
Buy there an object for your thought,
Emancipate yourselves. Be free[3]!"'

[1] Hînati-kumburê devotes a paragraph to each of these subjects for meditation.

[2] Of râga, dosa, and moha.

[3] This stanza has not yet been found in the Pi*t*akas. In the first line it does not seem quite clear at first sight why Karma, of all things, should be the price. That Indian word being too

7. 'And what, venerable Nâgasena, is the perfume bazaar of the Blessed One, the Buddha?'

'There are certain categories of virtue, O king, that have been made known by the Blessed One, and anointed by the perfume of that righteousness the children of the Blessed One fill with the fumes of the fragrant incense of the perfume of goodness the whole world of gods and men, in every direction, and to windward and to leeward, continuing to pervade it again and yet again. And which are those categories? The virtue of taking refuge[1],

full of meaning to be translateable, is necessarily retained, and hence the phrase 'taking Karma as the price' may convey no meaning at all. If so, in trying to escape Scylla the unhappy translator has fallen into Charybdis. But it must mean one of two things, either something to be abandoned, given up; or something good which the buyer possesses, and may exchange for the good he wants to buy. If our author means the first it must be Karma (as one of the Upadhis), as a basis for continued individuality, and be much the same as egoism. If he means the other, then Karma, though standing alone, must be here used in the sense of kusala-kamma, good Karma, that is, the effect of good deeds done in a former life. Now our author never elsewhere uses kamma, without any qualifying adjective, in the sense of good Karma. On pp. 7, 20, 67, 108 foll., 134, 151, 189, 302 of the Pâli the unqualified word means throughout bad Karma, the effect of bad deeds done in a former birth. In a few passages it is used of former deeds in a way that apparently includes both good and bad. See especially pp. 3, 10, 146, 268. Now a buyer, in the case put, could not give up either the bad or the good deeds he had already done in a former life—that would be beyond his power. He could only offer, in exchange for the good he wanted to buy, good Karma (that is, in the sense of good deeds) either in the present, or in the immediate future. Below, V, 21 (p. 341 of the Pâli), will be found instances given by our author himself. It is forced, no doubt, to call this 'a price,' but it is probably the sense intended, and so Hîna*t*i-kumburê takes it.

[1] Taking the threefold refuge in the Buddha, the Doctrine (Dharma), and the Order.

the virtue that is fivefold and eightfold and tenfold[1], and the virtue of self-restraint tabulated in the five recitations that compose the Pâtimokkha[2]. And this, O king, is what is called "The Blessed One's bazaar of perfumes." For it has been said, O king, by the Blessed One, the god over all gods:

"No flower's scent can go against the wind,
Not sandal wood's, nor musk's, nor jasmine flower's:
But the sweet perfume of the good doth go
Against the wind, and the good man pervades,
On every side, the sweetness of his life[3]."

"Red sandal wood, musk, and the lotus, and jasmine—
The perfume of goodness surpasseth them all.
Abundant the sweet scent of musk and of sandal wood—
Still stronger, the scent of the good mounts to heaven[4]!"'

8. 'And what, venerable Nâgasena, is the fruit bazaar of the Blessed One, the Buddha?'

'Certain fruits have been made known, O king, by the Blessed One. And they are these:—The fruit of the first stage of the Excellent Way (con-

---

[1] These are respectively the first five, the first eight, and the whole ten, of the Precepts set out in my 'Buddhism,' p. 160.

[2] The whole of this text is translated in vol. xiii of the 'Sacred Books of the East.' The sîlas here enumerated are only the lower morality. The higher ethics come below in § 12.

[3] From Aṅguttara Nikâya III, 79. The verse is quoted in the Dhammapada, verse 54, and also in the *G*âtaka Book, III, 291.

[4] It is not known where these lines originally stood. But they are quoted in the Dhammapada, verses 55, 56, and also in the *G*âtaka Book loc. cit., and in the Sumaṅgala Vilâsinî, p. 56.

version), and of the second stage, and of the third stage, and of the fourth (Arahatship)[1],—the fruit of the attainment of emptiness[2],—the fruit of the attainment of the absence of the three signs (of an unconverted life, lust, malice, and dullness)—and the truth of the attainment of that state in which no low aspirations survive. **[334]** And whosoever desires any one of these, he gives his Karma as the price, and buys the fruit he longs for—either conversion or any other.

9. 'Just, O king, as any man who has a mango-tree bearing fruit all the year round, he does not knock down the fruits until buyers come. But when a buyer has come, and the fruit-grower has taken the price, then he says: "Come, my good man, this tree is always in bearing (it has therefore fruits in all stages of growth), take from it the kind of fruit you prefer, whether unripe, or decayed[3], or hairy[4], or sour, or ripe[5]." And the buyer, for the price paid, takes the kind he likes the best—if that be unripe fruit then he takes that, if it be decayed fruit then that, if it be hairy fruit then that, if it be sour fruit then that, if it be ripe fruit then he takes a ripe one. Just so, O king, whosoever desires any one of those other fruits, he gives his Karma as the price, and buys the fruit he longs for—

[1] The details of these 'fruits' will be found in 'Buddhism,' pp. 108–110.

[2] As to in respect of what, see the note above on IV, 8, 69 (p. 219 of the Pâli).

[3] Dovila*m*, nilâta says the Si*m*halese, p. 484.

[4] Kesika. Hîna*t*i-kumburê merely repeats this word.

[5] The mango is used in all stages—when ripe for eating, and for pickles, curries, &c., in other stages.

either conversion or any other. And this, O king, is what is called "The Blessed One's bazaar of fruits."

"Men give their Karma as the price,
And buy the fruit ambrosia;
And happiness is theirs, and peace,
Who've bought the fruit ambrosia[1]."'

10. 'And what, venerable Nâgasena, is the antidote bazaar of the Blessed One, the Buddha?'

'Certain drugs, O king, have been made known by the Blessed One; drugs by which the Blessed One delivers the whole world of gods and men from the poison of evil dispositions. And what are these drugs? The four Noble Truths made known by the Blessed One, that is to say, the truth as to sorrow, and the truth as to the origin of sorrow, and the truth as to the cessation of sorrow, and the truth as to that path which leads to the cessation of sorrow[2]. And whosoever, longing for the highest insight (the insight of Arahatship)[3], hear this doctrine of the four truths, they are set quite free from rebirth, [335] they are set quite free from old age, they are set quite free from death, they are set quite free from grief, lamentation, pain, sorrow, and despair. And this, O king, is what is called "The Blessed One's bazaar of antidotes."

[1] These lines have not been traced as yet in the Pi*t*akas, and are probably not meant as a quotation. 'Ambrosia' is of course the ambrosia of Arahatship.

[2] For the full text of these 'Truths' see 'Buddhist Suttas,' pp. 148-150.

[3] A*ññ*â. The Si*m*halese, p. 486, has awabodhaya. The word is rare, but it occurs at *G*âtaka I, 140; II, 333; and at Dhammapada, verses 57, 96, always in this sense.

"Of all the drugs, in all the world,
The antidotes of poison dire,
Not one equals that Doctrine sweet.
Drink that, O brethren. Drink and live[1]!"'

11. 'And what, venerable Nâgasena, is the medicine bazaar of the Blessed One, the Buddha?'

'Certain medicines, O king, have been made known by the Blessed One, medicines by which he cures the whole world of gods and men. And they are these:—"The four Means of keeping oneself ready and mindful, and the fourfold Great Struggle, and the four Steps to Iddhi, and the five Organs of the moral sense, and the five moral Powers, and the seven Forms of the Wisdom of the Arahats, and the Noble Eightfold Path[2]." By these medicines the Blessed One purges men of wrong views, purges them of low aspirations, purges them of evil speaking, purges them of evil deeds, purges them of evil modes of livelihood, purges them of wrong endeavours, purges them of evil thoughts, purges them of erroneous meditation; and he gives emetics to the vomiting up of lusts, and of malice, and of dullness, and of doubt, and of self-righteousness, and of sloth of body and inertness of mind, and of shamelessness and hardness of heart, and of all evil. And this, O king, is what is called "The Blessed One's bazaar of medicine."

"Of all the medicines found in all the world,
Many in number, various in their powers,
Not one equals this medicine of the Truth.
Drink that, O brethren. Drink, and drinking, live!

[1] Not traced as yet.

[2] See the note above on V, 3 (p. 330 of the Pâli).

For having drunk that medicine of the Truth,
Ye shall have past beyond old age and death,
And—evil, lusts, and Karma rooted out—
Thoughtful and seeing, ye shall be at rest[1]!"'

12. 'And what, venerable Nâgasena, is the ambrosia bazaar of the Blessed One, the Buddha?'

'An ambrosia, O king, has been made known by the Blessed One, that ambrosia with which he besprinkles the whole world of gods and men—as men anoint a king on his coronation day—[**336**] and men and gods, when sprinkled with that ambrosia, are set free from rebirths, old age, disease, and death, from grief, and lamentation, and pain, and sorrow, and despair. And what is that ambrosia? That meditation which consists in active attention to, and leads to a true grasp of, the real conditions of corporeal things[2]. For it has been said, O king, by the Blessed One, the god over all gods:

"They, O brethren, feed on ambrosia who feed on active attention directed to corporeal things[3]." This, O king, is what is called "The Blessed One's ambrosia bazaar."'

[1] Nibbutâ, with allusion to the freedom and calm of Nirvâna. The verses have not been traced as yet in the Pitakas.

[2] Kâya-gatâ-sati-bhavanâ, where each term really requires a long commentary.

[3] It will be noticed that Nâgasena is here really going an inch beyond his text. In that text (which has not been traced) amata, ambrosia, means no doubt as elsewhere, the ambrosia of Nirvâna. And the text does not say that the active attention and the ambrosia are the same, but only that they who feed on the one feed also on the other. Even if we translate 'are feeding' instead of 'feed' (which is grammatically possible) a similar argument would hold good. But though it is impossible to say for certain, without knowing the context of the passage, the rendering above is more in accord with Pâli usage, and more likely therefore to be right.

"He saw mankind afflicted with disease,
He opened freely his ambrosia shop;
Go, then, O brethren, give your Karma for it,
And buy, and feed on, that ambrosial food[1].'"

13. 'And what, venerable Nâgasena, is the jewel bazaar of the Blessed One, the Buddha?'

'Certain jewels, O king, have been made known by the Blessed One, and adorned with those jewels the children of the Blessed One shine forth in splendour, illuminating the whole world of gods and men, brightening it in its heights, in its depths, from horizon to horizon, with a brilliant glory. And those jewels are these—the jewel of right conduct, and the jewel of meditation, and the jewel of knowledge, and the jewel of emancipation, and the jewel of the insight which arises from the assurance of emancipation, and the jewel of discrimination, and the jewel of the sevenfold wisdom of the Arahats[2].

14. 'And what, O king, is the Blessed One's jewel of right conduct[3]? The right conduct which follows on self-restraint according to the rules of the Pâtimokkha, the right conduct which follows on

---

[1] Not traced as yet. All these stanzas seem to belong together, and will doubtless be found in the same Sutta or poem.

[2] These seven jewels (or treasures, ratanâni) of the Buddha are intended of course to correspond to the seven treasures (also ratanâni) of the king of kings (the *k*akkavattî). They are different from the seven 'Treasures of the Noble Ones' (Ariyadhanâni) which are ethical qualities, whereas these jewels are means to the attainment of Arahatship.

[3] Sîla, a most difficult word to translate, as it includes so much that in English would be expressed by the varying phrases: goodness, virtue, righteousness, uprightness, morality, &c.

restraint of the bodily organs and the mind[1], the right conduct which results from a pure means of livelihood, the right conduct in relation to the four requisites of a recluse[2], the right conduct presented in the Short, and Middle, and Long Summonses[3], the right conduct of those who are walking in the Path, and the right conduct of those who have attained each of the various fruits thereof (beginning at conversion and ending at Arahatship)[4]. And all the beings in the world, O king, gods[5] and men, and the Mâras too (the spirits of evil), and the Brahmas (the very highest of the gods), and Sama*n*as and Brahmans are filled with longing and desire for a man who wears, as his ornament, this jewel of right conduct. And the Bhikkhu, O king, who puts it on shines forth in glory all around, upwards and downwards, and from side to side, surpassing in lustre all the jewels to be found from the Waveless Deep[6] below to the highest heavens above, excelling them all, overwhelming them all. Such, O king, are the jewels of right conduct set out for sale in the Blessed One's bazaar of gems. And this is what is called "The Blessed One's jewel of righteousness."

---

[1] Indriya; no doubt here the six organs, that is the usual five, and bhavaṅgo or mano as the sixth.

[2] Clothing, food, lodging, and medicine for the sick.

[3] Translated in 'Buddhist Suttas,' pp. 189–200.

[4] What we have here are the two higher stages of the three into which Buddhist ethics naturally falls. The morality of laymen has been included above, V, 7, where it already passes over into that of the ordinary, unconverted member of the Order. Here we begin with that, starting with the last item of the previous list, and go on, through the sîlas, to the highest ethics of Arahatship.

[5] The devas, those gods dwelling in Sakka's heaven, and, I think, the devatâs also (fairies, nyads, dryads, &c.).

[6] Avî*k*i, the lowest of the purgatories.

"Such are the virtues sold in that bazaar,
The shop of the Enlightened One, the Blest;
Pay Karma as the price, O ye ill-clad!
Buy, and put on, these lustrous Buddha-gems!"

[337] 15. 'And what, O king, is the Blessed One's jewel of meditation? The meditation that consists of specific conceptions, and of investigation regarding them[1];—the meditation that consists of reflection only, specific conceptions being lost sight of[2];—the meditation that continues after specific conceptions and reflection on them have both ceased[3];—the meditation that is void (of lusts, evil dispositions, and Karma);—the meditation from which three signs (of an unconverted life—lust, malice, and dullness) are absent;—the meditation in which no low aspirations remain[4]. And when a Bhikkhu, O king, has put on this jewel of meditation (Samâdhi), then ideas of lust, and ideas of anger, and ideas of cruelty, and all the various bad thoughts that have their basis in the evil dispositions of pride, self-righteousness, adhesion to wrong views, and doubt—all these, since they come into contact with meditation, flow off from him, disperse, and are dispelled, they stay not with him, adhere not to him. Just, O king, as when water has fallen on a lotus leaf it flows off from it, is dispersed and scattered

---

[1] I think the first *Gh*âna (see 'Buddhist Suttas,' p. 272) is meant.

[2] Apparently the passage over from the first to the second *Gh*âna.

[3] But insight, and the resulting bliss, remain. Compare above. II, 2, 3 (I, 67).

[4] Compare above, V, 8, on the last three.

away, stays not on it, adheres not to it[1]—so when a Bhikkhu has put on this jewel of meditation, then ideas of lust, and ideas of anger, and ideas of cruelty, and all the various bad thoughts that have their basis in the evil dispositions of pride, self-righteousness, obstinacy in wrong views, and doubt —these all, as soon as they come in contact with meditation, flow off, disperse, and are dispelled, stay not with him, adhere not to him. And why not? Because of the exceeding purity of the habit of meditation. This, O king, is what is called "The Blessed One's jewel of meditation," and such are the jewels of meditation set out for sale in the Blessed One's bazaar of gems.

"Bad thoughts can ne'er arise beneath the brow
Encircled by this coronet of gems.
It charms away perplexed and wandering thought.
Make it your own, buy it, put on the crown!"

16. 'And what, O king, is the Blessed One's jewel of knowledge? That knowledge by which the disciple of the noble ones knows thoroughly what is virtue, and what is not; what is blame-worthy, and what is not; what should be made a habit of, and what should not; what is mean, and what is exalted; [338] what is dark, and what is light, and what is both dark and light;—the knowledge by which he truly knows what sorrow is, and what the origin of sorrow is, and what the cessation of sorrow is, and what is the path that leads thereto. This, O king, is what is called "The Blessed One's jewel of knowledge."

[1] See the note upon IV, 8, 65.

"He who has knowledge as his jewelled wreath,
Will not continue long in outward form[1].
Soon will he reach Nirvâna, in rebirth
In any world[2] no longer take delight!"

17. 'And what, O king, is the Blessed One's jewel of emancipation? Arahatship is called the jewel of emancipation, and the Bhikkhu who has reached Arahatship is said to have decked himself with the jewel of emancipation. And just as a man, O king, who is decorated with ornaments made of strings of pearls, of diamonds and gold and corals; whose limbs are anointed with akalu[3], and with frankincense[4], and with Talis[5], and with red sandal wood; who is adorned with a garland of Ironwood blossoms, and Rottleria flowers, and flowers from the Sal tree, and the Salala[6], and the champak, and yellow jasmines[7], and Atimuttaka flowers[8], and

[1] Bhavo here equal to pañka skandha, according to Hînati-kumburê, p. 491.

[2] Bhave, here tri-widha-bhawa in the Simhalese.

[3] Akalu; only found here. The Simhalese has agaru kalu, and agaru according to Clough is Dalbergia.

[4] Tagara. Agil tuwaralâ, 'logwood frankincense.'

[5] Tâlîsaka. Clough says the Talis tree is Flacourtia cataphracta.

[6] Not in the Pâli dictionaries. But it is mentioned in Buddhavamsa II, 51 (there spelt salala). This verse is quoted at Gâtaka I, 13, verse 51, and the word is there spelt salala. The Simhalese has salala, and the Sanskrit lexicons have sarala. Clough identifies it, no doubt wrongly, with the last, the Anglo-Indian Hal tree, which the botanists call the Shorea robusta.

[7] Yûthikâ; sînidda, says Hînati-kumburê, p. 492, and Clough thinks this is oleander. But Böhtlingk-Roth say a sort of jasmine, Jasminum auriculatum.

[8] Yohombu in the Simhalese. Clough says this is a creeper called Borago Zeylanica. But does that grow in the North-West of India? According to Böhtlingk-Roth, Atimuttaka is the

trumpet flowers, and lotuses, and white and Arabian jasmines[1]—just as, with all this finery of garlands and perfumes and jewelry, he would outshine all other men, overwhelming them with brilliant glory and splendour—just so, O king, does he who has attained to Arahatship, he in whom the Great Evils (lusts, and becoming, delusion, and ignorance) are rooted out, he who has put on the diadem of emancipation of heart, just so does he outshine all other Bhikkhus from the lowest in attainment up to those even who are themselves emancipated[2], overwhelming them in brilliant glory and splendour. And why is that so? Because, O king, there is one diadem that is the chief of all, and that is this diadem of emancipation of heart! And this, O king, is what is called "The Blessed One's jewel of emancipation."

"All the people that dwell in a house look up
To their Lord when he wears his crown of gems—
The wide world of the gods and of men looks up
To the wearer of Freedom's diadem!"

18. 'And what, O king, is the Blessed One's jewel of the insight that follows on the assurance of emancipation? The knowledge arising out of looking back over the course[3]—that knowledge by

---

name of three plants, one of which is the Gaertnera Racemosa, much cultivated for the beauty and perfume of its flowers.

[1] The last four are the Pâ*t*alî, Uppala, Vassika, and Mallikâ, all of which are well known. Our author's flora and fauna are so numerous that one ought, if one had the necessary knowledge, to be able to draw conclusions as to his own 'habitat.'

[2] On the use of upâdây' upâdâya see above, p. 182, and below, p. 341 of the Pâli.

[3] Pa*kk*avekkhana-*ññ*â*nam*. That is, in looking back over the

which the disciple who is walking along the Excellent Way passes, from time to time, both the Way itself and the Fruits thereof up to Nirvâna in review, and is aware what evil dispositions he has got rid of, and what evil dispositions remain to be conquered—that is what [**339**] is called "The jewel of the assurance that follows on the knowledge of emancipation."

"The knowledge by which the Noble Ones know
The stages they've passed, and the road yet untrod;—
Strive, O ye sons of the Conqueror, strive
That jewel—'Assurance'—yourselves to obtain!"

19. 'And what, O king, is the Blessed One's jewel of discrimination? The discrimination of the sense of, and the discrimination of the deeper truths underlying the sense of the sacred writ, and the discrimination of philological peculiarities, and the discrimination of correct and ready exposition[1]. And the Bhikkhu, O king, who is adorned with these four jewels of discrimination, whatsoever company he enters into, whether of nobles, or brahmans, or merchants, or workpeople, enters it in confidence, neither put out nor shy; undaunted and undismayed, he enters the assembly without excitement or fear. Just, O king, as a warrior, a hero in the fight, when accoutred in all his harness

course he has followed along the Excellent Way, he becomes conscious of having got beyond each of the obstacles (the Samyoganas) that can beset him. It is the doctrine of 'final assurance' from the Buddhist point of view. Compare ñânadassana at Dîgha II, 83.

[1] Paisambhidâ. Hînai-kumburê merely repeats the ambiguous technical terms of the Pâli. Childers, sub voce, gives the various interpretations of other authorities. Compare above, I, 29, 34, 36. The third and fourth seem to me to be doubtful.

of war[1], goes down undismayed to the battle, in the confident thought: "If the enemy should remain afar off I can knock them down with my arrows, should they come thence towards me I can hit them with my javelins, should they come yet nearer I can reach them with my spear, should they come right up I can cleave them in two with my sabre[2], should they come to close quarters I can pierce them through and through with my dagger[3]"—just so, O king, does the Bhikkhu, when he wears the fourfold jewel of discernment, enter any assembly undismayed, in the confident thought: "Should any one put to me a puzzle turning on the discrimination of the sense, I shall be able to explain it, comparing sense with sense, explanation with explanation, reason with reason, argument with argument[4],—and thus shall I resolve his doubts,

---

[1] Pañkâvudho; literally 'with the five weapons on.' The expression is not infrequent; compare pañkâvudha-sannaddha, used of a hunter, at *G*âtaka III, 467; IV, 283, 437; and sannaddha-pañkâvudhâ, used of sailors fighting, at *G*âtaka IV, 160. But it is quite possible that weapons different from those here described are there meant, as they are not suited, for instance, to the hunter.

[2] Hîna*t*i-kumburê translates this weapon (ma*nd*alagga) simply by ka*d*uwa, sword; but 'bent blade' must mean a sabre.

[3] *Kh*urikâ. Childers has only 'knife.' The Si*m*halese, p. 493, has kirisaya, which is not in Clough, but is doubtless the Malay kreese. These five weapons are not mentioned elsewhere, and as three of the five words are rare, are probably those in special use in the country where our author lived. In this respect it is noteworthy that the Sanskrit kshurikâ is only mentioned, according to Böhtlingk-Roth, in the Râ*g*a Tarangînî of Kashmîr, and in the title of a late Upanishad. We shall therefore scarcely go far wrong if we understand by our author's *kh*urikâ the famous Afghan knife.

[4] Arthayen arthaya ga*l*apâ, &c., says the Si*m*halese. He

dispel his perplexity, and delight him by my exposition of the problem raised. Should any one put to me a puzzle turning on discrimination of the deeper truths, I shall be able to explain it by comparing truth with truth, and the various aspects and phases of Arahatship each with each [1], **[340]**—and thus his doubts too shall I be able to resolve, and, dispelling his perplexity, to delight him with my exposition of the problem raised. Should any one put to me a puzzle turning on the discrimination of philological peculiarities, I shall be able to explain it by comparing derivation with derivation [2], and word with word, and particle with particle, and letter with letter, and one modification of a letter by contact (sandhi) with another, and consonant with consonant, and vowel with vowel, and accent (intonation) with accent, and quantity with quantity, and rule with rule, and idiom with idiom;—and thus his doubts too shall I be able to resolve, and, dispelling his perplexity, to delight him with my exposition of the problem raised. Should any one put to me a puzzle turning on the discrimination of expositions, I shall be able to explain it by comparing metaphor with metaphor, and characteristic with characteristic [3], and sentiment with sentiment—and thus his doubts too shall I be able to resolve, and, dispelling his perplexity, to delight him with my exposition of the

will reply by adducing parallel passages, much in the style of modern scholarship.

[1] He gives the principal ones, as set out in his previous arguments.

[2] Nirutti. Hînati-kumburê unfortunately simply repeats all these technical terms.

[3] Lakkhana. As for instance above, I, 51–62.

problem raised. And this, O king, is what is called "The Blessed One's jewel of discrimination."

"First buy the jewel of discrimination,
Then cut[1] it with your knowledge and your skill;
So, free from all anxiety and fear,
Shall you illuminate both earth and heaven!"

20. 'And what, O king, is the Blessed One's jewel of the sevenfold wisdom of the Arahats? It is self-possession, and investigation of the system of doctrine, and zeal, and joy, and tranquillity, and contemplation, and equanimity[2]. And the Bhikkhu, O king, who is adorned with this sevenfold jewel of the divisions of the higher wisdom[3] shines forth over the whole world of gods and men, brightens it, illuminates it, and dispersing the darkness makes the light arise. This, O king, is what is called "The Blessed One's jewel of the sevenfold wisdom."

"The gods and men in reverence stand up
To him who wears this wisdom-diadem.
Show your good actions then,—that is the price,—
And buy, and wear, this wisdom-diadem!"'

[341] 21. 'And what, venerable Nâgasena, is the bazaar for all manner of merchandise set up by the Blessed One, the Buddha?'

'The Blessed One's bazaar for all manner of

---

[1] Phaseyya; literally 'he who having bought pa*t*isambhidâ shall touch it with his *ñ*â*n*a.' The Si*m*halese, p. 494, has spars*s*ako*t*a, which does not help us.

[2] The Si*m*halese again only repeats these seven technical terms, except the second Dhamma-vi*k*aya, which it renders by pra*gñ*â.

[3] Bodhi. Childers says, 'the supreme knowledge of a Buddha.' But this is wrong, as is evident even from the context here. The whole exposition is of Arahatship, not Buddhahood.

merchandise, O king, is the ninefold word of the Buddha; and the relics remaining of his body, and of the things he used; and the sacred mounds (*K*etiyâni, Dâgabas) erected over them[1]; and the jewel of his Order. And in that bazaar there are set out by the Blessed One the attainment (in a future birth) of high lineage, and of wealth, and of long life, and of good health, and of beauty, and of wisdom, and of worldly glory, and of heavenly glory, and of Nirvâ*n*a. And of these all they who desire either the one or the other, give Karma as the price, and so buy whichever glory they desire. And some buy with it a vow of right conduct, and some by observance of the Uposatha day, and so on down to the smallest Karma-price they buy the various glories from the greatest to the least. Just, O king, as in a trader's shop, oil, seed, and peas and beans can be either taken in barter for a small quantity of rice or peas or beans, or bought for a small price decreasing in order according to requirement—just so, O king, in the Blessed One's bazaar for all manner of merchandise advantages are to be bought for Karma according to requirement. And this, O king, is what is called "The Blessed One's bazaar of all manner of merchandise."

"Long life, good health, beauty, rebirth in heaven,
High birth, Nirvâ*n*a—all are found for sale—
There to be bought for Karma, great or small—
In the great Conqueror's world-famed bazaar.
Come; show your faith, O brethren, as the price,
Buy and enjoy such goods as you prefer[2]!"

---

[1] Hînan*-kumburê, characteristically enough for a Ceylon man, adds, 'and the Footprint and the Bo-tree.'

[2] The first line only of these verses is in the Sa*m*yutta III, 2, 7.

22. 'And the inhabitants that dwell in the Blessed One's City of Righteousness, O king, are such as these: Masters in the Suttantas, and masters in the Vinaya, and masters in the Abhidhamma; preachers of the faith; repeaters of the *G*âtakas, and repeaters of the Dîgha, and repeaters of the Ma*ggh*ima, [**342**] and repeaters of the Sa*m*yutta, and repeaters of the Aṅguttara, and repeaters of the Khuddaka Nikâya;—men endowed with right conduct, men accomplished in meditation, men full of knowledge, men taking delight in contemplation of the sevenfold wisdom of the Arahats, men of insight [1];—men who frequent the woods for meditation, or sit at the roots of trees, or dwell in the open air, or sleep on heaps of straw, or live near cemeteries, or lie not down to sleep,—men who have entered the Excellent Way [2], men who have attained one or more of the four fruits thereof, men who are still learners (have not yet reached Arahatship, but are close upon it), men enjoying the Fruits, that is, either Sotâpannas, or Sakadâgâmins, or Anâgâmins, or Arahats;—men of the threefold wisdom [3], men of the sixfold transcendental wisdom [4], men of the power of Iddhi, men who have reached perfection in knowledge, men

---

[1] Vipassakâ, not necessarily the insight of the Arahats, as Childers says. We have seen Vipassanâ ascribed above, p. 16 (of the Pâli), to a Sotâpanno.

[2] Pa*t*ipannakâ; so the Si*m*halese, p. 496 (but see otherwise below, V, 21, p. 344 of the Pâli).

[3] Tevi*gg*â, having the pubbe-nivâsânussati-*ñâ*na, the *k*etopariya-*ñâ*n*a, and the âsavâna*m* khaya-*ñâ*n*a. See Dîgha Nikâya II, 91-94 and 97.

[4] These are the last three, and besides them the so-called Divine Eye, and Divine Ear, and also the power of Iddhi. See Dîgha Nikâya II, 87-90, 95-96.

skilled in the maintenance of constant self-possession, in the Great Struggle, in the Steps to Iddhi, in the Organs of their moral sense, in the sevenfold wisdom, in the Excellent Way, in *Gh*âna, in Vimokkha, and in the attainment of the exalted and tranquil bliss that is independent of form or the absence of form —yea! like a forest full of bamboos, full of reeds, that City of Righteousness has been ever crowded and frequented by such Arahats as these! For it is said[1]:

(1) "Men devoid of passion, and of malice, and of dullness, men in whom the Great Evils (lust, becoming, delusion, and ignorance) are not, men who have neither craving thirst, nor grasping desires,—these are they who dwell in the City of Righteousness.

(2) "Men whose home is the forest, men who have taken on themselves the extra vows, men full of joy, men who are wearing rough garments, men rejoicing in solitude, heroes—these are they who dwell in the City of Righteousness.

(3) "Men who sleep sitting, or on any sleeping-place that comes, or spend their time standing or walking up and down in meditation, men who clad themselves in cast-off raiment—all these dwell in the City of Righteousness.

(4) "Men wearing the full set of three robes, tranquil, with a skin for the fourth, who rejoice in taking but one meal each day, the wise—these are they who dwell in the City of Righteousness.

(5) "The earnest and prudent, heroes who feed on little and know no greed, content whether they receive an alms or receive it not—these are they who dwell in the City of Righteousness.

[1] It is not known in what text.

(6) "The meditative, delighting in *Gh*âna, heroes of tranquil minds, and stedfast, looking forward to Nirvâ*n*a—these are they who dwell in the City of Righteousness.

(7) "Men walking in the path, and standing in the fruits thereof, those who have attained some fruits thereof but are yet learners as to the last, whose hope is directed to the utmost goal—these are they who dwell in the City of Righteousness.

(8) "Those who have entered the stream, and those who, free from stains, will only be reborn once more on earth, those who will never return again, and Arahats—these are they who dwell in the City of Righteousness.

(9) "Those skilled in the means of attaining undisturbed self-possession, and rejoicing in contemplation on the sevenfold wisdom, those who are full of insight, and bear the words of the Dharma in their hearts—these are they who dwell in the City of Righteousness.

[343] (10) "Those skilled in the Steps to Iddhi, and rejoicing in the meditations of Samâdhi, those who are devoted to the Great Struggle—these are they who dwell in the City of Righteousness.

(11) "Those perfect in the sixfold wisdom of the Abhi*ññ*âs, delighting in the sphere that is theirs by rightful inheritance[1], those having the power of flying through the air—these are they who dwell in the City of Righteousness.

(12) "Those of downcast eyes, and measured speech, the doors of whose senses are guarded, who

[1] Pettike go*k*are ratâ. That is in the four Sati-pa*tth*ânas. See the passage quoted below at VII, 1, 7, p. 368 of the Pâli.

are self-restrained, who are well trained according to the supreme Dhamma—these are they who dwell in the City of Righteousness.

(13) "Those of the threefold wisdom, and of the sixfold wisdom, those who have become perfect in Iddhi and perfect in knowledge—these are they who dwell in the City of Righteousness."

23. 'And furthermore, O king, those of the Bhikkhus who carry in their hearts the words of the excellent knowledge that is immeasurable, who are free from bonds, whose goodness and fame and power and glory no man can weigh, who (in imitation of their Master) [1] keep the royal chariot-wheel of the kingdom of righteousness rolling on, who have reached perfection in knowledge—such Bhikkhus are called, O king, "The Commanders of the Faith in the Blessed One's City of Righteousness."

'And furthermore, O king, those of the Bhikkhus, who have the power of Iddhi, who have learned the discriminations [2], who are full of confidence, who travel through the air, who are hard to oppose, hard to overcome, who can move without support, who can shake the broad earth and the waters on which it rests, who can touch the sun and the moon, who are skilful in transforming themselves and in making stedfast resolutions and high aspirations, who are perfect in Iddhi—such Bhikkhus are called, O king, "The royal chaplains in the Blessed One's City of Righteousness."

'And furthermore, O king, those of the Bhikkhus who have taken upon themselves the extra vows,

[1] Anuppavattakâ. See below, p. 363 of the Pâli.

[2] See above, V, 19.

who desire little and are content, who would loathe any breach of the regulations as to the manner of seeking an alms[1], and beg straight on from hut to hut, as a bee smells flower after flower[2], and then go away into the loneliness of the woods, those who are indifferent as to their body and as to life, those who have attained to Arahatship, those who place the highest value on the virtues of the practice of the extra vows—such Bhikkhus are called, O king, "The judges in the Blessed One's City of Righteousness."

'And furthermore, O king, those of the Bhikkhus who are pure and stainless, in whom no evil dispositions are left, who, skilful in the knowledge of the fall and rise of beings[3], have perfected themselves in the Divine Eye—such Bhikkhus are called, O king, "The givers of light[4] in the Blessed One's City of Righteousness."

'And furthermore, O king, those of the Bhikkhus [**344**] who are learned in the traditions, who hand on what has been handed down, the repeaters of the Discourses, and of the Canon Law, and of the tables of contents, those who are skilled in the exact determination of letters into surds and sonants, into

[1] Importunity, or even attracting attention in any way. See above, p. 229 of the Pâli.

[2] Compare Sigalovâda Sutta, p. 365, and Dhammapada, verse 49: 'As a bee, injuring not the flower or its colour or its scent, flies away, taking the nectar, so let a sage go through the village.'

[3] That is the fall of beings from one state of existence—their death in that state in other words—and their rise, their rebirth, in another.

[4] *G*otaka, as a city official, is something akin to torchbearer, lamplighter.

longs and short, as to lightness and heaviness[1], those who know by heart the ninefold word—such Bhikkhus are called, O king, "The peace officers[2] in the Blessed One's City of Righteousness."

'And furthermore, O king, those of the Bhikkhus who are learned in the Vinaya (Rules of the Order, Canon Law), wise in the Vinaya, skilled in detecting the source of offences[3], skilled in deciding whether any act is an offence or not, whether an offence is grievous or slight, whether it can be atoned for or not, skilled in deciding questions as to the rise, the acknowledgment, the absolution, or the confession of an offence[4]; as to the suspension, or the restoration, or the defence of an offender[5], who are perfect masters in the Vinaya—such Bhikkhus are called, O king, "The Rûpa-dakshas[6] in the Blessed One's City of Righteousness."

'And furthermore, O king, those of the Bhikkhus who wear on their brows the lotus garland of that noble Emancipation, who have attained to that

[1] These are six out of the ten divisions of Vyañgana-vuddhi, mentioned in the verse at Sumangala Vilâsinî I, 177. Hînañ-kumburê, p. 501, merely repeats the words.

[2] Dhamma-rakkhâ, 'dharmikawû âraksha-grahanayehi niyuktawû' in the Simhalese.

[3] Nidâna-pathana-kusalâ; 'Âpatti gena hœra dœkwî-mehi dakshawû,' says the Simhalese.

[4] One word, vutthâna, is here doubtful.

[5] See Mahâvagga IX, 4, 9. 10, &c.

[6] Literally 'skilled in form, shape, beauty.' The Simhalese repeats this ambiguous expression, adding the qualification amâtyayo, 'ministers, officials.' One would think that these would have been the judges, but our author has already made the Arahats the judges in his Dhamma-nagara. This only leaves him some minor official post to give away to those learned in Canon Law, and he has chosen one as unintelligible in Ceylon as it is to me.

highest and best and most exceeding excellent of all conditions, who are loved and longed for by the great multitudes—such Bhikkhus are called, O king, "Flower-sellers in the Blessed One's City of Righteousness."

'And furthermore, O king, those of the Bhikkhus who have penetrated to the comprehension of the four Truths, and have seen them with their eyes, who are wise in the teaching, who have passed beyond doubt as to the four fruits of Sama*n*aship, who having attained to the bliss thereof, share those fruits with others who have entered the paths[1]—such Bhikkhus are called, O king, "Fruit-dealers in the Blessed One's City of Righteousness."

'And furthermore, O king, those of the Bhikkhus who, being anointed with that most excellent perfume of right conduct, are gifted with many and various virtues, and are able to dispel the bad odour of sin and evil dispositions—such Bhikkhus are called, O king, "Perfume dealers in the Blessed One's City of Righteousness."

'And furthermore, O king, those of the Bhikkhus whose delight is in the Dhamma, and whose converse is pleasant, who find exceeding joy in the higher subtleties of the Dharma and the Vinaya[2], who either in the forest, or at the foot of trees, or in empty

---

[1] Pa*t*ipannâ, which Hîna*t*i-kumburê takes here to mean Arahats, but see the note above, V, 20 (p. 341 of the Pâli).

[2] Abhidhamme abhivinaye. A phrase very instructive as to the correct rendering of the much misunderstood word abhidhamma. As I pointed out already in the 'Hibbert Lectures' for 1881, it is a blunder to translate it, as is usually done, by 'metaphysics.' The whole context is taken from the Sangîti Sutta.

places, drink the sweet sap of the Dharma, who plunging themselves, as it were, in body, speech, and mind into the sweet juice [1] of the Dharma, excel in expounding it, in seeking and in detecting the deeper truths in the various doctrines, who—wheresoever and whensoever the discourse is of wishing for little, of contentment, of solitude, of retirement, of the exertion in zeal, of right conduct, of meditation, of knowledge, of emancipation, of the insight arising from the assurance of emancipation—[**345**] thither do they repair, and drink in the sweet savour of that discourse—such Bhikkhus are called, O king, "Thirsty and drunkards in the Blessed One's City of Righteousness."

'And furthermore, O king, those of the Bhikkhus who are addicted to the habit of wakefulness from the first watch of the night to the last, who spend day and night in sitting, standing, or walking up and down in meditation, who, addicted to the habit of contemplation, are devoted to their own advancement by the suppressing of evil dispositions—such Bhikkhus are called, O king, "Watchmen in the Blessed One's City of Righteousness."

'And furthermore, O king, those of the Bhikkhus who in the spirit and in the letter, in its arguments and explanations, in its reasons and examples, teach and repeat, utter forth and recapitulate the ninefold word of the Buddha—such Bhikkhus are called, O king, "Lawyers (dealers in Dharma [2]) in the Blessed One's City of Righteousness."

[1] 'The ambrosia of the Saddharma,' says Hînañ-kumburê, p. 502.

[2] Dhammâpanikâ. The Simhalese has Dhârmikâpanikayo.

'And furthermore, O king, those of the Bhikkhus who are wealthy and rich in the wealth of the treasures of the Doctrine, in the wealth of the traditions, and the text, and the learning thereof, who comprehend the signs, and vowels, and consonants thereof, in all their details, pervading all directions with their knowledge — such Bhikkhus are called, O king, "Bankers of the Dhamma[1] in the Blessed One's City of Righteousness."

'And furthermore, O king, those of the Bhikkhus who have penetrated to the sublimer teaching, who understand exposition and the divisions of objects of meditation to be practised, who are perfect in all the subtler points of training[2]—such Bhikkhus are called, O king, "Distinguished masters of law in the Blessed One's City of Righteousness."

24. 'Thus well planned out, O king, is the Blessed One's City of Righteousness, thus well built, thus well appointed, thus well provisioned, thus well established, thus well guarded, thus well protected, thus impregnable by enemies or foes. And by this explanation, O king, by this argument, by this reason, you may by inference know that the Blessed One did once exist.

(1) "As when they see a pleasant city, well planned out,
Men know, by inference, how great the founder was;
So when they see our Lord's 'City of Righteousness'
They know, by inference, that he did once exist.

[1] Dhamma-se*tth*ino, which the Si*m*halese repeats.

[2] Adhisîla, adhi*k*itta, and adhipa*ññ*â, says Hîna*t*i-kumburê.

[346] (2). "As men, seeing its waves, can judge, by inference,
The great extent and power of the world-embracing sea;
So may they judge the Buddha when they see the waves
That he set rolling through the world of gods and men—
He who, unconquered in the fight, allays all griefs,
Who rooted out, in his own heart, Craving's dread power,
And set his followers free from the whirlpool of rebirths—
'Far as the waves of the Good-Law extend and roll,
So great, so mighty, must our Lord, the Buddha, be.'

(3) "As men, seeing its mighty peaks that tower aloft,
Can judge, by inference, Himâlaya's wondrous height;
So when they see the Buddha's Mount-of-Righteousness—
Stedfast, unshaken by fierce passion's stormy blasts,
Towering aloft in wondrous heights of calm and peace,
Where lusts, evil, and Karma cannot breathe or live,—
They draw the inference: 'Great as this mountain high
That mighty Hero's power upon whose word it stands.'

(4) "As men, seeing the footprint of an elephant king,
Can judge, by inference: 'How great his size must be!'
So when they see the footprint of the elephant of men,
Buddha, the wise, upon the path that men have trod,
They know, by inference: 'How glorious Buddha was[1]!'

(5) "As when they see all living things crouching in fear,
Men know: ''Tis the roar of the king of the beasts that frightens them.'
So, seeing other teachers break and fly in fear,
They know: ''Tis a king of the truth hath uttered words sublime!'

(6) "Seeing the earth smiling, well watered, green with grass,
Men say: 'A great and pleasant rain hath fallen fast.'
So when they see this multitude rejoicing, peaceful, blest,
Men may infer: 'How sweet the rain that stilled their hearts!'

(7) "Seeing the wide earth soaked, boggy, a marsh of mud,
Men say: 'Mighty the mass of waters broken loose.'

[1] It is perhaps such poetical figures as this that have afforded foundation for the legend of Buddha's footprint.

So, when they see this mighty host, that once
were dazed
With the mud of sin, swept down in Dhamma's
stream, and left
In the wide sea of the Good-Law, some here,
some there,
All, gods and men alike, plunged in ambrosial
waves,
They may infer, and say: 'How great that
Dhamma is!'

(8) **[347]** "As when men, travelling, feel a glorious
perfume sweet
Pervading all the country side, and gladdening
them, infer at once,
'Surely, 'tis giant forest trees are flowering
now!'
So, conscious of this perfume sweet of righteous-
ness
That now pervades the earth and heavens,
they may infer:
'A Buddha, infinitely great, must once have
lived!'"

25. 'And it would be possible, O king, to show forth the Buddha's greatness, by a hundred or a thousand such examples, such reasons, such arguments, such metaphors. Just, O king, as a clever garland maker will, from one heap of all kinds of flowers, both following the instruction of his teacher, and also using his own individuality as a man, make many variegated and beautiful bouquets,—just so, O king, that Blessed One is, as it were, an infinite, immeasurable, heap of variegated flowers of virtue. And I now, a garland maker, as it were in the

church of the Conqueror, stringing those flowers together,—both following the path of our teachers of old, and also using such power of wisdom as in me is,—could show forth by inference the power of the Buddha in innumerable similes. But you, on the other hand, must show a desire to hear them[1].'

'Hard would it be, Nâgasena, for any other men thus to have shown by inference, drawn from such examples, the power of the Buddha. I am filled with satisfaction, venerable Nâgasena, at your so perfectly varied exposition of this problem.'

Here ends the problem of Inference[2].

---

[1] The Si*m*halese is here much expanded.

[2] Mr. Trenckner reads 'Anumâna pa*ñ*ha*m*,' the Si*m*halese has 'Mahâ Anumâna Pra*s*nayayi.'

BOOK VI.

THE DHUTAṄGAS.

[348] 1. The king saw Bhikkhus in the forest, lone
And far away from men, keeping hard vows.
And then he saw too householders, at home,
Eating the sweet fruits of the Noble Path [1].
Considering both of these, deep doubts he felt.
'If laymen also realise the Truth
Then surely vowing vows must be in vain.
Come! let me ask that best of teachers, wise
In the threefold basket of the Buddha's words,
Skilled to o'erthrow the arguments of the foe.
He will be able to resolve my doubts!'

---

2. Now Milinda the king went up to the place where Nâgasena was, and bowed down before him, and took his seat on one side. And when so seated, he said to Nâgasena: 'Venerable Nâgasena, is there any layman living at home, enjoying the pleasures of sense, occupying a dwelling encumbered with wife and children, enjoying the use of sandal wood from Benares, and of garlands, perfumes, and ointments, accepting gold and silver, with an embroidered head-dress on, set with diamonds and pearls and gold—is there any such who has seen face to face the calm, the supreme good, Nirvâ*n*a?'

'Not one hundred only, O king, nor two nor

[1] 'Standing in the Fruit of the Anâgâmins.' So they had already reached the third stage in the Excellent Way.

three nor five nor six hundred, not a thousand only, nor a hundred thousand, nor ten millions, nor ten thousand millions, not even only a billion laymen (have seen Nirvâ*n*a)—not to speak of twenty or thirty or a hundred or a thousand who have attained to clear understanding (of the four Truths)[1]. By

[1] I take this to mean, 'Not to speak of comparatively small numbers who have experienced Abhisamaya, an innumerable host of laymen have reached Nirvâ*n*a—that is, have reached, and during their lives remained in, the third stage of the Path, and attained Arahatship just before they died. Abhisamaya is used either absolutely or in composition. Mânâbhisamaya (A. IV, 38, 5=M. I, 12) certainly, and perhaps Atthâbhisamaya, is used of Arahats, but they do not occur in our author. He uses occasionally Dhammâbhisamaya (see pp. 255, 350, &c., of the Pâli) and *K*atu-sa*kk*âbhisamaya (see pp. 171, 334, &c.), but more frequently Abhisamaya absolutely. Dhammâbhisamaya, 'penetration into, clear understanding of, the Dhammas or Dhamma,' may refer to the four Dhammas of Aṅguttara IV, 1 (= M. P. S., IV, 2, 3), or to the comprehension of the qualities (Dhammas) of things, or (what is very much the same) to the comprehension of the principal doctrine (Dhamma) of the impermanence of all things. In the last case it would be the same thing, looked at from a slightly different point of view, as the Dhamma-*k*akkhu, the Eye for the Truths (see Sumaṅgala Vilâsinî I, 237), or as that insight (Vipassanâ) which is the entrance to the Path. But the four Truths (as to sorrow, &c.) are also important Dhammas, and as the expression *K*atu-sa*kk*âbhisamaya clearly refers to them and them only, this may also be the meaning of dhammâbhisamaya, or at any rate of abhisamaya standing above. So at least I take the latter here. We know that the 'Eye for the Dhamma,' the perception of the first only of the tî*n*i lakkha*n*âni (impermanence), implies and involves the entrance into the Path. Oddly enough there is as yet no evidence to show whether the perception of the cardinal doctrine of the four Truths necessarily does so too; or can do so alone, without the Dhamma-*k*akkhu. If the latter, then there are two gates to the Path. And this is not only quite possible, but is the inference one might fairly draw from the constant phrase 'After the exposition of the Truths had concluded so and so attained to' one or other of the phalâni.

what kind of exposition shall I lay before you evidence showing that I know this[1]?'

'Do you yourself tell me[2].'

3. 'Then, O king, I will explain it. All those passages in the ninefold word of the Buddha that deal with holiness of life, [349] and attainment of the path, and the divisions of the excellent habit of living under vows, shall be brought to bear in this connection[3]. Just, O king, as water which has rained down upon a country district, with both low-lying and high places, level land and undulations, dry ground and wet, will—all of it—flow off thence and meet together in the ocean of great waters; so will all those passages meet together, and be brought into connection, here. And a manifestation of reasons out of my experience and knowledge shall be also brought to bear. Thus will this matter be thoroughly analysed, its beauty will be brought out[4], it will be exhausted[5], brought home

---

[1] Literally 'shall I give you anuyoga,' which the Si*m*halese renders 'opportunity for speech' (!). Above, at p. 10 of the Pâli, the rendering is quite different, 'pâ*d*am dî samuge*n*a.' The only translation that fits the context in both of these places (the only ones in which the idiom has, so far, been found) is 'lay before you (proofs of my) mastery (over the subject),' or something of that sort. It is a disappointing satisfaction to find that the phrase was as unintelligible in Ceylon as it is to us. In my version above I should now prefer to write instead of 'repeated his lesson to his teacher for the last time,' 'gave his teacher proofs that he had understood what he had taught him.'

[2] Hîna*t*i-kumburê, p. 508, puts these words into the mouth of Nâgasena.

[3] Literally 'will come into connection here.'

[4] Vi*k*itto, which the Si*m*halese only repeats.

[5] Paripu*nn*o; literally 'filled' (paripûra wanneya).

to rest[1]. It will be, O king, as when an able writing-master, on exhibiting, by request, his skill in writing, will supplement the written signs by an explanation of reasons out of his experience and knowledge, and thus that writing of his becomes finished, perfect, without defect. So will I also bring to bear a manifestation of reasons out of my experience and knowledge; and thus shall this matter be thoroughly analysed, its beauty shall be brought out, it shall be exhausted, set at rest[2].

4. 'In the city of Sâvatthi, O king, about fifty millions of the disciples of the Blessed One, devout men and devout women, were walking in the paths, and out of those three hundred and fifty-seven thousand[3] were established in the fruit of the third path. And all of them were laity, not members of the Order. And there too, at the foot of the Ga*nd*amba tree, when the double miracle took place[4], two hundred millions of living beings[5] penetrated to an understanding (of the four Truths). And again on the delivery of the Râhulovâda[6] discourse, and of the Mahâ Mangala[7] discourse, and of the Sama*k*itta[8] exposition, and of the

---

[1] Samânîto, 'treated with respectful affection,' says Hîna*t*i-kumburê.

[2] I cannot hope to have solved all the difficulties with which the last two paragraphs bristle. But I think the general sense is clear, and the way smoothed for future translators.

[3] This curious number (like others below) must have a history and a meaning.

[4] See Sumangala Vilâsinî, p. 57; *G*âtaka I, 77, 78; IV, 263-266.

[5] Mostly gods of one sort or another.

[6] See the note above on I, 32 (p. 20 of the Pâli).

[7] In the Sutta Nipâta II, 4.

[8] See the note above, loc. cit.

Parâbhava[1] discourse, and of the Purâbheda[2] discourse, and of the Kalaha-vivâda discourse, and of the *K*ûla-vyûha[1] discourse, and of the Mahâ-vyûha[1] discourse, and of the Tuwa*t*aka[1] discourse, and of the Sâriputta[1] discourse, an innumerable number of celestial beings penetrated to knowledge (of the four Truths). In the city of Râ*g*agaha three hundred and fifty thousand devout laymen and devout laywomen, disciples of the Blessed One, were walking in the Paths. And there again at the taming of Dhanapâla the great elephant[3] nine hundred million living beings, and again at the meeting at the Pâsâ*n*ika *K*etiya on the occasion of the Pârâyana discourse[4] one hundred and forty million living beings, and again at the Indasâla cave eight hundred millions of gods, and again at Benares **[350]** in the deer park Isipatana at the first preaching of the Dhamma[5] one hundred and eighty million Brahma gods and innumerable others, and again in the heaven of the Thirty-Three at the preaching of the Abhidhamma on the Pa*nd*u Kambala Rock[6] eight hundred millions of the gods, and on the descent from the world of the gods at the gate of the city of Sankassa[6], at the miracle of the manifestation to the world[7],

---

[1] In the A*tth*akavagga of the Sutta Nipâta.

[2] Sutta Nipâta I, 6.

[3] See the note above on IV, 4, 44 (p. 207 of the Pâli), also below, p. 410 of the Pâli.

[4] Sutta Nipâta, pp. 185, 205 (of Professor Fausböll's edition for the Pâli Text Society).

[5] See 'Buddhist Suttas,' p. 154, and the note above on I, 38.

[6] *G*âtaka IV, 265.

[7] Loka-vivara*n*a-pâ*t*ihâriye, referred to at Dâ*th*ava*m*sa II, 120. The exact meaning of the second word, literally 'uncovering,'

three hundred millions of believing men and deities penetrated to a knowledge (of the four Truths). And again at Kapila-vatthu among the Sakyas, at the preaching of the Buddhava*m*sa [1] in the Nigrodha Arâma, and again at the preaching of the Mahâ Samaya Suttanta [2], gods in numbers that cannot be counted penetrated to a knowledge of the Dhamma. And again at the assemblies on the occasions of Sumana the garland maker [3], and of Garahadinna, and of Ânanda the rich man, and of *G*ambuka the naked ascetic [4], and of Ma*nd*ûka the god, and of Ma*tt*a-ku*nd*ali the god, and of Sulasâ the courtesan [5], and of Sirimâ the courtesan, and of the weaver's daughter, and of Subhaddâ, and of the spectacle of the cremation of the Brahman of Sâketa, and of the Sûnâparantas, and of the problem put by Sakka [6], and of the Tiroku*dd*a Sutta [7], and of the Ratana Sutta [8]—at each of these eighty-four thousand penetrated to a knowledge of the Dhamma. So long, O king, as the Blessed One remained in the world, so long wheresoever in the three great divisions

is doubtful. Alwis, in another connection, renders it 'prosperity.' See his quotation from Buddhaghosa's Papa*ñk*a Sûdanî quoted by Childers sub voce. The Si*m*halese has rûpa-kâya-sampat dakwâ dakwâ, 'continually manifesting (to all the world) the glory of his outward form.'

[1] See the commentary on that work quoted by Dr. Morris in his edition for the Pâli Text Society, pp. viii–x.

[2] See the opening words of that discourse, No. 20 in the Dîgha, in Grimblot.

[3] See above, pp. 115, 291 of the Pâli.

[4] Compare Thera Gâthâ 283–286.

[5] Her whole story is given, *G*âtaka III, 435 foll.

[6] The account of which is in the Dîgha, No. 21.

[7] In the Khuddaka Pâ*th*a.

[8] In the Sutta Nipâta and Khuddaka Pâ*th*a.

(of India)[1] or in the sixteen principal countries (in them)[2] he stayed, there, as a usual thing, two, three, four, or five hundred, or a thousand, or a hundred thousand, both gods and men, saw face to face the calm, the supreme good, Nirvâ*n*a. And all of those who were gods, O king, were laymen. They had not entered the Order. So these and many other billions of gods, O king,—even while they were yet laymen, living at home, enjoying the pleasures of sense,—saw face to face (realised in themselves) the condition of Peace, the Supreme Good, Nirvâ*n*a[3].'

5. 'If so, venerable Nâgasena,—if laymen, living at home and enjoying the pleasures of sense, can see Nirvâ*n*a,—what purpose then do these extra vows serve? That being so, rather must **[351]** the vows be workers of mischief. For, Nâgasena, if diseases would abate without medicine, what would be the advantage of weakening the body by emetics, by purges, and other like remedies?—if one's enemies could be subdued with one's fists only, where would be the need of swords and spears, of javelins and bows and cross-bows, of maces and of clubs?—if trees could be climbed by clambering up them with the aid of the knots and of the crooked and hollow places in them, of the thorny excrescences and creepers and branches growing on them, what would be the need of going in quest of ladders long and strong?—if sleeping on the bare ground gave

---

[1] That is, Pâ*k*îna, Avanti, and Dakkhi*n*âpatha (say the East, the Upper Ganges Valley, and the Dekkan).

[2] The full list is given in the note at 'Vinâya Texts,' II, 146.

[3] This Buddhist way of looking on the gods as laymen has been already referred to above in the note on p. 20 of the Pâli, I, 32 of the translation.

ease to the limbs[1], why should one seek after fine large beds, soft to the touch?—if one could cross the desert alone, inaccessible though it be, and full of danger and fear, why need one wait for a grand caravan, well armed and well equipped?—if a man were able by his own arms to cross a flowing river, what need he care for firm dykes or boats?—if he could provide board and lodging for himself out of his own property, why should he trouble to do service to others, to flatter with sweet words, to run to and fro?—when he can get water from a natural pool, why should he dig wells and tanks and artificial ponds? And just so, venerable Nâgasena, if laymen, living at home and enjoying the pleasures of sense, can realise in themselves the condition of Peace, the Supreme Good, Nirvâ*n*a, what is the need of taking upon oneself these vows?'

6. 'There are, O king, these twenty-eight good qualities in the vows, virtues really inherent in them; and on account of these all the Buddhas alike have longed for them and held them dear. And what are the twenty-eight? The keeping of the vows, O king, implies a mode of livelihood without evil, it has a blissful calm as its fruit, it avoids blame, it works no harm to others, it is free from danger, it brings no trouble on others, it is certain to bring with it growth in goodness, it wastes not away, it deludes not, it is in itself a protection[2], it works the satisfaction of desires and the taming of all beings, it is good for self-

[1] Dhâtu-samatâ, for which Hînan-kumburê (p. 511) has Dhâtu-samanaya.

[2] Hînan-kumburê, p. 512, takes ârakkhâ-patthitadada*m* as one compound.

control, it is appropriate[1], (he who keeps the vows) is self-dependent[2], is emancipated[3], the keeping of them is the destruction of lust, and of malice, and of dullness; it is the pulling away of pride, the cutting off of evil thoughts, the removal of doubts, the suppression of sloth, the putting away of discontent; it is long-suffering, its merit is beyond weight, and its virtue beyond measure, and it is the path that leads to the end of every grief. These, O king, are the twenty-eight good qualities in the vows; **[352]** and it is on account of these that all the Buddhas alike have longed for them and held them dear.

7. 'And whosoever, O king, thoroughly carry out the vows, they become completely endowed with eighteen good qualities. What are these eighteen? Their walk is pure, their path is accomplished, well guarded are they in deed and word, altogether pure are they in manners and in mind, their zeal flags not, all their fears are allayed, all delusions (as to the permanence and as to the degree) of their individuality have been put away, anger has died away while love (to all beings)[4] has arisen in their hearts, in taking nourishment they eat it with the three right views regarding food[5], they are honoured of

[1] Pa*t*irûpam, probably 'to the life of a recluse,' but the Sim*h*alese takes it to mean 'to the doctrine' (sâsana).

[2] Anissita*m*. See the note above on the translation of p. 321 of the Pâli. 'Independent of craving' (t*r*ish*n*â), says the Sim*h*alese.

[3] Vippamutta*m*. Of t*r*ish*n*â, says the Sim*h*alese again.

[4] Mettâ, which always has the connotation. Hîna*t*i-kumburê accordingly renders it sakala-satwayan kerehi maitreya.

[5] Âhâro pari*ññ*âto. The three right views are, 1 as to its nature, 2 as to its impurity, 3 as to the lust of taste.

all men, they are temperate in eating, they are full of watchfulness, they need no home, wheresoever is a pleasant spot there do they dwell, they loathe to do ill, they take delight in solitude, they are in earnest always. These, O king, are the good qualities with which they who carry out the vows are completely endowed.

8. 'And these ten, O king, are the individuals worthy of those advantages inherent in the vows—the man full of faith, ashamed to do wrong, full of courage, void of hypocrisy, master of himself, not unstable[1], desirous to learn, glad to undertake the task that is hard, not easy to take offence, of a loving heart. These, O king, are the ten individuals worthy of those advantages inherent in the vows.

9. 'And all they, O king, who as laymen, living at home and in the enjoyment of the pleasures of sense, realise in themselves the condition of Peace, the Supreme Good, Nirvâ*n*a,—all they had in former births accomplished their training, laid the foundation, in the practice of the thirteen vows, had purified their walk and conduct by means of them; and so now, even as laymen, living at home and in the enjoyment of the pleasures of sense, do they realise in themselves the condition of Peace, the Supreme Good, Nirvâ*n*a. Just, O king, as a clever archer first in regular succession teaches his pupils at the training ground the different kinds of bows, the manner of holding the bow up, and of keeping it in a firm grasp, and of bending the fingers, and of planting the feet, and of taking up the arrow, and of placing it on

[1] Alolo, 'not greedy after the four requisites of a recluse,' says the Si*m*halese, p. 514.

the string, and of drawing it back, and of restraining it, and of aiming at the mark, and thus of hitting[1] a man of straw, or targets made of the *Khanaka* plant[2], or of grass, or of straw, or of masses of clay, or of shields[3]—and after that, introducing them to the service of the king, he gains the reward of high-bred chargers and chariots and elephants and horses and money and corn and red gold and slave girls and slaves and wives and lands. **[353]** Just so, O king, all they who as laymen, living at home in the enjoyment of the pleasures of sense, realise in themselves the condition of Peace, the Supreme Good, Nirvâ*n*a,—all they had in former births accomplished their training, laid the foundation, in the practice of the thirteen vows, had purified their walk and conduct by means of them; and so now, even as laymen, and living at home in the enjoyment of the pleasures of sense, do they realise in themselves the condition of Peace, the Supreme Good, Nirvâ*n*a.

10. 'And there is no realisation of Arahatship, O king, in one single life, without a previous keeping of the vows. Only on the utmost zeal and the most devoted practice of righteousness, and with the aid of a suitable teacher, is the realisation of Arahatship attained. Just, O king, as a doctor or surgeon first procures for himself a teacher, either by the payment of a fee or by the performance of service, and then

[1] Vedhe. I follow Mr. Trenckner, but the Si*m*halese translation is based on the reading Vede.

[2] The Si*m*halese takes this word in composition with the following ti*n*a and spells it *G*anakaya. Compare *K*a*n*aka, 'a chick pea.'

[3] Phalaka. But Hîna*t*i-kumburê, p. 514, takes it in the technical sense of a kind of rough roller, made of the wood apple tree (dimbul porû), and used for levelling rice-fields.

thoroughly trains himself in holding the lancet, in cutting, marking, or piercing with it, in extracting darts, in cleansing wounds, in causing them to dry up, in the application of ointments, in the administration of emetics and purges and oily enemas, and only when he has thus gone through training, served his apprenticeship, made himself skilful, does he visit the sick to heal them. Just so, O king, all they who as laymen, living at home in the enjoyment of the pleasures of sense, realise in themselves the condition of Peace, the Supreme Good, Nirvâ*n*a,—all they had in former births accomplished their training, laid the foundation, in the practice of the thirteen vows, had purified their walk and conduct by means of them; and so now, even as laymen, and living at home in the enjoyment of the pleasures of sense, do they realise in themselves the condition of Peace, the Supreme Good, Nirvâ*n*a.

11. 'And there is no perception of the truth to those who are not purified by the virtues that depend on the keeping of the vows. Just as without water no seed will grow, so can there be no perception of the truth to those not purified by the practice of the vows. Just as there is no rebirth in bliss to those who have done no meritorious actions, no beautiful deeds, so is there no perception of the truth for those not purified by the practice of the vows.

12. 'Like the broad earth, O king, is the character resulting from the keeping of the vows, to serve as a basis to those who desire to be pure[1]. Like water is it, O king, to wash away the stain of all things

[1] Visuddhi-kâmânam, which Hîna*t*i-kumburê characteristically renders, 'who desire to attain to Nirvâ*n*a' (p. 516).

evil in those who desire to be pure. Like the fire is it, O king, to burn out the lust of all evil in those who desire to be pure [354]. Like the wind is it, O king, to carry away the dust of all evil in those desiring to be pure. Like medicine is it, O king, to allay the disease of evil in those desiring to be pure. Like ambrosia is it, O king, to act as an antidote to the poison of evil in those desiring to be pure. Like arable land is it, O king, on which to grow the crop of all the virtues of renunciation to those desiring to be pure. Like a wishing-gem[1] is it, O king, for conferring all the high attainments they long and crave for upon those who desire to be pure. Like a boat is it, O king, for carrying to the further shore of the mighty ocean of transmigration all those who desire to be pure. Like a place of refuge is it, O king, where those who desire to be pure can be safe from the fear of old age and death. Like a mother is it, O king, to comfort those who desire to be pure when afflicted with the sorrows of sin. Like a father is it, O king, to raise up in those who desire to be pure and to increase in goodness all the good qualities of those who have renounced the world Like a friend is it, O king, in not disappointing those who desire to be pure in their search after the good qualities of those who have renounced the world. Like a lotus flower, O king, is it, in not being tarnished by the stain of evil. Like costly perfume (of saffron and of jasmine and the Turkish incense and the Greek)[2]

[1] Manoharo. Childers does not give this meaning to the word, but it is confirmed by the passages above and below, pp. 118, 358 of the Pâli, and by the Si*m*halese.

[2] *K*atu-*g*âtiya-gandho. The two last are Yavana and Tarukkha. Böhtlingk-Roth explain both as Olibanum. Our

is it, O king, for counteracting the bad odour of evil for those who desire to be pure. Like a lofty mountain range is it, O king, for protecting those who desire to be pure from the onslaught of the winds of the eight conditions to which men are subject in this world (gain and loss, and fame and dishonour, and praise and blame, and happiness and woe)[1]. Like the space of heaven is it, O king, in the freedom from all obstruction, in the magnitude, in the great expanse and breadth it gives to those who desire to be pure. Like a stream is it, O king, in washing away for those who desire to be pure the stain of all evil. Like a guide is it, O king, in bringing safe out of the desert of rebirths, out of the jungle of lusts and sins, those who desire to be pure. Like a mighty caravan is it, O king, for bringing those who desire to be pure safe into that most blessed city of Nirvâ*n*a, peaceful and calm, where no fear dwells. **[355]** Like a well-polished spotless mirror is it, O king, for showing to those who desire to be pure the true nature of the constituent elements of all beings. Like a shield is it, O king, for warding off from those who desire to be pure the clubs and the arrows and the swords of evil dispositions. Like a sunshade is it, O king, for warding off from those who desire to be pure the scorching heat of the threefold fire[2]. Like

author does not give the details, but it is unlikely that he meant other perfumes than those usually comprised in the term 'perfume of four kinds.' The expression is not found in the Pi*t*akas, though it occurs in Buddhaghosa; and its use by our author may help to settle his date when we know its history, and the exact composition of the two foreign perfumes it includes.

[1] The eight Loka-dhammas.

[2] That is, of lust, malice, and dullness—that fire the 'going out' of which (in one's heart) is Nirvâ*n*a.

the moon is it, O king, as being longed and hoped for by those who desire to be pure. Like the sun is it, O king, as dispelling the blackness of the darkness of ignorance for those who desire to be pure. Like the ocean is it, O king, as causing to arise in those desiring to be pure the costly treasures of the virtues of those who have renounced the world, and by reason too of its immensity, of its being beyond measure and beyond count.

13. 'Thus is it, O king, of great service to those desiring to be pure, a remover of all sorrow and lamentation, an antidote to discontent; it puts an end to fear, and individuality, and imperviousness of mind; to evil, and to grief, and to pain, and to lust, and to malice, and to dullness, and to pride, and to heresy, and to all wrong dispositions; it brings with it honour and advantage and bliss; it fills them with ease and with love and with peace of mind; it is free from blame; it has happiness here as its fruit; it is a mine and treasure of goodness that is beyond measure and beyond count, costly above all things, and precious.

14. 'Just, O king, as men for nourishment seek after food, for health medicine, for assistance a friend, for crossing water a boat, for pleasant odours a perfume, for security a place of refuge, for support the earth, for instruction a teacher, for honours a king, and for whatever they desire a wishing-gem—just so, O king, do the Arahats seek after the virtues of the keeping of the vows for the attainment of all the advantages of renunciation of the world.

15. 'And what water is for the growth of seeds, [**356**] what fire is for burning, what food is for giving strength, what a creeper is for tying things up, what

a sword is for cutting, what water is for allaying thirst, what a treasure is for giving confidence, what a boat is for crossing to the further shore, what medicine is for allaying disease, what a carriage is for journeying at ease, what a place of refuge is for appeasing fear, what a king is for protection, what a shield is for warding off the blows of sticks and stakes, of clubs, of arrows, and of darts, what a teacher is for instruction, what a mother is for nourishing, what a mirror is for seeing, what a jewel is for ornament, what a dress is for clothing, what a ladder is for mounting up, what a pair of scales is for comparison[1], what a charm is for repetition, what a weapon is for warding off scorn, what a lamp is for dissipating darkness, what a breeze is for allaying fever, what knowledge of an art is for the accomplishment of business, what medicinal drugs are for the preservation of life, what a mine is for the production of jewels, what a gem is for ornament, what a command is for preventing transgression, what sovranty is for dominion—all that, O king, is the character-that-comes-of-keeping-the-vows for the good growth of the seed of renunciation, for the burning out of the stains of evil, for giving the strength of Iddhi, for tying up one's self in self-control and presence of mind, for the complete cutting off of doubt and mistrust, for allaying the thirst of craving, for giving confidence as to perception of the truth, for crossing to the further shore of the fourfold stream (of sensuality, individuality, delusion, and ignorance), for allaying the disease of evil dis-

[1] Nikkhepana; not in Childers, but compare Sa*m*yutta Nikâya XX, 22, 6.

positions, for attaining to the bliss of Nirvâ*n*a, for appeasing the fears that arise from birth, old age, decay and death, grief, pain, lamentation, woe, and despair, for being protected in the possession of the advantages of renunciation, for warding off discontent and evil thoughts, for instruction in all the good involved in the life of those who have renounced the world, for nourishment therein, for explaining to men quietude and insight, and the path and the fruits thereof and Nirvâ*n*a, for bestowing upon men a costly ornament high in the praise and admiration of the world, for closing the doors of all evil states, for mounting up to the peaks of the mountain heights of renunciation, for distinguishing crooked and cunning and evil intentions in others, for the proper recitation of those qualities which ought to be practised and those which ought not, for warding off as one's enemies all evil dispositions, for dissipating the darkness of ignorance, for allaying the fever arising from the scorching of the threefold fire, for the accomplishment of the attainment of the Condition of Peace—so gentle and so subtle,—for the protection of the virtues of the life of a recluse, for the production of the precious jewels of the sevenfold wisdom—self-possession, investigation of the truth, energy, joy, calm contemplation, and serenity,—for the adornment of the recluses, for the prevention of any transgression against that blameless, abstruse, delicate bliss **[357]** that comes of peace, for dominion over all the qualities that recluses and Arahats affect. Thus, O king, is it that keeping the vows is one and the same thing as attaining to all these qualities. And the advantage thereof, O king, cannot be weighed, neither measured; it has no equal, no rival, no superior, great is it and glorious, extensive and abundant, deep and broad, and large and wide, full of weight and worth and might.

16. 'And whosoever, O king, having evil cravings in his heart, being hypocritical, greedy, a slave to his stomach[1], seeking after material gain or worldly fame and glory, unfit (for the outward signs of Arahatship), not having reached the attainments, whose conduct is inconsistent (with membership in the Order), unworthy of it, inappropriate to it—whosoever being such shall take upon himself the vows, he shall incur a twofold punishment, suffering the loss of the good that may be in him. For in this world he shall receive disgrace, and scorn[2], and blame, and ridicule, and suspension, and excommunication[3], and expulsion, and he shall be outcast, rejected, dismissed; and in his next life he shall suffer torment in the great Avîki purgatory that is a hundred leagues in depth, and covered, as with a garland, with hot and scorching, fierce and fiery blazing flames; therein shall he rise and fall for myriads of years, upwards and downwards and across,—a foam-bubble, as it were, cast up and thrown from side to side in a boiling sea[4]. And, when released from thence, then as a mighty Preta (ghost), in the outward form of a monk, but with

[1] Odarika; not in Childers, and only found as yet at this passage and at the Thera Gâthâ, verse 101. It is the Sanskrit audarika. 'Who enters the Order for the sake of his stomach' says the Simhalese, p. 521.

[2] Khîlanam. Compare khîlito above, pp. 229, 288 of the Pâli.

[3] Compare the rules at *K*ullavagga I, 25, 1, &c.

[4] On Phen-uddehakam compare *G*âtaka III, 46; on samparivattakam above, p. 253 of the Pâli.

body and limbs lean and rugged and dark, with head swollen[1], bloated, and full of holes, hungry and thirsty, odd and dreadful in colour and form, his ears all torn, and his eyes ever winking, his limbs a mass of mortifying sores[2], his whole body the prey of maggots, his stomach all scorching and hot like a fiery furnace blazing in the breeze, yet with a mouth no larger than a needle so that his thirst can never cease, with no place of refuge to fly to, no protector to help him, groaning and weeping and crying out for mercy, shall he wander wailing o'er the earth!

17. 'Just, O king, as whosoever, being unfit for royalty, without having properly attained to it, being inappropriate to it, unworthy of it, unsuitable for it, a low-born man and base in lineage, should receive the consecration of a king, he would suffer mutilation, having his hands or his feet, or his hands and feet cut off, or his ears or his nose, or his ears and nose cut off, [358] or he would be tortured, being subjected to the Gruel Pot, or to the Chank Crown, or to the Râhu's Mouth, or to the Fire Garland, or to the Hand Torch, or to the Snake Strips, or to the Bark Dress, or to the Spotted Antelope, or to the Flesh Hooks, or to the Pennies, or to the Brine Slits, or to the Bar Turn, or to the Straw Seat[3], or he would be anointed with boiling oil, or be eaten by dogs, or be impaled alive, or be beheaded, or be subjected to punishments of various kinds. And why? Because he being unfit for it, without having properly attained to it, being inappropriate to it, unworthy of it, unsuitable for it, a low-born man

[1] Sûna (for sûna). See *K*ullavagga X, 1, 2, 3.

[2] Aru-gatto pakka-gatto. See Ma*gg*h*ima Nikâya I, 506.

[3] On all these see the notes above, I, 276, 277.

and base in lineage, he had placed himself in the seat of sovranty, and thus transgressed beyond his right limits. Just so, O king, whosoever having evil cravings in his heart, being hypocritical, greedy, a slave to his stomach, seeking after material gain or worldly fame and glory, unfit (for the outward signs of Arahatship), not having reached the attainments, whose conduct is inconsistent (with membership in the Order), unworthy of it, inappropriate to it—whosoever being such shall take upon himself the vows, he shall incur a twofold punishment, suffering the loss of the good that may be in him. For in this world he shall receive disgrace, and scorn, and blame, and ridicule, and suspension, and excommunication, and expulsion, and he shall be outcast, rejected, dismissed; and in his next life he shall suffer torment in the great Avî*k*i purgatory that is a hundred leagues in depth, and covered, as with a garland, with hot and scorching, fierce and fiery blazing flames; therein shall he rise and fall for myriads of years, upwards and downwards and across,—a foam-bubble, as it were, cast up and thrown from side to side in a boiling sea. And, when released from thence, then as a mighty Preta (ghost), in the outward form of a monk, but with body and limbs lean and rugged and dark, with head swollen, bloated, and full of holes, hungry and thirsty, odd and dreadful in colour and form, his ears all torn, and his eyes ever winking, his limbs a mass of mortifying sores, his whole body the prey of maggots, his stomach all scorching and hot like a fiery furnace blazing in the breeze, yet with a mouth no larger than a needle so that his thirst can never cease, with no place of refuge to fly to, no protector to help him, groaning and weeping and crying out for mercy, shall he wander wailing o'er the earth!

18. 'But whosoever, O king, is fit, who has reached the attainments, whose conduct is consistent with membership in the Order, who is worthy of it, appropriate to it, who desires little and is content, given to seclusion, not fond of society, alert in zeal, resolute of heart, without guile, without deceit, not a slave to his stomach, seeking neither material gain nor worldly fame or glory, full of faith, who has entered the Order from belief (in the doctrine, and not from worldly motives), and is full of desire for release from old age and death—whosoever being such shall take upon himself the vows with the idea of upholding the faith, he is deserving of twofold honour. For he is near and dear to, loved and longed for by both gods and men, dear as rare jasmine flowers to the man bathed and anointed, as sweet food to the hungry, as cool, clear, fragrant water to the thirsty, as a healing drug to a poisoned man, as a costly chariot drawn by high-bred steeds to the hurrying traveller, as a wishing-gem to the greedy for gain, as the pure white sunshade of sovranty to one ambitious for a throne, as the blessed attainment of the fruits of Arahatship to the seeker after holiness. It is he who attains to the fullest mastery over the four Earnest Meditations, the fourfold Great Struggle, the four Roads to Saintship, the five Organs of the moral sense, the five moral Powers, the seven forms of Wisdom, and the Noble Eightfold Path[1], quietude and insight reign in his heart, attainment

[1] For the details of these constituent elements of Arahatship, see my note in 'Buddhist Suttas,' pp. 60–63.

through study becomes easy to him, and the four fruits of the life of a recluse[1], [359] the four kinds of Discrimination[2], the threefold Knowledge[3], the sixfold higher Wisdom[4], in a word, the whole religion of the recluses becomes his very own, an anointed king is he, and over him is borne the pure white sunshade of emancipation!

19. 'Just, O king, as all the citizens and country folk in the land, the soldiers and the peons (royal messengers), wait in service upon a Kshatriya king, born to the purple, and on both sides of lineage high, when he has been consecrated with the inauguration ceremonies of the Kshatriyas[5]; the thirty-eight divisions of the royal retinue, and the dancing men, and acrobats, and the soothsayers[6],

---

[1] These are the four stages of the path to Arahatship.

[2] Pa*t*isambhidâ—in worldly things, and in religion, in intuitive knowledge, and in exposition.

[3] Tisso Vi*gg*â. One explanation of this term is the knowledge of the three limitations of individuality,—its impermanence, the pain involved in the struggle to maintain it, and the absence of any permanent principle (any soul) in any individual. But it is also explained in the Aṅguttara Nikâya III, 58, as meaning the knowledge firstly of one's own former births, secondly of other people's former births, and thirdly of the nature, the origin, and the right method of subduing sorrow and the âsavas (that is, lust, individuality, delusion, and ignorance). The first triplet is identical with the three lakkha*n*as, the second with the last three of the Dasabalas, the ten powers of a Buddha. So in the Sutta Vibhaṅga (Pârâ*g*ika I, 1–8) the last of these three is called tatiyâ vi*gg*a. Compare also 'Buddhist Suttas,' p. 162.

[4] The Abhi*ññ*âs.

[5] Some details of this are given in the Si*m*halese, p. 524.

[6] Mukha-maṅgalikâ, which the Si*m*halese repeats, and which apparently means 'panegyrists.' The exact connotation of both these terms has yet to be settled. So*tth*i vâ*k*akâ may correspond with the people who throw rice after a departing wedding pair;

and the heralds [1], and Samanas and Brahmans, and the followers of every sect, frequent his court, and he becomes the lord of every seaport, and treasure-mine, and town, and custom-house [2]—giving instructions as to the fate of every foreigner and criminal [3]—just so, O king, whoever is fit, who has reached the attainments, whose conduct is consistent with membership in the Order, who is worthy of it, appropriate to it, who desires little and is content, given to seclusion, not fond of society, alert in zeal, resolute of heart, without guile, without deceit, not a slave to his stomach, seeking neither material gain nor worldly fame or glory, full of faith, who has entered the Order from belief (in the doctrine, and not from worldly motives), and is full of desire for release from old age and

---

and Mukha-mangalikâ may be those who prophesy the lucky days on which a thing is to be commenced. But this is the only passage in which the phrases occur in Pâli, and in Sanskrit we have only much later authorities. See the Commentary on Sakuntalâ, quoted in the note on p. 152 of Sir M. Monier-Williams's edition, and Wilson's explanation in his Sanskrit Dictionary of swasti-vakânâ.

[1] Sotthi-vâkakâ, 'utterers of blessing.' The Simhalese has sôbhana-vâkanikayo (perhaps 'augurs').

[2] Sunkatthâna, 'taxing-place.' But the Simhalese, p. 524, has only samasthâna.

[3] I can only guess at the meaning of this enigmatical phrase, which the Simhalese again merely repeats, but a precisely similar passage occurs in the Sumangala Vilâsinî, p. 246; and though the exact course of proceedings in the ancient law courts of India is still, in many details, uncertain, it is yet clear that the actual apportionment of punishment (as well as the execution of it) was always held to be the sole prerogative of the king. This was more especially the case where mutilation or a death sentence was concerned. Minor punishments the judges could, no doubt, order without reference to the king. See Jolly, 'Beiträge zur indischen Rechts-geschichte,' in the 'Zeitschrift der deutschen morg. Gesellschaft,' 1890, pp. 344 foll.

death—whosoever being such shall take upon himself the vows with the idea of upholding the faith, he is deserving of twofold honour. For he is near and dear to, loved and longed for by both gods and men, dear as rare jasmine flowers to the man bathed and anointed, as sweet food to the hungry, as cool, clear, fragrant water to the thirsty, as a healing drug to a poisoned man, as a costly chariot drawn by high-bred steeds to the hurrying traveller, as a wishing-gem to the greedy for gain, as the pure white sunshade of sovranty to one ambitious for a throne, as the blessed attainment of the fruits of Arahatship to the seeker after holiness. It is he who attains to the fullest mastery over the four Earnest Meditations, the fourfold Great Struggle, the four Roads to Saintship, the five Organs of the moral sense, the five moral Powers, the seven forms of Wisdom, and the Noble Eightfold Path, quietude and insight reign in his heart, attainment through study becomes easy to him, and the four fruits of the life of a recluse, the four kinds of Discrimination, the threefold Knowledge, the sixfold higher Wisdom, in a word, the whole religion of the recluses becomes his very own, an anointed king is he, and over him is borne the pure white sunshade of emancipation!

20. 'Such, O king, are the thirteen vows purified by which a man shall bathe in the mighty waters of Nirvâ*n*a, and there indulge himself, as one sporting in the waves, with the manifold delights of religion, he shall addict himself to the eight modes of transcendental ecstacy, he shall acquire the powers of Iddhi, distant sounds, human and divine, shall greet his ear, he shall divine the thoughts of others, he

shall be able to call to mind his own previous births, and to watch the rise and fall from birth to birth of others, and he shall perceive the real nature and the origin of, he shall perceive the means of escape from sorrow, and from lust, individuality, delusion, and ignorance, the stains of life!

'And what are these thirteen? Wearing raiment made up of pieces taken from a dust-heap—Wearing three robes, and three robes only—Living on food received by begging—Begging straight on from house to house—Eating only once a day, at one sitting—Eating from one vessel only—Refusing food in excess of the regulations—Dwelling in the woods—Dwelling at the root of a tree—Dwelling in the open air—Dwelling in or near a cemetery—Not altering the mat or bed when it has once been spread out to sleep on—and sleeping in a sitting posture. It is he, O king, who, in former births, has undertaken and practised, followed and carried out, observed, framed his conduct according to, and fulfilled these thirteen vows, who acquires all the results of the life of a recluse, and all its ecstacy of peace and bliss becomes his very own[1].

---

[1] The Si*m*halese, pp. 525–531, goes at great length into the details of all these vows, each of which it divides into stages of greater or less severity, specifying the practice to be followed in each stage. As a matter of fact the members of the Buddhist Order have not observed them in any completeness. Like the Buddha himself, the majority have undertaken only the second of the thirteen—the wearing of three robes; and the others have only been occasionally practised, and then usually only one or more at a time, by isolated members. It is true that the *G*âtaka Commentary (Fausböll, vol. ii, p. 449) says that Upasena Vangantaputta kept the whole thirteen of the Dhutaṅgas. But this is at variance with the older text (in the Vinaya, Nissaggiya, No. XV) giving that account of the same episode on which the story in the

21. 'Just, O king, as a shipowner who has become wealthy by constantly levying freight in some seaport town, will be able to traverse the high seas, and go to Vanga, or Takkola, or China, or Sovîra, or Surat, or Alexandria, or the Koromandel coast, or Further India, or any other place where ships do congregate—just so, O king, [360] it is he who in former births has undertaken and practised, followed and carried out, observed, framed his conduct according to, and fulfilled these thirteen vows, who acquires all the results of the life of a recluse, and all its ecstacy of peace and bliss becomes his very own.

22. 'And just, O king, as a husbandman will first remove the defects in the soil—weeds, and thorns, and stones—and then by ploughing, and sowing,

---

*G*âtaka Commentary is based. The thirteen vows are not referred to at all in the rules of the Order, as translated in the three volumes of the Vinaya Texts, nor are they mentioned as a whole in any Pi*t*aka text yet published. But the thirteen names are given together in a different order in a passage twice repeated in the Parivâra, a late book, probably written in Ceylon (pp. 131, 193). It is there declared of each of the thirteen vows that five sorts of people undertake them—those who do so from stupidity, those who do so from vain desire, those who are mad, those who do so because the vows have been exalted by the Buddhas and their followers, those who do so from high motives. It is clear therefore that our author's doctrine of the thirteen Dhutangas is at variance with primitive Buddhism. It would require, however, a separate note on each of the thirteen to show the exact degree of this variance. The basis on which each of these observances rests can be found in the older teaching, and nearly all of them have been praised or followed, in a greater or less degree, from very early times,—not indeed as general rules binding on all members of the Order, but as supplementary or extra vows, conducive, but subsidiary to the ethical self-culture of the Arahat.

and irrigating, and fencing, and watching, and reaping, and grinding, will become the owner of much flour, and so the lord of whosoever are poor and needy, reduced to beggary and misery—just so, O king, it is he who in former births has undertaken and practised, followed and carried out, observed, framed his conduct according to, and fulfilled these thirteen vows, who acquires all the results of the life of a recluse, and all its ecstacy of peace and bliss becomes his very own.

23. 'And again, O king, just as an anointed monarch is master over the treatment of outlaws, is an independent ruler and lord, and does whatsoever he desires, and all the broad earth is subject to him—just so, O king, is he who has undertaken, practised, and fulfilled in former births these vows, master, ruler, and lord in the religion of the Conquerors, and all the virtues of the Sama*n*as are his.

24. 'And was not Upasena, the Elder, he of the sons of the Vangantas[1], from his having thoroughly practised all the purifying merits of the vows, able to neglect the agreement arrived at by the members of the Order resident at Sâvatthi, and to visit with his attendant brethren the Subduer of men, then retired into solitude, and when he had bowed down before him, to take his seat respectfully aside? And when the Blessed One saw how well trained his retinue was, then, delighted and glad and exalted in heart, he greeted them with courteous words, and said in his unbroken beautiful voice:

"Most pleasant, Upasena, is the deportment of

[1] According to the Si*m*halese this was a Brahman clan. But the derivation suggests the borders of Bengal, where it is somewhat strange to find Brahmans so early.

these brethren waiting upon you. How have you managed thus to train your followers?"

'And he, when so questioned by the omniscient Buddha, the god over all gods, spake thus to the Blessed One as to the real reason for the goodness of their nature: "Whosoever, Lord, may come to me to ask for admission to the Order or to become my disciple, to him do I say [361]: 'I, Sir, am a frequenter of the woods, who gain my food by begging, and wear but this robe pieced together from cast-off rags. If you will be the same, I can admit you to the Order and make you my disciple.' Then, if he agree thereto with joy, and abase himself[1], I thereupon admit him to the Order and to the company of my pupils. But if not, then neither do I admit him to the one nor to the other. Thus is it, Lord, that I train them[2]." And thus is it, O king, that he who has taken upon himself the vows becomes master, ruler, and lord in the religion of the Conquerors; and all its ecstacy of peace and bliss becomes his very own.

25. 'Just, O king, as a lotus flower of glorious, pure, and high descent and origin is glossy, soft, desirable, sweet-smelling, longed for, loved, and praised, untarnished by the water or the mud, graced with tiny petals and filaments and pericarps, the resort of many bees, a child of the clear cold

---

[1] Oramati. See *G*âtaka I, 492, where it is also used intransitively in the sense of 'abase oneself;' and *G*âtaka I, 498, where it is transitive, 'to lower' (the water in the ocean). But Hîna*t*i-kumburê, p. 533, has simply œlêda, 'and adheres thereto.'

[2] As remarked in the note, p. 268, this episode is taken from the introduction to the 15th Nissaggiya.

stream—just so is that disciple of the Noble Ones who in former births has undertaken and practised, followed and carried out, observed and framed his conduct according to, and fulfilled these thirteen vows, endowed with the thirty graces. And what are the thirty? His heart is full of affectionate, soft, and tender love, evil is killed, destroyed, cast out from within him, pride and self-righteousness are put an end to and cast down, stable and strong and established and undeviating is his faith, he enters into the enjoyment of the heart's refreshment, the highly praised and desirable peace and bliss of the ecstacies of contemplation fully felt, he exhales the most excellent and unequalled sweet savour of righteousness of life, near is he and dear to gods and men alike, exalted by the best of beings the Arahat Noble Ones themselves, gods and men delight to honour him, the enlightened, wise, and learned approve, esteem, appreciate, and praise him, untarnished is he by the love either of this world or the next[1], he sees the danger in the smallest tiniest offence, rich is he in the best of wealth—the wealth that is the fruit of the Path, the wealth of those who are seeking the highest of the attainments,—he is partaker of the best of the four requisites of a recluse that may be obtained by asking, he lives without a home addicted to that best austerity that is dependent on the meditation of the *Gh*ânas, **[362]** he has unravelled the whole net of evil, he has broken and burst through, doubled up and utterly destroyed both the possibility of rebirth in any of the five future states, and the five obstacles to the

[1] Compare 'Buddhist Suttas,' p. 10, and the note there.

higher life in this one (lust, malice, sloth, pride, and doubt), unalterable in character, excellent in conduct [1], transgressing none of the rules as to the four requisites of a recluse, he is set free from rebirths, he has passed beyond all perplexity, his mind is set upon complete emancipation, he has seen the truth [2], the sure and stedfast place of refuge from all fear has he gained, the seven evil inclinations (to lust, and malice, and heresy, and doubt, and pride, and desire for future life, and ignorance) are rooted out in him, he has reached the end of the Great Evils (lust, individuality, delusion, and ignorance), he abounds in the peace and the bliss of the ecstacies of contemplation, he is endowed with all the virtues a recluse should have. These, O king, are the thirty graces he is adorned withal.

26. 'And was not Sâriputta, the Elder, O king, the best man in the whole ten thousand world systems, the Teacher of the world himself alone excepted? And he who through endless ages had heaped up merit, and had been reborn in a Brahman family, relinquished all the delights of the pleasures of sense, and gave up boundless wealth [3], to enter the Order according to the teaching of the Conqueror, and having restrained his actions, words, and thoughts by these thirteen vows, became in this life of such exalted virtue that he was the one who, after the Master, set rolling on the royal chariot-

[1] Abhinîta-vâso, 'having the ten ariya-vâsas,' says the Simhalese.

[2] Di*tth*a-dhammo, 'seen the Four Truths,' says the Simhalese, p. 535.

[3] For saṅkha Hîna*t*i-kumburê has sahassa.

wheel of the kingdom of righteousness in the religion of Gotama, the Blessed One. So that this was said, O king, by the Blessed One, the god over all gods, in that most excellent collection, the Aṅguttara Nikâya[1]:

"I know, O brethren, of no other man who in succession to me sets rolling on the glorious chariot-wheel of the kingdom of righteousness so well as Sâriputta. Sâriputta, O brethren, sets rolling that wheel the best of all."'

'Most excellent, Nâgasena! The whole ninefold word of the Buddha, the most exalted conduct, the highest and best of the attainments to be gained in the world,—all these are wrapped up together in the virtues that result from the keeping of the vows.'

Here ends the Ninth Chapter[2].

Here ends the Solving of Puzzles.

[1] Aṅguttara I, 13, 7.

[2] The ninth, because the numbering of the Vaggas is carried on from the last book. But according to the divisions enumerated at the beginning of the work (translated at p. 4 of the previous volume) it is one of the principal divisions of the book that is here closed, and the chapters ought not to run on.

BOOK VII.

OPAMMA-KATHÂ-PAÑHO.

THE SIMILES.

CHAPTER 1.

1. [363] 'Venerable Nâgasena, with how many qualities must a member of the Order (a Bhikshu) be endowed to realise Arahatship?'

'The brother, O king, who wishes to attain Arahatship must take:—

1.	One quality of the ass	VII, 1, 2
2.	And five of the cock	3
3.	And one of the squirrel	8
4.	And one of the female panther	9
5.	And two of the male panther	10
6.	And five of the tortoise	12
7.	And one of the bamboo	17
8.	And one of the bow	18
9.	And two of the crow	19
10.	And two of the monkey	21
11.	And one of the gourd	VII, 2, 1
12.	And three of the lotus	2
13.	And two of seed	5
14.	And one of the Sal-tree	7
15.	And three of a ship	8
16.	And two of the anchor	11
17.	And one of the mast	13
18.	And three of the pilot	14
19.	And one of the sailor	17
20.	And five of the ocean	18
21.	And five of the earth	VII, 3, 1

22. And five of water . . . . VII, 3, 6
23. And five of fire 11
24. And five of wind 16
25. And five of rock 21
26. And five of space 26
27. And five of the moon 31
28. And seven of the sun 36
29. And three of Sakka 43
30. And four of a sovran overlord . . 46
31. And one of the white ant . . VII, 4, 1
32. And two of the cat 2
33. And one of the rat 4
34. And one of the scorpion 5
35. And one of the mungoose . . . 6
36. [364] And two of the old jackal . . 7
37. And three of the deer 9
38. And four of the bull 12
39. And two of the boar 16
40. And five of the elephant . . . 18
41. And seven of the lion . . . VII, 5, 1
42. And three of the *K*akravâka bird . . 8
43. And two of the Pe*n*âhikâ bird . . 11
44. And one of the house-pigeon . . . 13
45. And two of the owl 14
46. And one of the crane 16
47. And two of the bat 17
48. And one of the leech 19
49. And three of the serpent . . . 20
50. And one of the rock-snake . . . 23
51. And one of the road spider . . VII, 6, 1
52. And one of the child at the breast . . 2
53. And one of the land tortoise . . . 3
54. And five of the mountain height . . 4
55. And three of the tree 9

56. And five of the rain-cloud . VII, 6, 12
57. And three of the jewel 17
58. And four of the hunter 20
59. And two of the fisherman . . . 24
60. And two of the carpenter . . . 26
61. And one of the waterpot . . VII, 7, 1
62. And two of iron 2
63. And three of a sunshade . . . 4
64. And three of a rice field 7
65. And two of medicine 10
66. And three of food 12
67. And four of the archer[1] 15

And four of the king.
And two of the doorkeeper.
And one of a grindstone.
And two of a lamp.
And two of the peacock.
And two of the steed.
And two of the publican.
And two of a threshold.
And one of a balance.
And two of a sword.
And two of a fish.
[365] And one of a borrower.
And two of a sick man.
And two of a corpse.
And two of a river.
And one of a buffalo.
And two of a road.
And one of a tax-gatherer.
And three of a thief.

[1] The published text carries the details of these similes no further than this. See the remarks in the Introduction, pp. xxiv, xxv.

And one of the hawk.
And one of the dog.
And three of the physician.
And two of a woman with child.
And one of the yak cow.
And two of the hen.
And three of the dove.
And two of the one-eyed man.
And three of the husbandman.
And one of the female jackal [1].
And two of the dyers' straining-cloth [2].
And one of a spoon.
And one of the negociator of a loan.
And one of a collector.
And two of a charioteer.
And two of a village headman.
And one of a tailor.
And one of a helmsman.
And two of a bee.'

Here ends the Table of Contents.

---

[1] *G*ambuka-sigâliyâ. In *G*âtaka, No. 294, of Fausböll, the jackal is male. The reference therefore here is to a kind of jackal named after the *G*ambu fruit.

[2] *K*aṅgavârakassa. See Ma*ggh*ima Nikâya I, 142-4, and *G*âtaka V, 186, in both of which passages the Burmese MSS. read *k*aṅka-. The Si*m*halese, p. 540, has perahan ka*d*ê.

1. The Ass.

2. 'Venerable Nâgasena, that one quality of the harsh-voiced ass which you say he ought to take, which is that?'

'Just, O king, as the ass, wheresoever he may lie down—whether on a dust heap, or in the open space where four roads meet, or three [1], or at the entrance to a village, or on a heap of straw—**[366]**—nowhere is he given to resting long; just so, O king, should the strenuous Bhikshu, earnest in effort [2], wheresoever he may spread out his mat for repose—whether on strewed grass, or leaves, or on a bed of thorns, or on the bare earth—nowhere should he be given to sloth. This is the one quality of the ass he ought to have. For this has been said, O king, by the Blessed One, the god over all gods:

"Sleeping on pillows of chaff, my disciples, O brethren,
Keep themselves earnest and ardent in strenuous fight [3]."

---

[1] *K*atukke and singhâ*t*ake. I follow Hîna*t*i-kumburê in the distinction he makes between the meaning of these terms—satara and tun ma*m* sandhiyehi (p. 540).

[2] Yogî yogava*k*aro. The rendering of these words is quite inadequate, and has given me much trouble. Neither 'yogee' nor 'devotee' can be used, for they both have acquired connotations contradictory to what was in our author's mind. He means the Buddhist Bhikshu belonging to that class among the Bhikshus (by no means the majority) who had devoted themselves to a life of systematic effort according to the Buddhist scheme of self-training. But I have found it impossible to put into any English phrase sufficiently short for the constant repetition of the two Pâli words any full and accurate representation of all that they imply. See the note above on p. 43 of the Pâli, and *G*âtaka, vol. i, p. 303.

[3] Not traced as yet. Mr. Trenckner prints the passage as

'And this too, O king, was said by Sâriputta, the Elder, the Commander of the Faith:

"If it but raineth not knee-deep on him
When sitting in high meditations plunged—
What cares the man on Arahatship intent for ease[1]!"'

---

2. The Cock.

3. 'Venerable Nâgasena, those five qualities of the cock which you say he ought to take, what are they?'

'Just, O king, as a cock goes early and betimes to roost; so, O king, should the strenuous Bhikshu, earnest in effort, early and betimes sweep out the open space around the Dâgaba, and having got ready[2] the drinking-water for the day's use, and dressed himself[3], and taken his bath, he should bow

---

prose, but it is clearly two verses with a slight corruption in the first line. The point of the verses lies in the untranslateable pun of the words upadhâna, 'pillow,' and padhâna, 'strenuous fight.' The word etarahi seems to me suspect, and some such reading as ka*l*iṅgaropadhânâ va would restore the metre, and at the same time bring the play on the words more into prominence.

[1] This verse is found in the Thera Gâthâ, No. 985. Hîna*ń*-kumburê takes the na in the first line as a negative to abhivassati, and translates, 'So long as it does not rain knee-deep on him, when sitting in meditation, what cares the Bhikshu, who is bent on attaining Nirvâ*n*a, for ease!'—and this is, I think, preferable to Mr. Trenckner's division of the words.

[2] That is, 'filtered;' perahâ nagâ tabâ, says the Si*m*halese, p. 541.

[3] Sarîra*m* pa*t*igaggitvâ, 'rested a little to remove the weariness of his body,' says the Si*m*halese here, but adds below, § 4, siwuru hœnda.

down in reverence before the Dâgaba, and then pay visits to the senior Bhikshus, and, on his return, enter in due time into the chamber of solitude. This, O king, is the first of the qualities of the cock he ought to have.

4. 'And again, O king, as a cock rises early and betimes; so, O king, should the strenuous Bhikshu, earnest in effort, rise early and betimes to sweep out the open space around the Dâgaba, and get ready the drinking-water for the day's use, and dress himself, and pay his daily reverence to the Dâgaba, and enter into the chamber of solitude. This, O king, is the second of the qualities of the cock he ought to have.

5. 'And again, O king, as the cock is unremitting in scratching the earth to pick up what he can find to eat; so, O king, should the strenuous Bhikshu, earnest in effort, practise continual self-examination and circumspection in taking any nourishment he may find to eat, reminding himself: **[367]** "I eat this, seeking not after pleasure, nor after excitement, nor after beauty of body, nor after elegance of form, but merely for the preservation of my body, to keep myself alive, as a means of appeasing the pain of hunger, and of assisting me in the practice of the higher life. Thus shall I put an end to all former sorrow, and give no cause for future sorrow to arise; therein shall I be free from blame, and dwell at ease." This, O king, is the third of the qualities of the cock he ought to have. For it has been said, O king, by the Blessed One, the god over all gods:

"Like child's flesh in the desert wild,
Or smearing grease upon the wheel,

Solely to keep himself alive,
Does he, when feeling faint, take food [1]."

6. 'And again, O king, as the cock, though it has eyes, is blind by night; so, O king, should the strenuous Bhikshu, earnest in effort, though he is not blind, be as one blind. Whether in the woods, or on his daily walk for alms in search of food, blind should he be and deaf and dumb to all delights of form, or sound, or taste, or smell, or touch, should not make them the objects of his thought, should pay no special, detailed, attention to them [2]. This, O king, is the fourth of the qualities of the cock he ought to have. For it was said, O king, by Mahâ Ka*kk*âyana, the Elder:

"Let him with eyes be as one blind,
And he who hears be as the deaf,

[1] Not traced as yet. The verse is a riddle based on two parables. Of these the first is already published in the Sa*m*yutta Nikâya XII, 63, 5-8. It tells of a father and mother who in the desert (and of course only with the object of keeping themselves alive) ate their only child. The other is not yet published, but Mr. Trenckner points out that it occurs in the 34th Sa*m*yutta. Oiling wheels is done solely to keep the cart going. Compare the dying Buddha's comparison of himself to a worn-out cart, which can only with difficulty be made to move along. Like that, the body of the Tathâgata can only with difficulty be kept a little longer going ('Buddhist Suttas,' p. 37).

As to the last word, I take it, with Hîna*t*i-kumburê, p. 542, to be mu*kkh*ito, and not amu*kkh*ito as is printed in the text. That is also the reading adopted by Fausböll at *G*âtaka II, 294, where the verses are quoted.

[2] Na nimitta*m* gahetabba*m* nânubya*ñg*ana*m* gahetabba*m*. On these common expressions compare Aṅguttara I, 2, 6, &c.; Puggala Pa*ññ*atti II, 17, IV, 24, &c.; Dîgha II, 64, &c.; and Buddhaghosa as quoted in 'Vinaya Texts,' II, 9. Hîna*t*i-kumburê only repeats the first, but explains the second by nœwata nœwata wimasîme*m*.

He who can speak be as the dumb,
The man of strength as were he weak.
As each new object rises to his ken,
On the sweet couch of blest Nirvâ*n*a's peace
Let him lie down and rest[1]."

7. 'And again, O king, as the cock, even though persecuted[2] with clods and sticks and clubs[3] and cudgels, will not desert his home; just so, O king, should the strenuous Bhikshu, earnest in effort,—whether he be engaged in robemaking or in building-work, or in any of his daily duties, or in teaching, or in receiving instruction[4]—never give up his presence of mind. For that, O king—his presence of mind—is the home in which he dwells. This, O king, is the fifth of the qualities of the cock he ought to have. [368] And this, O king, has been said by the Blessed One, the god over all gods[5]:

"And which, O Bhikshus, is the Bhikshu's resort, the realm which is his own by right?—it is this, the four modes of being mindful and thoughtful[6]."

---

[1] From Thera Gâthâ 501. The Si*m*halese supports Mr. Trenckner in reading *g*ivhâv' in line three, but on the other hand has (twice) mana-sâyika*m* for mata-sâyika*m*. For the last line, of which a literal translation is impossible, it says, 'Let him make his couch on, fix his attention on, that Nirvâ*n*a which is mana-sâyika-*k*itta.' I think mata is the right reading, and that very possibly a riddle or pun is intended on the two meanings of that word.

[2] Paripâtiyanto. See above, p. 279 of the Pâli, and *G*âtaka II, 208. The Si*m*halese, p. 543, has he*l*anu labanneya.

[3] Laku*t*a. See above, pp. 255, 301 of the Pâli, and compare the Hindî.

[4] Hîna*t*i-kumburê expands all these details.

[5] In the Sa*m*yutta Nikâya XLVI, 7. See Mr. Trenckner's note.

[6] The four Satipa*tth*ânas. Compare above, p. 343 of the Pâli.

'And this too, O king, has been said by Sâriputta, the Elder, the Commander of the Faith:

"The elephant distinguishes good food
From bad, he knows what gives him sustenance,
And even when asleep he guards his trunk[1]—
So let each Buddha's son, earnest in zeal,
Never do violence to the Conqueror's word,
Nor injury to his self-possession, best of gifts[2]."'

3. The Squirrel.

8. 'Venerable Nâgasena, that one quality of the squirrel which you say he ought to take, which is that?'

'Just as the squirrel, O king, when an enemy falls upon him, beats his tail on the ground till it swells, and then with his own tail as a cudgel drives off the foe; just so, O king, should the strenuous Bhikshu, earnest in effort, when his enemy, sin, falls upon him, beat the cudgel of his self-possession till it swells, and then by the cudgel of self-possession drive all evil inclinations off. This, O king, is the one quality of the squirrel which he ought to have. For it was said, O king, by *K*ulla Panthaka, the Elder:

"When sins, those fell destroyers of the gains
Gained by the life of recluse, fall on us,
They should be slain, again and yet again,
By resolute self-possession as a club[3]."'

---

[1] As he does in war, according to Ma*gg*h*ima I, 415.

[2] Not traced as yet. It is not included in the collection of Sâriputta's verses preserved in the Thera Gâthâ.

[3] Not in the published texts.

4. The Panther (female)[1].

9. 'Venerable Nâgasena, that one quality of the female of the panther which you say he ought to take, which is that?'

'Just, O king, as the female of the panther conceives only once, and does not resort again and again to the male[2]; just so, O king, should the strenuous Bhikshu, earnest in effort,—seeing how future conceptions and births involve a period of gestation and a fall from each state as it is reached, and dissolution and death and destruction, seeing the horrors of transmigration and of rebirths in evil states, the annoyance of them, the torment of them,—he should stedfastly resolve never to enter upon any future life. [369] This, O king, is the one quality of the female panther which he ought to have. For it was said, O king, by the Blessed One, the god over all gods, in the Sutta Nipâta, in the Sutta of Dhaniya the cowherd:

"Like a strong bull who's burst the bonds that bound him,
Or elephant who's forced his way through jungle,
Thus shall I never more enter the womb—
And now, if it so please you, god, rain on[3]!"'

---

5. The Panther (male).

10. 'Venerable Nâgasena, those two qualities of the panther which you say he ought to take, which are they?'

---

[1] Dîpinî, perhaps 'leopardess.' The Si*m*halese has 'tigress,' which is certainly wrong.

[2] Because it realises the pains and sorrows of cub-bearing, says the Si*m*halese.

[3] Sutta Nipâta I, 2, 12.

'Just, O king, as the panther, lying in ambush in wild places, behind a thicket of long grass or brushwood, or among the rocks, catches the deer; so, O king, should the strenuous Bhikshu, earnest in effort, resort to solitary places in the woods, at the foot of a tree, on mountain heights, in caves and grottoes, in cemeteries, in forests, under the open sky, on beds of straw, in quiet, noiseless spots, free from strong winds, and hid from the haunts of men. For the strenuous Bhikshu, O king, earnest in effort, who frequents such solitudes, will soon become master of the six forms of transcendent insight. This, O king, is the first of the qualities of the panther he ought to have. For it was said, O king, by the Elders who collected the scriptures:

"As the panther by lying in ambush catches the deer,
So the sons of the Buddha, with insight and earnestness armed,
By resorting to solitudes gain that Fruit which is best [1]."

11. 'And again, O king, as the panther, whatever may be the beast he has killed, will never eat it if it has fallen on the left side; just so, O king, should the strenuous Bhikshu, earnest in effort, not partake of any food that has been procured by gifts of bamboos, or palms' leaves, or flowers, or fruits, or baths [2], or chunam, or tooth-sticks, **[370]** or water for washing; or by flattery, or by gaining the laity over by sugared

[1] That is, of course, Arahatship. The lines are not to be found in the published texts.

[2] Sinâna-dânena; omitted by the Sutta Vibhaṅga and by Hîna*t*i-kumburê (who quotes the Pâli of this passage).

words (literally by pea-soup-talk), suppressing the truth and suggesting the false [1], or by petting their children [2], or by taking messages as he walks from house to house [3], or by doctoring them, or by acting as a go-between, or as a messenger on matters of business or ceremony [4], or by exchanging with them things he has received as alms, or by giving back again to them as bribes robes or food once given to him [5], or by giving them hints as to lucky sites, or lucky days, or lucky signs (on their children's bodies at birth), or by any other of those wrong modes of obtaining a livelihood that have been condemned by the Buddha [6]—no food so procured should he eat, as the panther will not eat any prey that has fallen on its left side. This is the second of the qualities of the panther he ought to have. For it was said, O king, by Sâriputta, the Elder, the Commander of the Faith:

"This food, so sweet, has been procured
Through intimation given by speech.
Were I, then, to partake thereof,
My mode of livelihood would be blamed.

[1] Muggasuppatâ. So Hînati-kumburê, p. 546. The Sutta Vibhaṅga omits both this word and the next.

[2] Pâribhaṭṭakatâ.

[3] *G*aṅgha-pesaniyena. The Sutta Vibhaṅga I, 185, on which our whole paragraph here is based, reads -pesanikena. I have differentiated the three sorts of messages according to the Si*m*halese.

[4] Hînati-kumburê, both in his transcription of the Pâli (p. 546) and in his translation (p. 547), reads pahîna-gamana.

[5] Anuppadâna. Compare *G*âtaka III, 205. At Sigâlovâda Sutta, p. 307, and Milinda, p. 315, it means simply providing a person with things he wants. Childers's rendering, 'giving,' is inadequate in all the passages.

[6] Referring to the Sîlas.

Now though by hunger dire oppressed
My stomach seem to rise, to go,
Ne'er will I break my rule of life,
Not though my life I sacrifice[1]."'

6. The Tortoise.

12. 'Venerable Nâgasena, those five qualities of the tortoise which you say he ought to take, what are they?'

'Just, O king, as the tortoise, which is a water animal, keeps to the water; just so, O king, should the strenuous Bhikshu, earnest in effort, let his heart go out over the whole wide world with pity and with love—mighty, abounding, beyond measure, free from every feeling of hatred or of malice—towards all creatures that have life[2]. This, O king, is the first of the qualities of the tortoise he ought to have.

13. 'And again, O king, just as the tortoise, when, as he swims on the water and raises his head, he catches sight of any one, that moment sinks, and dives into the depths, lest they should see him again; just so, O king, should the strenuous Bhikshu, earnest in effort, when evil inclinations fall upon him, sink into the waters of meditation, dive down into the deeps thereof, lest those evil inclinations should catch sight of him again. This, O king, is the

[1] Not traced as yet. Hînań-kumburê gives a long account of the circumstances under which these verses were spoken. Sâriputta was ill. Moggallâna asked him what would be good for him to take. Sâriputta told him. His friend then, by intervention of the king of the gods, procured it. But Sâriputta refused to make use of it.

[2] The Brahma-vihâras (Nos. 1 and 2). See 'Buddhist Suttas, p. 201.

second of the qualities of the tortoise he ought to have.

14. [371] 'And again, O king, just as the tortoise gets up out of the water, and suns himself; just so, O king, should the strenuous Bhikshu, earnest in effort, when he rouses himself (withdraws his mind) out of meditation,—whether taken sitting, or lying down, or standing, or walking up and down,—sun his mind in the Great Struggle against evil dispositions. This, O king, is the third of the qualities of the tortoise he ought to have.

15. 'And again, O king, just as the tortoise, digging a hole in the ground, dwells alone; just so, O king, should the strenuous Bhikshu, earnest in effort, giving up worldly gain and honour and praise, take up his abode alone, plunging into the solitudes of empty lonely places in the groves and woods and hills, in caves and grottoes, noiseless and quiet. This, O king, is the fourth of the qualities of the tortoise he ought to have. For it was said, O king, by Upasena, the Elder, of the sons of the Vaṅgantas:

"Lonely and quiet places, haunts
Of the deer, and of wild beasts,
Should the Bhikshu seek as his abode,
For solitude's sweet sake [1]."

16. 'And again, O king, as the tortoise, when on his rounds he sees any one, draws in at once all his head and limbs into his shell, and hiding them there, keeps still in silence to save himself; just so, O king, should the strenuous Bhikshu, earnest in effort, wheresoever forms, or sounds, or odours, or tastes,

[1] Thera Gâthâ 577.

or feelings strike upon him, shut to the gate of self-restraint at the six doors of his senses, cover up his mind in self-control, and continue constant in mindfulness and thoughtfulness to save his Sama*n*a-ship. This, O king, is the fifth of the qualities of the tortoise he ought to have. For it was said, O king, by the Blessed One, the god over all gods, in the most excellent Sa*m*yutta Nikâya, in the Sutta of the parable of the tortoise :

"As the tortoise withdraws his limbs in his shell,
Let the Bhikshu bury the thoughts of his mind,
Himself Independent, injuring none,
Set free himself, speaking evil of none [1]."'

---

7. The Bamboo.

17. **[372]** 'Venerable Nâgasena, that one quality of the bamboo which you say he ought to take, which is it?'

'Just, O king, as the bamboo, whithersoever the gale blows, to that quarter does it bend accordingly, pursuing no other way of its own; just so, O king, should the strenuous Bhikshu, earnest in effort, conduct himself in accordance with the ninefold teaching of the Master, the word of the Buddha, the Blessed One, and stedfastly keeping to all things lawful and blameless, he should seek after the qualities of the Sama*n*aship itself. This, O king, is the one quality of the bamboo he ought to have. For it was said, O king, by Râhula, the Elder :

---

[1] The parable is in the 46th Sa*m*yutta. The verses are already published at vol. i, p. 7 of M. Feer's edition for the Pâli Text Society.

"In accord alway with Buddha's ninefold word
And stedfast in all lawful, blameless acts,
I have passed beyond rebirth in evil states [1]."'

---

8. The Bow.

18. 'Venerable Nâgasena, that one quality of the bow which you say he ought to have, which is it?'

'Just, O king, as a well-made and balanced bow bends equally from end to end, and does not resist stiffly, like a post; just so, O king, should the strenuous Bhikshu, earnest in effort, bend easily in accord with all his brethren—whether elders, juniors, of medium seniority, or of like standing with himself—and not repel them. This, O king, is the one quality of the bow he ought to have. For it was said, O king, by the Blessed One, the god over all gods, in the Vidhura Pu*nn*aka *G*âtaka:

"Let the wise bend as the bow, yield as the reed,
Not be contrary. He shall dwell in the home of kings [2]."'

---

9. The Crow.

19. 'Venerable Nâgasena, those two qualities of the crow that you say he ought to take, which are they?'

'Just, O king, as the crow goes about full of apprehension and suspicion, **[373]** always on watch and guard; just so, O king, should the strenuous Bhikshu, earnest in effort, go about full of apprehension and suspicion, always on watch and guard,

---

[1] Not traced as yet. Hîna*t*i-kumburê reads samuttarim.

[2] *G*âtaka, No. 545, verse 159.

in full self-possession, with his senses under control. This, O king, is the first of the qualities of the crow he ought to have.

20. 'And again, O king, as the crow, whatever food he catches sight of, eats it, sharing with his kind; just so, O king, should the strenuous Bhikshu, earnest in effort, never omit to share with virtuous co-religionists, and that without distinction of person or deliberation as to quantity [1], whatever lawful gifts he may have lawfully received, down even to the contents of his begging-bowl. This, O king, is the second of the qualities of the crow he ought to have. For it was said, O king, by Sâriputta, the Elder, the Commander of the Faith:

"Whate'er they may present to me, austere in life,
All that, just as it comes, do I divide
With all, and I myself then take my food [2]."'

---

10. The Monkey.

21. 'Venerable Nâgasena, those two qualities of the monkey which you say he ought to have, which are they?'

'Just, O king, as the monkey, when about to take up his abode does so in some such place as a mighty tree, in a lonely place covered all over with branches, a sure place of refuge; just so, O king, should the strenuous Bhikshu, earnest in effort, choose as the teacher under whom to live a man modest, amiable, righteous, of beauty of character, learned in tradition and in the scriptures, lovable, venerable, worthy of

---

[1] So Hînañ-kumburê understands this, his version agreeing with the quotation given by Mr. Trenckner from Buddhaghosa.

[2] Not traced as yet.

reverence, a speaker of profitable things, meek, clever in admonition, in instruction, and in education, able to arouse, to incite, to gladden [1]—such a friend should he choose as teacher. This, O king, is the first of the qualities of the monkey he ought to have.

22. 'And again, O king, as the monkey wanders about, and stands and sits, always on trees, and, if he goes to sleep, spends the night on them; just so, O king, should the strenuous Bhikshu, earnest in effort, stand and walk up and down thinking, **[374]** and lie down, and sleep, in the forest, and there enjoy the sense of self-possession. This, O king, is the second of the qualities of the monkey he ought to have. For it has been said, O king, by Sâriputta, the Elder, the Commander of the Faith:

"Walking, or standing, sitting, lying down,
'Tis in the forest that the Bhikshu shines.
To dwell in wildernesses far remote
Has been exalted by the Buddhas all [2]."'

Here ends the First Chapter [3].

---

[1] For the last six words, none of which are in Childers, see Ma*ggh*ima Nikâya I, 145, 6, and below, VII, 2, 20.

[2] Not traced as yet.

[3] The Kambojan MS., in the library of Trinity College, Cambridge, ends here.

Book VII. Chapter 2.

THE SIMILES (continued).

11. The Gourd.

1. 'Venerable Nâgasena, that one quality of the gourd which you say he ought to take, which is it?'

'Just, O king, as the gourd, climbing up with its tendrils[1] on to some other plant—whether a grass, or a thorn, or a creeper—grows all over it; just so, O king, should the strenuous Bhikshu, earnest in effort, who desires to grow up into Arahatship, do so by climbing up with his mind over the ideas that present themselves (as subjects for the Kamma*t*-*th*âna meditations). This, O king, is the one quality of the gourd which he ought to have. For it was said, O king, by Sâriputta, the Elder, the Commander of the Faith:

"As the gourd, clambering up with its tendrils, grows
O'er the grass, or the thorn-bush, or creeper wide-spread,
So the son of the Buddha on Ar'hatship bent,
Climbs up o'er ideas, to perfection and peace[2]."'

---

[1] So*n*d*i*kâhi, which must mean here the tentacles or feelers of the gourd-creeper. The Si*m*halese has simply So*n*d*im*. I have only found the word elsewhere in the connection So*n*d*i*kâ kila*ñg*â at Ma*ggh*ima I, 228 and Sa*m*yutta IV, 1, 6, 4.

[2] Not traced as yet. The last line is literally, 'By climbing up on the ârammanas should grow in the Fruit of those who have nothing left to learn' (that is, in Arahatship).

12. The Lotus.

2. 'Venerable Nâgasena, those three qualities of the lotus which you say he ought to take, which are they?'

[375] 'Just, O king, as the lotus, though it is born in the water, and grows up in the water, yet remains undefiled by the water (for no water adheres to it); just so, O king, should the strenuous Bhikshu, earnest in effort, remain undefiled by the support that he receives, or by the following of disciples that he obtains, or by fame, or by honour, or by veneration, or by the abundance of the requisites that he enjoys. This, O king, is the first of the qualities of the lotus that he ought to have.

3. 'And again, O king, as the lotus remains lifted up far above the water; just so, O king, should the strenuous Bhikshu, earnest in effort, remain far above all worldly things. This, O king, is the second of the qualities of the lotus that he ought to have.

4. 'And again, O king, as the lotus trembles when blown upon by the slightest breeze; just so, O king, should the strenuous Bhikshu, earnest in effort, exercise self-control in respect of the least of the evil dispositions, perceiving the danger (in the least offence). This, O king, is the third of the qualities of the lotus he ought to have. For it was said, O king, by the Blessed One, the god over all gods:

"Seeing danger in the least offence, he takes upon himself, trains himself in, the precepts[1]."'

---

[1] See Ma*gg*hima Nikâya I, 33; Dîgha II, 42, &c.

13. The Seed.

5. 'Venerable Nâgasena, those two qualities of seed which you say he ought to have, which are they?'

'Just, O king, as seed, tiny though it be, yet if sown in good soil, and if the god rains aright, will give abundant fruit; just so, O king, should the strenuous Bhikshu, earnest in effort, so conduct himself aright that the righteousness of his life may give abundantly of the fruits of Sama*n*aship. This, O king, is the first quality of seed which he ought to have.

6. 'And again, O king, as seed planted in well-weeded soil comes quickly to maturity; just so, O king, will his mind, when well-mastered[1], and well-purified in solitude, if it be cast by the strenuous Bhikshu, earnest in effort, into the excellent field of self-possession, come quickly to maturity. This, O king, is the second quality of seed which he ought to have. **[376]** For it was said, O king, by Anuruddha, the Elder:

"If seed be sown on a well-weeded field,
Its fruit, abounding, will rejoice the sower.
So the recluse's heart, in solitude made pure,
Matures full fast in self-possession's field[2]."'

14. The Sal-tree.

7. 'Venerable Nâgasena, that one quality of the Sal-tree which you say he ought to take, which is it?'

[1] Supariggahîta*m*, which the Si*m*halese, p. 553, omits.
[2] Not in the published texts.

'Just, O king, as the Sal-tree grows within the ground to the depth of a hundred cubits or more; just so, O king, should the strenuous Bhikshu, earnest in effort, perfect in solitude the four Fruits of Samanaship, the four Discriminations, the six forms of transcendental Insight, and all the qualities befitting a recluse. This, O king, is the one quality of the Sal-tree he ought to have. For it was said, O king, by Râhula, the Elder:

"The tree that's called the Sal-tree grows above the earth,
And shoots beneath, a hundred cubits deep.
As in the fullness of time, and at its highest growth
That tree shoots in one day[1] a hundred cubits high,
Just so do I, O Buddha, like the Sal,
Increase, in solitude, in inward good."'

15. The Ship.

8. 'Venerable Nâgasena, those three qualities of the ship that you say he ought to take, which are they?'

'Just, O king, as a ship, by the combination of the quantity of the different kinds of timber of which it is composed, conveys many folk across; just so, O king, should the strenuous Bhikshu, earnest in effort, cross the whole world of existence, whether in heaven, or on earth, by the combination of a number of qualities arising out of good conduct, righteousness, virtue, and the performance of duty.

[1] Ekâham. I follow the Simhalese (eka divasim), but confess myself very doubtful as to this being the meaning intended by the author.

This, O king, is the first of the qualities of a ship he ought to have.

9. 'And again, O king, just as a ship [**377**] can bear the onslaught of various thundering waves and of far-reaching whirlpools; so, O king, should the strenuous Bhikshu, earnest in effort, be able to bear the onslaught of the waves of various evil inclinations, and the onslaught of the waves of varied evils—veneration and contempt, support and honour, praise and exaltation, offerings and homage, blame and commendation in families not his own. This, O king, is the second of the qualities of the ship he ought to have.

10. 'And again, O king, as the ship journeys over the great ocean, immeasurable and infinite though it be, without a further shore, unshaken in its depths, roaring with a mighty noise, and filled with crowds of fish and monsters and dragons of all sorts; just so, O king, should the strenuous Bhikshu, earnest in effort, make his mind journey through to penetration into the four Truths in their triple order, in their twelvefold form[1]. This, O king, is the third of the qualities of the ship he ought to have. For it was said, O king, by the Blessed One, the god over all gods, in the most excellent Sa*m*yutta Nikâya, in the Sa*m*yutta on the Truths[2]:

"Whenever you are thinking, O Bhikkhus, you should think: 'Such is sorrow,'—you should think: 'Such is the origin of sorrow,'—you should think: 'Such is the end of sorrow,'—you should think: 'Such is the path that leads to the end of sorrow.'"'

[1] See 'Buddhist Suttas,' pp. 150–152, and especially § 21, from which the expressions here used are taken.

[2] This is the 55th Sa*m*yutta.

16. The Anchor.

11. 'Venerable Nâgasena, those two qualities of the anchor which you say he ought to take, which are they?'

'Just, O king, as the anchor, even in the mighty sea, in the expanse of waters agitated by the crowding of ever-varying waves, will fasten the ship, and keep it still, not letting the sea take it in one direction or another; just so, O king, should the strenuous Bhikshu, earnest in effort, keep his mind stedfast in the mighty struggle of thoughts, in the waters of the waves of lust and malice and dullness, not letting them divert it in one direction or another. This, O king, is the first quality of the anchor he ought to have.

12. 'And again, O king, as the anchor floats not, but sinks down, and even in water a hundred cubits deep holds the ship fast, brings it to rest; just so, O king, should the strenuous Bhikshu, earnest in effort, when he receives support, and fame, and honour, and veneration, and reverence, and offerings, and praise, [378] be not lifted up on the summit of the support or the fame, but keep his mind fixed on the idea of merely keeping his body alive. This, O king, is the second quality of the anchor he ought to have. For it was said, O king, by Sâriputta, the Elder, the Commander of the Faith:

"As the anchor floats not, but sinks down beneath the waves,
So be abased, not lifted up, by praise or gifts[1]."'

[1] Not traced as yet.

17. The Mast.

13. 'Venerable Nâgasena, that one quality of the mast which you say he ought to take, which is it?'

'Just, O king, as the mast carries ropes and braces and sails[1]; just so should the strenuous Bhikshu, earnest in effort, always have mindfulness and self-possession—when going out or coming back, when looking ahead or looking round, when stretching forth his arm or bending it back, when wearing clothes or carrying his bowl, when eating or drinking or swallowing or tasting, when easing himself or walking or standing or sitting, when asleep or awake, when talking and when silent, never should he lose his mindfulness and self-possession. This, O king, is the one quality of the mast he ought to have[2]. For it was said, O king, by the Blessed One, the god over all gods:

"Mindful, my brethren, should the Bhikshu remain, and self-possessed. This is my instruction to you[3]."'

18. The Pilot.

14. 'Venerable Nâgasena, those three qualities of the pilot which you say he ought to take, which are they?'

'Just, O king, as the pilot, day and night, with

[1] Lakâra. Childers says 'a part of a ship,' Dr. Morris ('Journal of the Pâli Text Society,' 1884, p. 101, note) says 'a chain attached to a well.' I follow the Simhalese, p. 556, which has ruwala. See *G*âtaka II, 112, and compare IV, 21.

[2] The Si*m*halese has here a page of matter not found in the Pâli.

[3] Dîgha Nikâya XVI, 2, 12.

continuous and unceasing zeal and effort, navigates[1] his ship; just so, O king, does the strenuous Bhikshu, earnest in effort, when regulating his mind, continue night and day unceasingly zealous and earnest in regulating his mind by careful thought. This, O king, is the one quality of the pilot he ought to have. For it was said, O king, by the Blessed One, the god over all gods, in the Dhammapada (the Collection of scripture verses):

"Be full of zeal, watch over your own thoughts;
Raise yourselves up out of the slough of endless births,
As the strong elephant engulphed in depths of mud[2]."

[379] 15. 'And again, O king, as the pilot knows all that is in the sea, whether good or bad; just so, O king, should the strenuous Bhikshu, earnest in effort, know good from evil, and what is an offence from what is not, and what is mean from what is exalted, and what is dark from what is light. This, O king, is the second quality of the pilot he ought to have.

16. 'And again, O king, as the pilot puts a seal on the steering apparatus[3] lest any one should touch it; so, O king, should the strenuous Bhikshu, earnest in effort, put the seal of self-control on his heart, lest any evil or wrong thoughts should arise within it. This is the third quality of the pilot he ought to have. For it was said, O king, by the

[1] Sâreti, 'makes go.' Not in Childers, but see Aṅguttara Nikâya III, 35, 4, and compare *K*ullavagga V, 11, 2.

[2] Dhammapada, verse 327.

[3] Yanta, which the Si*m*halese renders yantra (p. 559).

Blessed One, the god over all gods, in the most excellent Sa*m*yutta Nikâya:

"Think, O Bhikshus, no evil or wrong thoughts, such as thoughts of lust, or of malice, or of delusion[1].'"

19. The Sailor[2].

17. 'Venerable Nâgasena, that one quality of the sailor which you say he ought to take, which is it?'

'Just as the sailor on board ship, O king, thinks thus: "I am a hireling, and am working for my wage on board this ship. By means of this ship is it that I get food and clothing. I must not be lazy, but zealously navigate the ship;" just so, O king, should the strenuous Bhikshu, earnest in effort, think thus: "Gaining a thorough knowledge of this body of mine, put together of the four elements, continuously and unceasingly will I be self-possessed in mindfulness and thoughtfulness, and tranquil and peaceful will exert myself to be set free from births, old age, disease, and death, grief, lamentation, sorrow, suffering, and despair." This, O king, is the one quality of the sailor he ought to have. For it was said, O king, by Sâriputta, the Elder, the Commander of the Faith:

"Understand what the body is, realise that again
and again,
Seeing the nature of the body, put an end to
grief[3]."'

---

[1] Sa*m*yutta LV, 7.

[2] Kammakaro. Hîna*t*i-kumburê translates this 'handyman, artisan, ship's carpenter.'

[3] Not traced as yet.

20. THE SEA.

18. [380] 'Venerable Nâgasena, those five qualities of the sea you say he ought to take, which are they?'

'Just, O king, as the sea brooks no contact with a corpse[1]; just so, O king, should the strenuous Bhikshu, earnest in effort, brook no association with the stains of evil—lust and malice and dullness and pride and delusion, concealing the faults one has and claiming virtues one has not[2], envy and avarice, deceit and treachery and trickiness, wickedness and sinfulness of life. This, O king, is the first quality of the sea he ought to have.

19. 'And again, O king, just as the sea carries within it stores of all kinds of gems—pearls and diamonds and cat's-eyes, and chank shells, and quartz[3], and coral, and crystal, but conceals them all; just so, O king, should the strenuous Bhikshu, earnest in effort, though he have attained to the various gems of character—the Path, and the Fruits

[1] This curious belief has been made use of above, I, 259 of the translation. See also Divyâvadâna, p. 234.

[2] Makkho and pâlâso, 'hypocrisy and conceit.' See the notes above on IV, 8, 23.

[3] Silâ. Mr. Trenckner prints the passage as if sankhasilâ were to be taken together. But the use of the nominatives sankho silâ in the corresponding list at *K*ullavagga IX, 1, 3, 4 shows that by silâ, 'rock,' some kind of gem is meant. And that our author does not intend to deviate from the earlier authority is clear from his own work (above, p. 267 of the Pâli), where he also gives the two nominatives in a similar, though longer, list of gems. What may be the particular gem referred to under the name 'rock' is doubtful. Hîna*t*i-kumburê, p. 561, merely repeats the word silâ; and Clough, besides 'rock,' gives as special meaning only 'arsenic.' At *K*ullavagga ('Vinaya Texts,' III, 304) I have rendered it 'rock,' but 'quartz' now seems to me preferable.

thereof, and the four *Gh*ânas, and the eight Vimokkhas, and Samâdhi, and the five Attainments (forms of ecstatic contemplation and Insight), and the six forms of Transcendental Knowledge[1]—conceal them and not bring them to the light. This, O king, is the second quality of the sea he ought to have.

20. 'And again, O king, just as the sea associates with mighty creatures; just so, O king, should the strenuous Bhikshu, earnest in effort, associate himself with a fellow-disciple who desires little and is contented, who is pure in speech[2], whose conduct is directed to the eradication of evil, who is given to righteousness, modest, amiable, dignified, venerable, a speaker of profitable words, meek, one who will point out his associate's faults, and blame him when he does wrong, clever in admonition, in instruction, and in education, able to arouse, to incite, and to gladden—with such a man as a friend, in righteousness should he dwell. This, O king, is the third quality of the sea he ought to have.

21. 'And again, O king, as the sea, though filled with the fresh water brought down by the Ganges, and the Jumna, and the A*k*iravatî, and the Sarabhû, and the Mahî, and by other rivers a hundred thousand in number, and by the rains of heaven, yet

[1] It is very characteristic of our author that his interpretation of the gems into ethical conceptions is quite different from that of the *K*ullavagga, and much more mystic. In the older passage they are translated into the seven constituent characteristics of Arahatship. (See 'Vinaya Texts,' loc. cit., p. 305.) Compare also Divyâvadâna, pp. 115, 229.

[2] Dhuta-vâdo, not in Childers, and only found here. Perhaps 'who inculcates the keeping of the extra vows.' Dhutâṅgawâdiwû, says Hîna*n*-kumburê, p. 561.

never overflows its shore; just so, O king, should the strenuous Bhikshu, earnest in effort, never consciously transgress the precepts for the sake of support, or fame, or praise, or salutations, or reverence, or honour—no! not even for his life. This, O king, is the fourth of the qualities of the sea he ought to have. [**381**] For it was said, O king, by the Blessed One, the god over all gods[1]:

"Just, O king, as the great ocean has fixity as its characteristic, and never overflows its shores; just so, O king, should my disciples never overstep the regulations I have laid down for them—no! not even to save themselves alive[2]."

22. 'And again, O king, as the sea is not filled even by all the rivers—the Ganges, and the Jumna, and the A*k*iravatî, and the Sarabhû, and the Mahî—nor by the rains from heaven; just so, O king, should

[1] Devâtidevena. It is not known when this epithet, which our author so constantly applies to the Buddha, first came into use. It is not found in the Pi*t*akas, and the Milinda is the oldest book in which it has been traced. It is given in the Mahâvyutpatti, page 1, as a recognised epithet, but not in the corresponding Pâli list of epithets in the Abhidhâna Padîpikâ (though deva-deva occurs there). The origin of the appellation is solemnly explained in the Divyâvadâna, p. 391. It is there said to have been first bestowed on the Buddha (when, as a child, he was presented in the temple), because all the gods bowed down before him. There is nothing about this in the corresponding passage of the Lalita Vistara, pp. 136–138. The epithet is used of the Buddha in an inscription of Toramâna Shâhi ('Epigraphia Indica' for October, 1889). It occurs also in a verse preserved in the commentaries on the Dhammapada and the *G*âtaka (*G*âtaka IV, 158 = Dhammapada 148)—a verse not found in the Pi*t*aka versions of the same episode—and is used in a kind of pun in the Mahâva*m*sa, chap. i, verse 56. But these three passages are all of the fifth century A.D.

[2] Not traced as yet. A similar parable is used at the passage already quoted from the *K*ullavagga IX, 1, 3, 4.

the strenuous Bhikshu, earnest in effort, never be satisfied with receiving instruction, with asking and answering questions, with listening to the word, and learning it by heart, and examining into it, with hearing the Abhidhamma and the Vinaya, and the deep sayings of the Suttas, with analysis of forms, with learning the rules of right composition, conjunction, and grammatical construction[1], with listening to the ninefold teaching of the Conqueror. This, O king, is the fifth quality of the sea he ought to have. For it was said, O king, by the Blessed One, the god over all gods, in the Sutasoma *G*âtaka[2]:

"Just as the fire, in burning grass and sticks,
Is never satisfied, nor the great sea
Filled with the waters of all streams that flow—
So are these students wise, O king of kings,
Listening, ne'er sated with the words of truth[3]."'

Here ends the Second Chapter.

[1] The translation is here doubtful. The Si*m*halese apparently takes viggaha as qualifying pada, though it renders the whole by 'learning the rules of resolving words into their elements, and of building them up into compounds, and of Sandhi, and of conjugation, and of declension.'

[2] Not reached as yet in Professor Fausböll's edition. Mr. Trenckner says the verse quoted is No. 47 in the 537th *G*âtaka.

[3] The Si*m*halese reads Eva*m* hi me for Eva*m* h' ime, and renders 'listening to me.' Mr. Trenckner points out that the *G*âtaka MSS. read Evam pi te.

Book VII. Chapter 3.

THE SIMILES (continued).

21. The Earth.

1. **[382]** 'Venerable Nâgasena, those five qualities of the earth which you say he ought to take, which are they?'

'Just, O king, as the earth remains just the same whether one scatter upon it desirable things or the reverse—whether camphor and aloes and jasmine and sandal-wood and saffron, or whether bile and phlegm and pus and blood and sweat and fat and saliva and mucus and the fluid which lubricates the joints and urine and faeces—still it is the same; just so, O king, should the strenuous Bhikshu, earnest in effort, remain the same, unmoved at support or neglect, at fame or dishonour, at blame or praise, in happiness or in woe. This, O king, is the first of the qualities of the earth he ought to have.

2. 'And again, O king, as the earth has no adornment, no garlands, but is suffused with the odour of itself; just so, O king, should the strenuous Bhikshu, earnest in effort, wear no finery, but rather be set round with the sweet savour of his own righteousness of life. This, O king, is the second quality of the earth he ought to have.

3. 'And again, O king, as the earth is solid, without holes or interstices, thick, dense, and spreads itself out on every side; just so, O king, should the strenuous Bhikshu, earnest in effort, be endowed with an unbroken righteousness of life with no gaps

or cracks in it, thick, dense, and spreading itself out on every side. This, O king, is the third quality of the earth he ought to have.

4. 'And again, O king, as the earth is never weary, though it bears up the villages and towns and cities and countries, the trees and hills and rivers and ponds and lakes, the wild creatures and birds and men, multitudes of men and women; just so, O king, should the strenuous Bhikshu, earnest in effort, be never weary in giving exhortation and admonition and instruction and education, in rousing and inciting and gladdening, and at the expositions of the faith. This, O king, is the fourth quality of the earth he ought to have.

5. 'And again, O king, as the earth is free alike from fawning and from ill-will[1]; just so, O king, should the strenuous Bhikshu, earnest in effort, continue in spirit, like the earth, free alike from fawning upon any man, from ill-will to any man. This is the fifth quality of the earth he ought to have. **[383]** For it was said, O king, by the devoted woman, *K*ulla Subhaddâ, when she was exalting the recluses of her own sect[2]:

---

[1] This simile has already occurred above, I, 258, 259 (of the translation).

[2] The Si*m*halese (pp. 563, 564) gives the whole story. She was the daughter of Anâthapi*nd*ika (Sudatta), the famous supporter of the Buddha, and builder of the *G*etavana at Sâvatthi. On her marriage to a rich merchant at Sâketa (Audh) named Kâlaka, he invited the Brahman naked ascetics of his sect, the Â*g*îvakas, and asked her to go and entertain 'the Arahats.' Hearing the word Arahat she went quickly and full of delight to do so; and was shocked beyond measure to find a number of disorderly fakîrs, with neither modesty in their hearts, nor decency in their outward behaviour. So she fled from the hall, and on her husband remonstrating, was indignant. He then asked her what the recluses

"Were one, enraged, to cut their one arm with an axe,
Another, pleased, to anoint the other with sweet scent,
No ill-will would they bear the one, nor love the other.
Their hearts are like the earth, unmoved are my recluses[1]."'

22. WATER.

6. 'Venerable Nâgasena, the five qualities of water which you say he ought to take, which are they?'

'Just, O king, as water is firmly fixed (in pools, wells, &c.), shakes not, and (in its ordinary state) is not disturbed, and is pure by nature; just so, O king, should the strenuous Bhikshu, earnest in effort, putting away hypocrisy, and whining, and intimating their wants, and improper influences of all sorts, be fixed, unshaken, undisturbed, and pure in nature. This, O king, is the first quality of water he ought to have.

7. 'And again, O king, as water is always of a refreshing nature; just so, O king, should the strenuous Bhikshu, earnest in effort, be full of pity, and love, and kindness to all beings, seeking the good of all, in mercy to all. This, O king, is the second quality of water he ought to have.

8. 'And again, O king, as water makes the dirty clean; just so, O king, should the strenuous Bhikshu,

of her sect were like, and she told him. Another verse from her description is quoted below, p. 387 of the Pâli. The above story has been often repeated.

[1] Not traced. Hînań-kumburê reads ekań ke bâham (twice) and mânaso, pamodito; and he is no doubt right.

earnest in effort, be in all places, whether in the village or in the forest, free from disputes with, free from offence against his teachers, his masters, or those standing towards him like a teacher. This, O king, is the third quality of water he ought to have.

9. 'And again, O king, as water is desired of all men; just so, O king, should the strenuous Bhikshu, earnest in effort, wishing for little, content, given to solitude and retirement, be always an object of desire to all the world. This, O king, is the fourth quality of water he ought to have.

10. 'And again, O king, as water works no harm to any man; just so, O king, should the strenuous Bhikshu, earnest in effort, never do any wrong, whether in deed or word or thought, which would produce in others either strife, or quarrel, or contention, or dispute, or a feeling of emptiness, or anger[1], or discontent. [**384**] This, O king, is the fifth quality of water he ought to have. For it was said, O king, by the Blessed One, the god over all gods, in the Ka*n*ha *G*âtaka[2]:

"If you would grant a boon to me,
O Sakka, lord of every creature,—
Let none, Sakka, on my account,
Be harmed, whether in mind or body,
At any time or place. This, Sakka,
This would I choose as boon of boons[3]."'

---

[1] Ritta*ggh*âna, which Hîna*t*i-kumburê renders siswa kipîma.

[2] These words are in the original ascribed, not to the Buddha himself, but to Ka*n*ha-kumâro, the then Bodisat.

[3] *G*âtaka IV, 14. Professor Fausböll reads ma*m* kate, but the Si*m*halese (pp. 566, 567) confirms Mr. Trenckner's reading, ma*m* kâna, ma*m* nissâya, ma*m* anattha-kâmatâya.

23. Fire.

11. 'Venerable Nâgasena, those five qualities of fire which you say he ought to take, which are they?'

'Just, O king, as fire burns grass, and sticks, and branches, and leaves; just so, O king, should the strenuous Bhikshu, earnest in effort, burn out in the fire of wisdom all evil dispositions which feed on objects of thought, whether subjective or objective, whether desirable or the reverse. This, O king, is the first quality of fire he ought to have.

12. 'And again, O king, as fire has no pity, neither mercy; just so, O king, should the strenuous Bhikshu, earnest in effort, show no pity, neither mercy, to any evil dispositions. This, O king, is the second quality of fire he ought to have.

13. 'And again, O king, as fire destroys cold; just so, O king, should the strenuous Bhikshu, earnest in effort, lighting up in his heart the burning fire of zeal, destroy all evil dispositions therein. This, O king, is the third quality of fire he ought to have.

14. 'And again, O king, as fire, seeking no favour of any man, bearing no ill-will to any man, makes heat for all; just so, O king, should the strenuous Bhikshu, earnest in effort, dwell in spirit like the fire, fawning on none, bearing ill-will to none. This, O king, is the fourth quality of fire he ought to have.

15. 'And again, O king, as fire dispels darkness, and makes the light appear; just so, O king, should the strenuous Bhikshu, earnest in effort, dispel the

darkness of ignorance, and make the light of knowledge to appear. This is the fifth quality of fire he ought to have. For it was said, O king, by the Blessed One, the god over all gods, in his exhortation to Râhula, his son:

[385] "Practise thyself, Râhula, in that meditation which acts like fire. Thereby shall no wrong dispositions, which have not yet arisen, arise within thee, nor shall they that have arisen bear sway over thy heart[1]."'

---

24. Wind.

16. 'Venerable Nâgasena, those five qualities of wind which you say he ought to take, which are they?'

'Just, O king, as wind pervades the spaces in the woods and groves in flowering time; so, O king, should the strenuous Bhikshu, earnest in effort, rejoice in the groves of meditation that are all in blossom with the sweet flowers of emancipation. This, O king, is the first quality of wind he ought to have.

17. 'And again, O king, as wind sets all the trees that grow upon the earth in agitation, bends them

---

[1] Not traced as yet exactly in these words. But the passage at Ma*ggh*ima Nikâya I, 424, lines 3–6, agrees with it throughout, except that for akusalâ dhammâ here we have there manâpâmanâpâ phassâ, which comes to much the same thing. As the words are there addressed to Râhula, and as our passage here is introduced with the same formula as the quotation below (p. 388 of the Pâli) which is certainly taken from the same page of the Ma*ggh*ima, I think the above (M. I, 424, lines 3–6) is most probably the passage our author now intended to quote. If so, we have here a real case of difference in reading.

down; just so, O king, should the strenuous Bhikshu, earnest in effort, retiring into the midst of the woods, there examining into the true nature of all existing things (all phenomena, Saṁkhâras), beat down all evil dispositions. This, O king, is the second quality of wind he ought to have.

18. 'And again, O king, as the wind wanders through the sky; just so, O king, should the strenuous Bhikshu, earnest in effort, accustom his mind to wander among transcendental things. This is the third quality of wind he ought to have.

19. 'And again, O king, as wind carries perfume along; just so, O king, should the strenuous Bhikshu, earnest in effort, carry along with him alway the fragrant perfume of his own righteousness of life. This, O king, is the fourth quality of wind he ought to have.

20. 'And again, O king, as wind has no house, no home to dwell in; just so, O king, should the strenuous Bhikshu, earnest in effort, remain alway without a house, without a home to dwell in, not addicted to society, set free in mind. This, O king, is the fifth quality of wind he ought to have. For it was said, O king, by the Blessed One, the god over all gods, in the Sutta Nipâta:

"In friendship of the world anxiety is born,
In household life distraction's dust lies thick;
The state set free from home and friendship's
ties—
That, and that only, is the recluse's aim[1].'"

[1] Sutta Nipâta I, 12, 1. It has been already quoted above, IV, 5, 1 (p. 211 of the Pâli), where see the note.

25. The Rock.

21. 'Venerable Nâgasena, the five qualities of the rock that you say he ought to have, which are they?'

[386] 'Just, O king, as rock is firm, unshaken, immoveable; just so, O king, should the strenuous Bhikshu, earnest in effort, never be excited by alluring things—forms, or sounds, or scents, or tastes, or touch—by veneration or contempt, by support or by neglect, by reverence or its absence, by honour or dishonour, by praise or blame, nor should he be offended by things that give offence, nor bewildered on occasions of bewilderment, neither should he quake nor tremble, but like a rock should he be firm. This, O king, is the first quality of the rock he ought to have. For it was said, O king, by the Blessed One, the god over all gods:

"The solid rock's not shaken by the wind,
Just so the wise man falters not, nor shakes,
At praise or blame[1]."

22. 'And again, O king, as a rock is firm, unmixed with extraneous things; just so, O king, should the strenuous Bhikshu, earnest in effort, be firm and independent, given to association with none. This, O king, is the second quality of the rock he ought to have. For it was said, O king, by the Blessed One, the god over all gods:

"The man who mixes not with householders,
Nor with the homeless, but who wanders lone,
Without a home, and touched by few desires,—
That is the man I call a Brâhma*n*a[2]."

---

[1] Dhammapada 81. The first line recurs at Mahâvagga V, 1, 27.

[2] From the Sutta Nipâta III, 9, 35. It is also included in the Dhammapada collection of Scripture verses (No. 404).

23. 'And again, O king, as on the rock no seed will take root; just so, O king, should the strenuous Bhikshu, earnest in effort, never permit evil dispositions to take root in his mind. This, O king, is the third quality of rock that he ought to have. For it was said, O king, by Subhûti the Elder:

"When lustful thoughts arise within my heart,
Examining myself, alone I beat them down.
Thou who'rt by lust excited, who by things
That give offence, allowest of offence,
Feeling bewildered when strange things occur,
Thou shouldst retire far from the lonely woods.
For they're the dwelling-place of men made pure,
Austere in life, free from the stains of sin.
Defile not that pure place. Leave thou the woods[1]."

24. [**387**] 'And again, just as the rock rises aloft, just so should the strenuous Bhikshu, earnest in effort, rise aloft through knowledge. This is the fourth quality of the rock he ought to have. For it was said, O king, by the Blessed One, the god over all gods:

"When the wise man by earnestness has driven
Vanity far away, the terraced heights
Of wisdom doth he climb, and, free from care,
Looks over the vain world, the careworn crowd—
As he who standing on the mountain top
Can watch his fellow-men still toiling on the plain[2]."

25. 'And again, O king, just as the rock cannot

[1] Not traced as yet.

[2] This verse, not traced elsewhere as yet, is included in the Dhammapada collection as verse 28.

be lifted up nor bent down; just so, O king, should the strenuous Bhikshu, earnest in effort, be neither lifted up nor depressed. This, O king, is the fifth quality of the rock he ought to have. For it was said, O king, by the devout woman, *K*ulla Subhaddâ, when she was exalting the recluses of her own sect:

"The world is lifted up by gain, depressed by loss.
My Sama*n*as remain alike in gain or loss."'

---

26. Space.

26. 'Venerable Nâgasena, those five qualities of space which you say he ought to have, which are they?'

'Just, O king, as space is everywhere impossible to grasp; just so, O king, should it be impossible for the strenuous Bhikshu, earnest in effort, to be anywhere taken hold of by evil dispositions. This, O king, is the first quality of space he ought to have.

27. 'And again, O king, as space is the familiar resort of *Ri*shis, and ascetics, and gods[1], and flocks of birds; just so, O king, should the strenuous Bhikshu, earnest in effort, make his mind wander easily over all things with the knowledge that each individual (Sa*m*khâra) is impermanent, born to sorrow, and without any abiding principle (any soul). This, O king, is the second quality of space he ought to have.

---

[1] Bhûta, which the Si*m*halese, p. 572, renders yaksha. I think it means all kinds of gods (except the highest), demigods, fairies, superhuman beings, &c.

28. 'And again, O king, as space inspires terror; just so, O king [388], should the strenuous Bhikshu, earnest in effort, train his mind to be in terror of rebirths in any kind of existence. To seek no happiness therein. This, O king, is the third quality of space he ought to have.

29. 'And again, O king, as space is infinite, boundless, immeasurable; just so, O king, should the righteousness of the strenuous Bhikshu, earnest in effort, know no limit, and his knowledge be beyond measure. This, O king, is the fourth quality of space he ought to have.

30. 'And again, O king, as space does not hang on to anything, does not cling to anything, does not rest on anything, is not stopped by anything; just so, O king, should the strenuous Bhikshu, earnest in effort, neither in any way depend on, nor cling to, nor rest on, nor be hindered by either the families that minister to him, or the pupils who resort to him, or the support he receives, or the dwelling he occupies, or any obstacles to the religious life, or any requisites that he may want, or any kind of evil inclination. This, O king, is the fifth quality of space he ought to have. For it was said, O king, by the Blessed One, the god over all gods, in his exhortation to Râhula, his son:

"Just, Râhula, as space rests nowhere on anything, so shouldst thou practise thyself in that meditation which is like space. Thereby shall neither pleasant nor unpleasant sensations, as they severally arise, bear sway over thy heart[1]."'

---

[1] Ma*ggh*ima Nikâya I, 424. See the note above on VII, 3, 15.

27. The Moon.

31. 'Venerable Nâgasena, those five qualities of the moon which you say he ought to have, which are they?'

'Just, O king, as the moon, rising in the bright fortnight, waxes more and more; just so, O king, should the strenuous Bhikshu, earnest in effort, grow more and more in good conduct and righteousness and virtue and the constant performance of duty, and in knowledge of the scriptures and study[1], and in the habit of retirement, and in self-possession, and in keeping the doors of his senses guarded, and in moderation in food, and in the practice of vigils. This, O king, is the first quality of the moon he ought to have.

32. 'And again, O king, as the moon is a mighty lord[2]; just so, O king, should the strenuous Bhikshu, earnest in effort, be a mighty lord over his own will.

---

[1] Âgamâdhigame. These are two, not one. Âgama adhigama dekhi da says the Si*m*halese, p. 573.

[2] U*l*ârâdhipati. Dr. Morris in the 'Journal of the Pâli Text Society' (1880, p. 107) ingeniously proposes to read u*l*urâ*g*âdhipati, 'king and lord over the u*l*u's, the lunar mansions.' In that case the u*l*âra in the latter clause of the sentence would be a play upon words. But Mr. Trenckner's reading is confirmed by the Si*m*halese, which has *k*andra diwya-râ*g*a tema mahatwû sisiragu*n*aye*m* adhipati wûyeya, 'the moon, that heavenly king, is a lord by reason of his great coldness.' And the reading may well stand, for the mention, in the latter part of the clause, of the thing over which the Bhikshu is to be lord does not necessarily require a corresponding word in the first part. We have numerous instances in these similes of the ethical interpretation of the physical simile being an addition, with nothing corresponding to it in the type discussed. The moon was a god, lord over other things besides the lunar mansions.

This, O king, is the second quality of the moon he ought to have.

33. 'And again, O king, as the moon wanders at night; just so, O king, should the strenuous Bhikshu, earnest in effort, be given to solitude. [389] This, O king, is the third quality of the moon he ought to have.

34. 'And again, O king, as the moon hoists a standard over his mansion[1]; just so, O king, should the strenuous Bhikshu, earnest in effort, hoist the standard of righteousness. This, O king, is the fourth quality of the moon he ought to have.

35. 'And again, O king, as the moon rises when begged and prayed to do so; just so, O king, should the strenuous Bhikshu, earnest in effort, frequent for alms those families who have asked and invited him to do so[2]. This, O king, is the fifth quality of the moon he ought to have. For it was said, O king, by the Blessed One, the god over all gods, in the most excellent Sa*m*yutta Nikâya:

"Like the moon, O brethren, let your visits be paid to the laity. Drawing back alike in outward demeanour and in inward spirit, be ye always, as strangers on their first visit, retiring in the presence of the laity. [As the man who looks down a deep

---

[1] *K*ando vimâna-ketu. 'Has his mansion, forty-nine yo*g*anas in extent, as his banner,' says Hîna*t*i-kumburê. (A yo*g*ana is seven miles.) Vimâ*n*a does not mean lunar mansion, but the palace which every deity, and therefore also the moon, is supposed to inhabit.

[2] The Si*m*halese, p. 573, has the exact opposite. 'As the moon rises whether begged to do so or not, so should the Bhikshu visit the laity whether invited to do so or not.' But the Pâli must be right, as the subsequent quotation shows.

well, or a mountain precipice, or a river in flood, would be abashed alike in body and in mind; so be ye, O brethren, as the moon in your visits to the laity. Holding alike in your outward demeanour and your inward spirit, be ye alway, as strangers on their first visit, retiring in the presence of the laity][1].'"'

28. The Sun.

36. 'Venerable Nâgasena, the seven qualities of the sun you say he ought to have, which are they?'

'Just, O king, as the sun evaporates all water; just so, O king, should the strenuous Bhikshu, earnest in effort, cause all evil inclinations, without any exception, to dry up within him. This, O king, is the first quality of the sun he ought to have.

37. 'And again, O king, as the sun dispels the darkness; just so, O king, should the strenuous Bhikshu, earnest in effort, dispel all the darkness of lust, and of anger, and of dullness, and of pride, and of heresy, and of evil, and of all unrighteousness. This, O king, is the second quality of the sun he ought to have.

38. 'And again, O king, as the sun is always in motion; just so, O king, should the strenuous Bhikshu, earnest in effort, be ever thoughtful. This,

[1] Sa*m*yutta XVI, 3, 2, 3. The sentence in brackets is added from Hîna*t*i-kumburê, who gives here, p. 274, the Pâli text. Apakassa, the gerund of ava-karsh, and naviyâ, 'new-comers,' are only found in this passage. In three cases M. Léon Feer has here gone wrong, as he has so often elsewhere done, by putting the readings of the Si*m*halese MSS. only in the notes, and adopting the Burmese readings in the text. He should have read, as Hîna*t*i-kumburê does, ni*kk*a*m* naviyâ . . . . . gambhîrûdapâna*m*, ... nadî-dugga*m*.

O king, is the third quality of the sun he ought to have.

39. 'And again, O king, as the sun has a halo of rays; just so, O king, should the strenuous Bhikshu, earnest in effort, have a halo of meditation. This, O king, is the fourth quality of the sun he ought to have.

40. 'And again, O king, as the sun continually warms multitudes of people; just so, O king, should the strenuous Bhikshu, earnest in effort, rejoice the whole world of gods and men with good conduct, and righteousness, and virtue [**390**], and the performance of duty, and with the *Gh*ânas, and the Vimokkhas, and Samâdhi, and the Samâpattis (various modes of transcendental meditation or ecstacy), and with the five moral powers, and the seven kinds of wisdom, and the four modes of being mindful and self-possessed, and the fourfold great struggle against evil, and the pursuit of the four roads to saintship. This, O king, is the fifth quality of the sun he ought to have.

41. 'And again, O king, as the sun is terrified with the fear of Râhu (the demon of eclipses); just so, O king, should the strenuous Bhikshu, earnest in effort, seeing how beings are entangled in the waste wildernesses of evil life and rebirth in states of woe, caught in the net of the mournful results here of evil done in former births, or of punishment in purgatory, or of evil inclinations, terrify his mind with a great anxiety and fear. This, O king, is the sixth quality of the sun he ought to have.

42. 'And again, O king, as the sun makes manifest the evil and the good; just so, O king, should the strenuous Bhikshu, earnest in effort, make mani-

fest the moral powers, and the kinds of wisdom, and the modes of being mindful and self-possessed, and the struggle against evil, and the paths to saintship, and all qualities temporal and spiritual. This, O king, is the seventh quality of the sun he ought to have. For it was said, O king, by Vaṅgîsa, the Elder:

"As the rising sun makes plain to all that live
Forms pure and impure, forms both good and bad,
So should the Bhikshu, like the rising orb,
Bearing the scriptures ever in his mind,
Make manifest to men, in ignorance blind,
The many-sided Noble Path of bliss[1]."'

---

29. Sakka.

43. 'Venerable Nâgasena, the three qualities of Sakka (the king of the gods) which you say he ought to take, which are they?'

'Just, O king, as Sakka enjoys perfect bliss; just so, O king, should the strenuous Bhikshu, earnest in effort, rejoice in the perfect bliss of retirement. This, O king, is the first quality of Sakka he ought to have.

44. 'And again, O king, as when Sakka when he sees his gods around him keeps them in his favour, fills them with joy; just so, O king, should the strenuous Bhikshu, earnest in effort, keep his mind detached, alert, and tranquil, should make joy spring up within him, should rouse himself, exert himself, be full of zeal. [391] This, O king, is the second quality of Sakka he ought to have.

---

[1] Not traced as yet.

45. 'And again, O king, as Sakka feels no discontent; just so, O king, should the strenuous Bhikshu, earnest in effort, never allow himself to become discontented with solitude. This, O king, is the third quality of Sakka he ought to have. For it was said, O king, by Subhûti, the Elder:

"Since I, great hero, have renounced the world,
According to the doctrine that you teach,
I will not grant that any thought of lust
Or craving care has risen in my breast [1]."'

---

30. The Sovran Overlord.

46. 'Venerable Nâgasena, the four qualities of the sovran overlord which you say he ought to take, which are they?'

'Just, O king, as the sovran overlord gains the favour of the people by the four elements of popularity (liberality, affability, justice, and impartiality); just so, O king, should the strenuous Bhikshu, earnest in effort, find favour with, please, and gladden the hearts of the brethren and rulers of the Order and the laity of either sex. This, O king, is the quality of the sovran overlord he ought to have.

47. 'And again, O king, as the sovran overlord allows no robber bands to form in his realm; just so, O king, should the strenuous Bhikshu, earnest in effort, never allow lustful or angry or cruel ideas to arise within him. This, O king, is the second quality of the sovran overlord he ought to have. For it was said, O king, by the Blessed One the god over all gods:

---

[1] Not traced as yet.

"The man who takes delight in the suppression
Of evil thoughts, and alway self-possessed,
Reflects on the impurity of things
The world thinks beautiful, he will remove—
Nay, cleave in twain, the bonds of the Evil One[1]."

48. 'And again, O king, as the sovran overlord travels through[2] the whole world even to its ocean boundary, examining into the evil and the good; just so, O king, should the strenuous Bhikshu, earnest in effort, examine himself day by day as to his acts and words and thoughts, saying to himself: "How may I pass the day blameless in these three directions?" This, O king, [392] is the third quality of the sovran overlord he ought to have. For it was said, O king, by the Blessed One, the god over all gods, in the most excellent Ekuttara Nikâya:

"With constant care should the recluse
Himself examine day by day—
'As days and nights pass quickly by
How have they found me? and how left[3]?'"

---

[1] This verse has not been elsewhere traced as yet, but is included in the Dhammapada collection, verse 350. Vitakka, which, in accord with the context and with Hîna*t*i-kumburê, is rendered above 'evil thoughts,' and by Professor Max Müller 'doubts,' really means simply 'thoughts,' and is sometimes used without any bad connotation. In the Pâli the word Mâru, which spoils the metre, may possibly be an ancient gloss introduced by mistake into the text.

[2] Anuyâyati, which is only found here, and which the Si*m*halese, p. 577, renders anu*s*âsanâ karanneya. But compare ânuyâyin at Sutta Nipâta V, 7, 3–5, and Tela Ka*t*aha Gâthâ 25, anuyâyin above, p. 284 of the Pâli, and ânuyâto at Tela Ka*t*âha Gâthâ 41.

[3] Mr. Trenckner points out that this passage is taken from the Aṅguttara X, 5, 8. Hîna*t*i-kumburê, who gives the Pâli, prints it as verse, and translates the context at some length.

49. 'And again, O king, as the sovran overlord is completely provided with protection, both within and without; just so, O king, should the strenuous Bhikshu, earnest in effort, keep self-possession as his door-keeper for a protection against all evil, subjective and objective. This, O king, is the fourth quality of the sovran overlord he ought to have. For it was said, O king, by the Blessed One, the god over all gods:

"With self-possession as his door-keeper, O brethren, the disciple of the noble ones puts away evil and devotes himself to goodness, puts away what is matter of offence and devotes himself to blamelessness, preserves himself in purity of life [1]."'

Here ends the Third Chapter.

[1] Not traced as yet, but the same phrase from 'puts away evil' to the end occurs at *Gâtaka* I, 130, 131.

BOOK VII. CHAPTER 4.

THE SIMILES (continued).

31. THE WHITE ANT.

1. 'Venerable Nâgasena, that quality of the white ant which you say he ought to have, which is it?'

'Just, O king, as the white ant goes on with his work only when he has made a roof over himself, and covered himself up; just so, O king, should the strenuous Bhikshu, earnest in effort, on his round for alms, cover up his mind with righteousness and self-restraint as a roof. For in so doing, O king, will he have passed beyond all fear. This, O king, is the one quality of the white ant he ought to have. **[393]** For it was said, O king, by Upasena Vaṅganta-putta, the Elder:

"The devotee who covers up his mind,
Under the sheltering roof of righteousness
And self-control, untarnished by the world
Remains, and is set free from every fear [1]."'

---

32. THE CAT.

2. 'Venerable Nâgasena, those two qualities of the cat you say he ought to have, which are they?'

'Just, O king, as the cat, in frequenting caves and holes and the interiors of storied dwellings, does so only in the search after rats; just so, O king, should

---

[1] Not traced as yet. But as it is doubtless an old verse it is interesting that it contains the word yogî.

the strenuous Bhikshu, earnest in effort, whether he have gone to the village or to the woods or to the foot of trees or into an empty house[1], be continually and always zealous in the search after that which is his food, namely self-possession. This is the first quality of the cat he ought to have.

3. 'And again, O king, as the cat in pursuing its prey always crouches down[2]; just so, O king, should the strenuous Bhikshu, earnest in effort, continue conscious of the origin and end[3] of those five groups of the characteristic marks of individuality which arise out of clinging to existence, thinking to himself: "Such is form, such is its origin, such its end. Such is sensation, such is its origin, such its end. Such are ideas, such is their origin, such their end. Such are the mental potentialities (the Confections, Sa*m*khârâ), such is their origin, such their end. Such is self-consciousness, such is its origin, such its end[4]." This, O king, is the second quality of the cat he ought to have. For it was said, O king, by the Blessed One, the god over all gods:

---

[1] Hammiyantara. The Si*m*halese has Pi*t*a barânda œti u*d*u mahal prâsâda œtula*t*a giye da. 'Barânda,' which is not in Clough, I take to be simply 'verandah,' and the whole to mean: 'or goes into the interior of a mansion with an upper story to it on which is a verandah.' Buddhaghosa on *K*ullavagga VI, 1, 2, (putting only kû*t*âgâra, 'peaked chamber,' for barânda,) has the same explanation. Ten or twelve years is allowed in *K*ullavagga VI, 17, 1, for the building of such a prâsâda. See also Mahâvagga I, 30, 4, and VI, 33, 2.

[2] Âsanne is Mr. Trenckner's reading. But Hîna*t*i-kumburê, who translates deyat tabâ hindîme*m* ma, 'sitting with its fore-paws stretched out,' evidently read âsanena.

[3] Abbaya, not in Childers, is of course avyaya.

[4] The Si*m*halese expands this speech over ten pages, 580–589, and then omits the verse at the end.

"Seek not rebirths afar in future states.
Pray, what could heaven itself advantage you!
Now, in this present world, and in the state
In which you find yourselves, be conquerors!"'

33. The Rat.

4. 'Venerable Nâgasena, that one quality of the rat you say he ought to take, which is it?'

'Just, O king, as the rat, wandering about backwards and forwards, is always smelling after food[1]; just so, O king, [394] should the strenuous Bhikshu, earnest in effort, be ever in his wanderings to and fro, bent upon thought. This is the quality of the rat he ought to have. For it was said, O king, by Upasena Vaṅganta-putta, the Elder:

"Ever alert and calm, the man of insight,
Esteeming wisdom as the best of all things,
Keeps himself independent of all wants and cares[2]."'

34. The Scorpion.

5. 'Venerable Nâgasena, that one quality of the scorpion you say he ought to take, which is it?'

'Just, O king, as the scorpion, whose tail is its weapon, keeps its tail erect as it wanders about; just so, O king, should the strenuous Bhikshu, earnest in effort, have knowledge as his weapon,

---

[1] Upasi*m*sako. Dr. Morris, in the 'Journal of the Pâli Text Society' (1884, p. 75), suggests upasiṅghako. But the Si*m*halese in the first clause (p. 589, last line) has patami*m* ma, 'hoping for, seeking for,' and in the second (p. 590, line 2) pœtîme*m* ma, which is the same thing (from prârthanâ, which confirms Mr. Trenckner's reading).

[2] Not traced as yet.

and dwell with his weapon, knowledge, always drawn. This, O king, is the quality of the scorpion he ought to have. For it was said, O king, by Upasena Vaṅganta-putta, the Elder:

"With his sword of knowledge drawn, the man of insight
Should ever be unconquerable in the fight,
Set free from every fear[1]."'

35. THE MUNGOOSE.

6. 'Venerable Nâgasena, that one quality of the mungoose you say he ought to take, which is it?'

'Just, O king, as the mungoose, when attacking a snake, only does so when he has covered his body with an antidote; just so, O king, should the strenuous Bhikshu, earnest in effort, when going into the world where anger and hatred are rife, which is under the sway of quarrels, strife, disputes, and enmities, ever keep his mind anointed with the antidote of love. This, O king, is the quality of the mungoose he ought to have. For it was said, O king, by Sâriputta, the Elder, the Commander of the Faith:

"Therefore should love be felt for one's own kin,
And so for strangers too, and the whole wide world
Should be pervaded with a heart of love—
This is the doctrine of the Buddhas all."'

36. THE OLD MALE JACKAL.

7. **[395]** 'Venerable Nâgasena, the two qualities of the old male jackal you say he ought to take, which are they?'

[1] Not traced as yet.

'Just, O king, as the old male jackal, whatever kind of food he finds, feels no disgust, but eats of it as much as he requires; just so, O king, should the strenuous Bhikshu, earnest in effort, eat without disgust such food as he receives with the sole object of keeping himself alive. This, O king, is the first quality of the old male jackal he ought to have. For it was said, O king, by Mahâ Kassapa, the Elder:

"Leaving my dwelling-place, I entered once
Upon my round for alms, the village street.
A leper there I saw eating his meal,
And, as was meet, deliberately, in turn,
I stood beside him too that he might give a gift.
He, with his hand all leprous and diseased,
Put in my bowl—'twas all he had to give—
A ball of rice; and as he placed it there
A finger, mortifying, broke and fell.
Seated behind a wall, that ball of food
I ate, and neither when I ate it, nay,
Nor afterwards, did any loathing thought
Arise within my breast[1]."

8. 'And again, O king, as the old male jackal, when he gets any food, does not stop to examine it; just so, O king, should the strenuous Bhikshu, earnest in effort, never stop to find out whether food given to him is bitter or sweet, well-flavoured or ill—just as it is should he be satisfied with it. This, O king, is the second quality of the old male jackal

[1] Thera Gâthâ 1054–1056. The reading pakkena hatthena seems to me to be quite correct. Compare pakka-gatto, also of a leper, at M. I, 506; and above, p. 357 of the Pâli.

he ought to have. For it was said, O king, by Upasena Vaṅganta-putta, the Elder:

"Bitter food too should he enjoy,
Nor long for what is sweet to taste.
The mind disturbed by lust of taste
Can ne'er enjoy the ecstacies
Of meditations high. The man content
With anything that's given—in him alone
Is Samaṇaship made perfect[1].'"

37. The Deer.

9. 'Venerable Nâgasena, those three qualities of the deer you say he ought to take, which are they?'

'Just, O king, as the deer frequents the forest by day, and spends the night in the open air; just so, O king, should the strenuous Bhikshu, earnest in effort, pass the day in the forest, and the night under the open sky. This, O king, is the first quality of the deer he ought to have. [**396**] For it was said, O king, by the Blessed One, the god over all gods, in the exposition called the Lomahaṃsana Pariyâya:

"And I, Sâriputta, when the nights are cold and wintry, at the time of the eights (the Ashṭakâ festivals[2]), when the snow is falling, at such times did I pass the night under the open sky, and the day in the woods. And in the last month of the hot season I spent the day under the open sky, and the night in the woods[3]."

[1] Thera Gâthâ 580.

[2] So called because they were held on the 8th day after the full moon in the two winter months. See the notes in 'Vinaya Texts,' I, p. 130, and in the Maggḥima, p. 536.

[3] Maggḥima Nikâya I, p. 79. To quote this passage here as an authority the Bhikshu ought still to follow, is a striking instance of

10. 'And again, O king, as the deer, when a javelin or an arrow is falling upon him, dodges it and escapes, not allowing his body to remain in its way; just so, O king, should the strenuous Bhikshu, earnest in effort, when evil inclinations fall upon him, dodge them, and escape, placing not his mind in their way. This, O king, is the second quality of the deer he ought to have.

11. 'And again, O king, as the deer on catching sight of men escapes this way or that, that they may not see him; just so, O king, should the strenuous Bhikshu, earnest in effort, when he sees men of quarrelsome habits, given to contentions and strife and disputes, wicked men and inert, fond of society—then should he escape hither or thither that neither should they see him, nor he them[1]. This, O king, is the third quality of the deer he ought to have. For it was said, O king, by Sâriputta, the Elder, the Commander of the Faith:

"Let not the man with evil in his heart,
Inert, bereft of zeal, of wicked life,
Knowing but little of the sacred words—
Let not that man, at any time or place,
Be my companion, or associate with me[2]."'

---

the fatal habit of quoting texts of Scripture apart from their context. As it stands, it seems as if it supported the proposition of our author. But it is really just the contrary. For it occurs in the description given by Gotama of what he had done before he arrived at insight, when he was carrying out that system of penance which he afterwards abandoned as useless, and indeed worse than useless.

[1] See Ma*ggh*ima Nikâya I, 79, where the closing words are the same.

[2] Thera Gâthâ 987 (but the last words differ).

38. The Bull.

12. 'Venerable Nâgasena, those four qualities of the bull you say he ought to take, which are they?'

'Just, O king, as the bull never forsakes its own stall; just so, O king, should the strenuous Bhikshu, earnest in effort, never abandon his own body on the ground that its nature is only the decomposition, the wearing away, the dissolution, the destruction of that which is impermanent[1]. This, O king, is the first quality of the bull he ought to have.

13. 'And again, O king, as the bull, when he has once taken the yoke upon him, bears that yoke through all conditions of ease or of pain; just so, O king, should the strenuous Bhikshu, earnest in effort, **[397]** when he has once taken upon himself the life of a recluse, keep to it, in happiness or in woe, to the end of his life, to his latest breath. This, O king, is the second quality of the bull he ought to have.

14. 'And again, O king, as the bull drinks water with never satiated desire; just so, O king, should the strenuous Bhikshu, earnest in effort, receive the instruction of his teachers and masters with a desire, love, and pleasure that is never satiated[2]. This, O king, is the third quality of the bull he ought to have.

15. 'And again, O king, as the bull equally bears the yoke whoever puts it on him; just so, O king, should the strenuous Bhikshu, earnest in effort, accept with bowed head the admonitions and ex-

[1] See Dîgha Nikâya II, 83; *G*âtaka I, 146.

[2] Ghâyamânena, at*ri*ptikawa âghrâ*n*aye*m* in the Si*m*halese.

hortations of the elders, of the brethren of junior or of middle standing, and of the believing laity alike. This, O king, is the fourth quality of the bull he ought to have. For it was said, O king, by Sâriputta, the Elder, the Commander of the Faith :

"A novice, seven years of age, a boy
Only to-day received into our ranks,
He too may teach me, and with bended head,
His admonitions will I gladly bear.
Time after time, where'er I meet him, still
My strong approval, and my love, will I
Lavish upon him—if he be but good,—
And yield the honoured place of teacher to him [1]."'

---

39. The Boar.

16. 'Venerable Nâgasena, those two qualities of the boar you say he ought to take, which are they?'

'Just, O king, as the boar, in the sultry and scorching weather of the hot season, resorts to the water; just so, O king, should the strenuous Bhikshu, earnest in effort, when his heart is distracted and ready to fall, all in a whirl, inflamed by anger, resort to the cool, ambrosial, sweet water of the meditation on love. This, O king, is the first quality of the boar he ought to have.

17. 'And again, O king, as the boar, resorting to muddy water, digs into the swamp with his snout, and making a trough for himself, lies down therein; just so, O king, should the strenuous Bhikshu, earnest in effort, put his body away in his mind, and

[1] Not traced as yet. Hînati-kumburê, p. 594, takes santo in the sense of sat purusha guṇayem yukta wû.

lie down in the midst of contemplation. [398] This, O king, is the second quality of the boar he ought to have. For it was said, O king, by Pi*nd*ola Bhâradva*g*a, the Elder:

" Alone, with no one near, the man of insight,
Searching into and finding out the nature
Of this body, can lay him down to rest
On the sweet bed of contemplations deep[1]."'

---

40. The Elephant.

18. 'Venerable Nâgasena, the five qualities of the elephant he ought to take, which are they?'

'Just, O king, as the elephant, as he walks about, crushes the earth; just so, O king, should the strenuous Bhikshu, earnest in effort, mastering the nature of the body, crush out all evil. This, O king, is the first quality of the elephant he ought to have.

19. 'And again, O king, as the elephant turns his whole body when he looks, always looking straight before him, not glancing round this way and that[2]; just so, O king, should the strenuous Bhikshu, earnest in effort, turn his whole body when he looks, always looking straight before, not glancing round this way and that, not looking aloft, not looking at his feet, but keeping his eyes fixed about a yoke's length in front of him. This, O king, is the second quality of the elephant he ought to have.

20. 'And again, O king, as the elephant has no permanent lair, even in seeking his food does not always frequent the same spot, has no fixed place of

[1] Not traced as yet.
[2] On this curious belief, see 'Buddhist Suttas,' p. 64.

abode; just so, O king, should the strenuous Bhikshu, earnest in effort, have no permanent resting-place, but without a home should go his rounds for alms. Full of insight, wherever he sees a pleasant suitable agreeable place[1], whether in a hut or at the foot of a tree, or in a cave, or on a mountain side, there should he dwell, not taking up a fixed abode. This, O king, is the third quality of the elephant he ought to have.

21. 'And again, O king, as the elephant revels in the water, plunging into glorious lotus ponds full of clear pure cool water, and covered over with lotuses yellow, and blue, and red, and white, sporting there in the games in which the mighty beast delights; **[399]** just so, O king, should the strenuous Bhikshu, earnest in effort, plunge into the glorious pond of self-possession, covered with the flowers of emancipation, filled with the delicious waters of the pure and stainless clear and limpid Truth; there should he by knowledge shake off and drive away the Samkhâras[2], there should he revel in the sport that is the delight of the recluse. This, O king, is the fourth quality of the elephant he ought to have.

22. 'And again, O king, as the elephant lifts up his foot with care, and puts it down with care; just so, O king, should the strenuous Bhikshu, earnest in effort, be mindful and self-possessed in lifting

[1] For dese bhavam the Simhalese reads desa-bhâga.

[2] Samkhâra is here used in the sense in which they are said at Dhammapada, verse 203, to be paramâ dukkhâ. The word is there explained by the commentator (wrongly, I think) as the five Skandhas. The Simhalese, p. 596, simply has sarva samskâra dharmayam.

up his feet and in putting them down, in going or returning, in stretching his arm or drawing it back,—wherever he is he should be mindful and self-possessed. This, O king, is the fifth quality of the elephant he ought to have. For it was said, O king, by the Blessed One, the god over all gods, in the most excellent Sa*m*yutta Nikâya:

"Good is restraint in action,
And good restraint in speech,
Good is restraint in mind,
Restraint throughout is good.
Well guarded is he said to be
Who is ashamed of sin, in all things self-controlled [1].'"

Here ends the Fourth Chapter.

---

[1] From the Sa*m*yutta III, 1, 5, 6. The first four lines are also included in the Dhammapada collection, verse 361.

Book VII. Chapter 5.

THE SIMILES (continued).

[400] 41. The Lion.

1. 'Venerable Nâgasena, those seven qualities of the lion you say he ought to have, which are they?'

'Just, O king, as the lion is of a clear, stainless, and pure light yellow colour; just so, O king, should the strenuous Bhikshu, earnest in effort, be clear, stainless, and pure light in mind, free from anger and moroseness. This, O king, is the first quality of the lion he ought to have.

2. 'And again, O king, as the lion has four paws as his means of travelling, and is rapid in his gait; just so, O king, should the strenuous Bhikshu, earnest in effort, move along the four paths of saintship. This, O king, is the second quality of the lion he ought to have.

3. 'And again, O king, as the lion has a beautiful coat of hair, pleasant to behold; just so, O king, should the strenuous Bhikshu, earnest in effort, have a beautiful coat of righteousness, pleasant to behold. This, O king, is the third quality of the lion he ought to have.

4. 'And again, O king, as the lion, even were his life to cease, bows down before no man; just so, O king, should the strenuous Bhikshu, earnest in effort, even though he should cease to obtain all the requisites of a recluse—food and clothing and lodging and medicine for the sick—never bow down

to any man[1]. This is the fourth quality of the lion he ought to have.

5. 'And again, O king, as the lion eats regularly on, wheresoever his prey falls there does he eat whatever he requires, and seeks not out the best morsels of flesh; just so, O king, should the strenuous Bhikshu, earnest in effort, stand for alms at each hut in regular order, not seeking out the families where he would be given better food, not missing out any house upon his rounds[2], he should not pick and choose in eating, wheresoever he may have received a mouthful of rice there should he eat it, seeking not for the best morsels. This, O king, is the fifth quality of the lion he ought to have.

6. 'And again, O king, as the lion is not a storer up of what he eats, and when he has once eaten of his prey returns not again to it; just so, O king, should the strenuous Bhikshu, earnest in effort, never be a storer up of food. This is the sixth quality of the lion he ought to have.

7. [401] 'And again, O king, as the lion, even if he gets no food, is not alarmed, and if he does[3], then he eats it without craving, without faintness, without sinking[4]; just so, O king, should the

[1] This is an injunction the Bhikshus still observe. Some of them have been known to attend a levée in Ceylon (improperly, as I venture to think). But as they would bow to no one, not to governor or prince, the levée became, so far as they were concerned, a mere march-past.

[2] This is one of the Dhutangas, and is in the Sekhiyas (No. 33). Most Bhikshus never 'stand for alms' at all. But if they do, they observe this rule.

[3] 'If he does not,' says the Simhalese.

[4] Anagghâpanno. The MSS. in parallel passages (Tevigga I, 27; Anguttara II, 5, 7; III, 131; Udâna VII, 3, 10; Magghima I,

strenuous Bhikshu, earnest in effort, be not alarmed even if he gets no food, and if he does then should he eat it without craving, without faintness, without sinking, conscious of the danger in the lust of taste, in full knowledge of the right outcome of eating (the maintenance of life for the pursuit of holiness)[1]. This, O king, is the seventh quality of the lion he ought to have. For it was said, O king, by the Blessed One, the god over all gods, in the most excellent Sa*m*yutta Nikâya, when he was exalting Mahâ Kassapa, the Elder:

"This Kassapa, O Bhikshus, is content with such food as he receives, he magnifies the being content with whatever food one gets, he is not guilty of anything improper or unbecoming for the sake of an alms, if he receive none, yet is he not alarmed, and if he does then does he eat it without craving, without faintness, without sinking, conscious of danger, with full knowledge of the right object in taking food[2]."'

---

42. THE *K*AKRAVÂKA BIRD.

8. 'Venerable Nâgasena, those three qualities of the *K*akravâka bird you say he ought to take, which are they?'

'Just, O king, as the *K*akravâka bird never forsakes his mate even to the close of his life; just so, O king, should the strenuous Bhikshu, never, even

---

173; Sumangala I, 59) have usually a*ggh*opanno. The Simhalese has âhâra t*r*ish*n*âwehi no gœlî.

[1] Nissara*n*a-pa*ññ*ena. This Hîna*t*i-kumburê renders nissara*n*âkhyâtawû brahma*k*ariyânugraha pi*n*isa yanâdiwû pratyawekshâ *ññ*â*n*ayem yuktawû.

[2] Sa*m*yutta XVI, 1, 3 (vol. ii, p. 194 of M. Léon Feer's edition for the Pâli Text Society).

to the close of his life, give up the habit of thought. This, O king, is the first quality of the *K*akravâka bird he ought to have.

9. 'And again, O king, as the *K*akravâka bird feeds on the Sevâla and Pa*n*aka (water-plants so called), and derives satisfaction therefrom, and being so satisfied, neither his strength nor his beauty grows less; just so, O king, should the strenuous Bhikshu, earnest in effort, find satisfaction in whatever he receives. And if he does so find satisfaction, O king, then does he decrease neither in power of meditation, nor in wisdom, nor in emancipation, nor in the insight that arises from the consciousness of emancipation, nor in any kind of goodness. **[402]** This, O king, is the second quality of the *K*akravâka bird he ought to have.

10. 'And again, O king, as the *K*akravâka bird does no harm to living things; just so, O king, should the strenuous Bhikshu, earnest in effort, laying aside the cudgel, laying aside the sword, be full of modesty and pity, compassionate and kind to all creatures that have life[1]. This, O king, is the third quality of the *K*akravâka bird he ought to have. For it was said, O king, by the Blessed One, the god over all gods, in the *K*akravâka *G*âtaka:

"The man who kills not, nor destroys,
Oppresses not, nor causes other men
To take from men that which is rightly theirs[2]—

[1] This is from the first clause in the *K*ûla Sîla (translated in 'Buddhist Suttas,' p. 189).

[2] Na *g*inâti na *g*âpaye. Both these forms are to be derived, I venture to think, from *G*YÂ (or its more primitive form *G*Î), and not from *GI*. It is true that Childers gives *g*inâti as third person singular of *GI*, and that (through the influence of the

And this from kindness to all things that live—
No wrath with any man disturbs his peace[1].”’

43. The Pe*n*âhikâ[2] bird.

11. ‘Venerable Nâgasena, those two qualities of the Pe*n*âhikâ bird you say he ought to take, which are they?’

‘Just, O king, as the Pe*n*âhikâ bird, through jealousy of her mate, refuses to nourish her young[3]; just so, O king, should the strenuous Bhikshu, earnest in effort, be jealous of any evil dispositions

common word *G*ina) there has really, perhaps, been some confusion in Pâli writers between the two roots, closely allied as they are both in form and meaning. But whether or not that be so elsewhere, we have here at least another instance of the frequent association of a simple verb with its own causal. *G*âpeti, which occurs three times in the Milinda, and is always explained by Hîna*t*i-kumburê in the same way (see my notes above on pp. 171, 227 of the Pâli; here he has artha-hâni no karawâ da), i neither for *gh*âpeti (as Dr. Edward Müller suggests in his grammar, p. 37) nor for *g*âpayati, but for *g*yâpayati. For the apparent confusion between *G*I, *g*ayati, ‘conquer,’ and *G*YÂ, *g*inâti, (1) ‘overcome, bring into subjection,’ (2) ‘oppress, extort,’ see the commentary on *g*ine at Dhammapada, verse 103 (quoted also at *G*âtaka I, 314), which runs *g*initvâna *g*aya*m* âhareyya; and on *g*aya*m* at verse 201 (taken from Sa*m*yutta III, 2, 4, 7), which is explained by *g*inanto, and at verse 104 where *g*ita*m* is explained by *g*inâti. But in Pi*t*aka texts I know of no instance where the two roots cannot be kept quite distinct; and it is quite possible that the Dhammapada commentator, while interpreting the one root by the other, is still conscious of the difference between them. *G*îna (the p. p. p. of *g*inâti) is not given at all by Childers, but occurs *G*âtaka III, 153, 223, 335; V, 99.

[1] *G*âtaka IV, 71. One word differs, and the lines are not spoken by the Buddha, but by the bird.

[2] The Si*m*halese (p. 600) has kœndœttiya, a vord not in Clough.

[3] Hîna*t*i-kumburê's translation of this clause shows that he had a different reading in his Pâli text.

which arise within him, and putting them by his mindfulness into the excellent crevice of self-control, should dwell at the door of his mind in the constant practice of self-possession in all things relating to his body[1]. This, O king, is the first quality of the Pe*n*âhikâ bird he ought to have.

12. 'And again, O king, as the Pe*n*âhikâ bird spends the day in the forest in search of food, but at night time resorts for protection to the flock of birds to which she belongs; just so, O king, should the strenuous Bhikshu, earnest in effort, who has for a time resorted to solitary places for the purpose of emancipation from the ten Fetters, and found no satisfaction therein, repair back to the Order for protection against the danger of blame, and dwell under the shelter of the Order[2]. This, O king, is the second quality of the Pe*n*âhikâ bird he ought to have. For it was said, O king, by the Brahmâ Sahampati in the presence of the Blessed One:

"Seek lodgings distant from the haunts of men,
Live there in freedom from the bonds of sin;
But he who finds no peace in solitude
May with the Order dwell, guarded in heart,
Mindful and self-possessed[3].'"

---

[1] 'As the Pe*n*âhikâ, refusing to nourish her young in the nest, puts them into a crevice of a tree, and watches them there,' is the Si*m*halese interpretation. And the word susira would not have been used in the second clause unless something corresponding to it had originally stood also in the first.

[2] Here again it is probable from the Si*m*halese version that Hînati-kumburê reads ratti*m* for rati*m*.

[3] The verse occurs in the Thera Gâthâ 142, but is here quoted from the Sa*m*yutta Nikâya VI, 2, 3, 4, where the readings sa*k*e *k*a . . . . nâdhiga*kkh*aye . . . . . satimâ must be corrected according to the readings here.

44. The House-pigeon.

13. [403] 'Venerable Nâgasena, that one quality of the house-pigeon you say he ought to take, which is it?'

'Just, O king, as the house-pigeon, while dwelling in the abode of others, of men, does not become enamoured of anything that belongs to them, but remains neutral, taking notice only of things pertaining to birds; just so, O king, should the strenuous Bhikshu, earnest in effort, while resorting to other people's houses, never become enamoured of women or of men, of beds, or chairs, or garments, or jewelry, or things for use or enjoyment, or various forms of food that are there, but remain neutral always, addicted only to such ideas as become a recluse. This, O king, is the quality of the house-pigeon he ought to have. For it was said, O king, by the Blessed One, the god over all gods, in the *K*ulla Nânada *G*âtaka :

"Frequenting people's homes for food or drink,
In food and drink alike be temperate,
And let not beauty's form attract thy thoughts[1]."'

45. The Owl.

14. 'Venerable Nâgasena, those two qualities of the owl you say he ought to take, which are they?'

'Just, O king, as the owl, being at enmity with the crows, goes at night where the flocks of crows are, and kills numbers of them; just so, O king, should the strenuous Bhikshu, earnest in effort, be

[1] *G*âtaka IV, 223. There is a difference of reading, making no difference to the sense; and the words are put into the mouth, not of the Buddha, but of the old ascetic, the Bodisat of the story.

at enmity with ignorance; seated alone and in secret, he should crush it out of existence, cut it off at the root. This, O king, is the first quality of the owl he ought to have.

15. 'And again, O king, as the owl is a solitary bird; just so, O king, should the strenuous Bhikshu, earnest in effort, be devoted to solitude, take delight in solitude. This, O king, is the second quality of the owl he ought to have. For it was said, O king, by the Blessed One, the god over all gods, in the most excellent Sa*m*yutta Nikâya:

"Let the Bhikshu, my brethren, be devoted to solitude, take delight in solitude, to the end that he may realise what sorrow really is, and what the origin of sorrow really is, [**404**] and what the cessation of sorrow really is, and what the path that leads to the cessation of sorrow really is[1]."'

46. The Indian Crane[2].

16. 'Venerable Nâgasena, that one quality of the Indian crane you say he ought to take, which is it?'

'Just, O king, as the Indian crane by its cry makes known to other folk the good fortune or disaster that is about to happen to them; just so, O king, should the strenuous Bhikshu, earnest in effort, make known to others by his preaching of the Dhamma how dreadful a state is purgatory, and how blissful is Nirvâ*n*a. This, O king, is the quality of the Indian crane he ought to have. For it was said, O king, by Pi*nd*ola Bhâra-dvâ*g*a, the elder:

[1] Not traced as yet.

[2] Satapatto, literally 'the hundred-feathered one,' Si*m*halese kœrœl, quite different from the ordinary crane (bako). This one was a bird of ill omen. See *G*âtaka II, 153 foll.

"Two matters there are that the earnest recluse
Should ever to others be making clear—
How fearful, how terrible, purgatory is;
How great and how deep is Nirvâ*n*a's bliss[1]."'

---

47. The Bat.

17. 'Venerable Nâgasena, those two qualities of the bat you say he ought to take, which are they?'

'Just, O king, as the bat, though it enters into men's dwelling-places, and flies about in them, soon goes out from them, delays not therein; just so, O king, should the strenuous Bhikshu, earnest in effort, when he has entered the village for alms, and gone on his rounds in regular order, depart quickly with the alms he has received, and delay not therein. This, O king, is the first quality of the bat he ought to have.

18. 'And again, O king, as the bat, while frequenting other folk's houses, does them no harm; just so, O king, should the strenuous Bhikshu, earnest in effort, when visiting the houses of the laity, never give them cause for vexation by persistent requests, or by pointing out what he wants, or by wrong demeanour, or by chattering, or by being indifferent to their prosperity or adversity; he should never take them away from their chief business occupations, but desire their success in all things. This, O king, is the second quality of the bat he ought to have. For it was said, O king, [**405**] by the Blessed One, the god over all gods, in the Lakkha*n*a Suttanta:

"'Oh! How may others never suffer loss
Or diminution, whether in their faith,

---

[1] Not traced as yet.

Or righteousness, or knowledge of the word,
Or understanding, or self-sacrifice,
Or in religion, or in all good things,
Or in their stores of wealth, or corn, or lands,
Or tenements, or in their sons, or wives,
Or in their flocks and herds, or in their friends,
And relatives, and kinsmen, or in strength,
In beauty, and in joy'—'tis thus he thinks—
Longing for other men's advantage and success[1]!"'

---

48. The Leech.

19. 'Venerable Nâgasena, that one quality of the leech which you say he ought to take, which is it?'

'Just, O king, as the leech, wheresoever it is put on, there does it adhere firmly, drinking the blood; just so, O king, should the strenuous Bhikshu, earnest in effort, on whatsoever subject for meditation he may fix his mind, call that subject firmly up before him in respect of its colour, and shape, and position, and extension, and boundaries, and nature, and characteristic marks, drinking the delicious draught of the ambrosia of emancipation. This, O king, is the quality of the leech he ought to have. For it was said, O king, by Anuruddha, the Elder:

"With heart made pure, in meditation firm,
Drink deep of freedom's never-failing draught[2]."'

---

[1] This is from the 30th Sutta in the Dîgha Nikâya, where it occurs in the description of the Bodisat.

[2] Not traced as yet. Childers translates asek*a*na by 'charming,' &c., apparently on the authority of Subhûti's English gloss on Abhidhâna Padîpikâ 597. But that meaning is rather the point of union between all the synonyms given in the verse, and not the exact meaning of each of them. The word, either in its simple form, or with an added -ka, occurs in Theri Gâthâ 55; Ma*ggh*ima Nikâya I, 114.

49. The Serpent.

20. 'Venerable Nâgasena, those three qualities of the serpent you say he ought to take, which are they?'

'Just, O king, as the serpent progresses by means of its belly; just so, O king, should the strenuous Bhikshu, earnest in effort, progress by means of his knowledge. For the heart of the recluse, O king, who progresses by knowledge, continues in perception (of the four Truths), that which is inconsistent with the characteristics of a recluse[1] does he put away, that which is consistent with them does he develop in himself. This, [**406**] O king, is the first quality of the serpent he ought to have.

21. 'And again, O king, just as the serpent as it moves avoids drugs[2]; just so, O king, should the strenuous Bhikshu, earnest in effort, go on his way avoiding unrighteousness. This, O king, is the second quality of the serpent he ought to have.

22. 'And again, O king, as the serpent on catching sight of men is anxious, and pained, and seeks a way of escape[3]; just so, O king, should the strenuous Bhikshu, earnest in effort, when he finds himself thinking wrong thoughts, or discontent arising within him, be anxious and pained, and seek a way of escape, saying to himself: "This day must I have spent in carelessness, and never shall I be able to recover it." This, O king, is the third quality of the

[1] Vilakkha*n*am, not found elsewhere. Hîna*t*i-kumburê, p. 604, renders it simply 'dullness' (moha).

[2] 'Goes slanting, avoiding medicinal plants, trees, &c.,' says the Si*m*halese.

[3] *K*intayati, perhaps 'put out.' Gœlawî yanta sitanneya, says the Si*m*halese, p. 605.

serpent he ought to have. For it is a saying, O king, of the two fairy birds in the Bhallâ*t*iya *G*âtaka:

"'Tis one night only, hunter, that we've spent
Away from home, and that against our will,
And thinking all night through of one another,
Yet that one night is it that we bemoan,
And grieve; for nevermore can it return[1]!"'

---

50. The Rock-snake[2].

23. 'Venerable Nâgasena, that one quality of the rock-snake that you say he ought to take, which is it?'

'Just, O king, as the rock-snake, immense as is its length of body, will go many days with empty belly, and, wretched, get no food to fill its stomach, yet in spite of that it will just manage to keep itself alive; just so, O king, should the strenuous Bhikshu, earnest in effort, though he be addicted to obtaining his food by alms, dependent on the gifts that others may give, awaiting offers, abstaining from taking anything himself, and find it difficult to get his belly's-full, yet should he, if he seek after the highest good[3], even though he receive not so much as four or five mouthfuls to eat, fill up the void by water. This, O king, is the quality of the rock-snake he ought to have. For it was said, O king, [407] by Sâriputta, the Elder, the Commander of the Faith:

---

[1] *G*âtaka IV, 439.

[2] A*g*agara. Childers renders this 'boa-constrictor.' But Hîna*t*i-kumburê has pimburâ, which is a rock-snake, often confounded with the boa-constrictor on account of the size to which it grows.

[3] Atthavasikena, attha being rendered Nirvâ*n*a by the Si*m*halese.

"Whether it be dry food or wet he eats,
Let him to full repletion never eat.
The good recluse goes forth in emptiness,
And keeps to moderation in his food.
If but four mouthfuls or but five he get,
Let him drink water. For what cares the man
With mind on Arahatship fixed for ease[1]!"'

Here ends the Fifth Chapter.

[1] Thera Gâthâ 982, 983. The next verse but one has been already quoted above, p. 366 of the Pâli; and these recur at *G*âtaka II, 293, 294.

Book VII. Chapter 6.

the similes (continued).

51. The Road Spider.

1. 'Venerable Nâgasena, that one quality of the road spider you say he ought to have, which is it?'

'Just, O king, as the road spider weaves the curtain of its net on the road, and whatsoever is caught therein, whether worm, or fly, or beetle, that does he catch and eat; just so, O king, should the strenuous Bhikshu, earnest in effort, spread the curtain of the net of self-possession over the six doors (of his six senses), and if any of the flies of evil are caught therein, there should he seize them. This, O king, is the quality of the road spider he ought to have. For it was said, O king, by Anuruddha, the Elder:

"His heart should he shut in, at its six doors,
By self-possession, best and chief of gifts,
Should any evil thoughts be caught within,
Them by the sword of insight should he slay[1]."'

---

52. The Child at the Breast.

2. 'Venerable Nâgasena, that one quality of the child at the breast you say he ought to take, [408] which is it?'

'Just, O king, as the child at the breast sticks to its own advantage, and if it wants milk, cries for it;

[1] Not traced as yet.

just so, O king, should the strenuous Bhikshu, earnest in effort, adhere to his own good, and in everything—in teaching, in asking and answering questions, in the conduct of life, in the habit of solitude, in association with his teachers, in the cultivation of the friendship of the good—should he act with knowledge of the Truth. This, O king, is the quality of the child at the breast he ought to have. For it was said, O king, by the Blessed One, the god over all gods, in the Dîgha Nikâya, in the Suttanta of the Great Decease:

"Be zealous, rather, I beseech you, Ânanda, in your own behalf. Devote yourselves to your own good. Be earnest, all aglow, intent on your own good[1]!"'

---

53. The Land Tortoise[2].

3. 'Venerable Nâgasena, that one quality of the land tortoise which you say he ought to take, which is it?'

'Just, O king, as the land tortoise, being afraid of the water, frequents places far from it, and by that habit of avoiding water its length of life is kept undiminished; just so, O king, should the strenuous Bhikshu, earnest in effort, seeing the danger in the want of earnestness, be mindful of the advantages that distinguish earnestness. For by that perception of

---

[1] Mahâ-parinibbâna Suttanta V, 24, translated in 'Buddhist Suttas,' p. 91. The beginning of the exhortation has been already quoted above, p. 177 (of the Pâli).

[2] *K*ittaka-dhara-kummassa, literally 'of the tortoise who wears the sectarian mark (on his forehead).' The Si*m*halese repeats this phrase, which clearly distinguishes this tortoise from the other, the water tortoise, of VII, 1, 12.

danger in carelessness, his Samanaship fades not away, but rather does he go forward to Nirvâna itself. This, O king, is the quality of the land tortoise he ought to have. For it was said, O king, by the Blessed One, the god over all gods, in the Dhammapada:

"The Bhikshu who in earnestness delights,
Who sees the danger of indifference,
Shall fall not from his high estate away,
But in the presence of Nirvâna dwell[1].”'

---

54. The Mountain Height.

4. 'Venerable Nâgasena, those five qualities of the mountain height you say he ought to have, which are they?'

'Just, O king, as the mountain height is a hiding-place for the wicked; just so, O king, should the strenuous Bhikshu, earnest in effort, keep secret the offences and failings of others, revealing them not. This, O king, is the first of the qualities of the mountain height he ought to have.

5. 'And again, O king, just as the mountain height is void of many people; just so, O king, should the strenuous Bhikshu, [409] earnest in effort, be void of lust, angers, follies, and pride, of the net of (wrong) views[2], and of all evil dispositions. This, O king,

---

[1] Dhammapada, verse 32. The source from which the verse is taken is unknown now, and was also evidently unknown to our author. With the closing words nibbânass eva santike, compare verse 372, sa ve nibbâna-santike. Santike, 'immediate, close,' is always used with the connotation of being in the very presence of. The local qualification, 'near,' is upanissaya, avidûre.

[2] Ditthi-gâla, the net of delusions, those relating to the per-

is the second quality of the mountain height he ought to have.

6. 'And again, O king, just as the mountain height is a lonely spot, free from crowding of men; just so, O king, should the strenuous Bhikshu, earnest in effort, be given to solitude, and free from evil, unworthy qualities, from those that are not noble. This, O king, is the third quality of the mountain height he ought to have.

7. 'And again, O king, just as the mountain height is clean and pure; just so, O king, should the strenuous Bhikshu, earnest in effort, be good and pure, happy, and without self-righteousness. This, O king, is the fourth quality of the mountain height he ought to have.

8. 'And again, O king, just as the mountain height is the resort of the noble ones; just so, O king, should the strenuous Bhikshu, earnest in effort, be sought after by the noble ones. This, O king, is the fifth quality of the mountain height he ought to have. For it was said, O king, by the Blessed One, the god over all gods, in the most excellent Sa*m*yutta Nikâya:

"With solitary men, those noble ones,
Whose minds, on Arahatship strictly bent,
Rise easily to contemplation's heights,
Stedfast in zeal and wise in holy writ—
With such should he resort, with such commune[1].''

---

manence of any individuality, and the separateness of oneself from others, as well those now living as those in the future and the past.

[1] This is a favourite stanza. It occurs in the Sa*m*yutta XIV, 16-18, and is included in the verses ascribed, in the Thera Gâthâ, to the Arahats Somamitta and Vimala (verses 148, 266).

55. The Tree.

9. 'Venerable Nâgasena, those three qualities of the tree you say he ought to take, which are they?'

'Just, O king, as the tree bears fruits and flowers; just so, O king, should the strenuous Bhikshu, earnest in effort, bear the flowers of emancipation and the fruits of Sama*n*aship[1]. This, O king, is the first quality of the tree he ought to have.

10. 'And again, O king, as the tree casts its shadow over the men who come to it, and stay beneath it; just so, O king, should the strenuous Bhikshu, earnest in effort, receive with kindness, both as regards their bodily wants and their religious necessities, those that wait upon him, and remain near by him. This, O king, is the second quality of the tree he ought to have.

11. 'And again, O king, just as the tree makes no kind of distinction in the shadow it affords; **[410]** just so, O king, should the strenuous Bhikshu, earnest in effort, make no distinctions between all men, but nourish an equal love to those who rob, or hurt, or bear enmity to him, and to those who are like unto himself. This, O king, is the third quality of the tree he ought to have. For it was said, O king, by Sâriputta, the Elder, the Commander of the Faith:

"Devadatta, who tried to murder him;
Aṅgulimâla, highway robber chief;
The elephant set loose to take his life;
And Râhula, the good, his only son—
The sage is equal-minded to them all[2]."'

---

[1] The Si*m*halese, p. 610, is here greatly expanded.
[2] This stanza has only been traced at present in commentaries,

56. The Rain.

12. 'Venerable Nâgasena, those five qualities of the rain you say he ought to take, which are they?'

'Just, O king, as the rain lays any dust that arises; just so, O king, should the strenuous Bhikshu, earnest in effort, lay the dust and dirt of any evil dispositions that may arise within him. This, O king, is the first quality of the rain he ought to have.

13. 'And again, O king, just as the rain allays the heat of the ground; just so, O king, should the strenuous Bhikshu, earnest in effort, soothe the whole world of gods and men, with the feeling of his love. This, O king, is the second quality of the rain he ought to have.

14. 'And again, O king, as the rain makes all kinds of vegetation to grow; just so, O king, should the strenuous Bhikshu, earnest in effort, cause faith to spring up in all beings, and make that seed of faith grow up into the three Attainments, not only the lesser attainments of glorious rebirths in heaven or on earth, but also the attainment of the highest good, the bliss of Arahatship [1]. This, O king, is the third quality of the rain he ought to have.

15. 'And again, O king, just as the rain-cloud, rising up in the hot season, affords protection to the grass, and trees, and creepers, and shrubs, and medicinal herbs, and to the monarchs of the woods that grow on the surface of the earth; just so, O king, should the strenuous Bhikshu, earnest in effort,

where it is quoted with some variation. See the Commentary on the Dhammapada, p. 147.

[1] In my note above, I, 146, I might have referred to this passage.

cultivating the habit of thoughtfulness, afford protection by his thoughtfulness to his condition of Sama*n*aship, for in thoughtfulness is it that all good qualities have their root. This, O king, is the fourth quality of the rain he ought to have.

16. [**411**] 'And again, O king, as the rain when it pours down fills the rivers, and reservoirs, and artificial lakes, the caves, and chasms, and ponds, and holes, and wells, with water; just so, O king, should the strenuous Bhikshu, earnest in effort, pour down the rain of the Dhamma according to the texts handed down by tradition, and so fill to satisfaction the mind of those who are longing for instruction. This, O king, is the fifth quality of the rain he ought to have. For it was said, O king, by Sâriputta, the Elder, the Commander of the Faith:

"When the Great Sage perceives a man afar,
Were it a hundred or a thousand leagues,
Ripe for enlightenment, straightway he goes
And guides him gently to the path of Truth[1]."'

---

57. The Diamond.

17. 'Venerable Nâgasena, those three qualities of the diamond you say he ought to take, which are they?'

'Just, O king, as the diamond is pure throughout; just so, O king, should the strenuous Bhikshu, earnest in effort, be perfectly pure in his means of livelihood. This, O king, is the first quality of the diamond he ought to have.

18. 'And again, O king, as the diamond cannot

---

[1] Not traced as yet.

be alloyed with any other substance; just so, O king, should the strenuous Bhikshu, earnest in effort, never mix with wicked men as friends. This, O king, is the second quality of the diamond he ought to have.

19. 'And again, O king, just as the diamond is set together with the most costly gems; just so, O king, should the strenuous Bhikshu, earnest in effort, associate with those of the higher excellence, with men who have entered the first or the second or the third stage of the Noble Path, with the jewel treasures of the Arahats, of the recluses, of the threefold Wisdom, or of the sixfold Insight. This, O king, is the third quality of the diamond he ought to have. For it was said, O king, by the Blessed One, the god over all gods, in the Sutta Nipâta:

"Let the pure associate with the pure,
Ever in recollection firm;
Dwelling harmoniously wise
Thus shall ye put an end to griefs[1]."'

58. The Hunter.

20. [412] 'Venerable Nâgasena, those four qualities of the hunter you say he ought to have, which are they?'

'Just, O king, as the hunter is indefatigable, so also, O king, should the strenuous Bhikshu, earnest in effort, be indefatigable. This, O king, is the first quality of the hunter he ought to have.

21. 'And again, O king, just as the hunter keeps his attention fixed on the deer; just so, O king, should the strenuous Bhikshu, earnest in effort, keep his

[1] Sutta Nipâta II, 6, 10 (verse 282).

attention fixed on the particular object which is the subject of his thought. This, O king, is the second quality of the hunter he ought to have.

22. 'And again, O king, just as the hunter knows the right time for his work; just so, O king, should the strenuous Bhikshu, earnest in effort, know the right time for retirement, saying to himself: "Now is the right time to retire. Now is the right time to come out of retirement." This, O king, is the third quality of the hunter he ought to have.

23. 'And again, O king, just as the hunter on catching sight of a deer experiences joy at the thought: "Him shall I get!" just so, O king, should the strenuous Bhikshu, earnest in effort, rejoice at the sight of an object for contemplation, and experience joy at the thought: "Thereby shall I grasp the specific idea of which I am in search [1]." This, O king, is the fourth quality of the hunter he ought to have. For it was said, O king, by Mogharâ*g*a, the Elder:

---

[1] Uttari*m* visesa*m* udhiga*kkh*issâmi. Hîna*t*i-kumburê, p. 614, renders this, 'shall I arrive at the advantage of the attainment of the fruits of the path.' And he may be right, as the word uttari*m* is used. But the context seems to imply the rendering I have ventured to give, which preserves the usual connotation in this connection of the other two words of the phrase. A Bhikshu, for instance, on seeing a faded flower, will try to realise, to conjure up before his mind, the real fact of the transitoriness of all earthly (and of all heavenly) things. That is the specific idea of which he is in search, the deer he has to catch. No doubt it is only an intermediate step to the realisation of the fruits of the path. But as visesa*m* adhiga*kkh*ati is the technical term for success in such meditation, I cannot but think that the mind of our author was directed to the intermediate, rather than to the later stage of the Bhikshu's endeavour. The Si*m*halese has, perhaps, been guided by the verse, but there the word visesa*m* is omitted.

"The recluse who, with mind on Nirvâ*n*a bent,
Has acquired an object his thoughts to guide,
Should be filled with exceeding joy at the hope:
'By this my uttermost aim shall I gain [1].'"'

59. The Fisherman.

24. 'Venerable Nâgasena, those two qualities of the fisherman you say he ought to take, which are they?'

'Just, O king, as the fisherman draws up the fish on his hook; just so, O king, should the strenuous Bhikshu, earnest in effort, draw up by his knowledge, and that to the uttermost, the fruits of Sama*n*aship. This, O king, is the first quality of the fisherman he ought to have.

25. 'And again, O king, just as the fisherman by the sacrifice of a very little comes to great gain [2]; just so, O king, [**413**] should the strenuous Bhikshu, earnest in effort, renounce the mean baits of worldly things; then by that renunciation will he gain the mighty fruits of Sama*n*aship. This, O king, is the second quality of the fisherman he ought to have. For it was said, O king, by Râhula, the Elder:

"Renouncing the baits of the world he shall gain
The state that is void of lust, anger, and sin,—
Those conditions of sentient life—and be free,
Free from the cravings that mortals feel,
And the fruits of the stages of th' Excellent Way
And the six modes of Insight shall all be his [3]."'

[1] Not traced as yet. There are stanzas of Mogha-râ*g*a's both in the Sutta Nipâta and the Thera Gâthâ, but this is not one of them.

[2] By putting a small fish on his hook catches a big one.

[3] Not traced as yet.

60. The Carpenter.

26. 'Venerable Nâgasena, those two qualities of the carpenter he ought to take, which are they?'

'Just, O king, as the carpenter saws off the wood along the line of the blackened string (he has put round it to guide him)[1]; just so, O king, should the strenuous Bhikshu, earnest in effort, standing on righteousness as a basis, and holding in the hand of faith the saw of knowledge, cut off his evil dispositions according to the doctrine laid down by the Conquerors. This, O king, is the first quality of the carpenter he ought to have.

27. 'And again, O king, just as the carpenter, discarding the soft parts of the wood[2], takes the hard parts; just so, O king, should the strenuous Bhikshu, earnest in effort, forsaking the path of the discussion of useless theses, to wit:—the everlasting life theory—the let-us-eat-and-drink-for-tomorrow-we-die theory[3]—the theory that the soul and the body are one and the same—that the soul is one thing, the body another—that all teachings are alike

[1] Kâ*l*a-sutta*m*. See Dr. Morris's note in the 'Journal of the Pâli Text Society,' 1884, pp. 76–78, where he compares Mahâ Vastu, p. 17, and other passages.

[2] Phegg*u*m. See above, p. 267 (of the Pâli), and Ma*ggh*ima Nikâya I, 198, 434, 488, from which it is clear that pheggu is a technical term applied to the softer portions of every tree, no doubt the outside portions. Sâra, on the other hand, means not pith, but heart of a tree. The Si*m*halese words are sambulu and ara*t*uwa. Compare the ebony tree, the outside of which is as soft and white as deal, whereas the inside is black and hard.

[3] Sassata*m* and U*kkh*eda*m*. See 'Buddhist Suttas,' p. 149. Hîna*t*i-kumburê, p. 615, omits these two, and is very confused in his version of the others.

excellent[1]—that what is not done is of no avail—that men's actions are of no importance—that holiness of life does not matter—that on the destruction of beings nine new sorts of beings appear—that the constituent elements of being are eternal[2]—that he who commits an act experiences the result thereof—that one acts and another experiences the result of this action—and other such theories of Karma or wrong views on the result of actions—forsaking, I say, all such theses, paths which lead to heresy, he should learn what is the real nature of those constituent elements of which each individuality is, for the short term of its individuality, put together, and so reach forward to that state which is void of lusts, of malice, and of dullness, in which the excitements of individuality are known no more, and which is therefore designated the Void Supreme[3].

---

[1] Tad uttama*m* a*ññ*ad uttama*m*. The Si*m*halese omits the second uttama*m*.

[2] The Si*m*halese takes all the four previous phrases as qualifying this last one.

[3] This passage will be found of the greatest importance for the history of the development of early Buddhist belief. In the present state of our knowledge—or rather of our ignorance—of that subject, its obscure allusions are no doubt unintelligible. But they will not always remain so. And, when rightly understood, they will be expressly valuable inasmuch as they refer to that department of Buddhist belief of which we know, from other sources, the least. The development—or degeneration, if the expression be preferred—of Buddhist doctrine took place along three principal lines. Firstly, in the doctrine as to the person of the Buddha; secondly, in the pushing of Arahatship into the background and the elevation, in its place, of Bodisatship into the ideal; and thirdly, in the doctrine of the relation of man to the universe. We know a good deal of the growth of the legend of the Buddha, and of the change in the ethical standpoint. Of the evolution of the philosophic conceptions we know at present but little. It is on this last point that our author here lets us somewhat behind the scenes. The theses he

This, O king, is the second quality of the carpenter he ought to have. For it was said, O king, by the Blessed One, the god over all gods, in the Sutta Nipâta:

"Get rid of filth[1]! Put aside rubbish from you!
Winnow away the chaff[2], the men who hold
Those who are not so, as true Sama*n*as!
Get rid of those who harbour evil thoughts,
Who follow after evil modes of life!
Thoughtful yourselves, and pure, with those resort,
With those associate, who are pure themselves[3]!"'

Here ends the Sixth Chapter.

---

condemns are to some extent the same as those the discussion of which is condemned in the well-known passages in the Pi*t*akas, where similar lists occur. In other respects they are evidence of a different and later stage of thought than appears in those parts of the Pi*t*akas at present accessible. And on the positive side, in the closing words, though the author has evidently enough the old Arahatship in view, yet he chooses expressions which became the germ of the much later nihilism of the Mâdhyamika school, which has had so much influence in the more corrupt Buddhisms, more especially in China. As these later views never penetrated into Ceylon (or at least never had any vogue there, and were forgotten when Hîna*t*i-kumburê wrote), it is not surprising that the Si*m*halese scholar should be at fault in his interpretation of this difficult passage. Sanskrit Buddhist texts will be here the best commentary.

[1] Kâra*nd*ava*m*. In Childers, 'a sort of duck,' in the Si*m*halese, 'excrement.'

[2] Palâpe vâhetha. Chaff is so often used in Pâli of frivolous talk that it is given in the dictionaries as having that meaning. Hîna*t*i-kumburê takes it here in the sense of men of low caste, leprous *Kand*âlas.

[3] Not traced as yet. It is not in the Sutta Nipâta. This is the only passage in which our author gives the name of a book as the source from which he takes a passage, when the passage cannot be found in it. See Introduction, I, xliii.

Book VII. Chapter 7.

THE SIMILES (continued).

61. The Waterpot.

1. [414] 'Venerable Nâgasena, that one quality of the waterpot you say he ought to take, which is it?'

'Just, O king, as the waterpot when it is full gives forth no sound; just so, O king, should the strenuous Bhikshu, earnest in effort, even when he has reached the summit of Sama*n*aship, and knows all tradition and learning and interpretation, yet should give forth no sound, not pride himself thereon, not show himself puffed up, but putting away pride and self-righteousness, should be straightforward, not garrulous of himself, neither depreciating others. This, O king, is the quality of the waterpot he ought to have. For it was said, O king, by the Blessed One, the god over all gods, in the Sutta Nipâta:

"What is not full, that is the thing that sounds,
That which is full is noiseless and at rest;
The fool is like an empty waterpot,
The wise man like a deep pool, clear and full [1]."'

62. Black Iron [2].

2. 'Venerable Nâgasena, those two qualities of black iron you say he ought to take, which are they?'

[415] 'Just, O king, as black iron even when

[1] Sutta Nipâta III, 11, 43 (verse 721).

[2] Ka*l*âyasa. I suppose to distinguish it from bronze.

beaten out[1] carries weight; just so, O king, should the mind of the strenuous Bhikshu, earnest in effort, be able, by his habit of thoughtfulness, to carry heavy burdens. This, O king, is the first quality of black iron he ought to have.

3. 'And again, O king, as black iron does not vomit up the water it has once soaked in[2]; just so, O king, should the strenuous Bhikshu, earnest in effort, never give up the faith he has once felt in the greatness of the Blessed One, the Supreme Buddha, in the perfection of his Doctrine, in the excellence of the Order—never give up the knowledge he has once acquired of the impermanence of forms, or of sensations, or of ideas, or of qualities, or of modes of consciousness. This, O king, is the second quality of black iron he ought to have. For it was said, O king, by the Blessed One, the god over all gods:

"That man who is in insight purified,
Trained in the doctrine of the Noble Ones,
Grasping distinctions as they really are,
What need hath he to tremble? Not in part
Only, but in its full extent, shall he
To the clear heights of Arahatship attain[3]."'

63. The Sunshade.

4. 'Venerable Nâgasena, those three qualities of the sunshade[4] you say he ought to take, which are they?'

---

[1] Suthito. 'Like a thin, strong creeper,' says the Si*m*halese.

[2] There is no explanation in the Si*m*halese of this curious phrase.

[3] Not traced as yet. Hîna*t*i-kumburê (p. 618) reads visesagu*n*â pavedhati, and mukhabhâvam eva so.

[4] *Kh*atta. As used by high officials, a circular sunshade sup-

'Just, O king, as the sunshade goes along over one's head; just so, O king, should the strenuous Bhikshu, earnest in effort, be of a character above all evil dispositions. This, O king, is the first quality of the sunshade he ought to have.

5. 'And again, O king, just as the sunshade is held over the head by a handle; just so, O king, should the strenuous Bhikshu, earnest in effort, have thoughtfulness as his handle. This, O king, is the second quality of the sunshade he ought to have.

6. 'And again, O king, as the sunshade wards off winds and heat and storms of rain; just so, O king, should the strenuous Bhikshu, earnest in effort, ward off the empty winds of the opinions of the numerous Sama*n*as and Brahmans who hold forth their various and divergent nostrums, ward off the heat of the threefold fire (of lust, malice, and dullness), and ward off the rains of evil dispositions. [**416**] This, O king, is the third quality of the sunshade he ought to have. For it was said, O king, by Sâriputta, the Elder, the Commander of the Faith:

"As a broad sunshade spreading far and firm,
Without a hole from rim to rim, wards off
The burning heat, and the god's mighty rain;
So doth the Buddha's son, all pure within,
Bearing the sunshade brave of righteousness,
Ward off the rain of evil tendencies,
And the dread heat of all the threefold fire[1]."'

---

ported, not by a short stick fixed underneath its centre, but by a long stick fastened to a point on its circumference; and carried, not by the person it shades, but by an attendant behind him.

[1] Not traced as yet.

64. The Rice Field.

7. 'Venerable Nâgasena, those three qualities of the rice field you say he ought to have, which are they?'

'Just, O king, as the rice field is provided with canals for irrigation; just so, O king, should the strenuous Bhikshu, earnest in effort, be provided with the lists of the various duties incumbent on the righteous man—the canals that bring the water to the rice fields of the Buddha's doctrine[1]. This, O king, is the first of the qualities of the rice field he ought to have.

8. 'And again, O king, just as the rice field is provided with embankments whereby men keep the water in, and so bring the crop to maturity; just so, O king, should the strenuous Bhikshu, earnest in effort, be provided with the embankments of righteousness of life, and shame at sin, and thereby keep his Sama*n*aship intact, and gain the fruits thereof. This, O king, is the second quality of the rice field he ought to have.

9. 'And again, O king, just as the rice field is fruitful, filling the heart of the farmer with joy, so that if the seed be little the crop is great, and if the seed be much the crop is greater still; just so, O king, should the strenuous Bhikshu, earnest in effort, be fruitful to the bearing of much good fruit, making the hearts of those who support him to rejoice, so that where little is given the result is great, and where much is given the result is greater still.

[1] As the pun on the two secondary meanings of mâtikâ, 'rule, line,' is untranslateable, I add here Hîna*t*i-kumbu*r*ê's gloss on the simile.

This, O king, is the third quality of the rice field he ought to have. For it was said, O king, by Upâli, the Elder, he who carried the rules of the Order in his head:

"Be fruitful as a rice field, yea, be rich
In all good works! For that is the best field
Which yieldeth to the sower the goodliest crop [1].'"

65. Medicine.

10. [417] 'Venerable Nâgasena, those two qualities of medicine you say he ought to take, which are they?'

'Just, O king, as vermin are not produced in medicine; just so, O king, should no evil dispositions be allowed to arise in the mind of the strenuous Bhikshu, earnest in effort. This, O king, is the first of the qualities of medicine he ought to have.

11. 'And again, O king, just as medicine is an antidote to whatever poison may have been imparted by bites or contact, by eating or by drinking in any way; just so, O king, should the strenuous Bhikshu, earnest in effort, counteract in himself the poison of lusts, and malice, and dullness, and pride, and wrong belief. This, O king, is the second of the qualities of medicine he ought to have. For it was said, O king, by the Blessed One, the god over all the gods:

"The strenuous recluse who longs to see
Into the nature, and the meaning true,
Of the constituent elements of things,
Must as it were an antidote become,
To the destruction of all evil thoughts [1].'"

[1] Not traced as yet.

66. Food.

12. 'Venerable Nâgasena, those three qualities of food you say he ought to take, which are they?'

'Just, O king, as food is the support of all beings, just so, O king, should the strenuous Bhikshu, earnest in effort, be a handle, as it were, by which all beings may open the door of the noble eightfold path. This, O king, is the first of the qualities of food he ought to have.

13. 'And again, O king, just as food increases people's strength; just so, O king, should the strenuous Bhikshu, earnest in effort, grow in increase of virtue. This, O king, is the second of the qualities of food he ought to have.

14. 'And again, O king, just as food is a thing desired of all beings; just so, O king, should the strenuous Bhikshu, earnest in effort, be desired of all the world. This, O king, is the third of the qualities of food he ought to have. For it was said, O king, by Mahâ Moggallâna, the Elder:

"By self-restraint, training, and righteousness,
By duty done, and by attainments reached,
The strenuous recluse should make himself
To all men in the world a thing desired [1]."'

---

67. The Archer.

15. [418] 'Venerable Nâgasena, those four qualities of the archer you say he ought to take, which are they?'

'Just, O king, as the archer, when discharging

---

[1] Not traced as yet.

his arrows, plants both his feet firmly on the ground, keeps his knees straight, hangs his quiver against the narrow part of his waist, keeps his whole body steady, places both his hands firmly on the point of junction (of the arrow on the bow), closes his fists, leaves no openings between his fingers, stretches out his neck, shuts his mouth and one eye [1], and takes aim [2] in joy at the thought: "I shall hit it [3];" just so, O king, should the strenuous Bhikshu, earnest in effort, plant firmly the feet of his zeal on the basis of righteousness, keep intact his kindness and tenderness of heart, fix his mind on subjugation of the senses, keep himself steady by self-restraint and performance of duty, suppress excitement and sense of faintness, by continual thoughtfulness let no openings remain in his mind, reach forward in zeal, shut the six doors (of the five senses and the mind), and continue mindful and thoughtful in joy at the thought: "By the javelin of my knowledge will I slay all my evil dispositions." This, O king, is the first of the qualities of the archer he ought to have.

16. [4]'And again, O king, as the archer carries a vice [5] for straightening out bent and crooked and

[1] Literally 'and his eyes.'

[2] Nimitta*m* u*g*u*m* karoti. 'Keeps his mind directed,' says Hîna*t*i-kumburê, p. 621.

[3] On other technical terms of archery, compare above, p. 352 (of the Pâli).

[4] From this point to the end, Mr. Trenckner's text is taken from a MS. brought from Siam, as explained in his Introduction, pp. v, vi, and in my Introduction, I, xxiv. Hîna*t*i-kumburê gives no indication of any change here in the MSS. he used.

[5] Â*l*aka, which Hîna*t*i-kumburê, p. 622, merely repeats. But see Dr. Morris, in the 'Journal of the Pâli Text Society,' 1886, p. 158.

uneven arrows; just so, O king, should the strenuous Bhikshu, earnest in effort, carry about with him, so long as he is in the body, the vice of mindfulness and thoughtfulness, wherewith he may straighten out any crooked and bent and shifty ideas. This, O king, is the second of the qualities of the archer he ought to have.

17. 'And again, O king, as the archer practises[1] at a target; just so, O king, should the strenuous Bhikshu, earnest in effort, practise, so long as he is in the body. And how, O king, should he practise? He should practise himself in the idea of the impermanence of all things, of the sorrow inherent in individuality, in the absence in any thing or creature of any abiding principle (any soul); in the ideas of the diseases, sores, pains, aches, and ailments of the body that follow in the train of the necessary conditions of individuality; in the ideas of its dependence on others[2], and of its certain disintegration[3]; in the ideas of the calamities, dangers, fears, and misfortunes to which it is subject; of its instability under the changing conditions of life; of its liability to dissolution, its want of firmness, its being no true place of refuge, no cave of security, no home of protection, no right object of trust; of its vanity, emptiness, danger, and insubstantiality [**419**]; of its being the source of pains and subject to punish-

[1] Upâseti (only found here). Hînan-kumburê, p. 622, has abhyâsa karanneya. He gives the whole passage from katham maharâga yoginâ . . . . . . tatiyam angam gahetabbam in Pâli, and reads throughout upâsitabbam, without the omissions.

[2] Parato, not in Childers, but see Maggh*ima Nikâya I, 435, 500, where all these expressions occur together.

[3] Palokato, from rug.

ments[1] and full of impurity, a mongrel compound of conditions and qualities that have no coherence; of its being the food alike of evil and of the Evil One[2]; of its inherent liability to rebirths, old age, disease, and death, to griefs, lamentations, despair; and of the corruption of the cravings and delusions that are never absent from it. This, O king, is the third of the qualities of the archer he ought to have.

18. 'And again, O king, just as the archer practises early and late; just so, O king, should the strenuous Bhikshu, earnest in effort, practise meditation early and late. For it was said, O king, by Sâriputta, the Elder, the Commander of the Faith:

"Early and late the true archer will practise,
'Tis only by never neglecting his art,
That he earns the reward and the wage of his skill.
So the sons of the Buddha, too, practise their art.
It is just by never neglecting in thought
The conditions of life in this bodily frame
That they gain the rich fruits which the Arahats love[3].'"

Here ends the fifth riddle, the riddle of the archer.

Here end the two hundred and sixty-two questions of Milinda, as handed down in the book in its six parts, adorned with twenty-two chapters. Now those which have not been handed down are forty-

---

[1] Vadhakato, 'untrustworthy as the man who assassinates his friend,' says Hînati-kumburê, p. 623.

[2] Marâmisato, given by Hînati-kumburê both in the Pâli and Simhalese, but omitted by Mr. Trenckner. (Mrityu-mâra-klesa mârayanta âhâraya-wu-bœwim.)

[3] Not traced as yet.

two[1]. Taking together all those that have been, and those that have not been, handed down, there are three hundred plus four, all of which are reckoned as 'Questions of Milinda[2].'

---

19. On the conclusion of this putting of puzzles and giving of solutions between the king and the Elder, this great earth, eighty-four thousand leagues in extent, shook six times even to its ocean boundary, the lightnings flashed, the gods poured down a rainfall of flowers from heaven, Mahâ Brahmâ himself signified his applause, and there was a mighty roar like the crashing and thundering of a storm in the mighty deep. And on beholding that wonder, the five hundred high ministers of the king, and all the inhabitants of the city of Sâgala who were there, and the women of the king's palace, bowed down before Nâgasena, the great teacher, raising their clasped hands to their foreheads, and departed thence[3].

20. [420] But Milinda the king was filled with joy of heart, and all pride was suppressed within him. And he became aware of the virtue that lay in the religion of the Buddhas, he ceased to have any doubt at all in the Three Gems[4], he tarried no longer in the jungle of heresy, he renounced all obstinacy; and pleased beyond measure at the high

---

[1] There are only thirty-eight in the list at VII, 1, 1.

[2] Before these last sentences (Now those . . . . . Milinda), Hînan-kumburê has: 'Here ends that mirror of the good law called, "The Questions of Milinda."' Then he goes on as above.

[3] I here follow Hînan-kumburê, who has apparently had a fuller text before him.

[4] The Buddha, his religion, and his order.

qualities of the Elder, at the excellence of his manners befitting a recluse, he become filled with confidence, and free from cravings, and all his pride and self-righteousness left his heart; and like a cobra deprived of its fangs he said: 'Most excellent, most excellent, venerable Nâgasena! The puzzles, worthy of a Buddha to solve, have you made clear. There is none like you, amongst all the followers of the Buddha, in the solution of problems, save only Sâriputta, the Elder, himself, the Commander of the Faith. Pardon me, venerable Nâgasena, my faults. May the venerable Nâgasena accept me as a supporter of the faith, as a true convert from to-day onwards as long as life shall last!'

21. Thenceforward the king and his mighty men continued in paying honour to Nâgasena. And the king had a Wihâra built called 'The Milinda Wihâra,' and handed it over to Nâgasena, the Elder, and waited upon him and all the multitude of the Arahat Bhikshus of whom he was the chief with the four requisites of the Bhikshu's life. And afterwards, taking delight in the wisdom of the Elder, he handed over his kingdom to his son, and abandoning the household life for the houseless state, grew great in insight, and himself attained to Arahatship! Therefore is it said:

'Wisdom is magnified o'er all the world,
And preaching for the endurance of the Faith.
When they, by wisdom, have put doubt aside
The wise reach upward to that Tranquil State.

That man in whom wisdom is firmly set,
And mindful self-possession never fails,
He is the best of those who gifts receive,
The chief of men to whom distinction's given.

Let therefore able men, in due regard
To their own welfare[1], honour those who're wise,—
Worthy of honour like the sacred pile
Beneath whose solid dome the bones of the great
dead lie[2].'

Here ends the book of the puzzles and the solutions of Milinda and Nâgasena[3].

[1] This line is identical with the sixth line of the little poem on the gift of Wihâras preserved in the *K*ullavagga VI, 1, 5, and VI, 9, 2, and quoted as a whole in the *G*âtaka, book I, 93, and in part above IV, 5, 1. This line also occurs, in a third connection, at *G*âtaka IV, 354.

[2] These verses differ from those here given by Hînati-kumburê, which I have quoted in the Introduction to this volume.

[3] This closing title is omitted by Hînati-kumburê, who gives instead of it a second account of how he came to write his translation, and then adds as the closing title to his own book: 'Here ends the *S*rî Saddharmâdâsaya (the Mirror of the Good Law) made by Sînati-kumburê Sumangala, the Elder.' [Sînati is merely the Elu form of the Si*m*halese word Hînati, which is the name of a plant, coryza sativa; and Hînati-kumburê is the locative of the name of the place, Hînati-field, where he was born. Every unnânsê in Ceylon has such a local name in addition to his religious name. And the religious names being often identical (there are, for instance, many Sumangalas), the Bhikkhus are usually spoken of by the former, and not by the latter.]

ADDITIONS AND CORRECTIONS.

PART I.

P. xxv. For 'Mahâyâna' read 'Madhyamika.' There is a Nâgasena mentioned in the Bharhut Tope.

" 6, l. 1. Read 'to Tissa the Elder, the son of the Moggalî.' The whole sentence had better perhaps have been rendered: 'And these two also were foreseen by our Buddha (just as he foresaw Tissa the Elder, the son of the Moggalî), in that he foretold, saying, &c.'

" 30, n. 1. The phrase isi-vâta*m* parivâta*m* nagara*m* aka*m*su recurs at *G*âtaka III, 142; Samanta Pâsadikâ 316; Saddhamma Sa*m*gaha 41.

" 32, n. 1. Compare Saddhamma Sa*m*gaha, p. 42.

" 60, § 13. On the first simile, compare the Sa*m*yutta Nikâya XXII, 102, 7.

" 76, last line. For 'yoke' read 'yolk.'

" 78. It would have been better perhaps to have avoided the use of the words 'where' and 'there,' and to have rendered: 'In the case of beings who, having died, have been reborn elsewhere, time is. In the case of beings who, having died, have not been reborn elsewhere, time is not. And in the case of beings, &c.' The three cases are those of the Puthu*gg*ana, the Arahat when dead, and the Arahat alive. My note refers to the third case, not to the second; and should, I think, be modified accordingly. See Sa*m*yutta Nikâya III, 12, 35; Mahâ Parinibbâna Sutta IV, 3; Dhammapada, verse 89; Sutta Nipâta II, 13, 1, 12; Ma*ggh*ima Nikâya I, 235; *G*âtaka IV, 453; and compare Udâna, p. 80.

Hîna*t*i-kumburê gives only a literal translation. A similar question is discussed in the Kathâ Vatthu XV, 3.

" 99, n. 1. For 'chapter' read 'book, p. 39.'

" 107, l. 16. After 'brought about' insert a comma.

" 118, § 5. I now prefer 'initiation' instead of 'ordination' as the translation of Upasampadâ.

" 119, n. 1. This interpretation is confirmed by part ii, p. 197.

" 129, l. 7. The phrase, 'though his hands and feet were cut off,' seems, at first sight, out of place. But compare part ii, p. 147.

" 150, l. 2. Read 'and not accepting them.'

P. 153, § 18. Read '*Kiñkâ*:' and compare *G*âtaka IV, 189.
„ 164 (six lines from the bottom of the page). Read 'and then a subsequent ease to the pain he has given.'
„ 176, § 39. In accordance with the note at part ii, pp. 86, 87, we must read 'a huge and mighty cauldron, full of water and crowded with grains of rice, is placed over a fireplace.'
„ 179. On the problem of king Sivi and his new eyes, compare the question discussed in Kathâ Vatthu III, 7.
„ 229, n. 1, l. 6. For 'these' read 'those.'
„ 239, n. 2. For 'But I never think' read 'But I now think.'
„ 241, § 20. For 'The Master said, Nâgasena,' read 'The Master said, O king.'
„ 244, n. 2. For '*G*atharaggi' read '*Gath*araggi.'
„ 278, n. 1. For 'adika' read 'âdika.'
„ 288, n. 3. For 'purdhita' read 'purohita.'
„ 290, n. 2. This story, which I could not trace, is no doubt the one referred to in *K*ariyâ Pi*t*aka I, 7.
„ 291, l. 22. Read 'Uposatha.'

PART II.

P. 27, last line but two. Read 'kâma-loka.'
„ 29, n. 2, l. 7. Read 'sa*m*sâra.'
„ 139, l. 4. For 'sun and moon' read 'moon and sun.'
„ 148, two lines from the bottom. For 'O king' read 'Sir.'
„ 150, four lines from the bottom. For 'destructions' read 'distinctions.'
„ 166, n. 1. Read 'samâhato.'
„ 219, n. 2. Read 'bhâvanâ.'
„ 252, l. 4. For 'pulling' read 'putting.'
„ 271, n. 1. Compare the 'Journal of the Pâli Text Society,' 1887, p. 155.

INDEX OF PROPER NAMES.

'Æsop's' fables, page 180.
A*k*iravatî, river, 304.
Â/âra Kâlâma, ascetic, 43, 46.
Alexandria, 204, 211, 269.
Aṅgîrasa, physician, 109.
Aṅgulimâla, robber, 355.
Anuruddha, quoted, 296, 347, 351.
Arûpakâyikâ, gods, 188.
Attha Sâlinî, xviii.
Atula, physician, 109.
Avî*k*i, purgatory, 261.

Bactria, 211.
Bakkula, 8–12.
Barth, M.,
Benares, district, 204, 211.
Bhaddasâla, general, 147.
Bhâradvâ*g*a, brahman, 37.
Bhâruka*kk*ba, country, 211.
Brahmâ, god, 24.
Buddhaghosa, 26, 32, 282.
Burnouf, Eugène, 6.

China, 204, 211, 269.

Da Sylva, Mr. Lewis, 181 foll.
Devadatta, 5.
Dha*g*a, brahman, 44.
Dhammantari, physician, 109.
Dhanapâla, elephant, 248.
Dhaniya, cowherd, 285.
Divyâvadhana, quoted, 305.
D'Oldenbourg, S., xi, xvii.

Eka-sâ*t*aka, brahman, 147.

Fausböll, Professor, 1, 4, 16, 31, 146.
Feer, Léon, xvii.

Gandhâra, country, 204, 211.
Ganges, river, 304.
Gha*t*ikâra, potter, 21–25.
Gopâla-mâtâ, queen, 146.
Gough's 'Philosophy of the Upanishads,' 142.
Greeks, 204, 256.
Guttila, musician, 146.

*G*âli, prince, 131.
*G*otipâla, brahman, 20.

Hîna*t*i-kumburê, meaning of, 375.

Indasâla, cave, 248.

Jolly, Professor, 266.
Jumna, river, 304.

Ka*kk*âyana, physician, 109.
Kâliṅga, 81.
Ka*nd*araggisâma, physician, 109.
Ka*n*hâ*g*inâ, Vessantara's daughter, 125, 131.
Kapila, physician, 109.
Kashmîr, country, 204, 211.
Kassapa, the Buddha, 21.
Kathâ Vatthu, xx–xxvii.
Kola*ññ*a, king, 81.
Koromandel, coast, 269.
Kosala, country, 204, 211.
Ko*t*umbara, place, 211.
Kshemendra, xvii.

*K*akkhupâla, 9.
*K*andagutta, king, 147.
*K*andavatî, princess, 18, 19.

Lakkha*n*a, brahman, 44.
Lévi, Sylvain, xii–xvii.
Lomapâda, king, 17.
Lomasa Kassapa, rishi, 16.

Maddî, Vessantara's queen, 125.
Madhura, place, 211.
Magadha, country, 211.
Mâgandiya, ascetic, 183.
Mahâ Ka*kk*âyana, elder, 282.
Mahâ Kassapa, elder, 330.
Mahâ Va*m*sa, xviii.
Mahî, river, 304.
Mandhâtâ, king, 146.
Mantî, brahman, 44.
Milinda Wihâra, 374.
Moggallâna, thera, 36, 369.

Mogharâga, the elder, 354.
Morris, Rev. Dr., 5, 22, 122, 361.
Müller, Professor E., 128.

Nanda, king, 147.
Nârada, the physician, 109.
Nikumba, country, 204.
Nimi, king, 146.

Panthaka, elder, quoted, 284.
Pi*nd*ola Bhâradvâga, 335, 345.
Pu*nn*aka, slave, 146.

Râhu, demon, 321.
Râhula, Gotama's son, 290, 297, 317, 355, 361.
Râma, brahman, 44.

Sabbamitta, brahman, 45.
Sâdhîna, king, 146.
Sâgala, town, 373.
Sâketa, place, 211.
Sakka, god, 6, 24, 322, 323.
Samana Kola*ññ*a, king, 81.
Sarabhû, river, 304.
Sâriputta, thera, 36, 273, 280, 284, 287, 292, 293, 294, 299, 302, 329, 332, 333, 353, 357, 366, 372.
Scythians, 204, 211.
Sela, brahman, 25.
Sineru, mountain, 24.
Sovîra, seaport, 269.
Specht, E., xii–xiv.
Subhaddâ, quoted, 308, 316.
Subhoga, brahman, 44.
Subhûti, elder, 315, 323.
Sudatta, brahman, 44.
Suddhodana, king, 45.
Sumana, garland-maker, 146.
Sura*tth*a (Surat), 211, 269.
Suyâma, brahman, 44.

Takkola, seaport, 269.
Tartary, 204.
Tidasapura, in heaven, 145.
Trenckner, Mr., 13, 29, 147, 175, 183, 279, 327.
Turkey, incense from, 256.

Udâyi, 6.
Uddaka Râmuputta, ascetic, 46.
Udena, king, 146.
Udi*kk*a, country, 45.
Uggen, country, 211.
Upâli, the elder, 368.
Upasena Vangantaputta, 268, 269, 289, 326, 328, 329, 331.
Uposatha, elephant, 128.

Vanga, seaport, 269.
Vangîsa, quoted, 322.
Vasubandhu, xvii.
Vera*ñg*a, town, 37.
Vessantara, 114–132, 125.
Vilâta, country, 211.

Ya*ññ*a, brahman, 44.

INDEX OF SUBJECTS.

Agriculture, details of, pages 269, 270.
Anchor, simile of, 299.
Animals, list of, 101.
Ant, simile of the white, 326.
Arahats:—
laymen may become, 57, 96, 245; suffer bodily but never mental pain, 75; how far they can do wrong, 98–100; or be ignorant, 100; way to Arahatship confused with way to Buddhahood, 141; produce wonders at their graves, 174; the thirty-seven constituent qualities of Arahatship, 207, 218, 264; the seven jewels of the Arahats, 220–229; are the judges in the City of Righteousness, 235; no Arahatship without the vows, 254; description of the Arahat's character, 272, 273.
Archery, full details of, 253, 254, 370.
Arithmetic, 149.
Asceticism, 60–62.
Ass, riddle of, 279.
Assurance, final, 226.

Backsliders, 63–75.
Bamboo, simile of, 290.
Bat, compared to the Arahat, 346.
Bathing, 63.
Begging, forbidden to the members of the Buddhist Order, 33; allowed, 35.
Boar, simile of, 334.
Body, ten characteristics of the, 75.
Bow, simile of, 291.
Brahmans, 21, 26–28, 41.
Bull, simile of, 333.

Carpenter, riddle of, 361.
Carts, parts of, 49.
Cat, simile of, 326.
Champion, in battle, 149.
Charity, public feasts, 65, 68.
Children, no conversion of, 178.
Chinese books on Milinda, xi–xv.
Cloth manufacture, processes of, 52.
Cock, simile of, 280.
Confession, the one true, 55.
Conversion, who cannot reach, 177.
Corpse, the ocean does not keep a, 70.
'Corpse Dance,' 147.
Counties, list of, 53.
Crane (Indian), a bird of ill omen, 345.
Crow, riddle of, 291.

Dead, offerings for the, 151.
Death, premature, 162–174.
Debt, deposit of son as pledge for, 122.
Deer, simile of, 331.
Diamond polishing, 7; figuratively of knowledge, 229; has three qualities of the Arahat, 357.
Diseases, 8, 10, 62; causes of fatal, 164.
Dreams, 157–162.
'Drink of Triumph,' 16.
Drugs, magical, 129.

Earth, simile of, 307.
Elephant, the mystic royal, 128; and frog, parable of, 180; which attacked the Buddha, 248; has five qualities of the Arahat, 335.
Emancipation, the chief jewel of the Arahats, 225.
Evil One, the, 55.

Fairies, &c., various kinds of, 101.
Faith, the one true, 55.

Final assurance, 226.
Fire, by attrition, 203.
Fire, simile of, 311.
Fireplaces, form of, 86.
Fisherman, riddle of, 360.
Food, moderation in, 4-7.
Friendship of the world, 1.
Frog and elephant, parable of, 180.

Gem, the mystic royal, 14, 128; the wish-conferring, 59, 74, 119, 193, 258.
Gifts, how sanctified, 82-84.
God, the only one, 50.
Gourd, simile of, 294.
Graves, wonders at, 174 foll.
Gravitation, 80.
Gypsies, 87.

'Head Holocaust,' 147.
Heredity, 21.
Household cares, 1.
Hunter, has four qualities of the Arahat, 358.
Hyenas, 101.

Iddhi, 94, 96, 117, 231, 234, 259, 267.
Impermanence, law of, 102.
Imputed righteousness, 153-156.
Iron, 102, 364.

Jackal, simile of, 329.
Jasmine, the best of flowers, 73.

Karma, 11, 22, 38, 93, 95, 103, 108, 145-149, 163, 213, 214, 230.
Kings, their courtiers, &c., 41, 265; force of their example, 42; will fail if unworthy, 69, 262; custody of their seal, 124; seven mystic treasures of, 203; six royal insignia of, 207; powers and perquisites of, 266, 270; king has four qualities of the Arahat, 323.
Kingship of the Buddha, explained, 26-30.
Knowledge, Buddhist, described, 223.

Landowners, 15.
Laymen, can become Arahats, 57, 96; why admitted at once (before conversion) into the Order, 63-75, when they cannot enter the path, 78.
Leech, why like the Arahat, 347.
Lion, simile of, 338.
Looking-glass, simile of, 158.
Lotus, simile of, 70, 189, 222, 256, 295.
'Lower state,' the, 63-75.

Madness, wrong done in, 18, 19.
Magic. See Gem, Root, and Drugs.
Mankind will all become by nature pure, 95.
Mast, simile of, 300.
Matriarchate, 127 note.
Medicine (see Diseases):—
  tonic, use of, 7;
  purge, preparation for, 33;
  diagnosis, 64, 67;
  medicine of Nirvâ*n*a, 65, 190; of the vows, 256;
  a specific for all diseases, 67;
  the internal fire (for digestion), 97;
  list of old teachers of, 109;
  various divisions of medical knowledge, 109;
  verses on, 218, 219;
  training in surgery, 255;
  riddle about, 368.
Meditation, various sorts of, 212, 213; qualities of, 222.
Minister of State, 147, and see Seal.
Miracles, why the Buddhas work none, 24.
Monkey, simile of, 292.
Moon, simile of, 318.
Moon-worship, 127.
Mungoose, simile of, 329.

Nihilism, the explanation of Buddhist, 102; modern theories of, 142.
Nirvâ*n*a, is medicine, 65, 190;
  like space is without a cause, 103, 107;
  is unproducible, 102;
  is not put together of any qualities, 103;
  has no colour or form, 107;
  what it is, 181 note;
  has no pain involved in it, 181-185;
  has no form, or duration, or measure, 186-188;
  its qualities explained by similes, 189-195;
  how it can be known, 196;
  how attained to, 197-201;
  where attained to, 202-205.

Offerings for the dead, 151.

Order, the Buddhist:—
description of true member of, 5, 9;
the guilty member of, purifies gifts, 82, 83;
every member of, will reach Arahatship, ibid.;
why they should trouble themselves with study, and the business of the Order, 92;
why the rules of, were laid down gradually, 110;
description at length of the ideal member, 271–273.
Owl, has two qualities of the Arahat, 344.

Panther, similes of, 285.
Path, the ancient and the new, 13–19.
Patriarchal power to sell son, 122.
Penance, 141.
Physician, the Great, 8; description of an able, 67.
Pigeon, how like the Arahat, 344.
Pilot, simile of, 301.
Pledge, 122.
Poison, 80, 81.
Pupils, duties of, to teachers, 185.

Rain, why like the Arahat, 356.
Rat, simile of, 328.
Rebirth, 22, 83.
Recluse. See Order.
Relationship, terminology of, in Pâli, different from ours, 51.
Rice, sorts of, 73; riddle about, 367.
Righteousness, imputed, 153–156.
Rock, simile of, 314.
Root, with magical powers, 119.

Sailor, simile of, 302.
Sal-tree, simile of, 296.
Sandal-wood, simile of, 74.
'Sap of Life,' 37.
Scorpion, riddle of, 328.
Sea, simile of, 303–306.
Seal, the great, state custody of, 124.
Seasons, 103, 112.
Seed, riddle of, 296.
Ship, simile of, 297.
Sleep, theory of, 161.
Snakes, similes of, 348, 349.
Sons, may be sold or pledged, 122.
Space, simile of, 316.
Spider, simile of, 351.
Squirrel, simile of, 284.
Sun, heat of, how mitigated, 111; hotter in winter than summer, 112; has seven qualities of the Arahat, 320.
Sunshade, riddle of, 365.
Sun-worship, later than moon-worship, 127.

Teachers, the five, of the Buddha, 44–46; the Buddha has no, 6, 43, 46.
Tortoise, similes of, 288, 352.
Toys, various, 32.
'Tree of Wisdom,' 81.
Trees, how like the Arahat, 355.

Wage-earners despised, 210.
Water, simile of, 309.
Water, Soul in, 85–91.
Waterpots, curious form of, 86; adage of, 364.
Weapons, the five kinds of, 227; seven kinds of, 250.
Weaving, processes of, 52.
Wheel, the mystic royal, 137.
Wihâras, merit of building, 3.
Wind, simile of, 312.
Wonders at the graves of saints, 174 foll.
Writing, 9, 247.

Transliteration of Oriental Alphabets adopted for the Translations of the Sacred Books of the East.

CONSONANTS.	MISSIONARY ALPHABET. I Class.	II Class.	III Class.	Sanskrit.	Zend.	Pehlevi.	Persian.	Arabic.	Hebrew.	Chinese.
Gutturales.										
1 Tenuis	k	. . .	. . . .	क	𐬐	[illegible]	ک	ك	כּ	k
2 „ aspirata	kh	. . .	. . . .	ख	𐬑	[illegible]	. . .	. . .	כ	kh
3 Media	g	. . .	. . . .	ग	𐬔	[illegible]	گ	. . .	גּ	. . .
4 „ aspirata	gh	. . .	. . . .	घ	𐬖	[illegible]	. . .	. . .	ג	. . .
5 Gutturo-labialis	q	. . .	. . . .	. . .	. . . .	. . .	ق	ق	ק	. . .
6 Nasalis	ṅ (ng)	. . .	. . . .	ङ	{ 𐬢 (ng) / 𐬣 (N) }	. . .	. . .	. . .	. . .	. . .
7 Spiritus asper	h	. . .	. . . .	ह	𐬵 (𐬰𐬵 hv)	[illegible]	ه	ه	ה	h, hs
8 „ lenis	’	. . .	. . . .	. . .	. . . .	. . .	ا	ا	א	. . .
9 „ asper faucalis	‘h	. . .	. . . .	. . .	. . . .	. . .	ح	ح	ח	. . .
10 „ lenis faucalis	’h	. . .	. . . .	. . .	. . . .	. . .	ع	ع	ע	. . .
11 „ asper fricatus	. . .	*‘h*	. . . .	. . .	. . . .	. . .	خ	خ	ח	. . .
12 „ lenis fricatus	. . .	*’h*	. . . .	. . .	. . . .	. . .	. . .	. . .	. . .	. . .
Gutturales modificatae (palatales, &c.)										
13 Tenuis	. . .	*k*	. . . .	च	𐬗	[illegible]	چ	. . .	. . .	*k*
14 „ aspirata	. . .	*kh*	. . . .	छ	. . . .	. . .	. . .	. . .	. . .	*kh*
15 Media	. . .	*g*	. . . .	ज	𐬘	[illegible]	ج	ج	. . .	. . .
16 „ aspirata	. . .	*gh*	. . . .	झ	. . . .	. . .	ژ	غ	. . .	. . .
17 „ Nasalis	. . .	*ñ*	. . . .	ञ	. . . .	. . .	. . .	. . .	. . .	. . .

CONSONANTS (continued).	MISSIONARY ALPHABET. I Class.	II Class.	III Class.	Sanskrit.	Zend.	Pehlevi.	Persian.	Arabic.	Hebrew.	Chinese.
18 Semivocalis	y	...	....	य	[illegible] init. [illegible]	[illegible]	ي	ي	י	y
19 Spiritus asper	...	(y̔)	....	...	....	...	...	...	...	...
20 „ lenis	...	(y̓)	....	...	....	...	...	...	...	...
21 „ asper assibilatus	...	*š*	....	श	[illegible]	[illegible]	ش	ش	...	...
22 „ lenis assibilatus	...	*ž*	....	...	[illegible]	[illegible]	ژ	...	...	*ž*
Dentales.										
23 Tenuis	t	...	....	त	[illegible]	[illegible]	ت	ت	תּ	t
24 „ aspirata	th	...	....	थ	[illegible]	...	...	...	ת	th
25 „ assibilata	...	...	TH	...	....	...	ث	ث	...	...
26 Media	d	...	....	द	[illegible]	[illegible]	د	د	דּ	...
27 „ aspirata	dh	...	....	ध	[illegible]	...	...	...	ד	...
28 „ assibilata	...	...	DH	...	....	...	ذ	ذ	...	...
29 Nasalis	n	...	....	न	[illegible]	[illegible]	ن	ن	נ	n
30 Semivocalis	l	...	....	ल	....	[illegible]	ل	ل	ל	l
31 „ mollis 1	...	*l*	....	ळ	....	...	...	...	...	...
32 „ mollis 2	...	...	L	...	....	...	...	...	...	...
33 Spiritus asper 1	s	...	....	स	[illegible]	[illegible]	س (ث)	س	שׂ	s
34 „ asper 2	...	...	s (ʃ)	...	....	...	...	...	ס	...
35 „ lenis	z	...	....	...	[illegible]	[illegible]	ز (ذ)	ز	ז	z
36 „ asperrimus 1	...	...	z (ʒ)	...	....	...	ص	ص	צ	ʒ, ʒh
37 „ asperrimus 2	...	...	ẓ (ʒ)	...	....	...	ض	...	...	...

Dentales modificatae (lingualos, &c.)										
38 Tenuis	...	*t*	...	ट	...	...	ط	ط	ט	...
39 " aspirata	...	*th*	...	ठ	...	...	ط	ط	...	...
40 Media	...	*d*	...	ड	𐬛	𐭣	...	...	...	...
41 " aspirata	...	*dh*	...	ढ	...	...	...	ض	...	...
42 Nasalis	...	*n*	...	ण	𐬣	...	...	...	...	...
43 Semivocalis	r	...	...	र	𐬭	𐭥, 𐭫, ı	ر	ر	ר	...
44 " fricata	...	*r*	...	...	...	...	...	...	...	*r*
45 " diacritica	...	...	R	...	...	...	...	...	...	...
46 Spiritus asper	sh	...	...	ष	𐬴	𐭱	...	...	...	sh
47 " lenis	zh	...	...	...	...	...	...	...	...	...
Labiales.										
48 Tenuis	p	...	...	प	𐬞	𐭯	پ	...	פּ	p
49 " aspirata	ph	...	...	फ	...	...	...	...	פ	ph
50 Media	b	...	...	ब	𐬠	𐭡	ب	ب	בּ	...
51 " aspirata	bh	...	...	भ	...	...	...	...	ב	...
52 Tenuissima	...	*p*	...	...	...	...	...	...	...	...
53 Nasalis	m	...	...	म	𐬨	𐭬	م	م	מ	m
54 Semivocalis	w	...	...	...	𐬬	...	...	...	...	w
55 " aspirata	hw	...	...	...	...	...	...	...	...	...
56 Spiritus asper	f	...	...	...	𐬟	𐭯	ف	ف	...	f
57 " lenis	v	...	...	व	»	ı, 𐭥	و	و	ו	...
58 Anusvâra	...	*m*	...	अं	𐬄 ã	...	...	...	...	...
59 Visarga	...	*h*	...	अः	...	...	...	...	...	...

VOWELS.	MISSIONARY ALPHABET. I Class.	II Class.	III Class.	Sanskrit.	Zend.	Pehlevi.	Persian.	Arabic.	Hebrew.	Chinese.
1 Neutralis	0	...	....	...	....	...	...	...	◌ְ	ă
2 Laryngo-palatalis	ĕ	...	....	...	....	...	...	...	...	...
3 „ labialis	ŏ	...	....	...	....	ا fin.	...	...	...	...
4 Gutturalis brevis	a	...	....	अ	𐬀	𐭠 init.	ـَ	ـَ	◌ַ	a
5 „ longa	â	(*a*)	....	आ	𐬁	𐭠	ـَا	ـَا	◌ָ	â
6 Palatalis brevis	i	...	....	इ	𐬌	...	ـِ	ـِ	◌ִ	i
7 „ longa	î	(*î*)	....	ई	𐬍	𐭩	ـِي	ـِي	◌ִי	î
8 Dentalis brevis	*li*	...	....	ऌ	....	...	...	...	...	...
9 „ longa	*lî*	...	....	ॡ	....	...	...	...	...	...
10 Lingualis brevis	*ri*	...	....	ऋ	....	...	...	...	...	...
11 „ longa	*rî*	...	....	ॠ	....	...	...	...	...	...
12 Labialis brevis	u	...	....	उ	𐬎	...	ـُ	ـُ	◌ֻ	u
13 „ longa	û	(*u*)	....	ऊ	𐬏	𐭥	ـُو	ـُو	וּ	û
14 Gutturo-palatalis brevis	e	...	....	...	𐬈 (e) 𐬆 (*e*)	...	...	...	◌ֶ	e
15 „ longa	ê (ai)	(*e*)	....	ए	𐬉, 𐬀𐬉	𐭩	...	...	◌ֵ	ê̤
16 Diphthongus gutturo-palatalis	âi	(*ai*)	....	ऐ	....	...	ـَيْ	ـَيْ	...	âi
17 „ „	ei (ĕi)	...	....	...	....	...	...	...	...	ei, êi
18 „ „	oi (ŏu)	...	....	...	....	...	...	...	...	...
19 Gutturo-labialis brevis	o	...	....	...	𐬊	...	...	...	◌ָ	o
20 „ longa	ô (au)	(*o*)	....	ओ	𐬋	𐭥	...	...	וֹ	...
21 Diphthongus gutturo-labialis	âu	(*au*)	....	औ	𐬁𐬎 (*au*)	...	ـَوْ	ـَوْ	...	âu
22 „ „	eu (ĕu)	...	....	...	....	...	...	...	...	...
23 „ „	ou (ŏu)	...	....	...	....	...	...	...	...	...
24 Gutturalis fracta	ä	...	....	...	....	...	...	...	...	...
25 Palatalis fracta	ï	...	....	...	....	...	...	...	...	...
26 Labialis fracta	ü	...	....	...	....	...	...	...	...	ü
27 Gutturo-labialis fracta	ö	...	....	...	....	...	...	...	...	...